Open Education and Second Language Learning and Teaching

NEW PERSPECTIVES ON LANGUAGE AND EDUCATION
Founding Editor: Viv Edwards, *University of Reading, UK*

Series Editors: Phan Le Ha, *University of Hawaii at Manoa, USA* and Joel Windle, *Monash University, Australia.*

Two decades of research and development in language and literacy education have yielded a broad, multidisciplinary focus. Yet education systems face constant economic and technological change, with attendant issues of identity and power, community and culture. What are the implications for language education of new 'semiotic economies' and communications technologies? Of complex blendings of cultural and linguistic diversity in communities and institutions? Of new cultural, regional and national identities and practices? The New Perspectives on Language and Education series will feature critical and interpretive, disciplinary and multidisciplinary perspectives on teaching and learning, language and literacy in new times. New proposals, particularly for edited volumes, are expected to acknowledge and include perspectives from the Global South. Contributions from scholars from the Global South will be particularly sought out and welcomed, as well as those from marginalized communities within the Global North.

All books in this series are externally peer-reviewed.

Full details of all the books in this series and of all our other publications can be found on http://www.multilingual-matters.com, or by writing to Multilingual Matters, St Nicholas House, 31–34 High Street, Bristol BS1 2AW, UK.

NEW PERSPECTIVES ON LANGUAGE AND EDUCATION: 87

Open Education and Second Language Learning and Teaching

The Rise of a New Knowledge Ecology

Edited by
Carl S. Blyth and Joshua J. Thoms

MULTILINGUAL MATTERS
Bristol • Blue Ridge Summit

DOI https://doi.org/10.21832/BLYTH0992
Library of Congress Cataloging in Publication Data
A catalog record for this book is available from the Library of Congress.
Names: Blyth, Carl S. (Carl Stuart) – editor. | Thoms, Joshua J., editor.
Title: Open Education and Second Language Learning and Teaching: The Rise of a New Knowledge
  Ecology/Edited by Carl S. Blyth and Joshua J. Thoms.
Description: Bristol; Blue Ridge Summit: Multilingual Matters, [2021] |
  Series: New Perspectives on Language and Education: 87 | Includes bibliographical references and index. |
  Summary: "This book contextualizes open education in foreign language (FL) learning and teaching; fills a
  gap in the research by exploring aspects of open second language learning and teaching across a range of
  educational contexts; and illustrates new ways of creating freely shared FL materials. This book is open
  access under a CC BY ND license"—Provided by publisher.
Identifiers: LCCN 2020043613 (print) | LCCN 2020043614 (ebook) |
  ISBN 9781800410992 (hardback) | ISBN 9781800410985 (paperback) |
  ISBN 9781800411005 (pdf) | ISBN 9781800411012 (epub) |
  ISBN 9781800411029 (kindle edition) Subjects: LCSH: Second language acquisition. | Language and
  languages—Study and teaching. | Open educational resources.
Classification: LCC P118.2 .O64 20201 (print) | LCC P118.2 (ebook) |
  DDC 418.0071—dc23 LC record available at https://lccn.loc.gov/2020043613
LC ebook record available at https://lccn.loc.gov/2020043614

British Library Cataloguing in Publication Data
A catalogue entry for this book is available from the British Library.

ISBN-13: 978-1-80041-099-2 (hbk)
ISBN-13: 978-1-80041-098-5 (pbk)
ISBN-13: 978-1-80041-100-5 (pdf)
ISBN-13: 978-1-80041-101-2 (epub)

Open Access

 Except where otherwise noted, this work is licensed under the Creative
Commons Attribution-NoDerivatives 4.0 International License. To view a copy of this license, visit http://
creativecommons.org/licenses/by-nd/4.0/ or send a letter to Creative Commons, PO Box 1866, Mountain
View, CA 94042, USA.

Multilingual Matters
UK: St Nicholas House, 31–34 High Street, Bristol BS1 2AW, UK.
USA: NBN, Blue Ridge Summit, PA, USA.

Website: www.multilingual-matters.com
Twitter: Multi_Ling_Mat
Facebook: https://www.facebook.com/multilingualmatters
Blog: www.channelviewpublications.wordpress.com

Copyright © 2021 Carl S. Blyth, Joshua J. Thoms and the authors of individual chapters.

All rights reserved. No part of this work may be reproduced in any form or by any means without
permission in writing from the publisher.

The policy of Multilingual Matters/Channel View Publications is to use papers that are natural,
renewable and recyclable products, made from wood grown in sustainable forests. In the manufacturing
process of our books, and to further support our policy, preference is given to printers that have FSC and
PEFC Chain of Custody certification. The FSC and/or PEFC logos will appear on those books where full
certification has been granted to the printer concerned.

Typeset by Nova Techset Private Limited, Bengaluru and Chennai, India.

Contents

	Contributors	vii
	Introduction: Second Language Education as an Open Knowledge Ecology *Carl S. Blyth and Joshua J. Thoms*	1

Part 1: The Microsystem: Developing Knowledge in L2 Instructional Environments

1	Open Educational Resources in Heritage and L2 Spanish Classrooms: Design, Development and Implementation *Gabriela C. Zapata and Alessandra Ribota*	25
2	Open by Design: The *Cultura* Project *Sabine Levet and Stephen L. Tschudi*	47
3	Open Educational Resources as Tools to Teach the Indigenous Languages of Latin America: Where Technology, Pedagogy and Colonialism Meet *Sergio Romero*	69
4	Openness in a Crowdsourced Massive Online Language Community *Katerina Zourou and Anthippi Potolia*	87

Part 2: The Mesosystem: Developing Knowledge in L2 Teacher Education

5	Second Language Teachers and the Open Education Movement in the United States: A National Survey *Joshua J. Thoms and Frederick Poole*	109
6	Raising the Curtain on OER/OEP: Opening Pathways from Awareness to Engagement in a Graduate Course on Foreign Language Program Direction *Beatrice Dupuy*	130

7   The Role of OER in Promoting Critical Reflection and
    Professional Development: The Foreign Languages and the
    Literary in the Everyday Project   158
    Carl S. Blyth, Chantelle Warner and Joanna Luks

**Part 3: The Exosystem: Developing Knowledge in the
Field of L2 Education**

8   The Affordances and Challenges of Open-access Journals:
    The Case of an Applied Linguistics Journal   183
    Dorothy Chun and Trude Heift

9   Analysing Teachers' Tacit Professional Knowledge of OER:
    The Case of Languages Open Resources Online (LORO)   198
    Tita Beaven

10 Towards a Pedagogy of Openness: Bridging English-language
    and Foreign-language Digital Humanities   219
    Rebecca F. Davis and Carl S. Blyth

11 Finding and Using the Good Stuff: Open Educational Practices
    for Developing Open Educational Resources   245
    Christian Hilchey

    Appendix   266

    Index   270

Contributors

Dr Tita Beaven is Director of Innovation and e-learning at Sounds-Write, a provider of professional development for schoolteachers and other educational practitioners. Prior to that, she was a Senior Lecturer in Spanish at the School of Languages and Applied Linguistics at The Open University, UK. Her research is in the area of innovative pedagogy and technology in language learning and teaching, and Open Education. She holds a Doctorate in Education (Educational Technology) from The Open University.

Dr Carl S. Blyth is Associate Professor of French and Applied Linguistics. Since 2010, he has served as the Director of COERLL, a center at the University of Texas at Austin dedicated to promoting open solutions to the challenges of foreign language education. Interested in social approaches to language, he conducts research in interactional sociolinguistics, intercultural pragmatics and language technology. He is the co-editor (with Dale Koike) of the volume *Dialogue in Multilingual and Multimodal Communities* (John Benjamins, 2015). His articles have appeared in such journals as *L2 Journal, Language and Dialogue, The Modern Language Journal, CALICO Journal, Foreign Language Annals* and *ALSIC Revue*. He currently serves on the editorial boards of *Intercultural Pragmatics* (Mouton De Gruyter) and the open journal *Second Language Research and Practice* (AAUSC).

Dr Dorothy Chun is Professor of Applied Linguistics at the University of California, Santa Barbara. Her research areas include L2 phonology and intonation, CALL and telecollaboration for intercultural learning. She has conducted studies on cognitive process in learning with multimedia and on online intercultural exchanges. She edits the journal *Language Learning & Technology*.

Dr Rebecca Frost Davis, Director for Instructional and Emerging Technology at St. Edward's University, focuses on the intersections of digital pedagogy and liberal education. She is co-editor (with Matthew K. Gold, Katherine D. Harris and Jentery Sayers) of *Digital Pedagogy in the Humanities: Concepts, Models, and Experiments*. Recent publications include 'Pedagogy and Learning in a Digital Ecosystem' in Jessie Moore and Randy Bass (eds) *Understanding Writing Transfer and its Implications for Higher Education* and 'Redefining Learning Places in the Emerging Digital Ecosystem' in Deric Shannon and Jeffery Galle (eds) *From the Abstract to the Quotidian: Reflections on Pedagogy and Place*.

Dr Beatrice Dupuy is Professor of French and Applied Linguistics. She is Co-Director of the Center for Educational Resources in Culture, Language, and Literacy (CERCLL), a Title VI Center at the University of Arizona. Her research focuses on language teacher professional development, literacy-based approaches to teaching and learning and on experiential learning as a theoretical and practical framework for language education in home and study-abroad contexts. Her research has appeared in numerous journals including *Foreign Language Annals, Canadian Modern Language Review, System,* and *L2 Journal.*

Dr Trude Heift is Professor of Linguistics at Simon Fraser University, Canada. Her research area bridges applied and computational linguistics. She designs and studies online CALL systems by focusing on learner-computer interactions, learner modeling, corrective feedback and error analysis. She co-edits the journal *Language Learning & Technology.*

Dr Christian Hilchey is a Lecturer in the Department of Slavic and Eurasian studies at the University of Texas at Austin. A specialist in Slavic linguistics, he has taught Czech language classes at UT-Austin from Beginning to the Advanced levels (1st–5th year Czech). Interested in language pedagogy, he is currently writing an open textbook and online course entitled *Reality Czech* with the Center for Open Educational Resources and Language Learning (COERLL).

Dr Sabine Levet is Senior Lecturer in French in the Department of Global Studies and Languages at The Massachusetts Institute of Technology. She teaches all levels of French language and culture classes and is one of the original creators and developers of *Cultura*, which was funded by the National Endowment of Humanities and received a special recognition from the American Council on Education. She currently serves as the *Cultura* project director. She has written articles and chapters on telecollaboration and intercultural learning and has given numerous talks and workshops on intercultural communication and the integration of technology into the foreign language curriculum.

Joanna Luks is an independent scholar, who was most recently Senior Lecturer in the French Program in the Department of Romance Studies at Cornell University. Her pedagogical interests include transdisciplinarity in FL teaching with articulation of skills across language, literary and cultural studies, professional development and the (re)conceptualization of grammar drawing from theories in cognitive grammar. In 2013, she published *Le Littéraire dans le quotidien,* an open textbook funded by the Center for Open Educational Resources and Language Learning (COERLL). As part of an expansion of the approach, in 2014, Joanna became co-director of the FLLITE project (http://fllite.org/), a joint initiative between COERLL and the Center for Educational Resources in Culture, Language, and Literacy (CERCLL).

Dr Frederick Poole is an Assistant Professor at Michigan State University in the Master of Arts in Foreign Language Teaching Program. His research interests include digital game-based language learning, online collaborative reading environments and developing L2 literacy in dual language immersion programs.

Dr Anthippi Potolia is Senior Lecturer/Researcher at the University of Paris 8 – Vincennes Saint-Denis. Her main interests are Computer Assisted Language Learning and Discourse Analysis (representations about digital tools: social networks, online learning communities, distance education). Her research topics involve effects of computer mediation, as well as (intercultural) telecollaborative practices online. She co-edited the book *Thinking about the Didactics of Plurilingualism and its Mutations: Ideologies, Policies and Devices* in 2018 with Rennes University Press and has published articles in various journals. She is currently coordinating a book (with Martine Derivry) for Routledge, entitled *Virtual Exchange for Intercultural Language Learning and Teaching: Fostering Communication for the Digital Age*, which is scheduled to appear in 2021.

Alessandra C. Ribota is a doctoral student and graduate teaching assistant in the Department of Hispanic Studies at Texas A&M University. She holds an MEd in Curriculum and Instruction and has experience as a Spanish high school teacher. Her research interests are second language acquisition and pedagogy and teacher education.

Dr Sergio Romero is Associate Professor in the Dept. of Spanish and Portuguese at The University of Texas at Austin. He is a linguistic anthropologist with an interest in the structural and sociocultural aspects of language variation and change. His current work examines the diachronic development of dialectal variation, its social meaning and the emergence of pastoral registers in indigenous languages, using both ethnographic and philological methods. Much of his research focuses on Mayan languages, especially K'iche', Q'eqchi', Kaqchikel, and more recently Awakatek and Ixil. He has also published on Nahuatl, especially on dialects formerly spoken in colonial Guatemala, and has served as pro-bono translator for Maya migrants in the United States. Finally, he recently led a team of language instructors to create an open, online K'iche' language course (http://tzij.coerll.utexas.edu/).

Dr Joshua J. Thoms is an Associate Professor of Applied Linguistics and Spanish at Utah State University where he researches issues related to open education, second language (L2) digital social reading/literacy practices and the effects of classroom discourse on L2 learning and teaching. In 2013, he published a co-edited volume on hybrid language learning and teaching. In addition, he has published several articles appearing in journals such as *Language Learning & Technology, System, Modern Language Journal, Canadian Modern Language Review* and *Foreign Language Annals*. He serves on the editorial board of the open journal *Second Language Research and Practice* (AAUSC).

Stephen L. Tschudi, Specialist in Technology for Language Education, serves the University of Hawaii's Center for Language and Technology and National Foreign Resource Center by designing and delivering professional learning experiences for language educators on the topics of Project-Based Language Learning and Online Pedagogy. He is experienced in adapting *Cultura* to meet diverse instructional goals. His recent publications include Books 3 and 4 of *Encounters Global Chinese Language & Culture* from Yale University Press.

Dr Chantelle Warner is Associate Professor of German and Second Language Acquisition and Teaching at the University of Arizona, where she also co-directs the Center for Educational Resources in Culture, Language and Literacy (CERCLL), a Title VI National Language Resource Center. Since 2014, she directs the German Studies Language Program, which encompasses the first three years of language study. Her research crosses the fields of literary and applied linguistic inquiry and focuses on how language is involved in struggles for social and symbolic power and the educational potential of playful, literary language use and creative multilingualism.

Dr Gabriela C. Zapata is Associate Professor in the Department of Hispanic Studies at Texas A&M University. Her research foci are second (L2) and heritage language (HL) acquisition and pedagogy, bilingualism and teacher education. She is also interested in the development of OER materials for L2 and HL teaching and in language program direction. Dr Zapata has served as Director or Coordinator of five Spanish and Portuguese basic language programs in public and private universities in the United States and Canada. She has published articles in journals such as *Computer Assisted Language Learning, Hispania, Foreign Language Annals, International Journal of Bilingualism, Language Learning* and *Language Awareness*, among others, and in a variety of edited volumes.

She is also the co-editor (with Dr Manel Lacorte) of the volume *Multiliteracies Pedagogy and Language Learning: Teaching Spanish to Heritage Speakers* (Palgrave Macmillan, 2017).

Dr Katerina Zourou is a Senior Researcher interested in language learning/teaching from an open perspective (open educational resources and practices) and from the point of view of collaboration (collective learning) and networking (social media) and regularly gives graduate-level lectures on these topics (University of Grenoble Alpes, France, and Hellenic Open University, Greece). She is also head of Web2Learn, an SME acting as partner in transnational projects supported by the Council of Europe (ORD, e-lang), and by the European Commission (iPEN, INOS, CRETE, Catapult, BlockAdemic, MOONLITE, LangOER, etc.).

Introduction: Second Language Education as an Open Knowledge Ecology

Carl S. Blyth and Joshua J. Thoms

The Ecological Framework

Applied linguists have increasingly embraced an ecological framework developed by psychologists such as Bateson (1973), Bronfenbrenner (1979, 1993) and Gibson (1979) to investigate the complex interaction of variables affecting second language (L2) learning and teaching (e.g. Blyth, 2009; Chun, 2016; Douglas Fir Group, 2016; Guerrettaz & Johnston, 2013; Kramsch, 2002, 2008; Levine, 2020; Palalas & Hoven, 2013; Thoms & Poole, 2017; van Lier, 1996, 2000, 2004). Why ecology? Lam and Kramsch (2003) contend that the value of the ecological metaphor lies in its ability 'to capture the *interconnectedness* of psychological, social, and environmental processes of SLA' (144, italics in original). Put differently, an ecological perspective on L2 education frames the field as a complex adaptive system for generating and circulating disciplinary knowledge (Larsen-Freeman & Cameron, 2008). Furthermore, an ecological perspective helps L2 researchers grasp the dynamic relationships between the various subsystems of the overall system or field (Douglas Fir Group, 2016).

The general idea of conceptualizing human knowledge as a nested set of subsystems originates with the American psychologist Urie Bronfenbrenner (1979, 1993) who explores human development in terms of five separate but related levels of context: *the microsystem*, *the mesosystem*, *the exosystem*, *the macrosystem* and *the chronosystem*. Bronfenbrenner places the individual at the center of these nested systems. The microsystem refers to the individual's immediate environment and includes the individual's direct interactions with family members, friends and mentors. The mesosystem comprises activities and relationships between members other than the individual in the microsystem, for example, interactions between an individual's parents and teachers. The exosystem refers to social settings that are not in an individual's immediate environment and therefore exert an indirect influence on the individual's development, such as the school system, the government and the media. The macrosystem describes a set of attitudes, beliefs and values shared by the group at large, in other words, the culture that influences the individual's development. Finally, the chronosystem refers to changes in the culture that may affect the individual's development over time; for example, the growing acceptance of non-traditional gender roles in Western cultures.

The basic idea of ecology when applied to the field of L2 education is that different types of disciplinary knowledge are created and disseminated within different spaces or levels of the overall system: within the classroom, within teacher education programs, and within the field of L2 education at large (see Figure 0.1). In our application of ecological theory to L2 education, we conceive of the microsystem in terms of the direct interactions between learners and teachers in the immediate context of the language classroom. One step removed, the mesosystem refers to teacher education programs that do not include interactions with learners per se but that have a relatively direct impact on the classroom environment. Next, the exosystem refers to the field of L2 education that comprises many different language professionals who have an indirect if not tangential effect on the language learner, such as editors of scholarly journals, managers of open educational resources (OER) repositories and members of allied fields such as the Digital Humanities. Finally, the macrosystem refers to 'open education' as a set of ideologies and values that guide social and professional practices in the other subsystems (classrooms, teacher education programs and the field at large). Thus, by examining emergent forms of disciplinary knowledge in L2 education in terms of ecology, we hope to clarify the

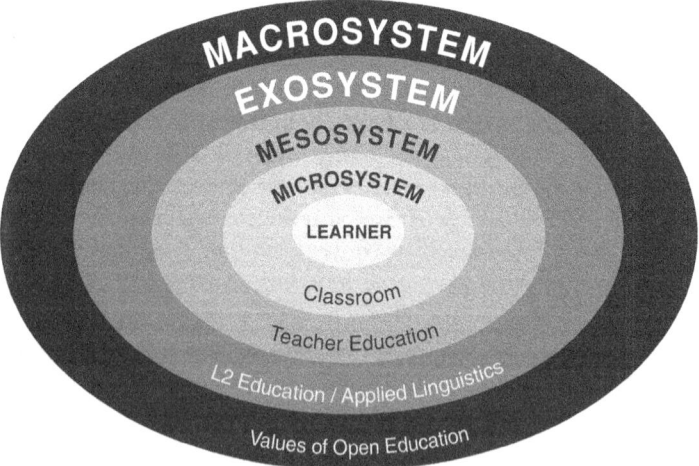

Figure 0.1 Ecological subsystems of L2 education

'instigative and debilitative forces between one ecosystem and another' (van Lier, 2000: 210). In brief, the general goal of this book is to explore how the disruptive forces of openness are giving rise to a new knowledge ecology within the interacting subsystems of L2 education.

As mentioned, applied linguists have recently begun to explore the application of ecological theory to the construction of second language acquisition (SLA) theories. In particular, the Douglas Fir Group (2016) outlines a transdisciplinary framework for SLA research that draws heavily on Bronfenbrenner's ecological approach to human development. Noting that SLA theories have traditionally favored cognitivist approaches due to the dominance of linguistics and psychology in the field, the Douglas Fir Group calls for a transdisciplinary approach that acknowledges the relevance of more socially oriented disciplines such as anthropology, education, sociology and cognitive science. To integrate research findings from multiple disciplines, the Douglas Fir Group frames L2 learning as an ecosystem that comprises 'three levels of mutually dependent influence' (2016: 24): the micro level of social activity in classrooms, the meso level of sociocultural institutions and communities and the macro level of ideological structures. According to the authors, such a transdisciplinary framework for SLA theory has two basic goals: 'to expand the perspectives of researchers and teachers of L2 learners with regard to learners' diverse multilingual repertoires of meaning-making resources and identities' and 'to foster in learners a profound awareness […] of the dynamic and evolving role their actions play in shaping their own and others' worlds' (2016: 25). In other words, by construing L2 learning in transdisciplinary terms, the Douglas Fir Group hopes to prompt scholars to frame their research in terms of the ecological affordances that may exist within and between the various levels. For instance, the Douglas Fir Group maintains that a transdisciplinary approach to SLA theorizing would help researchers to explore how language ideologies permeate all levels of the learning ecology: 'ideologies influence the access, investment, and agency into a new language that learners may or may not (be able or willing to) exert' (2016: 33). To support this assertion, the authors cite three areas in which ideologies directly affect L2 learning: language policies that constrain social patterns of language use, language ideologies that create unfavorable conditions for multilingualism and the belief systems of language learners themselves that affect their language development.

Closely related to the concept of open design in educational research, the Douglas Fir Group argues that one of the major affordances of an ecological approach to SLA theory is a clearer focus on language competencies as complex, dynamic and holistic phenomena (Douglas Fir Group, 2016: 26). As Larsen-Freeman has repeatedly argued (1997, 2006, 2012, 2017), languages and cultures are themselves complex, adaptive systems that are open to external influences. In other words, openness is a design feature of complex systems, whether that system be a language, a culture, or in the case of this book, a discipline. While SLA theory focuses on 'the processes by which school-aged children, adolescents and adults learn and use, at any point in life, an additional language, including second, foreign, indigenous, minority, or heritage languages [...]' (Douglas Fir Group, 2016: 19), the purview of this book is somewhat larger. Our focus is not only the knowledge created by language learners commonly referred to as *competence* in SLA studies, but rather different kinds of disciplinary knowledge that are central to different stakeholders in the field of L2 teaching and learning. Put differently, our book explores how different kinds of knowledge are created and disseminated by different stakeholders who reside at different levels of the ecosystem, including educational administrators, learners, teachers, teacher educators, textbook authors, textbook publishers and researchers. It bears repeating that some of these stakeholders may have little direct contact with language learners per se. We believe that an ecological approach allows for a more critical analysis of the indirect relationships between divergent types of knowledge typically associated with the field of L2 education. In summary, our book adopts a wider purview than the ecologically inspired studies of SLA that focus resolutely on the development of the learner's knowledge base.

In addition to applied linguists and SLA specialists, educators from many different fields have invoked the metaphor of ecology in their calls for a more democratic educational system (Iiyoshi & Kumar, 2008). For instance, Baraniuk (2007) employs the concept of 'knowledge ecosystem' to describe the relations between the various stakeholders in educational publishing: students, teachers, parents, administrators, textbook publishers and other businesses such as testing services. Baraniuk (2007: 230) contends that academic publishing constitutes a closed 'knowledge ecosystem' because it shuts out 'talented K-12 teachers, community college instructors, scientists and engineers out in industry, and the world majority who do not read and write English.' Baraniuk's claims raise important questions about power and hegemony in educational systems. His main contention is that educational publishing, as currently configured, is controlled by a small group of people in developed countries – publishers, editors and academics who are highly resistant to sharing control with the majority of end-users.

The contributors to this book view the field of L2 education as a diverse knowledge ecosystem, comprising ever-evolving approaches to L2 learning, teaching and publishing via a host of various learners, educators and other entities in the environment (e.g. L2 materials and tools, OER repositories, open-access journals), which, when examined together, provide for a more comprehensive understanding of our field in the 21st century. While L2 education has always been affected by a number of economic, political, theoretical and social forces that have led to changes over time, the field is currently experiencing the emergence of a new paradigm; that is, an open knowledge ecology brought about by the open education movement. The contributions of this book fill a void in the literature regarding the rise of this new paradigm by offering empirically grounded analyses of how open education is disrupting the study and teaching of second languages while also addressing issues related to open-access scholarship and similar work in the digital humanities. These new knowledge ecosystems, while different, are interrelated and collectively create an open and dynamic L2 education ecology.

To better understand the ecological metaphor and how it informs the work presented in this book, it is important to briefly highlight some of the central components of an ecological perspective as articulated by the applied linguist Leo van Lier (2000, 2004, 2010). First, an ecological approach aims to understand the complexity of the actions and activities of the organisms in any given environment via an analysis of the 'network of interdependencies among all the elements' (van Lier, 2010: 2). To understand a diverse ecosystem like L2 education, one must determine the relationships among the various actors and objects in the environment and investigate their on-going interactions. For instance, the values inherent in open education, such as collaboration and sharing, affect the ways in which L2 educators create pedagogical content, engage with students and disseminate scholarship. Furthermore, today's students are engaging more directly with each other via open L2 materials and tools.

In analyzing both the social actors (learners, teachers, administrators, publishers) and their objects (forms of scholarship) and the ways in which they interact in an ecosystem, one is able to understand the affordances that result, another important concept inherent in an ecological perspective. Van Lier (2004) indicates that affordances are not static features in an organism's environment but rather emerge from the interactions between the organisms and the environment. In the context of L2 education, 'the affordance perspective assumes an active learner establishing relationships with and within the environment. In terms of language learning, affordances arise out of participation and use, and learning opportunities arise as a consequence of participation and use' (Auyang, 2000, as cited in van Lier, 2004: 92). In the broadest sense, affordances can be viewed as 'relationships of possibility . . . they make action, interaction, and joint projects possible' (van Lier, 2010: 3). This book, in effect, explores the affordances of an open knowledge ecology for L2 educators, learners, researchers, publishers and the L2 learning community at large.

Another central aspect of an ecological perspective relates to agency. As mentioned above, a learner who is active in his or her environment (i.e. active with other elements in the environment such as learners, teachers or L2 artifacts) will inevitably encounter different kinds of affordances for learning. Learners must wield a certain amount of agency within their environment to take advantage of these affordances for their development and growth. Put another way, 'there must be room in a(n) . . .

environment for a variety of expressions of agency to flourish' (van Lier, 2010: 4). To that end, it is important to mention that ecological approaches are allied with complexity theoretic ideas and the conceptualization of L2 learning and teaching as a complex adaptive system (Larsen-Freeman, 2017). One of the characteristics or design features of complex adaptive systems is openness, which we believe is closely related to agency. As such, many of the chapters in this book examine how social actors in L2 environments demonstrate their agency by engaging in different open educational practices (OEP). This agency allows L2 students, teachers and researchers to participate more fully in the creation and sharing of new forms of knowledge with others. This increased level of participation, in turn, results in a positive disruption of L2 learning, teaching and academic publishing.

As alluded to above, open education advocates commonly assert that the educational system as currently configured is too closed, and as a consequence, creates 'shutouts,' people who are unable to gain full access to opportunities and knowledge (Baraniuk, 2007). For example, open educators frequently argue that the high costs of tuition and textbooks diminish the full participation of low-income students. According to advocates of open education, OER allow these students back into the educational system by reducing the cost of materials. In a similar fashion, researchers who do not have access to scholarly journals because their institutions cannot afford the ever-increasing subscription rates are unable to participate in the generation and dissemination of academic scholarship. Open-access journals are routinely offered as the solution to this problem. Finally, the many different social actors who populate academic fields often find themselves in 'silos,' a pejorative term that refers to isolated social networks defined by hyper-specialized interests. A solution to the common problem of academic isolation is the concept of the 'weak tie' (Granovetter, 1973), the occasional interaction between members of relatively closed social networks. In such a view, the more open an educational system, the more it promotes the common good by disseminating knowledge to more people. Note that the examples of lowered educational costs, improved access to scholarship and increased social connection construe openness as an instigative force for good. However, an ecological perspective on openness helps us adopt a more critical stance by assuming the existence of both instigative and debilitative forces in the analysis of systemic change. In other words, disruption is likely to have unintended consequences that play out differently at different levels of a discipline's systemic organization. Therefore, openness may solve a problem at one level while creating a problem at another level. The contributions of this book therefore explore both the benefits and the challenges of open education and its effects – both good and bad – on the L2 educational system.

Open Education: A Brief History

During the past 20 years, open education has evolved into a global movement affecting all levels of education. Early efforts focused on the creation and sharing of OER, defined as pedagogical materials 'that are openly available for use by educators and students, without an accompanying need to pay royalties or license fees' (Butcher, 2011: 5). Examples of OER include videos, images, podcasts, lesson plans, class activities, PowerPoint slides, full-length open textbooks, among many other resources. OER are often shared via a Creative Commons license (https://creativecommons.org/) that allows fellow educators to revise, remix, retain, reuse and redistribute the content by avoiding the usual restrictions of copyright (Wiley, 2014). More recent efforts have shifted the focus from OER to OEP such as open pedagogy, defined as an 'access-oriented commitment to learner-driven education AND as a process of designing architectures and using tools for learning that enable students to shape the public knowledge commons of which they are a part' (Jhangiani & DeRosa, 2017: 14, emphasis in original). Furthermore, OER and OEP typically draw upon 'open technologies that facilitate collaborative, flexible learning and the open sharing of teaching practices' (Cape Town Open Education Declaration, 2008: 1). In sum, the democratization of knowledge – both the creation and distribution of it – lies at the heart of the open education movement. When knowledge is severely limited or denied due to restrictive copyright or exorbitant access fees for students, teachers, researchers or the general public, it negatively affects those involved and restrains intellectual progress.

Until recently, the field of L2 education has only marginally embraced open education. Some of the reasons why L2 educators have been hesitant to participate in the open education movement relate to the dearth of research investigating the benefits and challenges of L2 learning and teaching in open environments, the effectiveness of OER when compared to traditional, publisher-produced materials and motivations as to why and how L2 educators engage in OEP at their institutions. While researchers have recently begun to explore aspects of OER and OEP in L2 education (e.g. Blyth, 2013; Comas-Quinn *et al.*, 2019; Thoms & Thoms, 2014), more investigation is needed. Furthermore, while both OER and OEP have the potential to create more engaged participants in L2 learning and teaching environments, hurdles still remain within this new open knowledge ecosystem. For instance, while there is ample evidence that teachers are beginning to develop their own materials, they appear unsure how to license and share their materials with others in the field (see Blyth, 2017 for other challenges). Thus, the dissemination of basic information about OER and OEP remains a major challenge.

Much of the research literature on the affordances of OER has focused on the economic savings that benefit students, instructors and institutions (e.g. Coleman-Prisco, 2017; Martin *et al.*, 2017; Weller *et al.*, 2017; Wiley, 2018). As previously mentioned, many open materials and tools typically carry a Creative Commons license, which enables OER to be freely shared with others thereby giving instructors and students access to content versus having to pay excessive fees for similar materials from traditional publishers. The average cost of textbooks and supplies in the US for a typical undergraduate student currently averages approximately $1300 per year (College Board, 2019), and there is ample evidence that OER significantly reduces or eliminates textbook costs for students (Wiley, 2018; Wiley & Green, 2012). While the cost-saving aspect of open education is compelling for students and administrators alike, the overall rise in the creation and/or adoption of OER in a variety of disciplines is motivated by many reasons.

First, the increasing number and availability of OER 'can contribute to more productive students and educators' (Butcher, 2011: 13). Many OER allow educators and/or students to adapt the materials so that they address context-specific educational needs (de los Arcos *et al.*, 2016), such as the diverse needs of foreign language (FL) learners (e.g. different content for heritage vs. non-heritage language learners) or filling a gap in a publisher-produced textbook or curriculum (e.g. incorporating authentic videos that assist in teaching a particular cultural or linguistic concept). In other words, one of the benefits of OER is that they are much easier to adapt and use when compared to traditional publisher-produced materials given that users don't need to worry about copyright issues when making changes to OER content. This kind of flexibility means that 'instructors, students and self-learners who use OER can replace "flat" educational experiences, where opportunity is a function of what one instructor or school can offer, with a constantly evolving multidimensional educational process' (Plotkin, 2010, para. 4). Data from the *Languages Open Resources Online* (LORO) project at The Open University in the United Kingdom (Comas-Quinn *et al.*, 2012) indicate that OER positively impact the skills and development of language teachers which can, in turn, result in L2 linguistic and cultural benefits for students (Comas-Quinn & Fitzgerald, 2013).

A second benefit of open education has resulted in language learning and teaching becoming more participatory for both instructors and students. That is, OER and OEP allow instructors and, in many cases, their students, to become active producers rather than passive consumers of course content. These changing instructor and student roles have the potential to create more effective learning environments (Butcher, 2011; Thoms & Thoms, 2014). Some researchers have found that the creation and use of OER can provide for a more student-centered learning experience, where students are more engaged and actively contributing to their learning, thereby creating meaningful educational experiences (DeRosa & Robison, 2017; Gruszczynska, 2012) versus traditional educational approaches where students simply 'consume' course content provided by instructors. These kinds of open learning and teaching experiences are inherent in open pedagogy, a term defined as 'an access-oriented commitment to learner-driven education AND as a process of designing architectures and using tools for learning that enable students to shape the public knowledge commons of which they are a part' (Jhangiani & DeRosa, 2017: 14, emphasis in original). In other words, L2 learning and teaching that relies on digital, open content (e.g. OER) and OEP can lead to the creation of a collaborative learning environment where learners are regularly exposed to and interact with authentic L2 resources and are provided opportunities to co-create and/or co-curate L2 content; all of which may lead to increasing motivation to learn and/or make use of the L2 in meaningful ways.

While more empirical work is needed that demonstrates the possible benefits of OER on student learning experiences, particularly in FL learning environments, the financial realities for many students and teachers in various parts of the world are pushing educators to create non-traditional materials like OER and engage in OEP to meet current and future educational challenges (de los Arcos & Weller, 2018). Furthermore, the ongoing COVID-19 health pandemic is yet another force that has resulted in efforts to open up access to OER, encourage OEP and freely share research related to L2 learning and teaching in distance education environments.

While the chapters in this book provide comprehensive descriptions of the features of the new knowledge ecology within L2 education, it is necessary to briefly describe some of the activities and collaborations that are becoming the norm due to the open movement. One example includes new approaches to disseminating scholarship. Specifically, the number of open-access journals dedicated to L2 scholarship is on the rise. Many university libraries around the world are also creating digital repositories where scholars can upload their digital work, thereby increasing access to and distribution of their research (see OpenDOAR http://v2.sherpa.ac.uk/opendoar/). In addition, more and more universities are adopting open-access mandates that generally grant institutions the ability to make researchers' work accessible to a wider audience via distribution through an open digital repository.

In the teaching realm, the creation and distribution of L2 materials and tools is made possible by an increase in online repositories of teaching-related content. For example, OER Commons (https://www.oercommons.org/) and MERLOT (https://www.merlot.org/merlot/) allow educators to openly share the content that they create with fellow educators and learners (see Appendix for a comprehensive list of OER and OEP L2 resources). In the United States, government-funded open initiatives and resources have also become important pieces of the open L2 education ecosystem. Examples of this type of investment include support for national foreign language resource centers dedicated to the creation and distribution of open L2 materials and research (e.g. the Center for Open Educational Resources and Language Learning at the University of Texas at Austin (https://www.coerll.utexas.edu/coerll/), the Open Language Resource Center at the University of Kansas (http://olrc.ku.edu) and the US Department of Education's *Go Open Initiative* and related policies concerning open data requirements for publicly funded research (https://tech.ed.gov/open/)). Similar open initiatives have also arisen in other parts of the world. One example is the Global OER Graduate Network (https://go-gn.net/), which brings together various PhD candidates throughout the world who carry out research on the development of OER, OEP and projects related to open learning and teaching environments (e.g. massive open online courses/MOOCs). The OER Hub (http://oerhub.net/), supported by and headquartered at the Open University in the United Kingdom, is yet another example of a center whose main goals include conducting research about open education and creating resources for the open education research community.

In summary, this book seeks to (a) contextualize open education as it pertains to L2 learning and teaching via in-depth explorations of how the open movement is affecting L2 education both in and beyond the classroom context, including the development of professional knowledge by L2 educators and the dissemination of L2 disciplinary knowledge via open journals, archives and repositories, (b) fill the research void by exploring aspects of open L2 learning and teaching across a range of educational environments and (c) illustrate new ways of creating, adapting and curating L2 materials that are openly licensed and freely shared among L2 educators and students.

Organization of Book

Each of the subsequent chapters draws on different kinds of knowledge associated with open education: the design and classroom implementation of OER, the application of OER and OEP to teacher education and the importance of new forms of disciplinary knowledge disseminated through open-access journals, OER repositories and open social networks. Despite commonalities, the chapters constitute different academic genres: empirical studies about the effects of openness on L2 learning and teaching, a survey of L2 teachers in the United States about OER and OEP, qualitative analyses of OER projects and essays about the kinds of knowledge needed to participate in the changing ecology of L2 education. In this book, we focus on the first three nested subsystems that together reflect the overall knowledge ecology of L2 education: (1) the microsystem of L2 instructional environments (Zapata & Ribota; Levet & Tschudi; Romero; Zourou & Potolia); (2) the mesosystem of L2 teacher education (Thoms & Poole; Dupuy; Blyth, Warner & Luks); and (3) the exosystem of the field of L2 education (Chun & Heift; Beaven; Davis & Blyth;

Hilchey). That said, we do not ignore the importance of the macrosystem that refers to the value system of open education. Rather, all chapters touch on open educational values that are embedded in various professional practices. As such, a shared belief may result in different OEP at different levels of the ecology. For example, open educators are generally in agreement that there should be no financial barriers to the access of scholarly knowledge. This democratic belief plays out in different ways in the L2 educational ecology. In the microsystem of the classroom, students and teachers are increasingly adopting OER rather than expensive commercial products. In the mesosystem of teacher education, L2 educators are beginning to learn the basics of OER creation and dissemination. And in the exosystem of the field at large, open-access journals are being promoted as a low-cost way to disseminate scholarship. The point is that these three different practices arise from the same fundamental belief in the importance of open access to education, knowledge and research.

The Microsystem: Developing Knowledge in L2 Instructional Environments

The first set of chapters focuses on how various kinds of knowledge are generated and circulated within instructional environments such as a traditional classroom or an online community. Viewing the instructional environment as the core microsystem of L2 education, these chapters reveal how open design changes L2 learning and teaching. Within these environments, the primary social actors are learners and teachers who employ OER and OEP as tools to mediate their cognitive and social behaviors. It is shown that OER and OEP not only change how learners and teachers interact in these L2 environments, but also what such interactions are about. In other words, the use of OER and OEP entails new pedagogical practices as well as new pedagogical content.

In their chapter 'Open Educational Resources in Heritage and L2 Spanish Classrooms: Design, Development and Implementation,' Gabriela Zapata and Alessandra Ribota describe the problems commonly associated with 'one-size-fits-all' textbooks in American higher education. In particular, Zapata and Ribota contend that commercial Spanish textbooks in the United States rarely reflect the life experiences of students outside the American mainstream. Furthermore, studies have found that commercial Spanish materials created for the general public may actually increase levels of linguistic and cultural insecurity among heritage Spanish speakers enrolled in general Spanish courses (Zapata, 2017). As a result, more and more L2 Spanish teachers are abandoning commercial materials in favor of teacher-generated OER. Along these lines, Zapata and Ribota contrast two case studies of the same instructor who designs and implements her own Spanish OER based on the multiliteracies-inspired pedagogy *Learning by Design* (L-by-D) (Cope & Kalantzis, 2015; Kalantzis *et al.*, 2005, 2016). Zapata and Ribota maintain that the inherent adaptability of OER is well suited to the L-by-D principles of *belonging* and *transformation* (Kalantzis *et al.*, 2005). For example, according to the L-by-D framework, instructional environments should incorporate resources that are directly connected to the learners' lifeworlds. Therefore, Zapata and Ribota urge L2 instructors to adapt all elements of the learning environment, including the pedagogical materials, to meet the specific needs of their learners as closely as possible.

Their first case study focuses on learners enrolled in a Spanish course for heritage speakers at a small, Hispanic-serving institution. In contrast, the second case study focuses on Spanish learners who belong to the American mainstream. While Zapata and Ribota view these OER projects as successful, they do not overlook the many challenges facing instructors who wish to create their own materials from scratch. For instance, in both case studies, the OER creator encountered significant resistance, initially from her students and later from her colleagues. In addition, the authors point out that the design and implementation of high-quality OER require more time and money than many language programs may be able to afford. Thus, Zapata and Ribota advise OER developers to secure proper funding and course release time from the outset of their projects.

In the next chapter 'Open by Design: The *Cultura* Project,' Sabine Levet and Stephen Tschudi describe how an innovative OER developed by three French instructors at MIT takes full advantage of its open pedagogical design. The general goal of the *Cultura* project's curriculum and platform is the development of an intercultural knowledge that leads to deeper understanding between two groups of L2 students from different cultures. Created in 1997 by a team of French instructors at MIT, *Cultura* has since been adapted to the teaching of many languages at many institutions, including secondary schools. After detailing the design of the original telecollaboration between students at MIT learning French and students at French universities learning English, Levet and Tschudi examine how the L2 teaching community has adapted various aspects of the *Cultura* project. One of the most salient features of the original *Cultura* model is the obligatory use of the L1 during the exchange of opinions in an online forum. While this feature results in naturally occurring linguistic data for cross-cultural analysis, many L2 teachers have preferred that their students practice the target language in the online forum, a significant adaptation of the model. The authors also describe how *Cultura* has been adapted to meet the needs of a greater variety of learning contexts, including the context of heritage language learning. Finally, the authors contend that the *Cultura* project exemplifies the OER ideal of pedagogical materials that are continuously adapted and updated by a community of users. Despite such affordances, Levet and Tschudi note that *Cultura's* open design places a heavy burden on its creators who must commit to curating the community and maintaining the materials and website.

Sergio Romero, in his chapter 'Open Educational Resources as Tools to Teach the Indigenous Languages of Latin America: Where Technology, Pedagogy and Colonialism Meet,' examines the development of an OER for K'iche' Mayan, a language spoken by more than 1 million people in the western highlands of Guatemala. Romero points out that the educational ecology of small indigenous languages differs significantly compared to global languages and cultures that are the usual objects of study in higher education. For instance, Romero emphasizes that the design of L2 pedagogical materials typically presupposes a standard language variety, but such an ideological construct is often hotly contested among speakers of indigenous languages. To complicate matters further, many publications about indigenous languages and cultures are difficult to adapt to the pedagogical needs of non-native learners, having been written by linguists and anthropologists for a scholarly audience. Romero details 'the distinctive articulations of language, culture and discourse in Mayan and other indigenous languages of Latin America' that present challenges for his American learners. In particular, Romero contends that university students with 'a Western mindset bring their own language ideologies and expectations to the experience of learning indigenous languages.' As such, indigenous language pedagogy differs in significant ways from general L2 pedagogy. In essence, students of indigenous languages are trained as linguists preparing to conduct field research. For instance, Romero describes how language variation is treated in his Ki'che' materials as something students learn to figure out for themselves with the partnership of native speakers. This kind of intellectual collaboration between learners and native speakers is a hallmark of indigenous language OER. In fact, Romero notes that direct community participation is critically important to the revitalization efforts of indigenous languages and cultures, of which OER plays a key role.

In the chapter 'Openness in a Crowdsourced Massive Online Language Community,' Katerina Zourou and Anthippi Potolia shift our focus away from traditional L2 classrooms towards 'the digital wilds' (Sauro & Zourou, 2019). More specifically, Zourou and Potolia examine Busuu and Duolingo, two online communities that mix OEP with commercial interests. The authors refer to Busuu and Duolingo as 'social network sites for language learning' (SNSLL) where massive numbers of users register to learn an L2. At issue is the concept of 'open washing,' a term that refers to a company or organization that adopts superficial practices of openness while rejecting the democratic ethos and values of the open education movement. Zourou and Potolia relate the concept of open washing to the freemium business model adopted by both Busuu and Duolingo. The freemium model allows users open access to free content at the beginning levels of engagement but requires them to pay for premium content at higher levels. Zourou and Potolia examine how the freemium model affects the design and delivery of content in SNSLLs and how it creates an ethical dilemma by violating pedagogical best practices. For example, the authors describe the 'exploitation of open content creation (in the form of peer correction) as a profit-making mechanism for the SNSLL without a corresponding remuneration for the producers – the downside of crowd-sourcing (Howe, 2006) – occurring in these open networked sites for language learning.' Based on a careful analysis of the reflective diaries of 21 users of Busuu and Duolingo, Zourou and Potolia conclude that some of the mechanisms of the freemium business model have negative implications for L2 learner participation and learning. In general, their study reflects a critical approach to openness, a design feature of complex, adaptive systems that can result in both good and bad outcomes.

The Mesosystem: Developing Knowledge in L2 Teacher Education

The second set of chapters focuses on the mesosystem of L2 teacher education and seeks to answer questions about how teacher education should introduce open education to beginning L2 teachers. What exactly do pre-service L2 teachers need to know about OER and OEP? How might contact with the ideas and practices of open education affect L2 teacher cognition? Finally, how can L2 teacher education programs help pre-service teachers to participate more fully in the new knowledge ecology of L2 education?

The first chapter of this section, 'Second Language Teachers and the Open Education Movement in the United States: A National Survey,' reports on a wide-scale survey about open education administered to 1,484 L2 educators in the US. In their survey, Joshua Thoms and Frederick Poole investigate four major aspects of OER and OEP in L2 education: (1) the variables affecting awareness and use of OER in language classrooms, (2) the reasons why language educators create, adapt, or use OER, (3) the kinds of OER most commonly used by language educators and (4) how the use of OER affects L2 teaching practice(s). The survey provides a snapshot of American L2 teachers' knowledge about OER and OEP, information of particular interest to academics in charge of L2 teacher education programs. The results of the survey show that L2 teachers working in blended/online classrooms tend to use OER more frequently than their colleagues in more traditional classrooms. In addition, K-12 teachers and community college teachers are more likely than university instructors to use OER. Finally, according to the survey results, English as a Second Language (ESL) teachers use OER at higher rates than their colleagues in foreign languages. Thoms and Poole report that the perceived shortcomings of publisher-produced textbooks is the primary reason L2 teachers give for using OER; L2 teachers tend to believe that user-generated materials are more current, relevant, and authentic than publisher-produced materials. In particular, L2 teachers prefer the use of videos and images to other forms of OER. Overall, 79% of the survey respondents reported that the use of OER had changed their teaching in positive ways. For example, many teachers attribute their belief in the importance of authentic pedagogical materials to their contact with OER. Characterizing their findings as 'hypothesis-generating,' Thoms and Poole call for further research into L2 teachers' knowledge of OER and OEP.

In 'Raising the Curtain on OER/OEP: Opening Pathways from Awareness to Engagement in a Graduate Course on Foreign Language Program Direction' (LPD), Beatrice Dupuy describes the impact of a thematic unit on OER and OEP in an applied linguistics course. Her study is based on a semester-long online graduate course on collegiate FL program direction at a large, public research university in the United States. Based on the case studies of three graduate students with different levels of OER awareness and engagement, the study is guided by four main research questions: (1) What did study participants know about OER/OEP before completing a course unit on a OER/OEP?; (2) What new knowledge about OER/OEP did study participants develop as a result of completing a course unit on OER/OEP?; (3) How did study participants approach the creation of their OER-based LPD resource sites?; and (4) What new practices did study participants engage in while creating their OER-based LPD resource sites?

After analyzing her students' self-reports, Dupuy notes that all three of the focal participants were familiar with the term OER at the outset of the course, but only one participant knew that the distinguishing feature of OER is an open copyright license. The other two participants associated OER with free online resources but not with open licenses. As for OEP, only one participant had heard of the term. Furthermore, the participants had relatively limited knowledge of OER repositories at the beginning of the course. An analysis of student data (e.g. readings, blog posts, reflective essays and OER assignments) leads Dupuy to claim that the unit greatly increased her students' knowledge of OER/OEP in measurable ways. In particular, Dupuy notes that the final project of designing an OER-based resource and sharing it with language program directors helped her students see themselves as legitimate contributors to the OER/OEP movement. That said, Dupuy ends her discussion with a cautionary note about the limits of teacher education coursework and calls for more extracurricular opportunities such as supervised classroom experiences or OER development experiences that would help L2 teachers become more active participants in the open education movement.

In the next chapter, 'The Role of OER in Promoting Critical Reflection and Professional Development: The Foreign Languages and the Literary in the Everyday Project,' Carl Blyth, Chantelle Warner and Joanna Luks describe a professional development opportunity for pre-service teachers that goes well beyond short-term course assignments as called for by Dupuy. The chapter focuses on the Foreign Languages and the Literary in the Everyday (FLLITE) project, a joint initiative of two national foreign language resource centers (US Department of Education). Guided by an hypothesis from the OER Hub's OER Evidence Report 2013–2014: 'Use of OER leads to critical reflection by educators, with evidence of improvement in their practice' (http://oerhub.net/research-outputs/reports/), the FLLITE project seeks to assist beginning FL teachers in the creation of their own OER that incorporate elements of literary language defined as playful uses of the target linguistic system. The OER life cycle refers to the typical phases involved in OER development: finding content for the OER, composing the OER, adapting the OER, using the OER in class and sharing the results with the community. As part of the project, graduate student developers receive feedback on their OER from more experienced members of a community of practice (e.g. university L2 faculty including language program directors). As such, the OER life cycle serves as a template for both OER development and teacher development. To demonstrate the impact of OER development on teacher cognition and professional development, Blyth, Warner and Luks describe two case studies of FLLITE participants who were both graduate student language instructors at the onset of their participation in the project. Based on interviews with the two participants as well as analyses of multiple drafts of their OER, the authors claim that OER development exposes beginning teachers to new ways of conceptualizing language and leads them to reflect on new ways of learning and teaching. Blyth, Warner and Luks contend that FLLITE is an example of social pedagogy in which students produce work for members of a community of practice who view the students as legitimate members of the community and who take the students' work seriously. As such, the social orientation towards peer review and publication is seen as a key element in the transformative impact of the FLLITE project on teacher education.

The Exosystem: Developing Knowledge in the Field of L2 Education

The final group of chapters ventures beyond the classroom and teacher education realms to explore how L2 educators develop their knowledge of open education through contact with colleagues and other information sources in the field at large. The focus of these chapters is on the tacit knowledge that L2 specialists gradually develop through engagement with the field's scholarly journals, OER repositories and professional networks. These sources of information are usually anchored in the home fields of applied linguistics and L2 education but may also include adjacent fields such as the Digital Humanities. The OEP that form the basis of this tacit knowledge include such things as knowing how to access scholarly information from open journals, knowing how to select OER from repositories, knowing how to develop and maintain 'weak ties' between professional networks, and knowing how to find high quality open content by conducting 'filtered' internet searches.

In their chapter, 'The Affordances and Challenges of Open-access Journals: The Case of an Applied Linguistics Journal,' Dorothy Chun and Trude Heift, co-editors of the open-access journal *Language Learning & Technology (LLT)* (https://www.lltjournal.org//), discuss open-access publishing as an integral part of the field's new knowledge ecology. Launched in 1997, *LLT* has rapidly expanded during the past 20 years and now ranks as the most impactful open-access journal in linguistics and the third most impactful open-access journal in Education. Comparing online journals to traditional print journals, the authors cite several affordances of open-access journals: broader dissemination; improved tracking of readership; unlimited virtual space for content; greater use of hyperlinks; lower production costs; shortened times between submission and publication; and most importantly, easier access. Current analytics show that *LLT* receives more than one million visitors per year from many different countries around the world (e.g. United States, China, Russia, Philippines, UK, Brazil, India, Germany, France and Canada). Chun and Heift discuss the effect of open access on *LLT's* 'impact factor' as measured by the number of citations of *LLT's* articles in other scholarly journals. According to the co-editors, *LLT* has established itself as a prestigious publication that competes with the best journals in the field. Furthermore, they point out that the citation indices on which *LLT's* impact factor is calculated are open and transparent to the public, in keeping with the open knowledge ecology. While *LLT* has overcome initial concerns about the quality of its published scholarship, there remains a general perception that print publications are viewed more favorably for tenure and promotion. However, Chun and Heift maintain that free, online journals are adopting more rigorous peer review processes (double-blind peer-review, copyright protection). As a result, open-access journals are no longer perceived as lacking in rigor and quality. However, *LLT*, like many open-access journals, still faces financial insecurities given its reliance on non-profit organizations largely funded by external grants. Chun and Heift conclude their chapter by emphasizing how *LLT* integrates the three branches of the open movement – open access, open data and open education, as advocated by the Scholarly Publishing and Academic Resources Coalition (SPARC). For example, *LLT* encourages authors to consider sharing their data with readers in an online repository used by second language researchers (http://www.iris-database.org). In addition, authors are asked to submit informal summaries of their work to make their research more accessible to L2 teachers, OER developers, language policy makers and the general public.

As noted, tacit pedagogical knowledge, also known as 'pedagogical know-how' is typically learned in an incidental fashion through practical classroom experience and interaction with one's professional colleagues.

In her chapter 'Analysing Teachers' Tacit Professional Knowledge of OER: The Case of Languages Open Resources Online (LORO),' Tita Beaven seeks to make explicit the tacit knowledge that teachers draw on when working through the five stages of the OER lifecycle: find, compose, adapt, use and share. Beaven's methods for uncovering this hidden knowledge are 'professional conversations' that she conducts with some of her colleagues who teach French and Spanish at the Open University in the United Kingdom. Beaven records, transcribes and codes these professional conversations according to Tait's (2000, 2003) categories of support that teachers give students in online learning: cognitive support (scaffolding pedagogical content), affective support (enhancing student self-esteem) and systemic support (establishing administrative processes). Beaven finds that teachers are highly aware of the kinds of support they give during all the phases of their engagement with the OER lifecycle. In other words, when locating and selecting OER for their teaching, teachers use their cognitive knowledge, such as their knowledge of language and linguistics and how to teach it, and their knowledge of what students already know or need more help with. Beaven's colleagues draw on their own previous experience of teaching in other contexts. They also use their knowledge of the course materials and resources in the LORO repository. Beaven suggests that future studies address how tacit pedagogical know-how can be made more explicit during the professional development of teachers.

In their chapter 'Towards a Pedagogy of Openness: Bridging English-language and Foreign-language Digital Humanities,' Rebecca Davis and Carl Blyth argue that instructors in the two major camps of digital humanities, English-language DH and foreign-language DH, would benefit from closer contact with each other. Davis and Blyth claim that the work of L2 scholars is unfortunately marginalized within the larger DH community because of the dominance of the English language in the field. Their chapter aims to bridge the gaps between the two DH communities by showing their many links and parallel developments. The authors frame their chapter in terms of Granovetter's (1973) concept of 'bridging weak ties' that facilitates the passing of information between relatively separated networks defined by strong ties. Taking themselves as an example of this phenomenon, the authors highlight their strong ties to their home professional networks, the DH community (Davis) and the foreign-language community (Blyth), and their weak ties to each other's network. The majority of their chapter is dedicated to describing the many open features of DH pedagogy and how these features might be profitably adapted to fit one's professional context. One characteristic of DH pedagogy is 'generative scholarship,' the practice of involving undergraduate students in classroom research projects that contribute to a larger research agenda. Davis and Blyth describe various examples of generative scholarship within the context of L2 classrooms in which students learn a new language and culture while contributing to an open, scholarly archive that can be used by others. Despite promising parallels, Davis and Blyth caution L2 educators to honor the important differences between the open practices of DH scholars in English departments and those in foreign language departments. While the two academic disciplines of English-language DH and foreign-language DH overlap significantly, they still comprise relatively discrete communities with different interests and different foci. For example, foreign-language DH instructors are typically more concerned with their students' variable linguistic and cultural proficiency than English-language DH instructors whose students are typically native speakers.

In the final chapter, 'Finding and Using the Good Stuff: Open Educational Practices for Developing Open Educational Resources,' Christian Hilchey, an OER developer and Czech teacher, shares the many valuable lessons he learned for finding open, authentic content on the internet and for using that content in the production of cutting-edge materials. Trained as a linguist, his personal narrative as an open educator is one of learning by doing, which includes a good deal of trial and error. Hilchey recounts how he set out to create an open Czech curriculum by carefully planning the scope and sequence of his pedagogical materials, the standard operating procedure for curriculum development projects. Next, he went to the Czech Republic to film interviews with native speakers. However, during the filming, he began to question whether his traditional approach to curriculum design would accurately reflect the lives of modern Czech speakers. For instance, he noticed that the reality depicted by Czech nationals in their own social media was far more hybrid and transnational than what he had been creating. As a result, he stopped producing 'Czech' content himself and embraced user-generated content created by Czech speakers. This led Hilchey to search the internet for what he calls 'the good stuff,' high-quality open content that meets various criteria of authenticity. That said, his experiences taught him that not all L2 content needs to be produced by native speakers. In fact, Hilchey revisits the definition of 'an authentic text' as something created by natives for natives. Hilchey points out that many digital genres today are transnational. In other words, transnational genres are not specific to a given language or culture but rather belong to deterritorialized forms of participatory culture common to the internet, for example, unboxing videos on YouTube. In addition, Hilchey provides the reader with a wealth of practical tips such as how to select the right search engine or online repository to find specific types of media, how to filter online searches in terms of open licenses, and when to use keywords in English or in the target language.

Conclusion

Collectively, the chapters of this book present a current view of an emerging knowledge ecology related to L2 learning and teaching that is more dynamic, inclusive and participatory in nature primarily due to the open education movement. The Covid-19 pandemic has underscored the importance of freely sharing knowledge and resources without restrictive barriers with an aim to improve pedagogy and students' educational experiences, both of which are fundamental components of open education. While L2 learning and teaching will continue to change due to a variety of educational, social, cultural, economic and political forces, this book illustrates that open education has and will remain an important factor in how L2 research, pedagogy and resources are produced, shared and disseminated.

References

Auyang, S. (2000) *Mind in Everyday Life and Cognitive Science*. Cambridge, MA: MIT Press.

Baraniuk, R. (2007) Challenges and opportunities for the open education movement: A Connexions case study. In T. Iiyoshi and M.S.V. Kumar (eds) *Opening Up Education* (pp. 229–246). Boston: MIT Press.

Bateson, G. (1973) *Steps to an Ecology of Mind*. London: Paladin Books.

Blyth, C. (2009) From textbook to online materials: The changing ecology of foreign language publishing in the era of digital technology. In M. Evans (ed.) *Foreign Language Learning with Digital Technology* (pp. 179–202). London: Continuum.

Blyth, C. (2013) Opening up foreign language education with OER: The case of *Français Interactif*. In F. Rubio and J. Thoms (eds) *Hybrid Language Teaching and Learning: Exploring Theoretical, Pedagogical and Curricular Issues* (pp. 196–218). Boston: Heinle Cengage.

Blyth, C. (2017) Open educational resources (OERs) for language learning. In S. May and S. Thorne (eds) *Language, Education, and Technology* (3rd edn) (pp. 169–180). Cham, Switzerland: Springer.

Bronfenbrenner, U. (1979) *The Ecology of Human Development*. Cambridge, MA: Harvard University Press.

Bronfenbrenner, U. (1993) The ecology of cognitive development: Research models and fugitive findings. In R. Wozniak and K.W. Fisher (eds) *Development in Context: Acting and Thinking in Specific Environments* (pp. 3–44). Hillsdale, NJ: Erlbaum.

Butcher, N. (2011) *A Basic Guide to Open Educational Resources (OER)*. Vancouver: Commonwealth of Learning.

Cape Town Open Education Declaration (2008) See http://www.capetowndeclaration.org/read-the-declaration

Chun, D. (2016) The role of technology in SLA research. *Language Learning & Technology* 20 (2), 98–115.

Coleman-Prisco, V. (2017) Factors influencing faculty innovation and adoption of open educational resources in United States higher education. *International Journal of Education and Human Developments* 3 (4), 1–12.

College Board (2019) Average estimated undergraduate budgets 2018–2019. See https://trends.collegeboard.org/college-pricing/figures-tables/average-estimated-undergraduate-budgets-2018-19

Comas-Quinn, A. and Fitzgerald, A. (2013) *Open Educational Resources in Language Teaching and Learning*. York: Higher Education Academy.

Comas-Quinn, A., Beaven, A. and Sawhill, B. (eds) (2019) *New Case Studies of Openness in and beyond the Language Classroom*. Research-publishing.net. https://doi.org/10.14705/rpnet.2019.37.9782490057511

Comas-Quinn, A., Beaven, A., Pleines, C., Pulker, H. and de los Arcos, B. (2012) Language open resources online (LORO): Fostering a culture of collaboration and sharing. *EUROCALL Review* 18, 2–14.

Cope, B. and Kalantzis, M. (2015) The things you do to know: An introduction to the pedagogy of Multiliteracies. In B. Cope and M. Kalantzis (eds) *A Pedagogy of Multiliteracies: Learning by Design* (pp. 1–36). London: Palgrave Macmillan.

de los Arcos, B. and Weller, M. (2018) A tale of two globes: Exploring the north/south divide in engagement with OER. In U. Herb and J. Schöpfel (eds) *Open Divide: Critical Studies on Open Access* (pp. 147–156). Sacramento, CA: Litwin Books.

de los Arcos, B., Farrow, R., Pitt, R., Weller, M. and McAndrew, P. (2016) Adapting the curriculum: How K-12 teachers perceive the role of open educational resources. *Journal of Online Learning Research* 2 (1), 23–40.

DeRosa, R. and Robison, S. (2017) From OER to open pedagogy: Harnessing the power of open. In R. Jhangiani and R. Biswas-Diener (eds) *Open: The Philosophy and Practices that are Revolutionizing Education and Science* (pp. 115–124). London: Ubiquity Press.

Douglas Fir Group. (2016) A transdisciplinary framework for SLA in a multilingual world. *Modern Language Journal* 100 (S1), 19–47.

Gibson, J. (1979) *The Ecological Approach to Visual Perception*. Boston: Houghton Mifflin.

Granovetter, M. (1973) The strength of weak ties. *The American Journal of Sociology* 78 (6), 1360–1380.

Gruszczynska, A. (2012) *HEA/JISC Open Educational Resources Case Study: Pedagogical Development from OER Practice*. York: Higher Education Academy.

Guerrettaz, A. and Johnston, B. (2013) Materials in the classroom ecology. *Modern Language Journal* 97 (3), 779–796.

Howe, J. (2006) The rise of crowdsourcing. *Wired*. See http://www.wired.com/wired/archive/14.06/crowds.html

Iiyoshi, T. and Kumar, M.S.V. (eds) (2008) *Opening Up Education*. Boston: MIT Press.

Jhangiani, R. and DeRosa, R. (2017) Open pedagogy. In E. Mays (ed.) *A Guide to Making Open Textbooks with Students* (pp. 6–21). Montreal: The Rebus Community for Open Textbook Creation.

Kalantzis, M., Cope, B. and the Learning by Design Project Group (2005) *Learning by Design*. Melbourne: Victorian Schools Innovation Commission and Common Ground Publishing.

Kalantzis, M., Cope, B., Chan, B. and Dalley-Trim, L. (2016) *Literacies* (2nd edn). Cambridge: Cambridge University Press.

Kramsch, C. (2002) *Language Acquisition and Language Socialization: Ecological Perspectives*. London: Continuum.

Kramsch, C. (2008) Ecological perspectives on foreign language education. *Language Teaching* 41 (3), 389–408.

Lam, W.S.E. and Kramsch, C. (2003) The ecology of an SLA community in a computer-mediated environment. In J. Leather and J. Van Dam (eds) *Ecology of Language Acquisition* (pp. 141–158). Dordrecht, Netherlands: Kluwer Academic.

Larsen-Freeman, D. (1997) Chaos/complexity science and second language acquisition. *Applied Linguistics* 18, 141–165.

Larsen-Freeman, D. (2006) The emergence of complexity, fluency, and accuracy in the oral and written production for five Chinese learners of English. *Applied Linguistics* 27, 590–619.

Larsen-Freeman, D. (2012) Complex, dynamic systems: A new transdisciplinary theme for applied linguistics? *Language Teaching* 45, 202–214.

Larsen-Freeman, D. (2017) Complexity theory: The lessons continue. In L. Ortega and Z.-H. Han (eds) *Complexity Theory and Language Development: In Celebration of Diane Larsen-Freeman* (pp. 11–50). Amsterdam and Philadelphia: John Benjamins.

Larsen-Freeman, D. and Cameron, L. (2008) *Complex Systems and Applied Linguistics*. Oxford: Oxford University Press.

Levine, G. (2020) A human ecological language pedagogy. *Modern Language Journal* 104 (1), 1–130.

Martin, M., Belikov, O., Hilton, J., Wiley, D. and Fischer, L. (2017) Analysis of student and faculty perceptions of textbook costs in higher education. *Open Praxis* 9 (1), 79–91. DOI: https://openpraxis.org/index.php/OpenPraxis/article/view/432

OER Evidence Report 2013–2014: Building Understanding of Open Education. (2014) See http://oerhub.net/research-outputs/reports/ (accessed 19 August 2019).

Palalas, A. and Hoven, D. (2013) Implications of using DBR to investigate the iterative design of a mobile-enabled language learning system. In J. Rodríguez and C. Pardo-Ballester (eds) *Design-based Research in CALL* (pp. 41–66). San Marcos, TX: CALICO.

Plotkin, H. (2010) Free to learn. San Francisco: Creative Commons. See http://wiki.creativecommons.org/Free_to_Learn_Guide

Sauro, S. and Zourou, K. (2019) What are the digital wilds? *Language Learning & Technology* 23 (1), 1–7.

Tait, A. (2000) Planning student support for open and distance learning. *Open Learning: The Journal of Open and Distance Learning* 15 (3), 287–299.

Tait, A. (2003) Reflections on student support in open and distance learning. *International Review of Research in Open and Distance Learning* 4 (1), 1–9.

Thoms, J. and Poole, F. (2017) Investigating linguistic, literary, and social affordances of L2 collaborative reading. *Language Learning & Technology* 21 (2), 139–156.

Thoms, J. and Thoms, B. (2014) Open educational resources in the United States: Insights from university foreign language directors. *System* 45, 138–146.

van Lier, L. (1996) *Interaction in the Language Curriculum: Awareness, Autonomy, and Authenticity*. London: Longman.

van Lier, L. (2000) From input to affordance: Social-interactive learning from an ecological perspective. In J. Lantolf (ed.) *Sociocultural Theory and Second Language Learning* (pp. 245–259). New York, NY: Oxford University Press.

van Lier, L. (2004) *The Ecology and Semiotics of Language Learning: A Sociocultural Perspective*. Boston, MA: Kluwer Academic Publishers.

van Lier, L. (2010) The ecology of language learning: Practice to theory, theory to practice. *Procedia Social and Behavioral Sciences* 3, 2–6.

Weller, M., de los Arcos, B., Farrow, R., Pitt, R. and McAndrew, P. (2017) What can OER do for me? Evaluating the claims for OER. In R. Jhangiani and R. Biswas-Diener (eds) *Open: The Philosophy and Practices that are Revolutionizing Education and Science* (pp. 67–77). London: Ubiquity Press. DOI: https://doi.org/10.5334/bbc.e.

Wiley, D. (2018) The evolving economics of educational materials and open educational resources: Toward closer alignment with the core values of education. In R. Reiser and J. Dempsey (eds) *Trends and Issues in Instructional Design and Technology* (4th edn) (pp. 316–322). New York, NY: Pearson.

Wiley, D. (2014) The access compromise and the 5th R. See http://opencontent.org/blog/archives/3221

Wiley, D. and Green, C. (2012) Why openness in education? In D.G. Oblinger (ed.) *Game Changers: Education and Information Technologies* (pp. 81–89). See http://www.educause.edu/research-publications/books/game-changers-education-and-information-technologies

Zapata, G. (2017) The role of digital, *Learning by Design* instructional materials in the development of Spanish heritage learners' literacy skills. In G. Zapata and M. Lacorte (eds) *Multiliteracies Pedagogy and Language Learning: Teaching Spanish to Heritage Speakers* (pp. 67–106). New York: Palgrave Macmillan.

Part 1

The Microsystem: Developing Knowledge in L2 Instructional Environments

1 Open Educational Resources in Heritage and L2 Spanish Classrooms: Design, Development and Implementation

Gabriela C. Zapata and Alessandra Ribota

In this chapter, we examine the application of the multiliteracies pedagogy Learning by Design (Cope & Kalantzis, 2015; Kalantzis *et al.*, 2005, 2016) to the design of open educational resources (OER) for the teaching of Spanish as a heritage (HL) and second language (L2). We first discuss the tenets of the framework, and the reasons why it is appropriate to guide the development of OER materials. We then compare two differing instructional initiatives. The first focuses on HL learners at a Hispanic-serving institution, and the second one, on L2 students at a basic language program at an R1 institution. Based on these two experiences, we address issues related to the design and development of materials such as the following: (1) the identification of students' needs (considering personal and institutional expectations and outcomes); (2) the development of materials (the determination of thematic and linguistic content); and (3) the implementation process at both institutions. Finally, we summarize the institutional and pedagogical factors that characterized both experiences.

Introduction

Interest in incorporating multiliteracies pedagogies (e.g. Blyth, 2018; Warner & Dupuy, 2018) and open educational resources (OER) (Chun *et al.*, 2016) to classroom instruction is growing. This is evidenced by articles in recent anniversary or special issues of influential journals in the field of second language (L2) pedagogy such as *Foreign Language Annals*, *L2 Journal* and *The Modern Language Journal*. The impetus behind this growth in interest seems to be the desire not only to offer L2 learners instruction that will allow them to move beyond the more limited opportunities for language use offered by more constrained methods such as communicative language teaching (CLT) (Allen & Paesani, 2010; Byrnes, 2006), but also to create opportunities for active use of the target language in a variety of social environments through engagement with different kinds of genres and modes. In other words, it seems that momentum is growing for the adoption of more comprehensive, discourse-oriented instructional approaches that will prepare L2 learners to work with and produce a variety of multimodal texts, rather than restricting use of the target language to interactions.

Also at the heart of this particular movement in L2 pedagogy is the important role that learner identity and investment play in the learning process, a role that the field has been discovering the importance of since the early 2000s (Norton, 2013; Pittaway, 2004). Indeed, the existing identity literature (e.g. Norton, 2010; Norton & Toohey, 2011) has emphasized the crucial need for L2 pedagogy not only to recognize learners as multidimensional beings, but also to engage them with instruction at a personal level, fostering both their investment in the learning process and their own legitimation as L2 meaning makers (Pittaway). Clearly, this type of instruction cannot rely (solely) on the use of commercial textbooks that offer one-size-fits-all materials that students might have a hard time relating to because the resources might not reflect their lifeworld (i.e. the personal and social aspects of their lives) (Swaffar, 2006). Also, generic materials can constrain opportunities to expose students to diverse multimodal texts. And this is where OER can help. Blyth (2014) argues that an OER-based curriculum can transform 'closed educational systems [(such as those found in traditional L2 classrooms) into open educational environments through] the use of... materials that are easily edited and personalized, [and an emphasis on...] a belief that knowledge is best understood as a creative process of co-constructed meaning' (2014: 662).

Even though a few researchers in the fields of heritage language (HL) and L2 teaching have explored the benefits of combining multiliteracies-based teaching practices and OER materials or applications (e.g. Blyth, 2018; Thoms & Poole, 2018; Zapata, 2017; Zapata & Mesa Morales, 2018), no one (to the best of the authors' knowledge) has looked at multiliteracies-based OER initiatives from conception to implementation. The purpose of this chapter is to do so by presenting two instructional projects, one with HL learners (HLLs) at a Hispanic-serving institution in California, and the other with L2 students at a basic language program at a public university in the southern region of the United States. The first section of the paper introduces the multiliteracies framework *Learning by Design* and justifies why it is an appropriate framework to guide development of OER materials. The subsequent two sections describe the two initiatives in detail, focusing on the identification of student needs, the development of materials and the implementation process. The concluding sections of the chapter examine important institutional and instructional factors, such as funding, technological support and teacher expertise – specifically, how they can limit or contribute to the success of this type of initiative.

Learning by Design and OER

Learning by Design (*L-by-D*) is a pedagogical framework developed in the early 2000s by Mary Kalantzis, Bill Cope and colleagues (Kalantzis *et al.*, 2005) in their native Australia. The framework is a reformulation of some earlier ideas on literacy proposed in 1996 by the New London Group, which Kalantzis and Cope were part of (New London Group, 1996). The focus of *L-by-D* is the development of learners' literacy, which (according to Kalantzis and her colleagues) needs to be 'recalibrated to align with contemporary conditions for meaning-making – including multimodality and the diverse forms of communication that we encounter in the wide range of social and cultural contexts in our daily life' (Kalantzis *et al.*, 2016: 73). This objective, they argue, can only be achieved by expanding the traditional view of literacy, which is based on the printed medium and 'a single, official, or standard form of language' (Cope & Kalantzis, 2015: 1), to that of *multiliteracies*, where, in order to be effective meaning-makers in contemporary society (i.e. to become *multiliterate*), learners need to work within the 'dynamic, culturally, and historically situated practices of using and interpreting diverse... [multimodal] texts to fulfil particular social purposes' (Kern, 2000: 6).

Students' multiliteracies development can only be accomplished through their involvement in activities that will allow them *to do* in order *to know*. This is what Cope and Kalantzis (2015) conceptualize as 'thinking-in-action,' dividing it into four knowledge-making processes: experiencing, conceptualizing, analyzing and applying, which are at the core of the *L-by-D* pedagogy. These processes allow for the organization, implementation, documentation and tracking of the learning process (Cope & Kalantzis, 2009). Also, they can be regarded as 'epistemic moves' that offer learners opportunities to *do* in order *to know* in different ways. Specifically, students do the following:

(1) experience known and new meanings (departing from known concepts and experiences, they move forward to explore new situations and/or information);
(2) conceptualize meanings either by naming (by grouping into categories, classifying and defining) and/or with theory (by formulating generalizations and establishing connections among concepts as well as by developing theories);
(3) analyze meanings both functionally (by focusing on structure and function, and establishing logical connections between form and meaning), and critically (by evaluating different perspectives, interests and motives); and

(4) apply meanings both appropriately (by engaging in real-life applications of knowledge, developing products similar to the ones they have been exposed to), and creatively (by applying new knowledge in innovative and creative ways). (Kalantzis & Cope, 2012)

Instructors can design tasks within these knowledge-making processes, thereby 'purposely and deliberately "weaving" backwards and forwards between a variety of activity types or forms of engagement in order to ensure specific subject matter and other learning goals' (Kalantzis & Cope, 2010: 208).

The active role that the *L-by-D* framework assigns to learners is directly connected to two core principles, *belonging* and *transformation* (Kalantzis *et al.*, 2005). Kalantzis and Cope (2012b) believe that instructional environments should not ignore who learners are and must incorporate resources that are connected to their lifeworld. In this way, instruction can be linked to the complex, diverse identities of learners, who in turn can feel recognized as 'designers of *uniquely* voiced meanings' (Kalantzis & Cope, 2012a: Kindle location 3899, emphasis added). This connection will foster *belonging to* and investment in the student learning process. Kalantzis and her colleagues argue that this type of in-depth investment (or engagement) is conducive to *transformation*, defined as learning that 'takes the learner into new places, and along the journey, acts as an agent of personal and cultural [change]' (Kalantzis *et al.*, 2005: 30).

Through its focus on the use of different multimodal ensembles that are connected to the personal experiences of students and/or those of their families/communities, *L-by-D* can thus make learner-centered, transformational, multiliteracies pedagogy possible. As learners work with different kinds of genres and non-linguistic resources associated with a variety of subjects in the four knowledge processes, they can analyze social function, structure and linguistic/non-linguistic meaning-making resources. Learners can then apply their new knowledge in the development of their own personal projects, expressing their identity and newly developed literacies. The principles and objectives of this kind of pedagogy are congruent with those advocated by open education practices and with the affordances they offer (Blyth, 2014; Thoms & Thoms, 2014).

Like the *L-by-D* framework, open education practices rely on the use of multimodal material that can be digitally reused, redistributed, revised and remixed to answer the needs of specific student populations (Wiley & Green, 2012). These practices also highlight the need to create instructional environments that 'promote innovative pedagogical models, and respect and empower learners as co-producers on their lifelong learning path' (ICDE, 2011). Thus, open teaching practices grounded in the tenets of *L-by-D* could have the potential not only to be conducive to learners' multiliteracies development, but also to result in belonging and transformation through the use of materials directly connected to students' lifeworlds and specifically adapted to answer their particular needs. Indeed, in a recent large-scale study (21,822 participants) at the University of Georgia on the impact of OER-based instruction on the learning outcomes of students from historically underserved groups (both in terms of ethnicity and socioeconomic status), Colvard et al. (2018) showed that this type of instruction can lead to positive results in terms of academic success and lower rates of withdrawal. This finding points to the potential of OER to bring more equity to educational environments. Another related important affordance of OER-based instruction is the financial benefit offered to learners, who do not need to invest in the purchase of what is normally an expensive textbook and/or purchase access to a commercial learning-management platform.

In what follows, we introduce two open education initiatives that were conceived, developed and implemented in accordance with the principles of *L-by-D*. The first focuses on an intermediate Spanish class for HLLs in a Hispanic-serving institution, and the second, on a fourth-semester L2 Spanish course in a public R1 university. Both experiences are discussed in detail.

Case #1: Intermediate Spanish for HLLs at a Small, Hispanic-serving Institution

Institutional background

The specific context of this OER project was a Hispanic-serving institution in Northern California, as classified by the Hispanic Association of Colleges and Universities.[1] Thirty-eight percent of the students at this institution are Hispanic, and have close ties with the Mexican-American communities in the county where the university is located, as well as the two most closely associated counties. Most of the residents in these counties live in rural communities and are employed in agriculture and industries related to it, such as packing (Regional Analysis and Planning Services, 2012). Therefore, a high percentage of the university's Hispanic students comes from households with parents whose main occupation is related to the cultivation of fruits and vegetables. These positions are generally low-paid, and, as a result, the annual per capita income in this region is quite low compared to other areas of California. For example, in 2016, the per capita figures in the three counties range from the mid $20,000 to the low $30,000 (United States Census Bureau, 2016).

Students with a Humanities-related major at the university where this project took place are required to fulfill a foreign language requirement. HLLs with an intermediate level of proficiency can do so by taking the only HL Spanish class offered at the institution. Until the 2014–2015 academic year, this class was based on its L2 equivalent, and thus, students worked with a textbook that was designed for L2 instruction but did not take into account HLLs' specific needs. As a result, every semester, in their course evaluations, the students enrolled in this class would voice their complaints about its content, particularly because they felt they had been asked to buy an expensive textbook that did not address their linguistic needs, did not reflect their bicultural identity, and did not discuss any issues that pertained to their community/ies. Also, that academic year, the existence of this pedagogical drawback had been noticed by the two scholars who had conducted the external review of the department where the class was housed, with the evaluation report recommending a reconsideration of the goals and content of this class, which included a change in the instructional materials used.

In order to address this recommendation and fulfill an important academic requirement as well as offer the most appropriate pedagogical program to strengthen/develop HLLs' multiliteracies skills in Spanish, the first author of this chapter, who at the time was coordinator of the L2 and HL classes in the department in question, decided to undertake a series of curricular actions. Also, since the majority of HLLs came from low-income families, another important goal was to relieve them from the financial cost of purchasing a commercially produced, and academically inadequate, textbook that most of them could not afford. Since the coordinator was also the undergraduate advisor for the department and had a teaching load of two classes per academic semester, the first step was to secure time release. The institution supported her efforts with a grant that, though it would not cover possible financial costs of the materials development effort, would at least provide this person with a course release. This support, though limited, was crucial for the success of the project.

Planning and design

Based on her knowledge of L2 and HL acquisition and pedagogy, and her experience working with Spanish HLLs at the institution (she had taught the HL class, and she had conducted studies with this population of students), the coordinator chose to develop open-source digital instructional resources under the tenets of the *L-by-D* pedagogy. There were three main reasons why she felt this was the most appropriate course of action. First, there was a body of existing literature that had shown how the framework had been successfully implemented in the Australian educational context for the teaching of English to learners from underrepresented groups with similar socioeconomic backgrounds as her students (e.g. Hepple *et al.*, 2014; Mills, 2010; Neville, 2008). She also believed that since the pedagogy emphasized both the individual needs of students and the essential connection between the learners' 'experiential world (lifeworld) [and] the formal learning [of which they would be part]' (Kalantzis *et al.*, 2005: 37), this emphasis would allow her to create OER materials that would reflect her students' realities and would allow them to connect to the instruction they were receiving at a personal level (*belonging*). The third reason was related to L-*by*-D's rejection of traditional views of 'literacy,' for the more current and realistic 'multiliteracies,' which reflects both of the following: (1) 'the variability of conventions of meaning in different cultural, social or domain-specific situations' (Kalantzis *et al.*, 2016: 1); and (2) the multimodal nature of modern communication and meaning making (e.g. video, audio, visual, printed, etc.). That is, even though the main objective of this class was the development of literacy skills among HLLs in the academic register, the coordinator believed it was pedagogically responsible to offer HLLs a comprehensive instructional environment that would nurture their use of Spanish not only in other registers (tying their language use to their community and life-world), but also in different multimodal forms of communication.

The next step was to design the content of the class. To achieve this goal, the coordinator followed a *backward design* (Wiggins & McTighe, 1998), the starting point of which was the determination of instructional outcomes. To that effect, and following Wiggins and McTighe's design steps, she outlined the class' curricular priorities in terms of both desired attained performance (i.e. what students would be able to do with the HL) and knowledge (linguistic, cultural, and multimodal). For example, she considered the following: (1) what was 'worth being familiar with;' (2) what was 'important to know and do;' and (3) what was essential for 'enduring understanding' (Wiggins & McTighe, 1998: 3). Other important institutional aspects that were considered were contact hours and available technology resources. The resulting outcomes included the following:

Students demonstrate:

Interpretive communication skills by reading, listening to and viewing authentic materials from authors belonging to Hispanic communities in the United States (focus on Mexican-American authors/artists);

An understanding of major ideas as well as important information using effective reading, listening and viewing strategies to interpret authentic and semi-authentic materials; and

Presentation skills in writing and speaking through essays, presentations and other multimodal projects.

When it came to content per se, the main point of reference was the demographic information introduced at the beginning of this section, which pointed to a clear thematic focus: The project needed to be based on the Mexican-American experience in the United States. This theme was divided into important social issues relevant to the lives of the HLLs and their community(ies). Thus, content was organized into four instructional modules centered on the following themes: (1) immigration (*la inmigración*); (2) labor (*el trabajo*), with an emphasis on agriculture; (3) family and cultural traditions (*la familia y las tradiciones culturales*); and

(4) my bilingual/bicultural identity (*mi identidad bilingüe/bicultural*). The materials used in the four modules were works of fiction (accessed by students through the institution's library) and non-fiction belonging to different genres, websites, works of art, comic strips, photos, interviews and documentaries. The materials-development process (research, design and development) took a period of six months, and it would not have been possible without the course release given by the institution.

The four modules included materials to be taught during one semester (the class met twice a week for 110 minutes per session), and approximately four weeks of instruction were devoted to each of them (more information is provided in the next section). Students' in-depth exploration of and work with the modules' multimodal resources was achieved through activities in *L-by-D*'s four knowledge processes: experiencing (the known and the new), conceptualizing (by naming and with theory), analyzing (functionally and critically) and applying (appropriately and creatively) (Cope & Kalantzis, 2015; Kalantzis & Cope, 2010, 2012a; Kalantzis *et al.*, 2005, 2016). The instructional activities developed allowed students to do the following: (1) reflect on their understanding of particular aspects of the four topics in the course and be exposed to new perspectives on those understandings; (2) conceptualize essential aspects of the content presented and formulate connections to other concepts and theory in general; (3) analyze and understand linguistic and discursive aspects from a functional perspective (how meaning is expressed) and critically (by examining what perspectives, interests and motives were presented in each resource); and (4) apply their new knowledge not only appropriately in related academic (e.g. producing similar texts on a different topic) and/or real-life tasks, but also creatively, in the development of innovative, multimodal (and thus, hybrid) projects (e.g. a digital comic book to explore the topic of their bilingual/bicultural identity). The materials in each module were interrelated thematically and instructionally.

All the activities in each module were created digitally on Google Docs, and they were organized in Google Drive (one folder per module).[2] The plan was for students to work on most tasks digitally; however, face-to-face classroom meetings would also be part of instruction. In addition, the course was structured to support students in the form of peer collaboration and instructor assistance through any or all of the following: (1) face-to-face interactions; (2) synchronous exchanges (via Google Hangouts); and (3) asynchronous exchanges (email and comments on Google documents). Assessment was based on learners' development of e-Portfolios on Weebly for Education sites (https://education.weebly.com/). That is, each student would be required to create a free Weebly for Education site where they would showcase their work throughout the semester. Learners could choose either to make their sites public or to keep them anonymous. Weebly was chosen because it was the department's preferred website-development platform for Capstone e-portfolios, and the coordinator was encouraged to use it for the initiative. Also, it was user-friendly (easier than Google sites), and there was no cost involved for the department, institution or students.

Implementation process

The newly developed resources were implemented in two sections of the Spanish as a HL class, but data were only collected in one section. The participants were 31 students. The instructor's first step was to collect information about her students' access to technology. To her dismay, she realized that more than half of her class did not have a computer or easy access to one when not at the university. Also, 40% of the students in her class had demanding part-time jobs. These circumstances forced her to adapt the syllabus and materials for the class in three different ways: (1) she moved her class to a computer lab for the rest of the semester (that way, all students had access to a computer); (2) she reserved class time for students' completion of digital projects; and (3) she provided free paper copies of the digital materials to those students who requested them. These changes resulted in a reduction in the number of tasks originally developed for the course and the planned forms of digital feedback. However, the new structure also brought about more in-class collaboration and technology use, which provided students with more opportunities to work with peers and to interact with the instructor in a face-to-face environment. Also, some students broadened their knowledge of Google Apps and other programs (e.g. Pixton) used in the class.

The instructional cycle followed the same pattern for all units, and the point of departure was always students' lifeworld (*L-by-D*'s experiencing the known). Resorting to multimodal ensembles, the instructor would trigger students' discussion and reflection on their views on and experiences with a particular topic, and she would then introduce a new perspective on it (*L-by-D*'s experiencing the new) through the use of a text (written, visual, or hybrid) developed by an author belonging to the same community as the students. The next instructional steps involved learners' work in the other three knowledge processes: conceptualizing, analyzing and applying (each process took approximately one week of instruction). Figure 1.1 provides an example of how these epistemic moves were pedagogically integrated in module #4: 'My Bilingual/Bicultural Identity' (*Mi identidad bilingüe/bicultural*). This module was organized around the autobiographical genre, and was based on the following instructional resources: (1) literary works (three poems) by two Latino writers; (2) photos; and (3) the web-based comics application Pixton (https://www.pixton.com/).[3]

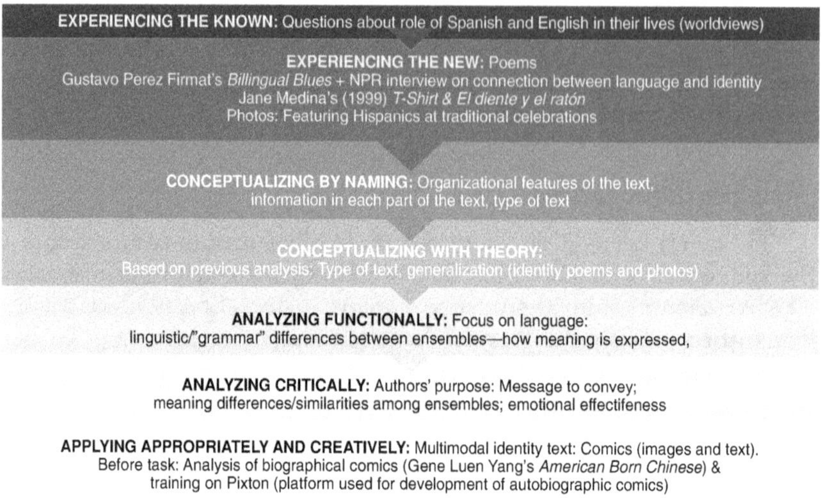

EXPERIENCING THE KNOWN: Questions about role of Spanish and English in their lives (worldviews)

EXPERIENCING THE NEW: Poems
Gustavo Perez Firmat's *Bilingual Blues* + NPR interview on connection between language and identity
Jane Medina's (1999) *T-Shirt & El diente y el ratón*
Photos: Featuring Hispanics at traditional celebrations

CONCEPTUALIZING BY NAMING: Organizational features of the text, information in each part of the text, type of text

CONCEPTUALIZING WITH THEORY: Based on previous analysis: Type of text, generalization (identity poems and photos)

ANALYZING FUNCTIONALLY: Focus on language: linguistic/"grammar" differences between ensembles—how meaning is expressed,

ANALYZING CRITICALLY: Authors' purpose: Message to convey; meaning differences/similarities among ensembles; emotional effectifeness

APPLYING APPROPRIATELY AND CREATIVELY: Multimodal identity text: Comics (images and text). Before task: Analysis of biographical comics (Gene Luen Yang's *American Born Chinese*) & training on Pixton (platform used for development of autobiographic comics)

Figure 1.1 Schematic representation of the activities in the module *Mi identidad bilingüe/bicultural* grounded in *Learning by Design*. Each knowledge process corresponds to those in the original model developed by Kalantzis and her colleagues (Kalantzis *et al.*, 2005, 2016)

Implementation results

The pedagogical experience that resulted from the implementation of OER materials had positive results in terms of students' literacy development (see Zapata, 2017) and attitudes towards instruction. For example, students praised the instructional resources not only for their financial benefit (i.e. not having had to purchase a commercial textbook), but also for the following pedagogical aspects: (1) the varied nature of the materials, ['which made the class fun. Class assignments were enjoyable and helped better understand material (sic)' – Student #4]; (2) their cultural value ['The assignments and class readings encouraged us to embrace our different Hispanic cultures' – Student #8]; (3) their academic value ['I was able to develop different skills in Spanish, such as writing and reading. We also learned about our Hispanic heritage' – Student #21]; (4) the opportunities for the collaborative construction of knowledge ['I liked how we worked with partners and could learn together' – Student #29]; and (5) their connection to themselves and their community ['Excellent choice of materials, resources, readings. They really allowed us to express our heritage and our background' - Student #30]. These positive opinions can be summarized in Student #2's words when describing the OER-based class: 'This course allowed me to better understand my culture while exercising and expanding the Spanish language. It helped me expand my vocabulary and also improved my written and oral skills. It really helped expand my knowledge about the cultural value of being a Spanish speaker.'

The comics developed by students in the bilingual/bicultural identity module, for example, provide evidence for these views. That is, the qualitative analysis of the multimodal resources in students' products reveals that, through this project, HLLs were able to use Spanish to express their emotions and perceptions of the topic and to connect to or reflect on their Mexican-American identities. Some students described feelings of confusion similar to the ones they had seen in Perez Firmat's (1995) work (Figure 1.2) while others felt that being bicultural was not an issue (Figure 1.3). Also, the meaningful, comprehensive combinations of images, written text and sometimes links to videos found in the comics show not only development at the level of literacy (e.g. most written texts were almost error free and exhibited grammatical complexity [use of complex clauses], which was not the case for the written assignments in module #1), but also the effective application of different modes of communication (an

Figure 1.2 Student-generated text expressing the emotional challenge of developing an identity

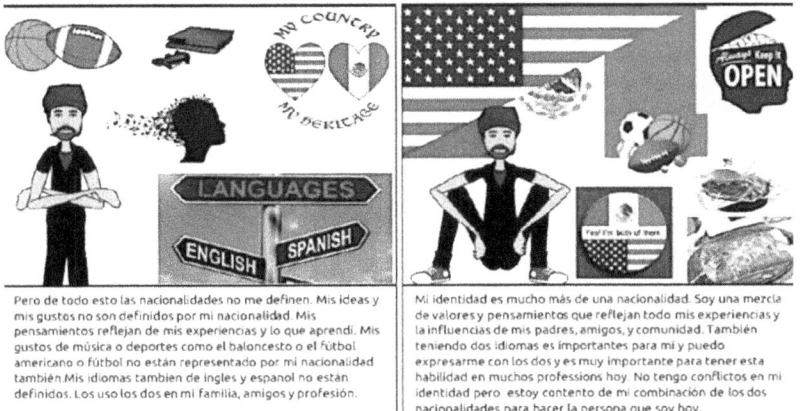

Figure 1.3 Student-generated text expressing pride in personal identity

Figure 1.4 Student-generated text that includes personal photos

affordance of digital OER instruction grounded in *L-by-D*) to express personal emotions (Figure 1.4). Finally, when asked what they had discovered about their Spanish through this activity, students referred to both positive aspects of their performance (e.g. their newly found pride in their use of the language, their ability to express complex feelings) and still challenging points (e.g. difficulties with limited vocabulary). Overall, 90% of the students seemed to like the activity, as they felt it had allowed them to exercise their creativity and grow both as Spanish writers and technology users. These benefits clearly point to the potential of this kind of instruction (and materials) for the development of not only HLLs' literacy in Spanish, but also both their multiliteracies and digital literacy.

This first OER experience for the coordinator broadened her knowledge of the development and implementation of open education resources, on the one hand, and the institutional and pedagogical aspects that can benefit or hinder the success of this type of educational practice on the other. These new data provided a good point of departure for the next OER project she initiated, which will be presented in the next few sections of the paper.

Case #2: Intermediate Spanish for L2 Learners at an R1 Institution

Institutional background and planning and design

This second OER initiative constituted a pilot study for a larger materials development effort, an OER beginning Spanish textbook, the main goal of which would be the use of solely open instructional materials for the teaching of L2 Spanish to university students. The authors of this paper were in charge of the textbook initiative, which was housed in an R1 university in the southern region of United States. The study was carried out in one section of a four-semester L2 Spanish class in Fall 2017, and it involved the participation of 23 students. The main objectives of this work were as follows: (1) to provide the authors with more experience as OER materials developers and implementers before embarking on the more comprehensive task of writing a full textbook; (2) to investigate students' attitudes towards OER instructional materials; and (3) to examine the development of L2 students' performance in the interpretive (reading) and presentational (writing) modes as compared to that of learners working with a commercial textbook.[4]

In summer 2017, the authors collaborated in the creation of four OER instructional units for the teaching of intermediate Spanish (American Council on the Teaching of Foreign Languages (ACTFL)'s intermediate-mid level of performance) by modifying and adapting existing open resources (e.g. authentic multimodal texts) and developing new ones. Prior to the beginning of this process, the first author visited the Center for Open Educational Resources and Language Learning at the University of Texas at Austin (COERLL; https://www.coerll.utexas.edu/coerll/), where she received guidance and suggestions for the use of Creative Commons licenses and ways to create open resources. This new knowledge, together with the second author's attendance of Center for Open Educational Resources and Language Learning (COERLL)-organized workshops, proved invaluable to their work.

As with the HL OER initiative, the materials-development process followed a backward design (Wiggins & McTighe, 1998), with the point of departure being the instructional outcomes (based on the theoretical and pedagogical bases of the program of which this class was part) expected in the four-semester class. The materials centered around four themes: (1) personal relationships (*Las relaciones personales*); (2) daily routines and other activities (*Las diversiones y la vida diaria*); (3) health and well-being (*La salud y el bienestar*); and (4) traveling (*Los viajes*). These topics matched those found in the commercial textbook (*Facetas*, 4th edn) used in other sections of the class. However, the open resources included not only more comprehensive and authentic material, but also content and tasks directly related to the lifeworld of the target student population. That is, the objective of the OER materials was twofold: (1) to expose students to multimodal ensembles created by members of the target cultures from a variety of social groups, and (2) to provide them with the opportunity to use Spanish to develop products for audiences that would go beyond the classroom environment (e.g. digital magazines that would be published in an online public platform), and that would allow for language use to express aspects of the self. In existing work, these two types of authenticity have been deemed essential for L2 learners' motivation and the success of their learning process (see Banegas *et al.*, 2019; Copland & Mann, 2012;

Pinner, 2019; Widdowson, 1990). Additionally, the open resources were designed to facilitate learners' work in *L-by-D*'s four knowledge processes: experiencing, conceptualizing, analyzing and applying (Kalantzis *et al.*, 2005, 2016). Even though the materials-development process ran smoothly, the authors still faced two challenges: (1) the determination of the way in which students would access the resources; and (2) the need to offer additional instructional practice akin to the one included in the commercial textbook's e-workbook.

In order to overcome the first challenge (students' access to materials), the two scholars in the project consulted with COERLL and the university's IT personnel. As with the HL OER initiative, it was determined that the most effective way for learners to work with the open resources would be through G Suite for Higher Education (Google Drive, Docs and Apps) (https://edu.google.com/higher-ed-solutions/g-suite/?modal_active=none), offered without additional cost to students (other than tuition) by the institution. This way, students would not only be able to have easy access to documents that they could download, modify and print, but they would also be able to collaborate synchronously and asynchronously with both their peers and instructor. In addition, Google allowed learners to create their own folders for the class where they would upload and store their work with private, instructor access. The four open units were therefore created in Google Doc format.[5]

The second challenge (the additional online practice) proved more taxing. Since both authors had other summer commitments, merely completing the main instructional material occupied most of their time and left little time to create extra workbook tasks. Therefore, they decided to solve this problem by agreeing to substitute the needed resources with existing online activities. In order to do so, they included links to those resources in the main Google documents, and asked students to submit screenshots of their completed assignments. Although at the time this seemed to be the most feasible and practical solution, it would become the main source of learner dissatisfaction during the implementation process, which is presented in the next section.

Implementation process

The newly developed instructional units were adopted in the section of the four-semester class taught by the second author of this paper in Fall 2017. Before the beginning of the semester, a Google folder was created for the section, with all the administrative (e.g. different criteria for assessment) and pedagogical resources organized into different subfolders (students were given view-only access to all the documents). The use of OER material was clearly stated in the syllabus, and the course instructor devoted most of the first week of classes to the following: familiarizing learners with the different course components; guiding them in the establishment of individual Google folders; showing them how to access and work with Google Docs; and informing them on how to complete the extra homework activities.

Overall, the implementation process worked well, even though the learners were at first a bit anxious about the lack of a commercial textbook and expressed this concern. Perhaps these feelings were related to their previous experiences with L2 learning in the department where the study took place, which had been centered around the use of a book. Fortunately, this situation was temporary, and by the end of the first OER unit, most students in the class (19 out of 23, or 83%) expressed positive opinions about the class's open practices. By the end of the semester, only one student disagreed with the idea of taking another OER-based instruction class, while the remaining 22 strongly agreed ($n = 10$) or agreed ($n = 12$) with this idea. Despite this overall positive response, a quite specific common complaint throughout the semester was the way in which the extra homework activities had been chosen and organized. For example, some students felt that the assigned exercises did not fully line up thematically with the topics that were being discussed in class, while others had difficulties with the chosen links, and/or did not quite understand the online activities, which were often more complex than the ones they had completed in the previous textbook's e-workbook. These opinions clearly pointed to the need for future material to incorporate extra practice more aligned with the OER instructional units.

Implementation results

In spite of the homework difficulties and the learners' initial reluctance when faced with a lack of a commercial textbook, overall student L2 development and attitudes in this pilot OER experience were positive. Preliminary analyses of the quantitative data collected in this pilot section and those of the textbook-based sections suggest slightly better results in terms of students' L2 performance in the presentational (writing) mode of communication. Also, in an end-of-the-semester survey, the learners praised the OER material for a variety of reasons. For example, students felt that the material was more connected to real life and their own personal experiences:

'[The material] was really helpful because it had more real-life situations in it rather than what would be presented in a textbook, and this helped so much for the social aspect of Spanish speaking.' (Student #6)

'I know how to talk about more things that I would normally talk about like in English, instead of foreign concepts or random vocab words.' (Student #18)

'I feel like the examples used were very realistic and could actually be used and be helpful in this day and age.' (Student #7)

> 'It has got me thinking in new ways that a traditional Spanish book hasn't before because it's very applicable to real life.' (Student #14)

Learners also believed that the resources not only had contributed to their L2 development, but, perhaps more importantly, had also boosted their confidence as Spanish speakers:

> 'A better vocabulary and more confidence in speaking Spanish in general.' (Student #5)

> 'It enhanced my knowledge of vocabulary in everyday situations A TON.' (Student #15; emphasis in original text)

> '[It] helped us hone our Spanish skills by practicing speaking, presentations, as well as writing.' (Student #2)

More practical, non-academic aspects of the material seemed to be important for these students as well, as can be seen in the following quotes:

> 'Not having to buy a book for this course was really convenient and a lot easier for me as a student. Instead of having to lug a book around and sheets of paper, it was easy to keep track of all my homework and class notes on my computer, ensuring that I was always prepared for class the next day.' (Student #10)

> 'The entire notion of a digitized book that does not involve a class code for a book exponentially helped in my understanding and accessibility of this course.' (Student #11)

> 'I love the fact that we had a free, online, open source book. It was very helpful and fiscally responsible.' (Student #12)

These comments show similarities with those expressed in the HL OER initiative covered in the previous section.

The L2 students' opinions on the impact of each of the instructional units on their individual learning were also submitted to sentiment analysis (SA) (Ignatow & Mihalcea, 2018). This type of analysis relies on 'the computational study of opinions, sentiments, emotions and attitude expressed in texts towards an entity [with the objective] of detecting, extracting and classifying opinions, sentiments and attitudes concerning different topics' (Ravi & Ravi, 2015: 14). In the last decade, SA has become a widely used tool in both industry and academics (e.g. see Zapata & Ribota, 2020, and, for a comprehensive review, Ravi & Ravi, 2015), and it has been deemed as an effective method in the analysis of students' motivation and views of instruction (Kim & Calvo, 2010; Ortigosa *et al.*, 2014). To conduct the SA in this study, the authors resorted to the online tool *Sentiment Analyzer* developed by Soper (n.d.). The main reasons behind this choice were the following: (1) the tool had been developed by an academic researcher, and (2) it had been highly ranked in the market (Fontanella, 2020). The SA scores resulting from the analysis of the four units showed a progression in the participants' perceived individual, instructional benefits. For example, units 1 and 2 rendered overall sentiment or tone scores of 61.3 and 75.8 respectively (quite positive / enthusiastic) while the scores in units 3 and 4 were, respectively, 99.2 and 97.2 (very positive / enthusiastic).

The attitudinal and opinion data from both the HL and L2 OER experiences seem to suggest that OER-based instruction benefitted students both academically (see also Zapata, 2017) and financially. The two initiatives were also beneficial for the authors, who not only grew as scholars and researchers, but also as materials developers, which provided them with the reassurance needed to undertake the now-completed textbook project. In the next sections, they summarized the lessons they learned from their involvement in these two projects.

Lessons Learned from These Experiences

The two OER experiences detailed in this chapter were characterized by the same benefits and drawbacks described in the existing literature on open practices. For example, the collected HL and L2 student opinions seem to confirm the fact that open resources promote three important dimensions of authenticity. The first one is HL and L2 learners' exposure to real, socially varied uses of the target language (Widdowson, 1990). The second one is the possibility of creating opportunities for more authentic language use that not only reflects real-life applications, but also facilitates students' communication with audiences beyond those present in the classroom, which, in itself, has been shown to have motivating effects for both students *and* instructors (Banegas *et al.*, 2019; Pinner, 2019). The third one is the opportunity to personally involve learners in both the curriculum and the learning process, which can result in belonging and investment (Beaven *et al.*, 2013; Copland & Mann, 2012; Pinner, 2019; Thoms & Thoms, 2014; Zapata, 2017). In addition, the resources encourage collaboration among students, instructors and materials developers, which is conducive not only towards a more democratic instructional environment (Blessinger & Bliss, 2016), but also towards 'the integration of knowledge and social networks in order to connect people to ideas…within a community of practice' (Blyth, 2014: 662). Two more beneficial effects brought about by the OER materials in these two experiences were financial and practical advantages (in terms of access to and portability of resources). Such effects have been highlighted elsewhere in the literature (e.g. Blessinger & Bliss, 2016; Tuomi, 2013). In our case, the HL students saved $197 and the L2 students, $164. Naturally, it is also important to note the positive academic benefits of the OER materials. Specifically, findings from the HL experience (Zapata, 2017) suggest that the adoption of open resources resulted in the development of different aspects of students' Spanish literacy, their multiliteracies (i.e. the effective application of different modes of communication to express personal meaning), and their digital literacy. In the case of the L2 learners, preliminary data analyses show that L2 development was similar in both the textbook-based and OER sections, which supports the results reported by Hilton (2016) and Clinton (2018) in their studies on the instructional effects of textbooks as compared to open materials.

The materials-development and -implementation processes also mirrored the existing literature. Both the success of the HL initiative and the difficulties that the authors faced in the two projects clearly point to the crucial role played by institutional support. It is undeniable that, without either release time and/or funding for, for example, additional personnel, it is extremely difficult for scholars to invest their expertise and effort into the creation of OER materials, a difficulty that has been emphasized in numerous publications (e.g. Carey & Hanley, 2008; Jhangiani *et al.*, 2016; McGowan, 2019; McMartin, 2008; Thoms & Thoms, 2014; Tuomi, 2013).

Another aspect of support that is often missing is the commitment of instructional units and their members to the adoption of open resources. That is, in both experiences, the authors faced resistance from either their department, or their colleagues, or both, which forced them to revisit their original plans and the ways in which they developed and implemented the OER materials. McGowan (2019) believes faculty resistance towards open education is connected to a variety of factors, such as their lack of knowledge of the affordances offered by this type of education and fears related to intellectual property and technology-based instruction.

Thus, if, as Blessinger and Bliss (2016) suggest, higher education is undergoing democratizing changes, and open education is at the core of those changes, it is essential for units across various levels of the university to provide incentives, information and training for faculty members to embark on and participate fully in open practices. Without this comprehensive kind of support, open education is limited, and this, in essence, goes against its very nature. We believe that a possible remedy for this situation would include not only the continued empirical investigation of OER experiences (Blyth, 2014), but also the wide dissemination of data (in local and scholarly environments), which can provide evidence of the many benefits that open practices can bring to higher education. It is also important that scholars advocate for these kinds of resources through collaborative efforts and participation in organizations such as the COERLL.

Finally, the two experiences offered further confirmation of the different kinds of expertise required from OER developers and implementers. First and foremost, it is essential for resources to be grounded in sound, research-guided theories and pedagogical practices in order to guarantee the quality of education offered to students (McGowan, 2019; Ossiannilsson *et al.*, 2016; Tuomi, 2013), which in turn points to the need for this kind of scholarly training. At the university level, this training could become part of methods classes for graduate teaching assistants in which open education, multiliteracies frameworks and OER-enabled pedagogy could become curricular topics. In addition, since open resources reside in the digital realm, it is important for developers to feel comfortable with the use of different technologies, and/or have the resources to hire experts that can provide the needed support. Developers will also need to understand how Creative Commons licenses work in order to prevent copyright infringements and protect scholars' intellectual property.

Yet another crucial piece of both the development and implementation process is methodology. The experiences presented in this article showed how essential it is for instructors to apply sound pedagogical techniques incorporating concepts, such as scaffolding (Wood *et al.*, 1976), to guide students' access to and work with material that either might be in a different format than they are used to, or might require the use of language in more comprehensive tasks. Also, creating instructional environments that promote work within Vygotsky's (1978) zone of proximal development can foster students' collaborative construction of knowledge, which, in turn, can facilitate learning and aid in the effective use of the OER. Of course, tying together all these factors are *L-by-D*'s *belonging* and *transformation*: Both developers and implementers need to fully understand who their target students are, not only academically, but also socially. And they need to use this knowledge to create open resources that will answer their learners' specific needs. Without this knowledge and the willingness to continue adapting and re-creating, open practices might not succeed.

Notes

(1) A Hispanic-serving institution is defined as a 2- or 4-year college/university which 'meets three criteria: (1) they must be accredited and nonprofit; (2) have at least 25% Latino/a undergraduate full-time equivalent enrollment; and (3) at least 50% of the Latino/a students are low income' (Contreras *et al.*, 2008: 72).
(2) At the end of the instructional period, the materials created for the class were revised and published in the Creative Commons site at the institution where this study took place. Further revisions were later undertaken, and the new versions of the units are now available at http://bit.ly/OERHerSpan.
(3) The three poems used were *Bilingual Blues* by Gustavo Pérez Firmat (Pérez Firmat, 1995), and *T-Shirt* and *El diente y el ratón* by Jane Medina (Medina, 1999). Students developed their hybrid autobiographical comics on Pixton, which was the only application that required paid licenses for use, and was financially supported by the university's Provost Office.
(4) The theoretical, pedagogical and methodological bases for the innovation were the *World-readiness standards for foreign language learning* (National Standards in Foreign Language Education Project, 2015), *ACTFL performance descriptors for language learners* (ACTFL, 2012), the 2013 Integrated Performance Assessment manual (Adair-Hauck *et al.*, 2013), and high-leverage teaching practices (Glisan & Donato, 2017).
(5) The units are now available for use at http://bit.ly/IML2Material.

References

Adair-Hauck, B., Glisan, E.W. and Troyan, F.J. (2013) *Implementing Integrated Performance Assessment*. Alexandria, VA: American Council on the Teaching of Foreign Languages.

American Council on the Teaching of Foreign Languages (ACTFL) (2012) *ACTFL Performance Descriptors for Language Learners*. Alexandria, VA: ACTFL.

Allen, H.W. and Paesani, K. (2010) Exploring the feasibility of a pedagogy of multiliteracies in introductory foreign language courses. *L2 Journal* 2, 119–142.

Banegas, D.R., Roberts, G., Colucci, R. and Sarsa, B.N. (2019) Authenticity and motivation: A writing for publication experience. *ELT Journal* 74 (1). DOI: 10.1093/elt/ccz056.

Beaven, A., Comas-Quinn, A. and Sawhill, B. (2013) Introduction on case studies of openness in the language classroom. In A. Beaven, A. Comas-Quinn and B. Sawhill (eds) *Case Studies of Openness in the Language Classroom* (pp. 1–8). Dublin: Research-publishing.net.

Blessinger, P. and Bliss, T.J. (2016) Introduction to open education: Towards a human rights theory. In P. Blessinger and T.J. Bliss (eds) *Open Education: International Perspectives in Higher Education* (pp. 11–26). Cambridge: Open Book Publishers.

Blyth, C. (2014) Open educational resources and the new classroom ecology. *The Modern Language Journal* 98, 662–664.

Blyth, C. (2018) Designing meaning and identity in multiliteracies pedagogy: From multilingual subjects to authentic speakers. *L2 Journal* 10 (2), 62–86.

Byrnes, H. (2006) Perspectives: Interrogating communicative competence as a framework for collegiate foreign language study. *The Modern Language Journal* 90, 244–266.

Carey, T. and Hanley, G.L. (2008) Extending the impact of open educational resources: Lessons learned from MERLOT. In T. Iiyoshi and M.S.V. Kumar (eds) *Opening Up Education: The Collective Advancement of Education through Open Technology, Open Content, and Open Knowledge* (pp. 181–195). Cambridge, MA: MIT Press.

Chun, D., Kern, R. and Smith, B. (2016) Technology in language use, language teaching, and language learning. *The Modern Language Journal* 100, 64–80.

Clinton, V. (2018) Savings without sacrifice: a case report on open-source textbook adoption. *Open Learning: The Journal of Open, Distance and e-Learning* 33, 177–189.

Colvard, N.B., Watson, C.E. and Park, H. (2018) The impact of Open Educational Resources on various student success metrics. *International Journal of Teaching and Learning in Higher Education* 30, 262–276.

Contreras, F.E., Malcom, L.E. and Bensimon, E.M. (2008) Hispanic-serving institutions: Closeted identity and the production of equitable outcomes for Latino/a students. In M. Gasman, B. Baez and C. Sotello Viernes Turner (eds) *Understanding Minority-Serving Institutions* (pp. 71–90). Albany: State University of New York Press.

Cope, B. and Kalantzis, M. (2009) Multiliteracies: New literacies, new learning. *Pedagogies: An International Journal* 4, 164–195.

Cope, B. and Kalantzis, M. (2015) The things you do to know: An introduction to the pedagogy of Multiliteracies. In B. Cope and M. Kalantzis (eds) *A Pedagogy of Multiliteracies: Learning by Design* (pp. 1–36). London: Palgrave Macmillan.

Copland, F. and Mann, S. (2012) *The Coursebook and Beyond: Choosing, Using and Teaching Outside the Text*. Tokyo: Abax.

Fontanella, C. (2020) *The Best 12 Sentiment Analysis Tools in 2020*. See https://blog.hubspot.com/service/sentiment-analysis-tools.

G Suite for Higher Education [Computer software]. https://edu.google.com/higher-ed-solutions/g-suite/?modal_active=none.

Glisan, E.W. and Donato, R. (2017). *Enacting the World of Language Instruction: High-Leverage Teaching Practices*. Alexandria, VA: ACTFL.

Hepple, E., Sockhill, M., Tan, A. and Alford J. (2014) Multiliteracies pedagogy: Creating claymations with adolescent, post-beginner English language learners. *Journal of Adolescent & Adult Literacy* 58 (3), 219–229.

Hilton, J. (2016) Open educational resources and college textbook choices: A review of research on efficacy and perceptions. *Educational Technology Research and Development* 64, 573–590.
ICDE (2011) *International Conference on Data Engineering.* See http://www.icde2011.org/.
Ignatow, G. and Mihalcea, R. (2018) *An Introduction to Text Mining: Research Design, Data Collection, and Analysis.* Los Angeles: Sage.
Jhangiani, R.S., Green, A.G. and Belshaw, J.D. (2016) Three approaches to open textbook development. In P. Blessinger and T.J. Bliss (eds) *Open Education: International Perspectives in Higher Education* (pp. 179–198). Cambridge: Open Book Publishers.
Kalantzis, M. and Cope, B. (2010) The teacher as designer: Pedagogy in the new media age. *E-Learning and Digital Media* 7 (3), 200–222.
Kalantzis, M. and Cope, B. (2012a) *Literacies.* Cambridge: Cambridge University Press.
Kalantzis, M. and Cope, B. (2012b) *New Learning: Elements of a Science of Education* (2nd edn). Cambridge: Cambridge University Press.
Kalantzis, M., Cope, B. and the Learning by Design Project Group (2005) *Learning by Design.* Melbourne: Victorian Schools Innovation Commission and Common Ground Publishing.
Kalantzis, M., Cope, B., Chan, B. and Dalley-Trim, L. (2016) *Literacies* (2nd edn). Cambridge: Cambridge University Press.
Kim, K. and Calvo, R. (2010) Sentiment analysis in student experiences of learning. In R.S.J. Baker, A. Merceron and P.I. Pavlik Jr. (eds) *Educational Data Mining* (pp. 111–120). Pittsburg: LearnLab and Carnegie Learning.
Kern, R. (2000) *Literacy and Language Teaching.* Oxford: Oxford University Press.
McGowan, V. (2019) Institution initiatives and support related to faculty development of open educational resources and alternative textbooks. *Open Learning: The Journal of Open, Distance and e-Learning.* DOI: 10.1080/02680513.2018.1562328.
McMartin, F. (2008) Open educational content: Transforming access to education. In T. Iiyoshi and M.S.V. Kumar (eds) *Opening Up Education: The Collective Advancement of Education through Open Technology, Open Content, and Open Knowledge* (pp. 135–147). Cambridge, MA: MIT Press.
Mills, K. (2010) What learners 'know' through digital media production: Learning by Design. *E–Learning and Digital Media* 7 (3), 223–236.
Moodle [Open source learning management system]. See https://moodle.org/.
National Standards in Foreign Language Education Project (2015) *World-Readiness Standards for Foreign Language Learning.* Alexandria, VA: ACTFL.
Neville, M. (2008) *Teaching Multimodal Literacy Using the Learning by Design Approach to Pedagogy: Case Studies from Selected Queensland Schools.* Altona, Australia: Common Ground.
New London Group (1996) A pedagogy of Multiliteracies: Designing social futures. *Harvard Educational Review* 66, 60–92.
Norton, B. (2010) Language and identity. In N.H. Hornberger and S.L. McKay (eds) *Sociolinguistics and Language Education* (pp. 349–369). Bristol: Multilingual Matters.
Norton, B. (2013) *Identity and Language Learning: Extending the Conversation* (2nd edn). Bristol: Multilingual Matters.
Norton, B. and Toohey, K. (2011) Identity, language learning, and social change. *Language Teaching* 44, 412–446.
Ossiannilsson, E., Altinay, Z. and Altinay, F. (2016) Transformation of teaching and learning in higher education towards open arenas: A question of quality. In P. Blessinger and T.J. Bliss (eds) *Open Education: International Perspectives in Higher Education* (pp. 159–178). Cambridge: Open Book Publishers.
Ortigosa, A., Martín, J.M. and Carro, R.M. (2014) Sentiment analysis in Facebook and its application to e-learning. *Computers in Human Behaviour* 31, 527–541. https://doi.org/10.1016/j.chb.2013.05.024

Pérez Firmat, G. (1995) *Bilingual Blues*. Tempe, AZ: Bilingual Press.
Pinner, R. (2019) *Authenticity and Teacher-Student Motivational Synergy: A Narrative of Language Teaching*. New York: Routledge.
Pittaway, D.S. (2004) Investment and second language acquisition. *Critical Inquiry in Language Studies: An International Journal* 1 (4), 203–218.
Pixton [Computer software]. See https://www.pixton.com/.
Ravi, K. and Ravi, V. (2015) A survey on opinion mining and sentiment analysis: Tasks, approaches and applications. *Knowledge-Based Systems* 89, 14–46. See https://doi.org/10.1016/j.knosys.2015.06.015.
Soper, D. (n.d.) *Sentiment Analyzer* [Computer software]. See https://www.danielsoper.com/sentimentanalysis/default.aspx.
Swaffar, J.K. (2006) Terminology and its discontents: Some caveats about communicative competence. *Modern Language Journal* 90, 246–249.
Thoms, J.J. and Poole, F. (2018) Exploring digital literacy practices via L2 social reading. *L2 Journal* 10 (2), 36–61.
Thoms, J.J. and Thoms, B.L. (2014) Open educational resources in the United States: Insights from university foreign language directors. *System* 45, 138–146.
Tuomi, I. (2013) Open educational resources and the transformation of education. *European Journal of Education* 48, 58–78.
United States Census Bureau (2016) *QuickFacts*. See https://www.census.gov.
Vygotsky, L.S. (1978) *Mind in Society: The Development of Higher Psychological Processes*. Cambridge, MA: Harvard University Press.
Warner, C. and Dupuy, B. (2018) Moving toward multiliteracies in foreign language teaching: Past and present perspectives...and beyond. *Foreign Language Annals* 51, 116–128.
Widdowson, H.G. (1990). *Aspects of Language Teaching*. Oxford: Oxford University Press.
Weebly for Education [Online platform for website development]. (https://education.weebly.com/)
Wiggins, G. and McTighe, J. (1998) *Understanding by Design* (1st edn). Upper Saddle River, NJ: Merrill Prentice Hall.
Wiley, D. and Green, C. (2012) Why openness in education? In D.G. Oblinger (ed.) *Game Changers: Education and Information Technologies* (pp. 81–89). See http://www.educause.edu/research-publications/books/game-changers-education-and-information-technologies (accessed March 22, 2018).
Wood, D.J., Bruner, J.S. and Ross, G. (1976) The role of tutoring in problem solving. *Journal of Child Psychiatry and Psychology* 17, 89–100.
Zapata, G.C. (2017) The role of digital, *Learning by Design* instructional materials in the development of Spanish heritage learners' literacy skills. In G.C. Zapata and M. Lacorte (eds) *Multiliteracies Pedagogy and Language Learning: Teaching Spanish to Heritage Speakers* (pp. 67–106). New York: Palgrave Macmillan.
Zapata, G.C. and Mesa-Morales, M. (2018) The beneficial effects of technology-based social reading in L2 classes. *Lenguas en Contexto* 9 (Suplemento 2018–2019), 40–50. See http://www.facultaddelenguas.com/lencontexto/?idrevista=25#25.40.
Zapata, G.C. and Ribota, A. (2020) The instructional benefits of identity texts and learning by design for learner motivation in required second language classes. *Pedagogies: An International Journal*. https://doi.org/10.1080/1554480X.2020.1738937.

2 Open by Design: The *Cultura* Project

Sabine Levet and Stephen L. Tschudi

This chapter examines the *Cultura* project from the perspective of open education. *Cultura* is a telecollaborative project to develop intercultural understanding between groups of students from different cultures. Initially developed in French at MIT, it has been widely adapted by instructors at other institutions. After examining the main features of a *Cultura* exchange, the chapter looks at how the intrinsically open design of the project creates affordances for both learners and educators in four main areas: pedagogy, materials development, technology and professional development. 'Openness' is manifest both in the particular features of a *Cultura* exchange, where students are engaged in the co-creation of knowledge, and in the systematic ways the *Cultura* model, technological platform, associated materials and classroom methodologies have been made available to instructors who have in turn adapted them to their own contexts. As an open system and part of a culture of openness, *Cultura* contributes significantly to pedagogy, technology, materials development and professional development in world language education.

Introduction

Cultura is a telecollaborative project aimed at developing intercultural understanding between groups of students from different cultures. First created in a French language class at MIT by a team of three instructors (Gilberte Furstenberg, Sabine Levet and Shoggy Waryn), it initially connected students in the US and in France. Since its inception in 1997, it has been widely adapted in other languages at other institutions and received a Special Recognition Award from the American Council on Education for its 'Innovative Use of Technology to Promote Internationalization' (American Council on Education, 2010).

Two emerging technologies that became widely available in the mid-1990s were essential to *Cultura*: the web made it possible for remote groups of students to access the same documents posted online, and online discussion forums enabled communication between these groups. *Cultura* benefited from open source web technology for developing its website, and from a collaborative, web-based environment developed at MIT (MetaMedia) available to the whole MIT community to enable communication via online forums.

In turn, since its creation, *Cultura* has been openly accessible to instructors and the community at large through multiple channels: a website that provides both pedagogical resources (including an archive of past exchanges) and open technology tools to easily manage exchanges; conferences and workshops; and one-on-one support via email, phone or Skype. The commitment to offer concrete support to instructors who want to adapt *Cultura* has been part of every stage of the project's development over the years. For instance, when, after receiving initial funding from the Consortium for Language Teaching and Learning (1997), Cultura received a three-year grant from the National Endowment from the Humanities (1998), part of its stated mission was to make *Cultura* open. In 2008, *Cultura* received additional funding from the French Initiatives Endowment Funds at MIT to make its website more user-friendly and interactive, and to reconfigure the MIT-developed program enabling instructors to easily manage a *Cultura* exchange (Exchange Management Tool) so that it would be available for free to instructors lacking technology support at their own institutions. It also offered the possibility to have their exchanges hosted at MIT.

In the first part of this chapter, we will look at the main features of a *Cultura* exchange, examining how *Cultura's* collaborative, comparative and constructivist approach is consistent with the foundational values of Open Pedagogy, such as 'autonomy and interdependence; freedom and responsibility; democracy and participation' (Paquette, 1979, as cited in Jhangiani & DeRosa, 2017), and will show how its modular design effectively makes this project highly adaptable to different contexts. In the second part, we will discuss different ways in which *Cultura* has actively been made available, accessible and usable by the FL community at large. In the final part, we will reflect on how *Cultura* has evolved through multiple collaborations and adaptations and see what types of discussions have been taking place among instructors, partners, developers and adopters in this open context.

Main Features of a *Cultura* Exchange

In this section, we will first look at how a *Cultura* exchange is structured, present its approach and methodology, describe the types of materials used and explain how students, working with these materials in an open environment, collaborate with one another to co-create knowledge. Illustrating the process with examples from the forums, we will show how this model of telecollaboration enables dynamic open interactions between students and allows a multiplicity of voices into the classroom. It enables students to reflect on the materials both on their own and with others, choose freely in what discussions they want to participate and what particular ideas they want to explore, and lets them bring outside sources into the conversation and decide how far they want to pursue a topic.

Need

The call for teaching culture in language classes has been central to the profession for many years. The *Standards for Foreign Language Learning*, published by the National Standards in Foreign Language Education Project, US Dept. of Education (1996) in collaboration with the American Council on the Teaching for Foreign Languages (ACTFL), gave a large place to culture. The fourth edition of the *World-Readiness Standards for Learning Languages* (National Standards Collaborative Board, 2015) specifies that learners meeting the *Cultures Standards* must be able to 'interact with cultural competence and understanding' and 'use the language to investigate, explain, and reflect on the relationship between the products...practices and perspectives of the cultures studied' (2015: 1).

Similar recommendations were issued by the Modern Language Association (MLA) Ad Hoc Committee on Foreign Languages, 'New Structures for a Changed World,' which in its 2007 report stressed the need to train students to become 'educated speakers who have deep translingual and transcultural competence' and called for a curricular reform that would 'situate language study in cultural, historical, geographic and cross-cultural frames within the context of humanistic learning.' One of the recommendations of the report was that students should be 'trained to reflect on the world and themselves through the lens of another language and culture' (MLA Ad Hoc Committee on Foreign Languages, 2007).

Since the mid-1990s, the Council of Europe as well has been calling for the development of intercultural competence. Stressing that intercultural competence (ICC) is not acquired automatically and needs to be learned and practiced, it has been supporting instructors through a number of publications on intercultural learning, such as *Developing the Intercultural Dimension in Language Teaching: A Practical Introduction for Teachers* (Byram *et al.*, 2002).

Approach

Developing intercultural understanding, in *Cultura*, means engaging in a dynamic online interaction with partners from another culture. In a *Cultura* exchange, two groups of students from two different cultures compare similar materials from their respective cultures juxtaposed online, such as student-generated answers to intercultural questionnaires, statistics and surveys, films and their remakes, images, commercials, newspaper articles or websites of international companies. They discuss the materials with their own group in class and with their online partners via asynchronous forums (Levet *et al.*, 2001) in which their interaction is self-directed and self-regulated.

The ability to communicate online would not, in and of itself, automatically result in intercultural understanding. The pedagogy behind *Cultura* is built upon a learner-centered constructivist approach where students actively construct their knowledge as it unfolds around specific materials and tasks (Furstenberg & Levet, 2010). The description that follows presents a 'classic' *Cultura* exchange. Because *Cultura* can be freely adapted to different contexts and cultures, there have been multiple variations regarding materials, language use, and types of partnerships (NFLRC, National Foreign Language Resource Center, 2010 / 2012). But it is important to understand how the process unfolds, to appreciate how technology supports the pedagogical goal.

Methodology

In the first stage of a *Cultura* exchange, the students are asked to respond online, anonymously and in their L1, to a series of three questionnaires. For instance, in an exchange between MIT and a French university, the MIT students will answer in English to prompts in English, and the French university students will answer in French to prompts in French. For the first questionnaire, students are asked what words they would associate with different word prompts, such as 'family,' 'success,' 'individualism.' For the second questionnaire, they complete sentences such as 'A good parent is someone who …,' 'A rude person is someone who …,' 'A good job is…' For the third questionnaire, they have to say how they would react in various hypothetical situations such as: 'You see a student cheating during an exam,' or 'You have been waiting in line, and someone cuts in front of you.' The goal of these questionnaires is to collect raw materials that the students will then analyze and discuss. There might not be a perfect choice of equivalent words and expressions in both languages for the prompts, but this lack of exact equivalency is often discussed in the forums – an apt example of how *Cultura* students have ample opportunities to reflect on the very issue of translation and adaptation.

The decision to have students answer in L1, and later in the exchange to write their comments on the forums in L1 as well (which means that the forums happen in two languages, with both sides of the exchange writing in L1, and consequently reading in L2), was linked from the start to the notion that language is culture. 'Language shapes who you are' (Kramsch & Gerhards, 2012: 75). In Claire Kramsch's formulation, passing between languages implies moving between different modes of thought, and different modes of being (Kramsch, 2018). Language is not only about getting your message across. In the words of famed semiotician Mikhail Bakhtin, 'Language is not a neutral medium… it is populated – overpopulated – with the intentions of others' (Bakhtin, 1982: 294). As the MLA Report recognized, 'Culture is represented not only in events, texts, buildings, artworks, cuisines and many other artifacts but also in language itself. Expressions such as 'the pursuit of happiness,' 'liberté, égalité, fraternité' and 'la Raza' connote cultural dimensions that extend well beyond their immediate translation' (MLA Ad Hoc Committee on Foreign Languages, 2007).

When the responses from each group in the exchange are published online side-by-side, the juxtaposition allows differences to emerge, as shown in Figure 2.1.

This example from a US/France exchange contains many cognates on the French side, which will make it easier for non-readers of French to get a sense of the effects of juxtaposition. The reader will note that on the English side, words with positive connotations dominate the word associations produced in response to the stimulus word 'individualism,' while on the French side, words with negative valences are quite frequent. Students' noticing of this obvious difference forms the kernel for their continued exploration, through discussion with their partners of more finely nuanced differences in the two cultures' associations with the

Cultura Archived Exchanges   2006   Spring   MIT   École Polytechnique   Word Association

Individualism	Individualisme
awareness, self-determination	argent, vitesse
beliefs, strength	égoïsme, américain
independence, freedom	égoïsme, argent
independence, selfish	égoïsme, vision à court terme, moderne
independence, sovereignty, pride	égoïste, défaut, méchant
intelligence, ideas	égoïsme, nécessaire, modernité
liberal, integrity	égoïsme, requin
loneliness, stubbornness	décadence, antipathie, perte
motivation, isolation, pioneering	défaut, développé
narcissism	démocratie, capitalisme, majorité
necessary, enlightening	mal moderne, français, à combattre
open-mindedness, independence	méchanceté, égoïsme
political	Polytechnique, égoïsme, fermé
school of thought, weird	racisme, égoïsme , mépris
self, modern	se battre
society, reality, self	solitude, opportunisme
success, drive	solitude,égoïsme,société
understatement, values	survie, force, honnêteté
uniqueness, autonomy	
United States, personality, freedom	

Figure 2.1 Archived exchange from the *Cultura* website

concept of individualism. Other examples with many different prompts and in different languages are available on the *Cultura* archived exchanges (http://cultura.mit.edu/cultura-exchanges-archive).

These responses to the intercultural questionnaires provide an entry point into both cultures, and are the first items analyzed by students, both online and in class, over a period of three weeks. The first week, students discuss the word associations; the second week, the sentence completions; and the third week, the reactions to situations.

The first task for students is to analyze and compare the answers to three prompts of their choice in the category assigned for the week. On average, there are about 10–12 prompts per category, so usually all the different topics are covered, even if the instructor does not assign them specifically. Performing this comparison by themselves in advance prepares students to work with their peers in class as well as online. The step-by-step process is carefully scaffolded, and starts with asking students to take a close look at the materials: after printing the juxtaposed answers, they work on the vocabulary, count and circle words to see what answers are used most often on each side, which ones appear on one side only. They regroup the responses and try to decide if they have a rather positive, neutral or negative connotation – a question which is occasionally brought back in the classroom discussions. For instance, the notion of power (*puissance*) that the French university students sometimes associate with the prompt 'USA' can be seen as having a positive, neutral or negative connotation.

The students' task is organized around three questions, essential to the scaffolding process: (a) What did you notice? Write down your observations; (b) Why do you think the students from (other school) gave these answers? Make a hypothesis; (c) What questions could you ask them to verify your hypothesis? Asking students to go through observations, hypotheses and questions enables them to analyze the materials and takes them out of the right/wrong duality with which they are familiar, while empowering them to navigate their own path toward new insights. They can always revise their hypotheses and understanding in the light of new elements brought into the conversation by their classmates or their online partners in the forums. During the classroom discussions (in L2), they are encouraged to always support their analysis with direct observations, and to directly quote the answers to the questionnaires and comments on the forums as evidence to support their point. In order to avoid generalizations or oversimplifications, whenever students come up with an observation about the other culture, they are encouraged to consider within what situations it seems to apply, and if there are situations where it does not apply. The whole group in class is important for this type of exercise, since all students can bring together, contrast and combine their different observations and interpretations.

There is a forum attached to each prompt. They are all open to all students, so that anyone can follow an entire conversation at a glance. Forum responses are written in L1, outside of class, but are referred to during class. Occasionally, forum postings allude to classroom discussions, as students bring back online what they have discussed with their peers. Even though the forums are asynchronous, it is expected that all students on both sides of the exchange will contribute within a specific period of time, generally a week, to ensure that there is truly a back and forth between them.

The instructors do not intervene directly in the forums, but again scaffold the process by providing expectations for participation. For example, they request that students post their observations, share their hypotheses and ask questions to verify them. Students also need to answer their partners' questions and react to their comments. When first joining a new topic, they need to read what has been said so far, so as to help move the conversation and not just repeat observations that might have already been made. Over a week, they are expected to visit the same topics multiple times to continue the conversation.

The end goal of the forums is not to create a consensus among all students, but to enable them to engage with their online partners and progressively build a more nuanced view of the others' culture. They are never asked to come up with any definitive statement about the other culture, but to always re-examine their findings in the light of new materials and new points of view. Since the process is reciprocal, answering questions or reacting to hypotheses from their partners enables them to put their own culture in perspective.

Examples from the archived exchanges

Although each exchange unfolds differently, it is almost always possible to observe an arc of developing understanding as discussion progresses. In a foundational stage, learners typically begin by offering or soliciting clarification or confirmation of observed differences in the objects under examination. As these differences come into focus, learners are encouraged by their instructors to offer and solicit hypotheses and opinions regarding possible underlying cultural values. Exposure to the full range of opinions and hypotheses, and the subsequent discussion in which these are tested, allows learners to gain a nuanced understanding of the partner culture.

The following examples from the archived exchanges (between students in the US and in France) will illustrate the types of interactions taking place between the two groups and will show how the forums open the classroom to multiple voices.

Discussing observed differences through comparisons, hypotheses and questions

The conversation often starts with students focusing on specific words and expressions that appear in the juxtaposed answers. For instance, looking at the prompt 'Work,' a student notices that one side associates it with 'exhaustion' and the other one with 'obligation.'

> 'I noticed the emphasis of exhaustion in the opinions of American students and the emphasis on obligation regarding 'work' for the French' (Z., Work, Spring 2017).

Another one sees that the prompt 'A good parent' is associated on one side with 'unconditional love,' whereas for the other side a good parent is 'a guide.'

> 'It seems to me, when I'm reading the answers, that for the Americans, the most important thing for a father or a mother is unconditional love, whereas for the French, their role as a guide comes up more often.' (Il me semble, en lisant les réponses, que pour les américains, la chose la plus importante chez un père ou une mère est un amour inconditionnel, alors que pour les français, le rôle de guide revient plus souvent pour les parents.) (A., Good parent, Spring 2013)

Doing a close reading of the answers leads them to ask clarifying questions, as in the example below, where a student in the US realizes that the word 'education' appearing on the French side with the prompt 'A good parent' might have to do either with 'schoolwork' or 'moral education.'

> 'The word 'education' seems only to appear on the French side. Does this refer to moral education or education related to schoolwork when children are young?' (M., Good parent, Spring 2016).

They make hypotheses about what the answers seem to reveal, drawing on their understanding of certain concepts in the other culture. Here for instance a student in the US wonders about a possible connection between how the students in France answered the prompt 'Individualism' and what he perceives to be 'the French value of equality.'

> 'It is possible that the idea of individualism goes against the French value of equality?' (E., Individualism, Spring 2016)

Pursuing a nuanced understanding

The conversations on the forums and in the classroom are part of a process. Students learn to follow through and go beyond first impressions. For instance, in the comment below, a student in the US wondered if the notion of not following others, just doing things to fit in (that appeared in their own answers to 'Individualism') might exist in France, but under a different name.

> 'It seems to me that most of the American students find individualism positive, creative; meanwhile, the French seem to see it as negative [...]. Is there a better word in French that describes someone who doesn't follow others/just do things to fit in?' (S., Individualism, Spring 2016)

The answer from a French student confirmed that this was the case.

> 'S., I would say that the word equivalent to 'individualism' in French would be 'non-conformiste.'' (S., je dirais que le mot qui équivaut à 'individualism' serait 'non-conformiste.') (M., Individualism, Spring 2016)

Students are aware of the risk of oversimplification, and do not hesitate to disagree with comments from participants in their own group and call for more nuance.

> 'I disagree with what has been said so far about the relationship between parents and children in France. I think that we – us as much as you – give an overly simplistic view of it.' (Je ne suis pas d'accord avec ce qui a été dit sur la relation parent-enfant en France. Je trouve qu'on – nous comme vous – en donne une image trop caricaturale [...].) (A., Good parent, Spring 2017).

This call for more nuance means also looking at stereotypes in their own culture. For instance, in a discussion about 'Suburbs,' where the associations on the French side were mostly negative, a French student expressed frustration with the ways suburbs are presented in the media, which does not represent her own experience.

> 'I come from the suburbs of Paris and see that the French have a negative opinion about them. What annoys me the most is that the media in France as well as abroad give a negative view of the suburbs. They give the impression that all suburbs are ghettos, but that is not the case. Most of them are nice places to live, and that's where I feel best.' (Je viens de la banlieue parisienne et je constate que les Français ont une vision négative. Ce qui me désole le plus, c'est la vision négative de la banlieue véhiculée par les médias aussi bien en France qu'à l'étranger. Ils donnent l'impression que toutes les banlieues sont des ghettos, alors que ce n'est pas le cas. La majorité sont des lieux de vie agréables, et c'est là que je me sens le mieux.) (S., Suburbs, Spring 2013)

Students actively engage and try both to understand the others and be understood. They often reformulate their comments when trying to work past apparent misunderstandings, grounding their exchange in specific examples or other participants' comments.

> 'I think the difference that I was trying to articulate has to do with the way French and American parents support their children.' (C., Good parent, Spring 2017)

Skill development and skill transfer

The types of interactions illustrated above demonstrate how, in keeping with Open Pedagogy principles as embodied in open educational practices, Cultura moves intercultural learning 'beyond a content-cent[e]red approach, shifting the focus from resources to practices, with learners and teachers sharing the process of knowledge creation' (Cronin, 2017: 3). Students, engaging with others on the forums, become aware that language and culture play a role in the way they perceive the world, and that learning is a co-construction; that it is necessary to question assumptions and stereotypes and one's own culture; that the frame of reference, or context, is important; that they all occupy multiple positions. As they learn to interpret text and reflect on the different meanings attached to different contexts, they develop literacy skills that they can apply when working with different materials.

The intercultural questionnaires are just the starting point. Depending on their pedagogical goals, instructors can decide to include different modules in the exchange. Such modules always center around the comparison of artifacts from the two cultures that correspond to one another but are produced within the respective cultural contexts. Comparisons may range from works of fiction in the same genre, to hard data on similar social phenomena, to images of related (but distinct) cultural phenomena – the possibilities are endless.

Comparing a French film and its American remake was part of the very early *Cultura* exchanges at MIT, as a way to look at the underlying cultural frameworks revealed by the two versions of a film. It can be easily adapted to different cultures, as a large number of foreign films have been adapted, over the years, for an American audience. A scene-by-scene comparative analysis enables students, focusing on the story and the characters, to observe what has been changed in the remake, and reflect on what this reveals about each culture.

Working with statistics and surveys after the questionnaires leads students to open up their range of investigation. Their informants for the first three weeks of an exchange are a small number of students from their partner school who cannot be seen as representative of an entire cultural group. Thus, students are asked to look for statistics and national surveys and say how, in their opinion, they illustrate, explain, or seem to contradict an aspect of the other – or their own – culture that was discussed in the first part of the exchange.

Working with images makes students think about how to communicate about their culture visually. For instance, they can illustrate different aspects of their daily life, such as where they live, eat and study, take pictures of their schedules and photograph visuals found around campus. They can also try to clarify visually the meaning of a concept in their own culture, or work on advertising pages in magazines or websites. This can be done in cross-cultural teams, each one contributing images around a similar topic, and then reflecting and commenting on what these pictures reveal about both cultures.

Work with commercials can focus on the differences in the way similar products are advertised in the two cultures. Students can also analyze commercials that draw heavily on cultural images from each culture. This work is not necessarily done in partnership. It often happens at the end of the semester and can be used as a way to see how what students have discussed with their partners is reflected in such documents.

While the archived discussions reflect what happens between students online, it is important to stress the less visible but essential work that happens between instructors before any conversation can take place between their two groups of students. A *Cultura* exchange is first a collaboration between two instructors across cultures. They must agree on a common calendar; select the materials the students will compare and discuss; review and select the best technological tools to facilitate the students' collaboration. Most importantly, they must discuss expectations, especially regarding students' participation. The question of timely participation on the forums, which is essential but sometimes difficult to achieve, reveals that coordinating work across cultures, between two groups with very different sets of constraints and expectations, can be tricky. It is an opportunity, for both groups, to become aware of the others' context and actively work across differences.

How *Cultura* has been made Available, Accessible and Usable by the FL Teaching Community at Large

Cultura is a freely available open educational resource. There are several dimensions to the concept of free availability, however. Even if a resource is *free*, if it is not known to potential users, it cannot be considered *available* in any practical sense. To help *Cultura* serve effectively as an open resource, the creators of *Cultura* and those who have worked closely with them have set forth the principles and practices of this model of intercultural telecollaborative exchange in various professional publications. In addition, researchers have examined *Cultura* as an object of study, and practitioners have reported on their experiences applying or adapting the model. This section focuses on *Cultura*-related works of these various types.

Cultura: Foundational resources

The *Cultura* online platform at MIT, which has been available since 2008 (with some interruption) as an open resource for educators conducting exchanges, facilitates both (1) the administration of surveys, such as word association and sentence completion, and (2) the conduct of learners' bilingual discussions, in which they compare survey results or other juxtaposed artifacts, then put forward and test hypotheses about cultural values based on their comparisons. Past survey results and the ensuing discussions are retained in the site's publicly available *Cultura* archives. The website is an appropriate starting point for interested practitioners who are seeking guidance in the implementation of their own intercultural online exchanges.

A seminal publication introducing the *Cultura* model, Furstenberg and Levet *et al.* (2001), appeared in *Language Learning and Technology*, an open journal with a Journal Impact Factor that hovers around the 90th percentile (Clarivate Analytics, 2018). Additional overviews of *Cultura* can be found in Furstenberg and Levet (2010), Furstenberg and Levet (2014) and Furstenberg and English (2016). These publications provide both theoretical orientation and practical exposition of how the model can be implemented.

Publications exploring *Cultura*

The foundational publications mentioned above provide guidance in the use of the *Cultura* model as an open resource for practitioners of intercultural exchange. Such presentations of the 'classic' *Cultura* model represent just one type of resource available to interested practitioners, however. In addition, a number of publications have assessed the efficacy of *Cultura* as a resource for intercultural learning, focusing variously on learner acquisition of ICC or on features of *Cultura* that motivate and constrain learner behaviors. Other publications, using *Cultura* as a springboard, have offered extensions of the *Cultura* model into educational environments, situations or populations where it had not previously been employed. Both types of publications reveal the value of *Cultura* as an open resource, both for (1) the examination of the process of the acquisition of intercultural competence and for (2) the development of innovations in educators' praxis as they seek to facilitate said acquisition. In this section, we will examine selected publications assessing *Cultura* as an educational tool, and in the following section we will examine adaptations and extensions of *Cultura*.

Cultura: *Intercultural learning in the open*

The open records at the *Cultura* website have provided a dataset for researchers examining the effectiveness of *Cultura* as a resource for intercultural learning. Of the research publications that have relied on this dataset, a few have notably focused on markers of learner acquisition of intercultural competence, while most publications have focused more on possible effects of the design of *Cultura* itself, or on *Cultura*'s contributions to the online teaching and learning of world languages.

One notable publication focusing on learner acquisition in *Cultura* is Blyth (2012), a study that used the archive to examine French and American stancetaking in online environments, based on many semesters of *Cultura* exchanges between students at MIT and Brown Universities and students at four French universities (Université de Brest, Université de Lille, ENSAM Lille and ENSEIRB-MATMECA). Based on the importance ascribed by John Du Bois (2007) to stancetaking in language use, Blyth (2012) examined 'cultural, grammatical, and interactional features of the opinions expressed by French and American college students during telecollaborative discussions of individualism' (2012: 49). Analysis of cumulative data from a number of exchanges revealed that culture-based differences in the pragmatics of taking a position posed challenges to students' cross-cultural communication. Blyth (2012) saw evidence that French and American students' models of the discussion topic were culturally conditioned, and he described the strategies students on both sides of the exchanges used to negotiate their 'mismatched' stances (based in their respective home cultures) during online interaction.

Chun (2014b) also examined learner acquisition in a *Cultura*-style exchange between students in the US and in Germany, focusing on ICC. She found that there was 'ample evidence of many students' emerging ICC' (2014b: 121). In this study, Chun used a modification of the *Cultura* model that combined interaction in the asynchronous forums typical of *Cultura* with additional synchronous chats; moreover, among her subjects a high proportion were multilingual and multicultural, 'present[ing] a potentially confounding variable' (2014b: 105). Chun's focus in this study on genre differences between learners' chat and forum postings, and the links between these genre differences and students' post-hoc assessments of the degree of 'success' of specific conversations, is suggestive of the complexity inherent both in assessing learner acquisition in *Cultura* and *Cultura*-like environments and in comparing studies of said acquisition.

Other publications have examined the design of *Cultura* and its effects. Some investigators have identified a salient strength of *Cultura* in contrast to other models for intercultural exchange, namely, the non-prescriptive and emergent nature of cultural knowledge in *Cultura* exchanges in which participants present hypotheses of cultural difference and test them through discussion. Levy (2007), for example, stressed how *Cultura* managed the risk of intercultural conflict through its emphasis on exploratory dialogue. In this assessment, *Cultura* is seen as mitigating cultural conflict through negotiation, which would suggest that the emergent knowledge is not presented as monolithic or essentializing.

However, because *Cultura* invites comparison and contrast of phenomena identified with established cultures (e.g. French, American) by students situated in those cultures (though not assumed to be native speakers), and leads them initially to frame this comparison and contrast in terms of those established cultures, *Cultura* has been criticized as facilitating 'culturalist discourses' that essentialize cultural differences (Trémion, 2013). This question about the effects of *Cultura*'s structural design was also raised in Koike and Lacorte (2014). In their own publications, the creators of *Cultura* contend that, far from essentializing, *Cultura* attempts to draw students away from stereotyping:

> We are not trying to lead our students into believing that, if they write a long enough list of 'cultural facts,' they will know any better what the other culture is about. We lead them into recognizing a process, and train them to look, make hypotheses, ask questions, reflect on what 'culture' is, identifying along the way their own culturally encoded behaviors, becoming more alert and open towards another culture, more flexible, and enriching the way they perceive the world. (Furstenberg *et al*., 2001: 85)

Furstenberg and Levet (2014) note that while the initial cultural questionnaires may give a sense of 'simplistic… duality', the subsequent discussions allow for 'a much more nuanced and complex view of the cultures at hand' (2014: 14). *Cultura*'s positioning as an open educational resource has facilitated the testing of this proposition 'in the open,' that is, using the abovementioned publicly available *Cultura* archives.

Blyth (2015) tested this critique of *Cultura*'s structure, querying whether *Cultura* leads participants inexorably to frame their discourse in culturally essentialist terms by examining the 'influence of affordances of the design of *Cultura*'s instructional design on the participants' discursive perspectives on language and culture' (2015: 139). This examination contrasts with Blyth's (2012) earlier publication by shifting the focus somewhat from learner acquisition to features of the *Cultura* model. Using selections from the same open dataset, Blyth (2015) evaluates whether the parameters established for learner inquiry in the *Cultura* model provide affordances for learners to 'explicitly contest culturalist discourses' (2015: 141) and to 'avoid constructing monolithic representations of national cultures' (2015: 161) while exploring differences seen in responses on the French and the American sides of an exchange. Blyth (2015) concludes that 'while *Cultura*'s instructional design focuses participants on cultural differences that lead them to construe language and culture as relatively static phenomena' (2015: 160), nevertheless, this does 'not always lead to essentialist discourses as predicted by the critics' (2015: 160). It is interesting to note that the contestation of 'essentializing' in *Cultura* can take place very much in the open, both in the sense that the model is freely available and adaptable, and in the sense that the data that serve as a basis for the debate are also freely available.

Cultura *as referential resource*

Apart from publications that examine learner acquisition and the efficacy of *Cultura* in facilitating it, there are a considerable number of works in which *Cultura* is referred to as a potential resource or tool, an exemplar of best practices, or simply as a source of ideas. Since *Cultura* encompasses teacher praxis, the role of the student, the use of technology, the co-construction of knowledge, the definition of 'culture,' and many other facets of educational theory and practice, the emphasis on what is 'best' about *Cultura* may vary. A number of authors have focused on the integration of technology that enables students in *Cultura* exchanges to connect and communicate. Shrum and Glisan (2016), for example, held up *Cultura* as an effective model for the integration of technology in education. In their instructions for an exercise for pre-service teachers, they shone a spotlight on what they characterized as a serendipitous confluence of practices described in *Cultura* and the student standards developed by the International Society for Technology in Education: 'What makes Cultura a useful example for ISTE-S is that it does not set out to meet these standards but yet does so through skillfully crafted scaffolded exercises' (Shrum & Glisan, 2016: 431). Finkbeiner and Knierim (2006), in their professional development-oriented volume on cultural exchange, made use of *Cultura* as a model for transitioning another model for intercultural exchange to an online format: 'we decided to first collect ideas by following and adapting the *Cultura* design... This helped us gain highly valuable insights into intercultural learning online... allow[ing] for the implementation [of] a web-based learning design' (2006: 213–214). Blake (2008) recognized *Cultura* for having effectively met the challenge of how to use technology to bring learners to a greater understanding of culturally rooted sociolinguistic markers and morphosyntactic structures found in social media.

Other practitioners referring to *Cultura* have focused on pedagogic aspects. Perry (2016), after referring to the word-association comparisons that often constitute the first stage in a *Cultura* exchange, stated 'I used this idea in my own classroom to challenge the connotations of some words I felt to be charged with cultural interpretation for Italians and Americans' (2016: 17). Orsini-Jones and Lee (2018) cited task designs found in the *Cultura* model, such as the questionnaires, as an inspiration for the design of features of an intercultural telecollaborative project called *CoCo*.

Adaptations and Extensions of *Cultura*

From its beginnings, the *Cultura* project has positioned itself not only as a free and open resource enabling creative adaptation without concern for breaching copyright, but also as a creative hub for the extension of principles and practices that characterize *Cultura* into new domains for telecollaborative exchange. One important result has been the adaptation of the 'classic' *Cultura* model into variant forms suited to populations of learners with profiles distinct from the 'pioneer' group of university-level learners of French at MIT and their exchange partners in France. From *Cultura*'s early days, educators who have made use of the model as a framework for engaging in intercultural telecollaboration have *adapted* the model to fit the needs of learners in their classes, varying the model along a number of different dimensions. Practitioners have also *extended* the model beyond its original context of foreign language study into the study of language for specific purposes or heritage language learning. Variations in practice in such adaptations and extensions can be motivated by differences in the overarching purpose or topical focus of each exchange, characteristics of student populations, motivations of the instructor and available instructional resources. As noted in Furstenberg and Levet (2014), 'changes in some of the parameters of the original model [might include] the use of L1 or L2 in the forums[,] the type of documents used for comparison[,] the role of the teacher in the online forums[,] and classroom face-to-face discussions' (2014: 27). To these we might add the length of the exchange; the use of various tools for communication, such as the mix of synchronous chat and asynchronous forums cited in Chun (2014b) above; the numbers of students on each side of the exchange; and the role the exchange plays in the instructional program or curriculum. In this section we will examine dimensions of variation in adaptations of the *Cultura* model.

Extension to new languages and contexts of study

The first and most obvious type of variation from the original *Cultura* context, which joined learners of French and English as foreign languages in the United States and France, respectively, was the extension of the model into other languages. Examples of language pairings in *Cultura*-inspired exchanges have now become too numerous to cite; for a study performed on *Cultura*-inspired exchanges in Spanish and Russian, see Bauer *et al.* (2006). Beyond variation in language, extensions of the *Cultura* model into educational contexts beyond postsecondary-level foreign language study are worth mentioning; these include extension into lower (secondary) levels, into heritage language learning contexts and into language for specific purposes (LSP) contexts. The NFLRC at the University of Hawai'i at Mānoa (nflrc.hawaii.edu) has, through several professional development events, served as an incubator for the design and delivery of various extensions and adaptations of the *Cultura* model, which are described at the website 'Online Cafés: Creating Language and Culture Learning Communities' (National Foreign Language Resource Center, 2010 / 2012) (http://nflrc.hawaii.edu/onlinecafes/).

By the time the NFLRC proposed the extension of the *Cultura* model into the domain of heritage language learning as the theme of its 2008 Summer Institute, *Cultura* had already been tried at the secondary level. This extension, and other adaptations of the *Cultura* model, were detailed by Gilberte Furstenberg in a PowerPoint presentation (Furstenberg, 2008) that oriented Institute participants to the kinds of adaptations that had been made by *Cultura*-inspired practitioners up to that point, preparing them to think about how they would apply the *Cultura* model to exchanges between groups representing heritage members of the same culture either in different locations in diaspora (e.g. Filipino-Americans in Hawai'i and in California), or in-country and in diaspora (e.g. Samoans in American Sāmoa and in Hawai'i). With the aim of 'acculturating' learners in these groups to cultural practices and language use as realized in their distinct communities, while facilitating learning of the heritage language (even Samoans in American Sāmoa had limited proficiency in their heritage language), Institute participants designed online exchanges that extended and adapted the *Cultura* model. While these exchanges were not 'cross-cultural' in the same sense as 'classic' *Cultura*, they used the same strategies of comparison and discussion to uncover areas of similarity and difference and to test hypotheses about variation in their local 'microcultures.' The Filipino-American Heritage Café is treated in detail in Domingo (2014).

One of the working groups in the NFLRC 2008 Summer Institute worked to extend the *Cultura* model into a business-language LSP context joining students learning Business Chinese in Hawai'i with students learning Business English in China. Adaptations to the *Cultura* model made in this extension centered around the choice of topics and artifacts specific to business; the project is detailed in Jiang *et al*. (2014).

Adaptations based on purpose and population

One feature of *Cultura* that often surprises new practitioners is the use of L1, both to answer questionnaires and to engage partners in discussion. This 'least understood and most widely ignored feature of *Cultura*' (Furstenberg & Levet, 2014: 7) serves the functions of equalizing groups (no matter their L2 proficiency level, they are all highly proficient in L1), enabling full freedom of expression (no groping for the *mot juste*), and ensuring authenticity in linguistic input as well as full embodiment of culture-in-language for the benefit of the collaborative partners. Despite these compelling justifications, quite a number of adaptations of *Cultura* choose to tweak this parameter, most commonly with the aim of providing learners with the chance to develop their productive skills in the L2. Various solutions have included splitting the exchange schedule into blocks of time in which one or the other language is used exclusively, using a lingua franca (as when learners of English language from two different cultures have used English exclusively in *Cultura*-inspired exchanges), or even – in what might justly be termed a distortion of the model – having both sides use L2 exclusively in the exchange.

While topics in *Cultura* exchanges at MIT typically involve what might be termed core cultural values, including abstract concepts such as 'individualism' or what makes a 'good parent,' other exchanges have varied in their topic selection. Exchanges for specific populations may focus on topics of particular interest, such as nurturance of the heritage culture among the heritage students described above. Exchanges of shorter length or among younger learners may narrow topical focus (school and family), while exchanges among highly proficient learners, such as students in the Language Flagships (thelanguageflagship.org), have gone in-depth into topics such as the media in society.

Since *Cultura* is freely available and adaptable, variations often end up looking quite different from the original model – to the point that it is sometimes difficult to say where '*Cultura*-based adaptations' become something else entirely. For example, Vaskivska (2015) involved only one group of students in a cultural-learning activity that made use of archived word-association responses; they were not given the opportunity to engage in hypothesis formation and testing with a partner group. While Vaskivska concludes that 'the cultural awareness of L2 learners can also be raised by using archived data from… native speakers' (2015: 99), she concedes that 'online exchanges would help clarify any incorrect assumptions L2 students might make about the target language and culture based on responses from native speakers' (2015: 100). Such latitude in variation is to be expected in the open education landscape.

Cultura and the open education ecosystem

Models for open education stress the benefits of the free and open exchange of ideas and materials, as exemplified in the 'About' pages of the Open Education Consortium (2018) and Opensource.com (2018). The gates and controls on academic exchange that characterize the for-profit educational marketplace, such as high textbook prices or paywalls controlling access to publications, are absent or greatly reduced in open education, allowing dialogue about evolving educational models and materials to proceed at a pace limited only by the medium of exchange. In the case of *Cultura*, scholarly exchange and the development of new ideas and resources have taken place through publications and conferences as well as one-on-one communication initiated through the 'contact us' link on the website by instructors who have heard about Cultura via different channels and are thinking about adapting it. Offering support through direct engagement with potential users is central to the open design philosophy of *Cultura*.

Communication with instructors focuses first on determining what they need: what they know about Cultura, where they heard about it, if they have experience with telecollaboration. Instructors planning an exchange may have questions about the different options offered on the website: downloading the *Cultura* Exchange Tool on their own school's server vs. being hosted at MIT or using other tools such as blogs and Google forms. They check if using *Cultura* is free, how to find a partner and how much support they can expect. They may have questions on how to manage their exchange, or sometimes need direct assistance with managing their website. This is an opportunity to engage with the instructors and discuss their pedagogical goals and particular challenges, having to do with a wide range of topics: use of L1 and L2, the role of the teacher, what happens in the classroom, exploration of themes from the archives, the types of instructions students need, rules of conduct online. This type of direct support for instructors, developing their exchanges is often time-sensitive and therefore assumes the availability of a supporting team. Keeping *Cultura* going as an open resource entails an investment on the part of MIT, the host institution, in institutional infrastructure, including human resources. In turn, the *Cultura* Project helps to fulfill MIT's institutional commitment to open educational resources. Cultura's sustainability depends on this commitment.

Conclusion

Cultura's contribution to open education is multifold. It opens the classroom to the world, creating 'an open source textbook' (Cha, 2006) generated by students. As the same author notes, 'it is not about the technology.' It is about an approach and methodology, embodying key features of Open Pedagogy, that have been actively shared with educators over the past 20 years. Each *Cultura* exchange is unique, since adaptations in different languages often lead to variations in content and form. But some elements, which constitute the essential aspects of *Cultura*, tend to be present in most exchanges inspired by the original model: the approach is comparative; discussions happen online and in the classroom; the student-generated intercultural questionnaires are usually the first items to be discussed. Because of *Cultura*'s modular structure, instructors incorporate into their exchanges different types of documents closely tied to their pedagogical goals and vary elements of the model to fit their distinct needs.

While *Cultura* has made contributions in the arena of open educational resources and practices, further progress is far from guaranteed. First of all, as with all resources in open education, the sustainability of the resource depends on the presence of supporting infrastructure, both technological (institutional hosting) and socioeconomic (the ability of creators and contributors to find sources of funding for developing the project). Secondly, creators and contributors need to strive for greater transparency and reciprocity in practice, so that new users can access best practices more easily. On the part of the developers, this means improving practitioners' access to the elements of *Cultura* that take place away from the online platform, so that teachers new to *Cultura* better understand the in-class praxis that, in concert with learners' online discussions, supports learners' progress toward intercultural competence. On the part of users, this means 'giving back'; that is, rather than simply using the model, participating actively in a loop of user innovation. Ideally all the different variations and adaptations of *Cultura* would be accessible online, as was the initial project, to encourage the distribution and exchange of ideas, in keeping with the open philosophy of the project. Finally, further engaged scholarship around *Cultura* will increase the value of the resource and serve to draw additional users into the community.

Cultura's active commitment to open education has not only enabled a community of educators to engage with this model but has also engendered valuable discussion among educators about technology and teaching, the teaching of culture and language, telecollaboration and now open education.

References

American Council on Education (2010) Bringing the World into the Classroom: ACE award to recognize the innovative use of technology to promote internationalization. PDF document. See http://www.acenet.edu/news-room/Documents/BringTheWorld Final.pdf

Bakhtin, M. (1982) On dialogism and heteroglossia. In M. Holquist (ed.) *The Dialogic Imagination: Four Essays by M. M. Bakhtin*. Austin: University of Texas Press.

Bauer, B., deBenedette, L., Furstenberg, G., Levet, S. and Waryn, S. (2006) Internet-mediated intercultural foreign language education: The *Cultura* Project. In J.A. Belz and S.L. Thorne (eds) *Internet-mediated Intercultural Foreign Language Education* (pp. 31–62). Boston: Heinle & Heinle. See http://citeseerx.ist.psu.edu/viewdoc/down load?doi=10.1.1.556.4118&rep=rep1&type=pdf

Blake, R.J. (2008) *Brave New Digital Classroom: Technology and Foreign Language Learning*. Washington, DC: Georgetown University Press.

Blyth, C. (2012) Cross-cultural stances in online discussion: Pragmatic variations in French and American ways of expressing opinions. In J.C.F. Brasdefer and D. Koike (eds) *Pragmatic Variation in First and Second Language Contexts: Methodological Issues* (pp. 49–80). Amsterdam: John Benjamins.

Blyth, C. (2015) Exploring the complex nature of language and culture through intercultural dialogue: The case of *Cultura*. In D. Koike and C.S. Blyth (eds) *Dialogue in Multilingual and Multimodal Communities* (pp. 139–165). Amsterdam: John Benjamins.

Byram, M., Gribkova, B. and Starkey, H. (2002) *Developing the Intercultural Dimension in Language Teaching: A Practical Introduction for Teachers*. Strasbourg: Council of Europe.

Cha, R. (2006) *Cultura: A Glimpse at the Future of the Student Generated Textbook*. See http://www.futureofthebook.org/next/text/2006/04/cultura_a_glimpse_at_the_futur_1.html

Chun, D.M. (2014b) Developing intercultural communicative competence through online exchanges. In D.M. Chun (ed.) *Cultura-inspired Intercultural Exchanges: Focus on Asian and Pacific Languages* (pp. 97–123). Honolulu, HI: NFLRC, University of Hawai'i.

Clarivate Analytics (2018) InCites Journal Citation Reports dataset, updated June 06, 2018.

Cronin, C. (2017) Openness and praxis: Exploring the use of open educational practices in higher education. *The International Review of Research in Open and Distributed Learning* 18 (5). http://dx.doi.org/10.19173/irrodl.v18i5.3096

Domingo, N.P. (2014) UH-UCLA Filipino Heritage Café and the Fil-Ams' quest for identity. In D.M. Chun (ed.) *Cultura-inspired Intercultural Exchanges: Focus on Asian and Pacific Languages* (pp. 145–161). Honolulu, HI: NFLRC, University of Hawai'i.

Du Bois, J. (2007) The stance triangle. In R. Englebretson (ed.) *Stancetaking in Discourse: Subjectivity, Evaluation, Interaction* (pp. 139–182). Amsterdam: John Benjamins.

Finkbeiner, C. and Knierim, M. (2006) The ABC's as a starting point and goal: The Online Intercultural Exchange Project (ICE). In P.R. Schmidt and C. Finkbeiner (eds) *ABC's of Cultural Understanding and Communication: National and International Adaptations* (pp. 213–244). Charlotte, NC: Information Age Publishing.

Furstenberg, G. (2008) *Online Cafés for Heritage Learners: The Different Parameters* [PowerPoint slides]. See http://nflrc.hawaii.edu/onlinecafes/wp-content/uploads/2010/01/GC03Furstenberg.ppt

Furstenberg, G. and English, K. (2016) Cultura revisited. *Language Learning & Technology* 20 (2), 172–178. http://dx.doi.org/10125/44471

Furstenberg, G. and Levet, S. (2010) Integrating telecollaboration into the language classroom: Some insights. In M. Dooly and R. O'Dowd (eds) *Telecollaboration 2.0 for Language and Intercultural Learning* (pp. 305–336). New York: Peter Lang Publishing Group.

Furstenberg, G. and Levet, S. (2014) Cultura: From then to now. Its origins, key features, methodology, and how it has evolved. Reflections on the past and musings on the future. In D.M. Chun (ed.) *Cultura-inspired Intercultural Exchanges: Focus on Asian and Pacific Languages* (pp. 1–32). Honolulu, HI: NFLRC, University of Hawai'i.

Furstenberg, G., Levet, S., English, K. and Maillet, K. (2001) Giving a virtual voice to the silent language of culture: The Cultura project. *Language Learning & Technology* 5 (1), 55–102. http://dx.doi.org/10125/25113

Jhangiani, R. and DeRosa, R. (2017, August 29) Open Pedagogy. See https://press.rebus.community/makingopentextbookswithstudents/chapter/open-pedagogy/

Jiang, S., Wang, H. and Tschudi, S. (2014) Intercultural learning on the web: Reflections on practice. In D.M. Chun (ed.) *Cultura-inspired Intercultural Exchanges: Focus on Asian and Pacific Languages* (pp. 127–143). Honolulu, HI: NFLRC, University of Hawai'i.

Koike, D. and Lacorte, M. (2014) Toward intercultural competence: From questions to practices and perspectives of the target culture. *Journal of Spanish Language Teaching* 1 (1), 15–30.

Kramsch, C. (2018) Third Place: How a French Germanist became an applied linguist in America. In P.M. Lützeler and P. Höyng (eds) *Transatlantic German Studies: Testimonies to the Profession*. Martlesham: Boydell & Brewer / Camden House.

Kramsch, C. and Gerhards, S. (2012) Im Gespräch: An interview with Claire Kramsch on the 'multilingual subject.' *Die Unterrichtspraxis* 45 (1), 74–82.

Levy, M. (2007) Culture, culture learning and new technologies: Towards a pedagogical framework. *Language Learning and Technology* 11 (2), 104–127. http://dx.doi.org/10125/44106

MLA Ad Hoc Committee on Foreign Languages (2007) Foreign languages and higher education: New structures for a changed world. See https://www.mla.org/Resources/Research/Surveys-Reports-and-Other-Documents/Teaching-Enrollments-and-Programs/Foreign-Languages-and-Higher-Education-New-Structures-for-a-Changed-World

National Foreign Language Resource Center (2010/2012) Online Cafés: Creating language & culture learning communities. See http://nflrc.hawaii.edu/onlinecafes/

National Standards Collaborative Board (2015) *World-Readiness Standards for Learning Languages* (4th edn). Alexandria, VA: National Standards Collaborative Board.

National Standards in Foreign Language Education Project, US Dept. of Education (1996) *Standards for Foreign Language Learning: Preparing for the 21st Century*. Lawrence, KS: Allen Press.

Open Education Consortium (2018) About the Open Education Consortium. See http://www.oeconsortium.org/about-oec/

Opensource.com (2018) The open source way. See https://opensource.com/open-source-way

Orsini-Jones, M. and Lee, F. (2018) The *CoCo* Telecollaborative Project: Internationalisation at home to foster global citizenship competences. In M. Orsini-Jones and F. Lee (eds) *Intercultural Communicative Competence for Global Citizenship: Identifying Cyberpragmatic Rules of Engagement in Telecollaboration* (pp. 39–52). London: Palgrave Macmillan.

Paquette, C. (1979) Quelques fondements d'une pédagogie ouverte. *Québec français* (36), 20–21. See https://www.erudit.org/fr/revues/qf/1979-n36-qf1208689/51334ac.pdf

Perry, P.C. (2016) Fostering intercultural teaching through film. In P.C. Perry and E.B. Foley (eds) *Fostering Culture Through Film: A Resource for Teaching Foreign Languages* (pp. 7–26). Newcastle-upon-Tyne: Cambridge Scholars Publishing.

Shrum, J.L. and Gleason, E.W. (2016) *Teacher's Handbook: Contextualized Language Instruction* (5th edn). Boston: Cengage Learning.

Trémion, V. (2013) Constructing a relationship to otherness in web-based exchanges for language and culture learning. In F. Dervin and A. Liddicoat (eds) *Linguistics for Intercultural Education* (pp. 161–174). Amsterdam: John Benjamins.

Vaskivska, T. (2015) *Evaluation of a State of Intercultural Competence through Completion of* Cultura *Project Tasks* (Master's thesis). Arizona State University. See https://repository.asu.edu/attachments/150745/content/Vaskivska_asu_0010N_14809.pdf

3 Open Educational Resources as Tools to Teach the Indigenous Languages of Latin America: Where Technology, Pedagogy and Colonialism Meet

Sergio Romero

Based on a case study of K'iche' Maya, this chapter will examine the pedagogical, cultural and political challenges of producing open educational resources (OER) to teach indigenous languages of Latin America and will suggest a few solutions. First, I will consider the social role of regional variation and the challenges involved in linguistic standardization of indigenous languages. Second, I will examine the available linguistic and pedagogical works on indigenous languages, their strengths and limitations as foundations for online OER. Whereas scholarly publications on indigenous languages are often detailed and abundant, they are not easily adapted to the needs of non-native language learners. Third, I will consider the challenges for non-indigenous learners of the peculiar articulations of language, culture and discourse that we find in Mayan and other indigenous languages of Latin America. Students with a Western mind-set bring their own language ideologies and expectations about the role of teacher and instructor to the experience of learning indigenous languages. Unfortunately, many are unprepared to make the adjustments required by pedagogies cognizant of the cultural values held by speakers of indigenous languages and the marginalization in which they are held by mainstream societies in Latin America. Finally, I will discuss the future of indigenous languages in Latin America and the role that OER can have in revitalization efforts.

Indigenous Languages and Digital Technology Today

Digital technology and the internet have been hailed as critical innovations that could substantially improve the conditions under which indigenous languages are transmitted, revitalized and preserved. Long afflicted by a lack of affordable, accessible pedagogical materials, many indigenous language activists have turned to open, digital platforms as key resources for teachers, students and intellectuals (Bischoff & Fountain, 2013; Nicholas, 2009; Romero, 2016). Digital platforms have been argued to enhance the capacities of indigenous communities to access, design and disseminate materials in their own languages. Some scholars, however, have also criticized the role that corporations have played as gatekeepers, as well as the language ideologies undergirding their interventions, which have proved damaging to community consensus on language policy (Romero, 2018, 2016; Tan & Rubdy, 2008; Whiteside, 2007). The teaching of indigenous languages as second or third languages, in particular, has seen a substantial expansion in the last decade, both in the United States and Latin America. As the number of indigenous children and adults for whom their native language is not their primary language, and as the number of non-indigenous students interested in indigenous languages continues to increase, access to quality pedagogical materials is crucial to sustain this trend. Indigenous language activists are not of one mind concerning the ways traditional knowledge, especially native languages, should be shared, if at all, with non-natives. Nevertheless, it is undeniable that an increase in the number of learners affords visibility, more committed scholars trained in fields relevant to language revitalization and more students of indigenous background acquiring for the first time or recovering fluency in their native language (Maxwell, 2012; Romero, 2018, 2016).

As Blyth (2013) argues, the foreign language publishing industry does not do justice to the needs, values and practices of less commonly taught language (LCTL) teaching in general, and of indigenous languages in particular. Very few North American or European presses have published quality pedagogical materials for L2 indigenous language instruction. Furthermore, concerning Mesoamerican languages, for example, a substantial number of published L2 materials assume a Eurocentric, colonialist positionality in which indigenous peoples are either stereotyped as poor and uneducated, or exoticized as inhabiting cultural and linguistic worlds unintelligible to the non-indigenous. To avoid the pitfalls of colonialism and orientalism, pedagogical materials for indigenous language instruction should only be developed on the basis of long-term ethnographic experience, a consideration of the educational needs of indigenous communities, and in partnership with indigenous co-authors, as discussed in the second and third below. As a linguistic anthropologist, my ethnographic experience in K'iche'-Maya communities provided me with the cultural knowledge and linguistic proficiency to collaborate successfully with K'iche' co-authors in the development of L2 K'iche' materials. Such collaborative methods of creating and disseminating pedagogical materials reflects efforts within the open education community to increase access to scholarship and participation in educational opportunities.

A further issue hindering access to quality L2 materials for indigenous languages is the high cost of books and digital materials published in mainstream presses. Colleges, universities and public libraries often do not purchase these volumes for their collection due to their relatively small readership. These limitations are especially acute in the countries where indigenous languages are spoken in Latin America. Baraniuk (2007: 230) refers to academic publishing as a 'knowledge ecosystem' that shuts out 'talented K-12 teachers, community college instructors, scientists and engineers out in industry, and the world majority who do not read and write English.' The judicious use of ethnographic knowledge and the participation of native speakers of indigenous languages as co-authors in the production of L2 pedagogical materials expand this knowledge ecosystem. In summary, the open publishing process that gives rise to open educational resources (OER) allows for the irruption of indigenous knowledge, ways of speaking and language ideologies into academic spaces where they have traditionally been excluded.

The rest of this chapter will examine the pedagogical, cultural and political challenges of teaching and producing OER to teach indigenous languages of Latin America and will suggest a few solutions. Although I will concentrate on K'iche' Mayan, a Mayan language spoken by more than one million speakers in the western highlands of Guatemala, my remarks can be extended with some qualifications to many Mesoamerican and Andean languages. The current sociopolitical situation of Native American languages in North America, however, merits a separate discussion and my remarks should not be assumed to be relevant for the latter (Nicholas, 2009). In the rest of the chapter, I will consider first the social role of regional variation and the challenges involved in linguistic standardization of indigenous languages. The latter is almost always presupposed in the design of L2 pedagogical materials but is often a contentious topic among speakers of indigenous languages. Second, I will consider the available linguistic and pedagogical works on indigenous languages, their strengths and limitations as pedagogical materials. Whereas scholarly publications are often detailed and abundant, they are not easily adapted to the needs of non-native language learners. Third, I will consider the challenges for non-indigenous learners of the distinctive articulations of language, culture and discourse that we find in Mayan and other indigenous languages of Latin America. Students with a Western mindset bring their own language ideologies and expectations to the experience of learning indigenous languages. However, Western language ideologies construct speech and linguistic communication in ways that are not always congruent with those practiced by speakers of indigenous languages.

Many Spanish- or English-speaking students, for example, find challenging the adjustments required by a pedagogy cognizant of the cultural values held by speakers of indigenous languages. Finally, I will discuss the future of indigenous language instruction and the role that OER have in revitalization efforts.

'Accent', Regional Variation and the Teaching of Indigenous Languages of Latin America

The majority of indigenous languages spoken in Latin America today show substantial regional variation. From the highlands of Mexico and Guatemala, to the snow-capped peaks of the Andes, substantial lexical and structural variation is a defining sociolinguistic feature of indigenous languages. Usually, it does not interfere with mutual intelligibility between speakers of different varieties. Indeed, regional 'accents' frequently act as ethno-linguistic markers, operating also as shifters that cue interlocutors to transitions in style or discourse genre. Regional variation is thus deeply ingrained culturally and discursively (Mannheim, 2011; Romero, 2018, 2017, 2015, 2012). Standardized varieties unifying widely different varieties of the same language are indeed a relatively recent phenomenon in indigenous Latin America. Often accompanying the emergence of pan-indigenous social movements, linguistic standardization has made great strides in the last three decades, but its actual impact on speakers' language practices is limited. Until very recently, the exclusion of indigenous languages from schools and universities, a widespread stigmatization of indigenous languages outside indigenous communities and a small number of available publications have been obstacles to the expansion of standardized varieties (Barrett, 2016; Cojtí, 1995; England, 1996; French, 2010; Jiménez, 1997; Maxwell, 1996; Romero, 2017; Warren, 1997). This complex sociolinguistic picture can be illustrated with K'iche', a Mayan language spoken in the western highlands of Guatemala by more than one million speakers. Using phonological differences as diagnostics, dialectologists divide K'iche' into at least 12 different regional varieties (see Figure 3.1). However, even this high number underestimates the scope of actual variation as lexical and even syntactic differences are involved. Dialectal differences act as linguistic markers strongly tied to local ethnic landscapes (Romero, 2015).

Many K'iche' speakers feel uncomfortable with Standard K'iche' as it involves recent lexical coinages or words not present in their own native variety. New word coinages, also called neologisms, are prescriptively preferred as an alternative to Spanish loanwords to protect Mayan languages from massive borrowing from Spanish, Guatemala's official language (French, 2010; Kaqchikel Cholchi', 1997; Maxwell, 1996; Romero, 2015). For non-native K'iche' learners and instructors, this situation creates challenges rarely found in the teaching of politically dominant languages such

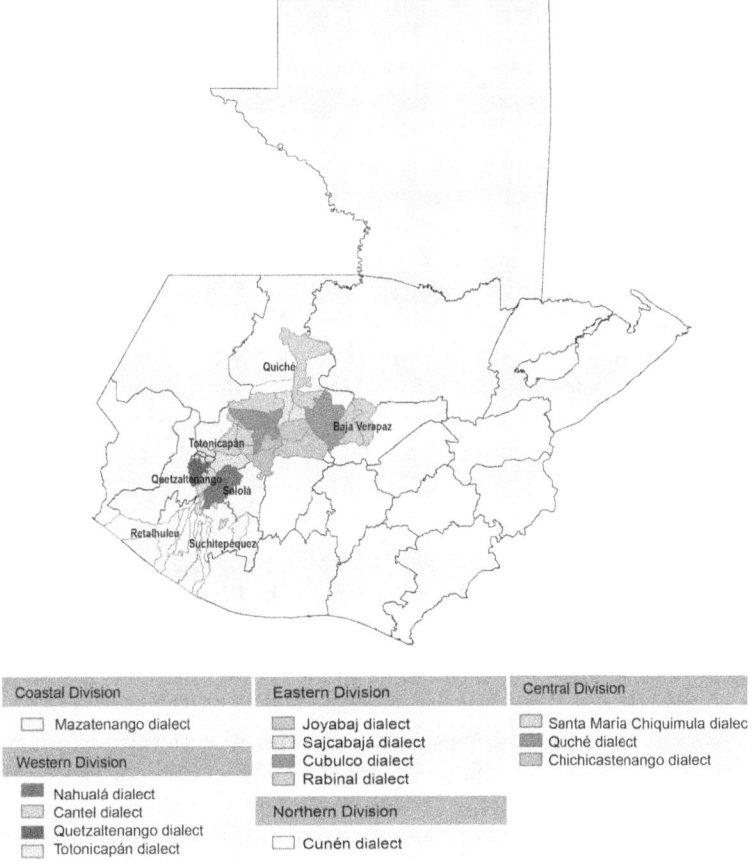

Figure 3.1 The dialects of K'iche' Maya (Romero, 2015)

as Spanish or English. First, the restricted use of standardized varieties limits their practical value in L2 classrooms. In my experience of teaching standardized varieties, many students were frustrated with the difficulty of communicating with native speakers who were unfamiliar with standardized forms, which is the large majority today. Most students come with the expectation that the variety they learn in class will be effective when engaging speakers of all varieties of the target language. As I said earlier, intelligibility across different varieties is usually not an issue for native speakers, but for beginning learners it can be very challenging. Students' previous language learning experiences and a language ideology that imagines the standard prescriptive 'prestige' variety as better or more 'correct' than others, clashes with a linguistic ecology in which substantial regional variation is the rule. Second, although teaching a specific regional variety may allow beginning students to start practicing their new skills in natural settings, it can also lead to frustration and disappointment when engaging speakers of divergent dialects. The expectation that the sort of standardized one-size-fits-all forms taught in most Spanish or English classes, for example, will also be used in L2 instruction in indigenous languages can thus be an obstacle for an effective, satisfying learning experience. In my years as co-instructor in K'iche' courses in the US and Guatemala, I have always stressed to students the differences between the ecologies of Standard Average European Languages and indigenous languages of Latin America. Making students aware of the social value of dialectal differences and their role in discourse is key to developing a constructive attitude towards linguistic variation and regional 'accents'. Introducing variation as pedagogical resource, however, is not easy. Many regional varieties have not been systematically studied, and therefore neither appropriate examples nor detailed descriptions are available for most. Despite the relatively superficial treatment of dialectal variation, however, the scholarly literature on indigenous languages is vast and much of it is of the highest quality. It is definitely a valuable teaching resource, although little of it has a pedagogical intent, as we will see in the following section.

Scholarly Literature and the Teaching of Indigenous Languages as L2

Indigenous languages have been the focus of scholarly attention since the middle of the sixteenth century when Franciscan and Dominican Friars wrote the first *artes* 'descriptive grammars' with the goal of teaching the Spanish clergy in charge of Christianization (Acuña, 1983; Farris, 2018; Romero, 2011; Sachse, 2014). Today, thousands of publications focus on different aspects of their grammar, vocabulary, regional variation and discourse. Linguists and anthropologists have made impressive strides in the documentation and description of indigenous languages of Latin America. However, most of these materials were written in an academic style packed with technical jargon unknown to most educated readers. Also, scholarly works are not pedagogical in the sense that they do not necessarily seek to develop readers' communicative competence. Instead, they describe particular aspects of the grammar or engage theoretical issues using data from indigenous languages. Scholarly articles and books may be used as additional teaching resources by instructors trained in linguistics but are generally of limited use for L2 learners. Very few specialist publications are pedagogical in the sense I use above. Furthermore, pedagogical materials are scarce and available only for languages with large numbers of speakers, such as Quechua or K'iche' Maya with more than one million speakers each, or for languages with sizable colonial manuscript corpora such as Nahuatl and Yucatec Maya, which many historians and ethnologists peruse as primary sources in historical research (Andrews, 1975; Bricker, 2019; Dürr, 2006; Mondloch, 2017; Romero, 2014). Furthermore, available pedagogical publications often focus on developing students' readings skills rather than their oral, communicative competence. These structural weaknesses are sometimes compounded by an authorial perspective that cannot be characterized as anything but colonialist. Often written by clergy, government officials or even tourist guides, the selection of texts and examples constructs indigenous subjects as inhabiting only a limited number of stereotyped interactive roles, such as domestic servants, participants in catechism classes or market vendors. Ample semantic domains, discourse styles and idioms are treated superficially. Indeed, the participation of native speakers does not go beyond acting as 'informants' of non-native linguists/missionaries. Rarely are they acknowledged as co-authors (Eachus & Carlson, 1980; Haeserijn, 1966; Romero, 2014).

Despite these limitations, scholarly works can be useful in developing L2 instruction materials with an open, inclusive and participatory perspective. Given the substantial differences in sound, grammar and lexicon between indigenous and Standard Average European Languages, Spanish- and English-speaking students, for example, face considerable challenges in acquiring a basic communicative knowledge of the target indigenous language. Learning to vocalize ejective and non-ejective articulations of uvular, velar and alveopalatal consonants – a phonemic distinction in K'iche' – demands regular student practice, for example. And the morphological marking of subjects as well as objects on transitive verbs is a challenging aspect of K'iche' grammar for English- and Spanish-speaking students to master. Instruction is much more effective when differences between students' native language and the target indigenous language are systematically addressed. In this regard, a judicious and explicit use of grammar and practice exercises is a necessary condition for successful L2 acquisition, perhaps more so than in Standard Average European Languages. It provides the basic auditive and interpretive skills to make the target language perceptible, even when not completely comprehensible. In my experience designing pedagogical materials for K'iche' Mayan, scholarly publications were a useful resource for the systematic presentation of phonemic inventories and verbal morphology, for instance. They were also a source of relevant textual examples, especially from regional varieties I have not covered in my own research.

A caveat is necessary at this point: the linguistic literature is not exhaustive and there are often gaps in the description of the grammar of particular languages. Conscientious instructors will sometimes need to do research of their own to be able to present elements of the grammar missing in reference grammars in a systematic way. For example, until recently, no available publication examined the syntax of conditional sentences in K'iche', which of course can be heard in many naturally occurring conversations. Such descriptive gaps in the literature are unavoidable given the traditional methods used by many field linguists.[1] An emphasis on phonology and morphology, on the one hand, combined with little attention to naturally occurring discourse, on the other, unavoidably leads to descriptive gaps, as we have seen above. Instructors should prepare students for the experience of encountering ways of speaking, words or even syntactic patterns that no one has systematically described before. Zach Blume, an undergraduate student participating in one of my K'iche' Mayan classes at Vanderbilt University, was to the best of my knowledge the first to describe a semantically intentional verbal nominalization in the Nahualá variety. This construction does not occur in every regional dialect and no other linguist or scholar before Zach had discussed it.

Learning an indigenous language can be a profound personal and intellectual experience, but it should be undertaken with humility, patience and awareness of challenges integral to their current social situation. It should not be distorted, forcing indigenous languages through the dominant L2 instruction models developed for Spanish or English, for example. As we will see in more detail in the next section, the speech communities where indigenous languages are spoken experience and construct speech, interactive conversation and communication very differently from those of Standard Average European Languages. Recognizing the differences is crucial for the success of L2 instruction of indigenous languages.

Language Ideologies, Culture and Indigenous Language Instruction

Language ideologies are the body of attitudes, affects, conceptions and ideas about language and linguistic communication shared by members of a speech community. They form a fundamental ideational and attitudinal background for linguistic practice in any society (Dorian, 1998; Irvine & Gal, 2000; Schieffelin *et al.*, 1998; Silverstein, 2003). In indigenous societies of Latin America, language ideologies are embodied in speech acts, speech events, politeness and interaction norms substantially different from those found in Western societies. Communicative competence entails the execution of speech acts, discourse patterns, politeness norms and cultural values in ways unfamiliar for most Spanish- or English-speaking students (Kroskrity, 2000; Mannheim, 2011; Romero, 2015; Silverstein, 2000). For example, greetings in K'iche' are complex routines organized in terms of traditional ideas of authority, kinship, but also determined by speech event and by the specific role played by the speaker and his/her audience. The choice of pronominal address form, verbal inflection, intonation contour or specific salutation formula are crucial in greeting an interlocutor in culturally appropriate ways (Romero, 2015). Needless to say, this requires substantial cultural knowledge and competence in body language, gesture, etc. in ways unfamiliar to most Spanish- or English-speaking students. Students' cultural background and expectations about language instruction can actively interfere with the development of such cultural skills. The traditional classroom is not necessarily effective in this regard, unless accompanied by the experience of living in indigenous communities. Intensive summer programs, for example, where students live with native speaker families can be transformative, providing not only experiential knowledge but also fostering a self-critical approach to learning. When such opportunities are lacking, alternative strategies are required to provide the necessary cultural content. In my teaching, I have focused on three spaces of cultural and linguistic practice to stress differences between students' expectations and speech in indigenous societies: vocabulary, oral tradition and onomastics.

First, lexical incommensurability between languages is due to different conceptual partitions of human experience (Lee, 1996). For example, Ixhil Mayan has three transitive verbs meaning 'to eat' depending on the texture of the food to be consumed. When food is corn-based (tortillas, tamales, etc.) the verb [-tx'aa'][2] is always used; if the consistency of comestibles is soft (fruit, flan, desert) then [-low] is selected; for other solid foodstuffs [-eechb'u] is required. As we see, the semantics of ingestion verbs is inseparable from Ixhil gastronomy, and students should understand the latter before they can use this verb class with comfort. New vocabulary is thus always an opportunity for instructors to introduce the cultural knowledge needed to communicate in indigenous languages. Images, video recordings or explanatory sections in textbooks are effective channels to foster cultural awareness. Second, oral tradition is a central element of indigenous culture, which can be used judiciously to educate students about indigenous ways of speaking. Let us bear in mind that most indigenous cultures are oral cultures in the sense that writing is marginal for the acquisition of communicative competence. Among the K'iche' Maya, for example, the ancestors are believed to bequeath in oral tradition a set of effective cultural principles that undergird, among other things, the production and interpretation of language (Romero, 2017). In this regard, in my classes I use oral narratives as key entry points to discuss indigenous cosmovision, language metaphors, local history and constructions of gender/authority. K'iche' oral tradition is enormously diverse and many texts are accessible, with appropriate directions, even to beginning–intermediate students with the caveat that consultation with native speakers and ritual specialists is a must before oral traditions are used in class. Certain myths and ritual texts are considered secret or at least inappropriate for teaching purposes. Finally, onomastics – naming practices – embodies both cultural principles and history. In my own instruction practice, place names and personal names are presented in terms of the general principles that govern their selection. The use of calendric names to name hills, for example, springs from an intimate ritual relationship between community and sacred landscape, which is considered a deity. Calendric names, based on the sacred 260-day calendar, are still used by ritual specialists to make prognostications and heal illnesses. The privileged use of certain Spanish names in

Nahualá, a K'iche' community in the western highlands of Guatemala, is a consequence of the prestige accrued by cultural heroes tied to local histories (Romero, 2017; Tedlock, 1992).

To summarize, the acquisition of cultural knowledge should be a transversal axis in indigenous language L2 instruction. The sharp cultural, grammatical and political differences between Western and indigenous ways of speaking require a direct engagement in class, as well as the appropriate use of texts of different genres. The acquisition of communicative skills must go through a serious personal and political engagement with the target culture beyond a mere listing of interesting, 'exotic' facts. We have discussed above three challenges faced by instructors and students of indigenous language today: regional variation, lack of appropriate pedagogical materials and the differences between western and indigenous language practices and related language ideologies. Based on my personal experience as co-instructor and co-designer of pedagogical materials, I will examine in the following section the ways in which digital platforms and OER can be used to meet these challenges.

OER as a Solution to the Challenges of Teaching Indigenous Languages

OER offer solutions to the challenges of indigenous language instruction that traditional academic publishing and traditional classroom instruction would be hard-pressed to provide. Promoting the systematic, comparative presentation of regional variation, making quality pedagogical materials readily accessible and providing a multimedia stage for the delivery of cultural content are three of the strengths offered by virtual, online open-access platforms. In contrast to traditional, academic publishing, the open practices inherent in the creation and dissemination of OER call for the participation of native speakers in different locations to simultaneously collaborate in the design and execution of L2 instructional materials. Such an open publishing process makes indigenous language instruction possible on a global scale. I will discuss each of the solutions to the challenges discussed above based on my experience collaborating in the design of OER in K'iche' Maya.

As explained earlier, the challenges of regional variation in L2 instruction are twofold. On the one hand, regional varieties play an important role as ethnolinguistic markers and stylistic cues, and on the other, standardized varieties are rarely used by speakers of indigenous languages, especially in oral exchanges. Students are confronted with substantial regional variation once they start using their newly acquired linguistic skills. Open-access, online materials are an ideal platform to introduce students to variation in gradual, pedagogical ways. As I mentioned earlier, the goal is not to document variation systematically, but to encourage students to explore it, understand its cultural role and develop personal strategies to cope with it. The presentation of systematic lexical or phonological contrasts between target and neighboring varieties, when such data is available, helps students' awareness of the scale of variation they can find across the K'iche'-speaking world. Technically, it is easy to incorporate examples of variation in vocabulary or grammar in any virtual platform. The K'iche' OER developed at the University of Texas with assistance from the Center for Open Educational Resources and Language Learning (COERLL) illustrate two aspects of this strategy.[3] First, in order to grapple with the sociolinguistic complexity of K'iche', a focus on one particular variety, in our case the one spoken in the township of Nahualá, Guatemala, seemed to us a pedagogical necessity (see Figure 3.1). The Nahualá variety offers two key advantages, both grammatical and social. On the one hand, it is a phonologically and lexically conservative dialect that has had relatively little influence from Spanish. On the other hand, it continues to be the everyday language of at least 120,000 speakers in the townships of Nahualá and Santa Catarina Ixtahuacán in the highlands and piedmont of Guatemala. Children are socialized in K'iche' and the majority of speakers of all ages comfortably use a diverse repertoire of styles and ways of speaking (Romero, 2015). Our materials try to do justice to this rich social life using audios and videos, presenting K'iche' as a language that is both traditional and modern, an artifact decisive for the transmission of culture and ethnic identity, but also the linguistic code used to engage our post-modern present. A critic may argue that our decision to design our OER based on the Nahualá variety is at odds with the centrality of regional variation in K'iche' linguistic economies. However, the advantages of a focus on this particular variety, as argued above, outweigh the disadvantages. Furthermore, online OER provide a practical solution to this apparent contradiction, allowing the gradual, introduction of comparisons with other regional varieties. We will soon begin to complement each of our units with illustrative vocabulary and pronunciation contrasts such as those found in Table 3.1.

Table 3.1 A few lexical comparisons between the Santa Maria Chiquimula and neighboring K'iche' varieties (Romero, 2015)[4]

Idiom/word	Township	Santa María Chiquimula equivalent	Gloss
Noya	San Antonio Ilotenango	Ali	Girl
ʃinna wiɓ	Momostenango	ʃinʃeʔx wiɓ	I got scared
Yeʔ	San Francisco El Alto	Xeʔ	Yes
Minaweqleʔex	San Francisco El Alto	Minaʃakopix	Don't push me!
Mamaʔ akʼ	Patzite	Amaʔ akʼ	Rooster
ʧin	Chichicastenango	Nicʼ	Little
Baxʧiʔ	Chichicastenango	Atam	Early

As I have said earlier, our goal is not to address variation systematically but to develop student awareness of its cultural role and an adaptive, inquisitive attitude to differences between what is learned in the classroom and what is actually found in markets and homes through the K'iche'-speaking world.

Another crucial strength of OER for indigenous language instruction is their unparalleled reach. OER can effectively address the scarcity of quality pedagogical materials. The University of Texas' K'iche' OER, for example, present K'iche' grammar in 40 units with as much detail as the best published reference grammars. It does so, however, in a gradual, student-friendly manner, avoiding complex technical language as much as possible, and also including appropriate examples and exercises. We are aware of the fact that many students feel discouraged by 'grammar', but given the structural differences between K'iche' and Standard Average European Languages, it is hard to imagine an effective language course that does not address it.[5] Our materials stress pragmatics, unlike most treatments of K'iche' grammar in the literature that focus almost exclusively on phonology, morphology and syntax (Lopez Ixcoy, 1997; Mondloch, 1978). Unit 3, for example, includes a discussion of the pragmatics of K'iche' greeting formulas (see Figure 3.2).

As alluded to above, published reference grammars of K'iche' Mayan unwittingly leave out important phrases and idiomatic expressions, such as conditional constructions. In order to write the sections on conditional constructions for our online materials, hours of observation, elicitation and analysis with native speaker collaborators were required. As far as I know, our materials contain the only systematic treatment of K'iche'

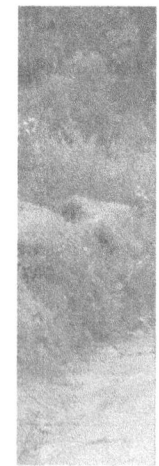

Figure 3.2 Unit 3 of the University of Texas' online K'iche' materials: Pragmatics of K'iche' greeting formulas (https://tzij.coerll.utexas.edu/tijonik-3/)

conditionals in the literature. Our critical engagement with the published literature has enhanced the quality of our materials, and has also made them a useful resource for scholars themselves.

OER and open-access platforms are also effective in delivering cultural knowledge and foster a self-critical student attitude necessary for successful, culturally appropriate communication in indigenous languages. From the earliest units, our materials focus on key aspects of K'iche' life and cultural values that students with a Western mindset would find challenging. In order to actively discourage the exoticization of highland Maya culture, our collaborators have led the way in the design and presentation of pedagogically appropriate topics such as traditional food, textiles, feasts, sacred landscape, markets, etc. (see Figure 3.3). We use native speaker-designed and executed videos and audios accompanied by transcriptions/translations as stimuli to engage our students in active discussion of difference, systematic discrimination and cultural stigmatization. Without an open, honest discussion of the history and the current social context in which the K'iche' find themselves, our OER would only perpetuate a caricature of the Maya as a people frozen in time, a figment of the Western imagination rather than a living, complex and thoroughly modern society (Carmack, 1995; Cook, 2000; Falla, 1980).

As explained above, vocabulary differences are key to understanding the divisions between the materials and social worlds that distinguish different societies' cultural practices (Lee, 1996). Unit 11 of the University of Texas' online K'iche' materials, for example, introduces traditional textiles. A weaver from Nahualá makes a visual presentation of traditional *po't* 'traditional blouses', their designs, figures and meanings. The video

Figure 3.3 Unit 9 of the University of Texas' online K'iche' materials: 'Market Day' (https://tzij.coerll.utexas.edu/tijonik-9/)

82 Part 1: The Microsystem: Developing Knowledge in L2 Instructional Environments

Figure 3.4 Unit 11 of the University of Texas' online K'iche' materials: 'This is our clothing' (https://tzij.coerll.utexas.edu/tijonik-11/)

is also rich in words and expressions used in the domain of textiles and clothing, illustrating the linguistic articulation between traditional outfit, technology and gender (see Figure 3.4).

Our materials also engage the relationship between oral traditions and local landscapes. The two are intimately intertwined in highland Maya societies in origin myths, ritual cycles, local geography and in the grammar of directional constructions themselves, what scholars have called 'referential practice' (Hanks, 1990; Romero, 2017). Unit 17, for example, starts with a video in which one of our collaborators speaks about the spatial organization of the town of Nahualá in relationship to surrounding hills, and rural settlements. Quite remarkable is also his use of directional markers – a group of clitics added to verbal expressions- to mark spatial relationships between himself, local geography, and movement (https://tzij.coerll.utexas.edu/tijonik-17-lesson-17-in-ko-pa-ukux-tinamit-i-am-at-the-center-of-town-prepositions/).

Finally, OER can also be part of an alternative, inclusive online platform in which native speakers can not only participate but utilize materials according to their own personal and community agendas. The videos posted as part of our online materials, for example, are popular in YouTube among members of the K'iche' diaspora in the United States, according to user comments we have received. They are used by K'iche' speakers to teach themselves how to write in their own language, and also, surprisingly, as auxiliary resources for English self-instruction. The materials are also used by L2 instructors in Guatemala to teach non-native speakers, both Guatemalan and foreign, and also by primary school teachers in some bilingual schools in rural Guatemala. Online media are much easier to access in indigenous communities than published materials as almost every Guatemalan owns a smartphone today. Online platforms also enable native speakers to participate directly in the design and delivery of pedagogical content. For example, the University of Texas' materials were largely designed and executed by native speaking co-authors from Nahualá, Guatemala. Delivery format, audio and video scripts and recording, as well as the selection and elaboration of illustrative examples and practice exercises received crucial input from our Nahualá co-authors.

Open-access Platforms and the Future of L2 Indigenous Language Instruction

The future of L2 indigenous language instruction is undoubtedly tied to open digital platforms and direct community participation. The University of Texas K'iche' OER offer an example of successful collaboration between US-based academic institutions and indigenous communities in Latin America engaged in linguistic revitalization. Our work with OER is moving us towards partnerships with indigenous communities in which L2 instruction will be in the hands of native speaking instructors with online textbooks and pedagogical materials relevant also for language revitalization.[6] We see a dual institutional role for ourselves: First, as committed long-term web hosts, and second, as providers of pedagogical and technical support. Unfortunately, some interesting indigenous language online instructional initiatives have passed away as host institutions have lost interest after the demise of their original authors.[7] Securing long-term, engaged web hosts is therefore critical for the visibility and success of online indigenous language initiatives. Also important to the long-term viability of indigenous language materials will be the adoption of open licenses, the distinguishing feature of OER, that explicitly tell end users what rights are shared. Many indigenous language scholars who have create pedagogical materials and posted them online are unfamiliar with open licenses and do not adopt a copyright license at all. Materials that do not carry an explicit copyright – open or closed – create an ambiguous situation for end users who do not know what they are legally allowed to do with the materials.

We envision the future of L2 instruction of indigenous languages as a new kind of knowledge ecosystem based on a collaborative, dynamic, community strategy for self-empowerment and cultural preservation, rather than a mere surrender of traditional knowledge to interested non-natives. Needless to say, this new knowledge ecosystem is built on OER and OEP, that is, on open-access online materials and indigenous participation and co-ownership of content and online platforms.

Notes

(1) Until recently, documentary linguistics did not systematically address discourse and pragmatics, and rarely used naturally occurring speech as primary data. Sociolinguistic variation is also generally neglected by documentary linguists.
(2) Unless otherwise stated, words in Mayan languages will be written in the official unified alphabet used in Guatemala.
(3) The website, called *Chqeta'maj le Qach'ab'al K'iche'* 'Let us learn the K'iche' language!', consists of 40 units including conversation, readings and grammar sections. It uses written texts, audio, video and practice exercises, with participation of native speaking instructors and non-native students. The website may be accessed at https://tzij.coerll.utexas.edu
(4) K'iche' words are in IPA script in order to represent subphonemic features.
(5) Grammar is also subject to variation across the K'iche'-speaking world, especially in syntax. Nevertheless, at this stage we have not directly addressed this in our materials.
(6) We are currently in the planning stage to extend this model to Huasteca Nahuatl and Cochabamba Quechua.
(7) These include the University of Chicago's Aymara materials website, and UCLA's Digital Resources for the Study of Quechua (Pers. Communication: Anonymous Reviewer).

References

Acuña, R. (1983) Introducción. In R. Acuña (ed.) *Thesaurus Verborum*. Mexico City: UNAM.
Andrews, J.R. (1975) *Introduction to Classical Nahuatl*. Austin: University of Texas Press.
Baraniuk, R. (2007) Challenges and opportunities for the open education movement: A Connexions case study. In T. Iiyoshi and M.S.V. Kumar (eds) *Opening Up Education*. Boston, MA: MIT Press.
Barrett, R. (2016) Mayan language revitalization, hip hop, and ethnic identity in Guatemala. *Language & Communication* 47, 144–153.
Bischoff, S. and Fountain, A. (2013) A case study in grass roots development of web resources for language workers: The Coeur d'Alene Archive and Online Language Resources (CAOLR). In S.T. Bischoff, D. Cole, A. Fountain and M. Miyashita (eds) *The Persistence of Language: Constructing and Confronting the Past and Present in the Voices of Jane H. Hill*. Amsterdam/Philadelphia: John Benjamins Publishing Company.
Blyth, C. (2013) LCTLs and technology: The promise of open education. *Language Learning & Technology* 17 (1), 1–6.
Bricker, V. (2019) *A Historical Grammar of the Maya Language of Yucatan: 1557–2000*. Salt Lake City: University of Utah Press.
Carmack, R. (1995) *Rebels of Highland Guatemala: The Quiche-Mayas of Momostenango*. Norman: University of Oklahoma Press.
Cojtí, D. (1995) *Ub'aniik ri Una'ooj Uchomab'aal ri Maya' Tinamit: Configuracion del Pensamiento Politico del Pueblo Maya (2da. parte)*. Guatemala City: Cholsamaj.
Cook, G. (2000) *Renewing the Maya World: Expressive Culture in a Highland Town*. Austin: University of Texas Press.
Dorian, N. (1998) Western language ideologies and small-language prospects. In L. Grenoble and L. Whaley (eds) *Endangered Languages: Current Issues and Future Prospects*. Cambridge: Cambridge University Press.
Dürr, M. (2006) Einführung in das Kolonialzeitliche Quiché (K'iche'). Berlin: FU Berlin, Lateinamerika-Institut. See http://home.snafu.de/duerr/download.html.

Eachus, F. and Carlson, R. (1980) *Aprendamos Kekchí: Gramática Pedagógica Popular de Kekchí.* Guatemala City: Instituto Lingüístico de Verano.

England, N. (1996) The role of language standardization in revitalization. In E. Fischer and R. McKenna Brown (eds) *Maya Cultural Activism in Guatemala.* Austin: University of Texas Press.

Falla, R. (1980) *Quiché Rebelde: Estudio de un Movimiento de Conversión Religiosa, Rebelde a las Creencias Tradicionales, en San Antonio Ilotenango, Quiché (1948–1970).* Guatemala City: Editorial Universitaria.

Farris, N. (2018) *Tongues of Fire: Language and Evangelization in Colonial Mexico.* New York: University Press.

French, B. (2010) *Maya Ethnolinguistic Identity: Violence, Modernity and Cultural Rights in Highland Guatemala.* Tucson: University of Arizona Press.

Haeserijn, E. (1966) *Ensayo de la Gramática del K'ekchi.* Purulhá, Baja Verapaz: Suquinay.

Hanks, W. (1990) *Referential Practice: Language and Lived Space Among the Maya.* Chicago: University of Chicago Press.

Irvine, J. and Gal, S. (2000) Language ideology and linguistic differentiation. In P. Kroskrity (ed) *Regimes of Language: Ideologies, Polities, and Identities.* Santa Fe: School of American Research.

Jiménez, O. (1997) Tensión entre idiomas: Situación actual de los idiomas mayas y el español en Guatemala. In *Latin American Studies Association.* Guadalajara, Mexico.

Kaqchikel Cholchi'. (1997) *Rukemik K'ak'a' Taq Tzij (Criterios para la creación de neologismos en kaqchikel).* Guatemala City: Academia de las Lenguas Mayas de Guatemala.

Kroskrity, P. (2000) *Regimes of Language: Ideologies, Politics and Identities.* Santa Fe: School of American Research.

Lee, P. (1996) *The Whorf Theory Complex: A Critical Reconstruction.* Amsterdam/Philadelphia: John Benjamins Publishing Company.

Lopez Ixcoy, C. (1997) *Gramatica K'iche'.* Guatemala City: Cholsamaj.

Mannheim, B. (2011) *The Language of the Inka Since the European Invasion.* Austin: University of Texas Press.

Maxwell, J. (1996) Prescriptive grammar and Kaqchikel revitalization. In E.F. Fischer and R. McKenna Brown (eds) *Maya Cultural Activism in Guatemala.* Austin: University of Texas Press.

Maxwell, J. (2012) Memory, remembering and the construction of truth among Maya groups in highland Guatemala. In S. Wood and A. Megged (eds) *Mesoamerican Memory: Enduring Systems of Remembrance.* Norman: University of Oklahoma Press.

Mondloch, J. (2017) *Basic K'ichee' Grammar* (Revised Edition). Boulder, CO: University of Colorado Press.

Nicholas, S. (2009) 'I Live Hopi, I Just Don't Speak It' – The critical intersection of language, culture, and identity in the lives of contemporary hopi youth. *Journal of Language, Identity, and Education* 8 (5), 321.

Romero, S. (2011) Language, Catechisms and Mesoamerican lords in highland Guatemala: Addressing 'God' after the Spanish conquest. In *XIII European Maya Conference.* Copenhagen.

Romero, S. (2012) 'They don't get speak our language right': Language standardization, power and migration among the Q'eqchi' Maya. *Journal of Linguistic Anthropology* 22 (2), 21–41.

Romero, S. (2014) '¡Cuánto sufrir! Solo la fe de indio me ha mantenido firme...': Jorge Ubico y el indigenismo del presbítero Celso Narciso Teletor. *Mesoamérica* 56, 1–23.

Romero, S. (2015) *Language and Ethnicity among the K'ichee' Maya.* Provo: University of Utah Press.

Romero, S. (2016) 'Bill Gates speaks K'ichee'! The corporatization of linguistic revitalization in Guatemala. *Language & Communication* 47, 154–166.

Romero, S. (2017) 'Brujos', mitos y modernidad en la historia oral k'iche'. *Estudios de Cultura Maya* 50, 249–270.

Romero, S. (2017) The labyrinth of diversity: The sociolinguistics of Mayan languages. In J. Aissen, N. England and R. Zavala (eds) *The Mayan Languages* (pp. 379–400). New York: Routledge.

Romero, S. (2018) Ethnicity and regional stereotypes in standard Ixhil (Ixil) Mayan. *Language & Communication* 61, 102–112.

Sachse, F. (2014) The expression of Christian concepts in colonial K'iche' missionary texts. In S. Dedenbach-Salazar Sáenz (ed.) *La Transmisión de Conceptos Cristianos a las Lenguas Amerindias: Estudios Sobre Textos y Contextos en la Epoca Colonial*. St. Augustin, Germany: Anthropos.

Schieffelin, B., Woolard, K. and Kroskrity, P. (1998) *Language Ideologies: Practice and Theory*. New York/Oxford: Oxford University Press.

Silverstein, M. (2000) Whorfianism and the linguistic imagination of nationalism. In P. Kroskrity (ed.) *Regimes of Language: Ideologies, Politics and Identities*. Santa Fe, NM: School of American Research Press.

Silverstein, M. (2003) The whens and wheres – as well as hows – of ethnolinguistic ecognition. *Public Culture* 15 (3), 531–557.

Tan, P. and Rubdy, R. (eds) (2008) *Language as Commodity: Global Structures, Local Marketplaces*. London: Continuum.

Tedlock, B. (1992) *Time and the Highland Maya*. Albuquerque: University of New Mexico Press.

Warren, K. (1997) *Indigenous Movements and their Critics: Pan-Maya Activism in Guatemala*. Princeton: Princeton University Press.

Whiteside, A. (2007) 'Transnational' Yucatecans and language practices in San Francisco, California: Results from a participatory research survey. *Kroeber Anthropology Society Papers* 96, 55–73.

4 Openness in a Crowd-sourced Massive Online Language Community

Katerina Zourou and Anthippi Potolia

This chapter explores dimensions of openness (and lack of) as experienced by users in two massive online language communities (Busuu and Duolingo). These communities are widely known as social network sites for language learning (SNSLL) where massive numbers of users register to learn a second language (L2). Based on the reflective diaries of 21 SNSLL users, master's students at the Hellenic Open University, this study draws its theoretical framework from studies that critically address open, massive online education (Farrow, 2015; Weller, 2014). Pertaining to a content analytical approach, we offer a critical account of dimensions of openness (and closedness) as experienced by participants. As both SNSLL adopt the freemium business model by allowing or prohibiting access to content and to services depending on user status (free account users and Premium ones), we analyse the effect of this model on learning and user engagement. We focus in particular on the exploitation of open content creation (in the form of peer correction) as a profit-making mechanism for the SNSLL without a corresponding remuneration for the producers – the downside of crowdsourcing (Howe, 2006) – occurring in these open networked sites for language learning.

Open Access to Knowledge and Business Intricacies

Open education has gained more and more traction in the last decades, with advocates paving the way towards more cost-free learning opportunities and educational materials. The term 'open educational resources' (OER) was coined at the 2002 UNESCO Forum to indicate digital learning resources 'that have been released under an open license that permits no-cost access, use, adaptation and redistribution by others with no or limited restrictions' (UNESCO, 2012: 1). Apart from focusing on the free accessibility of resources, this definition for which we opt in our study, emphasizes the 'use, adaptation and redistribution' of resources released under a Creative Commons (or other) license, thus enabling the re-use and repurposing of resources in other learning contexts within a transparent and legal framework (see also Cronin & MacLaren, 2018; Knox, 2013; Wiley, 2014). This understanding of openness (freely accessible resources/services suitably licensed to enable re-use/repurposing) is fundamental in the analysis which will follow and in the general positioning of collaborative knowledge building in digital environments for language education that we explore in this study.

Recently, research has started focusing on what happens to resources after they are made openly accessible, giving rise to a conceptual shift from OER, as mere content, to open educational practice (OEP), as content created, adapted and repurposed by users (Conole & Ehlers, 2010). In Computer Assisted Language Learning (CALL) studies, research on OER/OEP is fairly new yet remarkable with regards to the variety of scholar activity, such as journal special issues and books (Thomas & Evans, 2014; Zourou, 2016), advocacy (Blyth *et al.*, 2015; COERLL, 2012; Kurek & Skowron, 2015) and transnational collaboration projects (LangOER and TELL-OP to name just a few). The development of digital materials for language learning and teaching is one of CALL's most substantial topics of interest, hence the natural connection with research on creation, sharing and (re-) use of resources in the open.

In the next section, we discuss ways in which public and private institutions benefit from the potential of digital technologies to offer language materials and services online, containing exclusively or partially open resources. This will lead to the examination of the underlying business models of for-profit organisations in embracing openness and to current trends in digital social participation such as crowdsourcing. We then move to an overview of the two communities under scrutiny (Busuu and Duolingo) and of their use as training opportunities for teachers in language learning beyond the classroom, before moving into the context of investigation, the research questions and the methodology. The paper ends with a data analysis and a conclusion.

'Openwashing' and the freemium model

It is quite understandable that the creation, availability and sustainability of open resources calls for adequate financial resources. However, confusion arises from the various understandings of the term 'open', with several studies critically appraising the adoption of the term, 'open' for marketing reasons. Weller, in his seminal book *The Battle of Open* (2014), provides an insightful picture of the multifaceted phenomenon of openness and ways it affects the scope and orientation of open education as initially conceptualised. The author shows how different interpretations of the term in some cases contradict each other and are often beset by companies offering resources which may appear open, while continuing to be proprietary (preventing re-use and repurposing). Along the same lines, Farrow (2015) critically examines how the term, 'open' becomes misleading with the development of Massive Open Online Courses (MOOCs), for the majority of which free access is provided but content remains copyright protected.

'Open' content is mostly advertised by institutions offering fee-based educational services. This is generally known as 'openwashing.' The term may have been first adopted in 2009 by Michelle Thorne meaning, 'to spin a product or company as open, although it is not' (Pomerantz & Peek, 2016). Watters (2014) explains the motive of openwashing in the following way: 'industry forces are quick to wrap themselves in language and imagery in the hopes it makes them appear more palatable, more friendly, more progressive. More "green," for example, more "open."' Thus, several for-profit institutions claim to offer open content but in fact rely on copyright-restricted, 'closed' content rather than using an open licence.

Moving the openwashing principle further and connecting it to profit-generating activity, open access to content is often used by companies, mostly internet start-ups, as an incentive to get internet users to pay a fee for an upgrade service and/or content. Unlocking open content as a trigger to buy a subscription or an upgraded service (e.g. Premium service) is a business model known as *freemium*, a combination of the terms, *free* and *premium* service. (For an overview of business models applied on internet services and products in education sector, see De Langen, 2013; Osipov et al., 2015).

In online language education, the freemium model is mostly applied by start-ups offering digital (language) resources and courses for a fee. The two communities scrutinised in this chapter, Busuu and Duolingo, are developed and maintained by start-ups, which both adopt the freemium model. As such, free access and paid content co-exist, with the former serving as an incentive to sign up to the Premium version to gain access to paid language resources and tutorial support.

Whereas in our analysis we will analyse user understandings of the freemium model on their learning activity, here we show how the freemium model is implemented technically. This happens namely through notifications by email and notifications on the community portal. Figure 4.1(a) shows an invitation to subscribe to a Premium account sent to the email address of the free account holder in Busuu. Figure 4.1(b) shows an incentive to become a Premium user on the main page of the free account holder.

Free access and paid content coexist within the same clusters of content (lessons). As shown in Figure 4.2, content accessible to users with a free account is in dark grey, and content reserved for Premium users is in light grey. The degree of free/paid content varies among lessons and without a clear explanation as to the different proportions of free and paid content, despite the fact that the unit of comparison is the same (a lesson). After a set of three lessons, the community offers a Review, namely

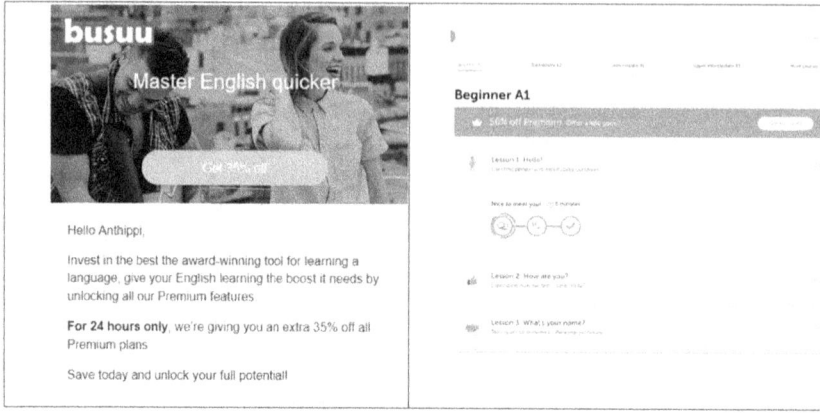

Figure 4.1(a) An email notification to subscribe to a Premium account in Busuu
Figure 4.1(b) An incentive to buy a Premium account (red banner, '50% off Premium. Offer ends soon') on the main page of a non-Premium user

revision of knowledge acquired in the previous lessons. All Reviews are reserved for Premium users only.

Finally, incentives to upgrade to a Premium account appear as a hover box over a piece of paid content (Figure 4.3).

In CALL, very few studies have explored the implications of the freemium model for L2 learning in digital language learning environments. Loiseau *et al.* (2011) claim that 'Busuu and Livemocha are equipped with an economic model of free admission combining freemium formula and advertising financing. In these models, profitability is derived above all from the free aspect: freemium requires a basic offer accessible to anyone,

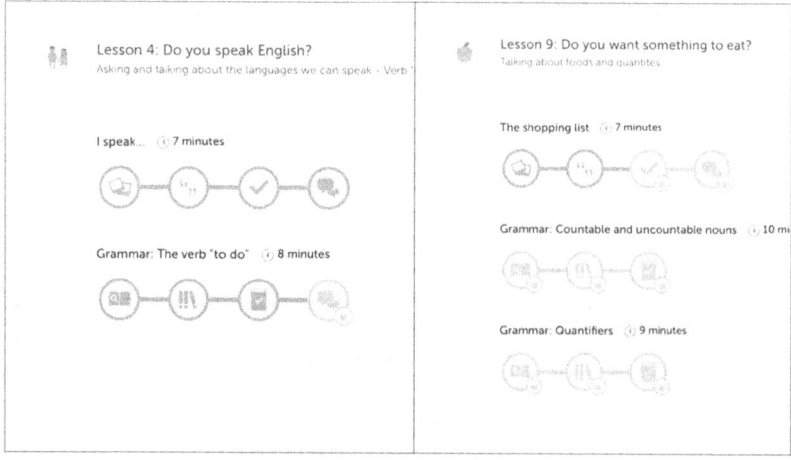

Figure 4.2 Examples of free (dark grey) and paid (light grey) content

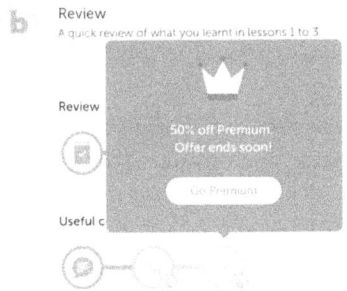

Figure 4.3 A pop-up window appearing when the user moves over a subscription-only zone

leading certain users to subscribe to a more complete paid offer'. In a later study, Zourou and Lamy (2013) have explored the design of social networking and gamification features of language learning communities and how this affects content prioritisation. They offer two examples where being a Premium user disrupts the egalitarian approach often marketed in these communities.

The first example comes from Lang-8, a language correction site (inactive since 2016), where users post short 'journals,' namely L2 productions, that other users correct for free. What is more, Premium users receive corrections faster than free account users. This happens because in Lang-8, the algorithms of the Premium User system prioritise L2 productions of Premium customers on other users' screens, ensuring faster correction than the journals of holders of free accounts (Zourou & Lamy, 2013). Thus, Premium users' posts are noticed and reviewed/corrected as a priority by native speakers who do so for free but with a clear benefit for the company that maintains the community (Premium subscriptions as revenue generation). This also happens in Livemocha (inactive since 2016) where instructions to peer learners make it clear that grading is for paying customers, and are commanding in tone (Zourou & Lamy, 2013: para 72):

> Note to Reviewers: This exercise is a Premium exercise called Role Play (...). Please watch the video and comment on the user's speech and pronunciation.

This system of prioritising Premium user productions in the correction process, while preventing free account users from submitting as many productions as Premium users, was identified in our 2013 study. This is still common practice, if we take into consideration the Busuu website in May 2019:

> 'Premium members of the Busuu community can send as many Conversation exercises as they want. If you are not a Premium subscriber, you can only send a limited number of Conversation exercises. [...]

Premium customers are prioritised in the queue for corrections, and should receive feedback fairly quickly (sometimes within a few minutes). Free members of the community may have to wait for longer to receive a correction'.

In what precedes, we outlined the concepts of openwashing and its extreme practice in the attempt to monetize open content, the freemium model. We shared concrete examples of how the freemium model is technically implemented in various SNSLL. As SNSLL offer language learning content and services (feedback, certificates, revisions) to their users, in the following section we offer an overview of crowdsourcing and the role that users (language learners) play in generating content and services.

Crowdsourcing

Contemporary forms of networked participation provide various types of user-generated activity, arising from individuals and groups that support knowledge creation and sharing in the open. Open scholarship, open science and open governance are a few examples of the approaches and practices evolving in freely accessible, distributed spaces, which enable public engagement, novice–expert interaction and collaboration and horizontal production of content and services. The term 'produsage' is a compound word (production + usage) often employed to designate the dynamics of user roles (user but also producer of content) and the artifact produced, as 'development is evolutionary, iterative, and palimpsestic' (Bruns, 2007).

Within this context of open, distributed social participation, the term crowdsourcing was coined by Howe (2006) and refers to the engagement of individuals who voluntarily offer their knowledge to a knowledge seeker (such as a social group, an organisation, a company, etc.). Crowdsourcing implies favouring the commitment of highly motivated users in the production process. Depending on the context it can be seen not only as a movement towards massive user engagement in an unrestricted and collaborative manner, but also as a means by which companies exploit users' collective efforts of knowledge building, without corresponding remuneration, '[by] tap[ping] the latent talent of the crowd' (Howe, 2006). It is a concept analysed from an educational perspective as well (Paulin & Haythornthwaite, 2016).

In CALL research, studies on crowdsourced practices are scarce. A paper by Zourou and Lamy (2013) offers a critical appraisal of ways that SNSLL roll out sophisticated game mechanics (badges, points, stars, rewards, etc.) designed to encourage the crowd (L2 learners – registered users of the SNSLL) to produce content (learning materials and corrections) while at the same time commercialising the result of this process with almost no remuneration or compensation for the users who generate it.

The authors claim that 'crowdsourcing, a notion that is in some cases considered as a "generous" ideal that enhances social action (...) plays out in some of these (SNSLL) in ways that owe nothing to generosity and everything to industrial exploitation' (Zourou & Lamy, 2013). While the 2013 study on crowdsourcing in SNSLL looks at game mechanics from a design point of view, the current study addresses crowdsourcing from the viewpoint of users engaged in the process.

Social Network Sites for Language Learning

Busuu, Duolingo and the now defunct Livemocha and Lang-8 are examples of environments known as SNSLL, web 2.0 language learning communities or massive online language communities. In this study, we shall not debate possible differences pertaining to definition, as this has been done previously (Chik & Ho, 2017; Loiseau et al., 2011; Reinhardt, 2017). We shall therefore use them interchangeably. There is a growing body of literature on SNSLL (Alvarez Valencia, 2016; Potolia & Zourou, 2019; Stevenson & Liu, 2010) which demonstrates the interest brought into this field by L2 scholars and practitioners.

The two SNSLL explored in this study, Busuu and Duolingo, were chosen for their similarities, in particular their belonging to the same sub-category of 'structured community with learning pathways' (Loiseau et al., 2011). This refers to the existence of language learning materials structured in lessons and units, following clearly depicted learning pathways.

Users are encouraged to take on the role of tutor in their L1, although the main objective of the communities in question is to learn an L2. More specifically, social networking and gaming mechanisms foster interaction and participation – essential to learning – and allow users to move from an individual learning stance to a social autonomy one (Zourou et al., 2017). Feedback is provided by any user, be it a native speaker or a competent user of the target language.

Regarding SNSLL, a short definition is provided on what is understood by services and content and how peer feedback is situated vis-à-vis those two strongly interrelated components. By 'services' we refer to what is offered apart from language content, such as accreditation (language certificates). By 'content' we refer to the language learning content, either delivered by the SNSLL (lessons), or generated by users (peer corrections attached to L2 productions posted on the SNSLL).

Peer corrections can be considered as belonging to both content and service categories; to services, because it is mainly Premium users who subscribe for a fee in order to receive regular peer corrections; to content, because peer corrections are displayed in the same manner (position, layout) as proprietary content of the SNSLL and also because it is publicly accessible just like content delivered by the SNSLL. The difference, or rather, the nuance, is situated at the level of authorship. While proprietary content is exclusively created and delivered by the SNSLL, corrections are exclusively generated by community members. However, because the latter are encapsulated within proprietary content, peer corrections become fully part of the content and are thus exploited accordingly (cf. freemium offer and crowdsourcing).

Regarding differences of the two SNSLL, in Duolingo all content is freely accessible, whereas in Busuu content is also paywalled. Thus, the distinction made between free and paid content (see section on Data analysis) concerns only Busuu. In addition, in Duolingo, to our knowledge, there are no oral or written productions. There are discussions, enabling peer interaction, embedded in exercises. We consider those differences minor and not affecting the analysis undertaken of both SNSLL.

There are few studies aiming to familiarise pre- and in-service language teachers with the 'wilderness' (Thorne, 2010) of out-of-class language learning, or language learning beyond the classroom (Benson, 2011; Reinders & Benson, 2017; Whyte, 2016). Whereas there is a solid body of literature on teacher training through digital technologies, in the majority of cases pre- and in-service teachers are trained within formal education settings (classroom-based learning), as is the case with Telecollaboration or Online Intercultural Exchange projects. Very few studies (cf. Liu *et al.*, 2015; Orsini-Jones, 2015; Stevenson & Liu, 2010) exist for pre-service language teachers to familiarize themselves with language learning in dynamic, unpredictable, erratic sociodigital contexts (cf. Sauro & Zourou, 2019) as SNSLL are. The present study, along with ones outlined above, moves in this direction.

Method

Context of investigation

As part of the Hellenic Open University Master's degree on French as a Second Language, a group of 21 teachers attended the course 'Computer Assisted Language Learning' during the academic year 2017–2018. Students had varying degrees of experience in teaching French and different ages: participants thus ranging from young graduates without experience to experienced teachers (active in either the private or public sector), aged about 55. For six weeks in Spring 2018, they were asked to keep a reflective journal during their activity in a community of their choice (Duolingo or Busuu). Each reflective journal was approximately 4000 words long.

All participants registered for free (they were not Premium users). As for the content of the reflective diary, we proposed a short series of questions in order to allow the participants to reflect on three topics – motivation, pedagogy and technology – from the learner's viewpoint and from the teacher's viewpoint. Nineteen participants freely chose Busuu, while two opted for Duolingo.

Research questions

Our study explores understandings of openness (and lack of openness) with respect to language learning content and services in SNSLL. Interest in SNSLL is motivated by the massive number of registered users (100 million for Busuu, 300 million for Duolingo, July 2020 data) and languages (12 for Busuu, 23 for Duolingo), as well as their approach to learning (peer correction, social learning, gamification), although there is no underlying learning theory, rather a blend of innovative and much less innovative features. The goal of this paper is to analyse how open access to content and services is experienced by language learners registered in the SNSLL. To do so, we refer to the freemium model and to crowdsourcing, both relying on open resources to trigger user activity. This brings us to the research questions of the study:

- How open/closed is access to language content and how are services experienced by users?
- How are users engaged in open content creation and peer feedback (cf. content and service) and what are the implications for L2 learning?

Methodology

Content analysis (Bardin, 2013; Mucchielli, 2006) serves as a methodological framework for this qualitative, interpretative study. More precisely, according to Schreier (2014: 170) it consists of 'a method for systematically describing the meaning of qualitative data'.

After skimming the journal corpora a number of times (open coding, Elo & Kyngäs, 2008), we were able to isolate extracts related to openness in the broad sense of the term (cf. section Openwashing and the freemium model) and more particularly those statements with some appraisal, followed by an explanation of the subjective stance. We then compared our viewpoints and came up with one corpus on the theme of openness, from which three subcategories emerged (cf. section on Data analysis). Throughout this process, we respected the three specificities of content analysis identified by Schreier (2014). These correspond to (a) reduction of the amount of material (focus on selected aspects of meaning, especially those relating to the research questions), (b) the systematic character of the approach (the examination of every single part of the material that is relevant to the research question as a means to avoid a bias from the researchers' own assumptions and expectations) and (c) flexibility (the data-driven character of the categories, as a guarantee that categories reflect the data).

Participants were asked their permission to use their reflective diaries for research purposes. All participants signed the written consent form containing clauses of anonymity, data access and processing and duration of use. All data were anonymised; the attribution of initials in the extracts below is random and does not correspond to participants' initials. Translation of journal extracts from French into English has been done by the researchers.

Data Analysis

Our analysis is structured around the various materialisations of openness as they are reflected in the participants' reflective diaries. Recall that the adjective 'open' is understood as free (gratis) access to materials, as the SNSLL do not allow any re-use of user data.

Data are organised into three categories for analysis. First, 'openness as a misconception', pertains to tensions surrounding access to open content. Second, 'openness as an obligation' relates to tensions surrounding the requirements made by the SNSLL in return for open-access content. Third, 'openness as exploitation' refers to the exploitation of open content for commercial purposes, highlighting the downside of crowdsourcing in the SNSLL.

Openness as a misconception

This category includes understandings of openness which pertain to open-access content. It is further broken down into openness as disappointment, as restriction and as a craving.

Openness as disappointment

In '"Openwashing" and the freemium model' we outlined studies in OER literature that point to openwashing, namely misuse of the term, 'open' to conceal commercial practices which are not open. In what follows, participants express their frustrations when they become aware of the separation of content into free and fee-based.

(E) What leads to boredom is that a learner with a free account is highly demotivated as he cannot keep up with the progress of the lessons. He does not have access to production activities, to many grammatical phenomena, to testing, to community conversations and to lesson revisions unlike users of the paid version.

When they realise that important components of the learning process are reserved for Premium users, free account users formulate their annoyance and loss of motivation. This is further accentuated when they realise that the separation of content into free and fee-based is based on type of learning resource, as discussed in the following paragraph.

Openness as restriction

Free account users quickly become aware of the fact that they cannot access certain types of materials, interaction and production possibilities.

For this reason, we have labelled this category as restriction, in the sense of not only restricting access to content but doing so for specific types of content and services, which happen to be fundamental for L2 acquisition.

(G) The freely accessible lessons are usually vocabulary lessons. Without additional help, it is difficult to advance in other areas of language acquisition.

Vocabulary items can be freely accessed (cf. extract above), but not grammar units, production activities, or reviews (a revision of three lessons), as illustrated in the light grey (paywalled) pieces in Figure 4.2. Free access to vocabulary items is discussed by participants in their journals:

(N) Although I can correctly complete vocabulary exercises, I cannot understand the sentence because I have not been taught all the words and conjugation of the verbs.

(L) The exercises are repetitive: the same countries again and again! It's a bit boring.

As the extracts above indicate, vocabulary acquisition accessible to free account users is limited to oral and written repetition and to the memorisation of words out of context. The impact on learning is described hereafter:

(M) The words I've learned so far are easy, but I don't think I can use them in communication in Italian because I have only memorised words and I do not know how to use them in a sentence.

This approach to learning vocabulary may be considered as going against contemporary pedagogical frameworks of vocabulary acquisition (Ma, 2017) that disapprove of fragmentation and decontextualisation. Participants further explain the disconnect between vocabulary learning and decontextualised word memorisation, mistakenly called 'vocabulary' in the SNSLL:

(R) The activities are easy, we feel that we are very strong in terms of language, we learn easily and it gives us the desire to continue. Yet this is not true. We learn by repeating, by using a traditional method. Vocabulary learning involves the repetition of words and not the construction of sentences.

Whereas the aforementioned extracts highlight issues related to vocabulary, the following ones emphasise the scarcity of opportunities for L2 production for free account users:

(K) The (freely accessible) activities always follow the same pattern. I'm starting to get bored. (…) Only at the end of lesson 11 did the platform allow me to make a written or oral production and send it to

the community. During the last ten lessons, I did not have this opportunity because this kind of activity was reserved for premium learners.

(R) There are no spontaneous and open oral productions.

(I) I'm starting to find the activities and exercises very monotonous!!!!! There is no communication or interaction with other learners! It's just a computer correcting our exercises! This kind of language learning is totally different from classroom learning!!!!!! Classroom learning like this would be disastrous!

This leads inevitably to a reconsideration of the nature of open resources and their value for learning purposes, as the following participant points out:

(D) On the one hand, it's clear that in general, the exercises are not very relevant in pedagogical terms, but at least they are easy. Thus, learners think that by doing all the activities they are satisfying their language needs. Nevertheless, speech, illustrated through real-life communication situations, as well as the appropriation / systematisation stage are missing. This creates a false impression of language skill acquisition.

In summary, we analysed openness as restriction, corresponding to the predictable nature of freely accessible learning materials, a lack of interaction with the community during the initial weeks of activity and a lack of L2 production possibilities. This materialisation of openness is critically addressed by the participants from a pedagogical point of view and from a motivational point of view in the above extracts. What follows is an interpretation of open content as a craving.

Openness as a craving

The freemium model adopted by the two SNSLL is manifested through notifications (appearing on a user profile on the SNSLL and sent by email), and through a gamified incentive, consisting in the invitation and subsequent sign up of three new users in return for week-long access to Premium content. In this section we highlight the experience shared by one participant, who seems to have been won over by this incentive:

(U) I invited three friends to sign up to Busuu so that I could gain one week's free access to the Premium version. The three friends signed up using my link but although I received a notification saying I could start my free week nothing has changed. I'm angry. The blocked parts are still blocked.

The user finally reaches out for technical assistance to the community forum and successfully activates her Premium account for a week. Yet what is worth discussing is this 'anger' that the participant expresses, for having done what is necessary to obtain one week's Premium access while being impeded by a technical bug (fixed in the end). This longing for Premium access is indicative of the longing for something unattainable (unless paid for) that the SNSLL exposes users to through the carefully designed gamified feature that ensures the Premium version is considered something worth competing for. 'Openness as a craving', from our viewpoint, relates to the acquisition of something regarded as valuable for users (Premium access), partly because of its acquisition for free, when access is normally fee-based, and an addiction to the gamified environment of the SNSLL. Access to the Premium account aside, the commercial trick of offering only one week's access, seems to become a goal in itself for this participant. Through this gamification mechanism, Premium access (paid content) is designed to be seen as something desirable, still accessible to free account users. Undoubtedly, the SNSLL in return for (only) one week's access to Premium, succeeds in increasing its user base and traffic through the sign up of new users.

Openness as an obligation

Openness as an obligation is understood as something in return for free access to content and to the community. This takes two forms, the obligation to provide feedback and the incentives to buy a subscription. This may act as a disincentive to learn.

Openness as a service in exchange

Peer correction appears as an obligation to serve the community, as a type of service in exchange for the free materials accessible. This requirement to provide feedback is illustrated in Figure 4.4, which is an example of an email notification that users regularly receive.

By framing peer correction as a condition for becoming part of the community ('Be part of the Busuu community by helping others'), the SNSLL place peer correction in the social sphere of the community, as a means to strengthen social bonds.

Regular notifications to provide feedback are reported in our dataset:

(E) *I must point out that it is rather annoying to receive daily e-mails seeing as I visit the platform quite frequently and offer corrections.*

Because peer correction is provided in a user's L1, it goes against the very objective of registering for an SNSLL:

(A) *I receive one email per day from Busuu asking me to correct other users' exercises. It's annoying. We sign up to this platform to learn a language. It's true that we're members of a virtual community, and that's good. It's reassuring to know that you're not alone. Learning a language is sometimes difficult. But I constantly feel obliged to show that I belong to the community by correcting the exercises of others.*

Figure 4.4 Email notification to provide peer correction

The give-and-take mechanism concretised in making peer feedback in one's L1 of equal importance with one's objective of L2 learning is undeniably a value making mechanism for the SNSLL, which receives traffic and popularity due to peer feedback activity. However, users see themselves attributed a role that has not been foreseen (providing feedback in one's L1), which affects their user activity, especially due to the incessant nature of the notifications. This is further connected to the crowdsourcing practices of the SNSLL discussed in section 'Openness as exploitation'.

Openness as a disincentive to pay

One may reasonably inquire as to the effectiveness of the freemium model in these two SNSLL, namely whether the free access to materials and the regular notifications to upgrade to the Premium version succeed in convincing users to pay for a subscription. According to our analysis, among the 21 participants, none expressed the wish to subscribe to Premium. On the contrary, participants expressed complete unwillingness to do so:

(Q) *The course revisions are also restricted to Premium members. The free version is probably just a way of getting users to subscribe to the paid version. Commercial behaviour to make money – very negative in my opinion.*

(U) *One disadvantage is that I cannot practice pronominal verbs or frequency adverbs because I have to become a Premium member. It's a little disincentivising and I do not want to pay.*

Although participants recognise the value of the items behind a paywall (grammar, revision) they clearly express their reluctance to pay to subscribe. An explanation of this objection is given in the following extract:

(N) Receiving emails quite often, either to connect to the Busuu community or to buy the premium edition, is quite annoying. Sending promotional emails to buy the Premium offer does not cause me to buy it.

(I) The community offers this possibility of free learning, but it bombards us with notifications and emails to benefit from the premium subscription that is fee-based and gives us access to everything!!!!!!! It's like a trap ...

In both extracts above, the frequency of notifications ('we're bombarded by,' 'it's annoying') and the obvious marketing objective of the strategy ('it's like a trap,' 'it's commercial behaviour to earn money – it's very negative') clearly discourage people from purchasing a Premium account and instead of encouraging people to become Premium users, the freemium approach has a negative effect among this population (disturbance, distress, disillusion expressed in the extracts above).

Openness as a disincentive to learn

As participant A in 'Openness as a service in exchange' points out, the combination of, on the one hand, limited and decontextualised free resources, lack of interaction and limited opportunities for L2 production and, on the other hand, constant notifications to pay for a subscription and provide L1 feedback, affects the very purpose of activity in the SNSLL. This clearly represents a gap between one's own learning objectives and learning practice as it unfolds in the SNSLL:

(Q) It's very annoying that the Busuu platform attempts to convince me to buy a Premium subscription. It gives me the impression that it's not a free learning platform and that its purpose is to attract more users for commercial reasons.

(B) Busuu's constant reminders to subscribe to the Premium version, which offers 50% off the monthly subscription, were extremely annoying and unpleasant and disoriented me several times in achieving my goals.

(N) On the one hand I find that this practice encourages me to connect to the platform, but on the other hand I find the large number of emails that I receive, stressful and disincentivising.

For some users, the obvious commercial nature of these SNSLL distorts participation, engagement and smooth interaction. Paywalled content and services disincentivises users who defy the revenue model of the SNSLL.

Openness as exploitation

In connection to various materialisations of openness, it is worth investigating the status of user-generated content (as peer corrections are) and ownership of this content by their creators. Despite the user-generated character of the corrections, they belong to the copyright protected content of the system. Thus, peer learners as content authors do not have rights over the content they generate. What is more, peer correction is the feature that SNSLL users value the most when joining an SNSLL (Zourou *et al.*, 2017). It may be seen as the driving force behind the community, as L2 learners reach their objective within the social environment of the SNSLL. At the same time, peer correction aptly serves the crowdsourcing mechanism of the SNSLL, as corrections become pieces of content, originally user-generated, ultimately appropriated by the SNSLL.

Since peer correction takes place effectively, the SNSLL have an additional selling point (besides access to all parts of learning resources and services), as they can claim that the learning process is secured, at least theoretically (L2 productions are being corrected). The point that is worth investigating, which relates to the discussion on openness and exploitation of open content for commercial purposes, is that Premium users receive many more and quicker corrections to their productions than free account users; whereas the latter provide feedback but rarely receive corrections (see section '"Openwashing" and the freemium model').

It is clear that the relationship between productions and corrections is more unbalanced for free account users despite the fact that they supply corrections. A more fine-grained analysis, based on a larger dataset would undoubtedly offer more insights into this phenomenon, yet this exploratory study offers indications that substantiate this claim. More precisely, in 'Openness as restriction' we heard from one dissatisfied free account user, K, who complained about the lack of production opportunities before lesson 11. In other words, although participant K supplied corrections in her L1 along with completing lessons 1–11, she was denied opportunities to receive correction, because all L2 production possibilities for her were disabled until lesson 11. This is in sharp contrast with participant U in 'Openness as a craving', who is the user who received a Premium account for one week, as compensation for bringing three new users to register to the SNSLL. In her journal she notes:

(U) Thanks to the free Premium week I was able to complete 100% of the lessons. I asked for corrections for an activity I had done. Three people corrected it (…) It was nice to see the same correction by three different people.

The significant increase in number of corrections received once the user became Premium (three corrections for the same L2 production) compared with the exclusion of any L2 production (and the subsequent loss of corrections), the monotony of learning resources for free account holders, lack of interaction and rare L2 production opportunities (cf. 'Openness as restriction'), leaves little doubt as to the exploitation of open content (peer corrections) as a value making mechanism for the SNSLL. L2 productions of Premium users are prioritised in the algorithms of the SNSLL, to the detriment of productions from free account users, despite their contribution as suppliers of content. We can thus claim that the crowdsourcing model adopted by the SNSLL takes advantage of free account users, by exploiting their user-generated open content in the form of corrections, from which only Premium account holders usually benefit. Through our analysis, we are able to provide some tangible data regarding crowdsourcing and its downside, namely the fact of 'tapping the latent talent of the crowd' (Howe, 2006) in a profit-making fashion. It echoes Jones arguing that 'corporate misappropriation of free labour and exploitation of work supplied for moral reasons' (2014: 344; Selwyn, 2014).

Conclusion

Before sharing some concluding remarks, the limitations of the current study should be considered. First, the analysis is exploratory in nature and based on a small sample of users, offering only some understanding of the phenomena under scrutiny. Second, the analysis focuses on understandings of openness and neglects positive outcomes from the three-month experience of participants – views of participants are more positive regarding other dimensions of the SNSLL (especially social aspects and engagement), analysed in another contribution (Potolia & Zourou, 2019). Third, content restricted to Premium users occurs in Busuu only (cf. second section), which is the community that 19 out of 21 students opted for, thus data regarding open/closed content does not apply for both SNSLL. Fourth, it is worth re-contextualising the experience, as participants (L2 learners) were language teachers engaged in this experience as part of their teacher training. It may be that their degree of criticality is part of their teacher identity which has affected their interpretation of L2 learning in SNSLL.

Our study examined aspects of openness (and lack thereof) by discussing commercial practices around open content and services. Although it is natural for a start-up operating an SNSLL to generate revenue, some of the mechanisms used to reach this objective sometimes have negative implications for language learning, participation and engagement. We were able to come to the following conclusions through the content analysis of reflective diaries that we carried out.

First, openness is a complex phenomenon to be dealt with, as previous scholars have pointed out (Collier & Ross, 2017; Pomerantz & Peek, 2016). In our study, we were able to depict 3 materialisations (openness as a misconception, openness as an obligation and openness as exploitation) and their subcategories.

Second, the freemium model does not encourage free account users to pay a subscription, rather the contrary, as notifications to become a Premium member are numerous and disincentivising, affecting user engagement and *in fine*, L2 learning.

Third, open content available to free account users is predictable, and more importantly, typified. Although the freemium model as revenue-generation strategy is, by definition, built on a separation between free and paid content and services, the choice of providing for free only some types of content and by prohibiting access to valuable components (revision, L2 productions, grammar, conversations), acts firstly as a disincentive to learn, and secondly, presents serious flaws in terms of how online language learning is conceptualised in SNSLL. This means that from a pedagogical point of view, language learning resources should not be fragmented, and should not be constructed on capitalisable autonomous units. In our opinion, it would make more sense to ban access to certain language levels or at least to find a suitable freemium model that does not go against fundamental concepts in L2 acquisition. Openness would have been better understood and embraced with fewer misconceptions and obligations for users who were confronted with a lack of pedagogy overruled by the overly obvious revenue model.

Crowdsourcing in SNSLL has been explored in previous studies, one of which pointed out its failings in terms of language content creation and concluded with these words: 'In this economic triangle (company, customer, reviewer) the customer [Premium account holder] pays the company in order to profit from the time and skill invested by peer learners, who receive very little if any part of the financial benefit' (Zourou & Lamy, 2013). We were able to validate this claim by juxtaposing it with user perspectives collected in this study. Overall, what we witness is the upkeep of the unbalanced scheme of content provision and lack of corresponding remuneration or compensation identified in previous studies. Our paper calls for more research on the implications on learning, agency and social participation in massive online language communities.

Finally, in connection to CALL research, there is growing interest surrounding informal technology-mediated language learning and teaching (Dressman & Sadler, 2020) to which the current paper contributes. By bringing to light practices and expectations of different actors (users and commercial players), this study underscores and calls for further research on complex phenomena that emerge in informal learning contexts.

References

Álvarez Valencia, J.A. (2016) Language views on social networking sites for language learning: the case of Busuu. *Computer Assisted Language Learning* 29 (5), 853–867.
Bardin, L. (2013) *L'analyse de contenu* (2nd edn). Paris: Presses Universitaires de France (original work published 1977).
Benson, P. (2011) *Beyond the Language Classroom*. London: Palgrave Macmillan.

Blyth, C., Thoms, J. and Zourou, K. (2015) 'Out in the Open, Reaching for the Stars': EU-US Insights into Open Educational Practices in Language Education. Webinar held on September 15.

Bruns, A. (2007) Produsage: Towards a broader framework for user-led content creation. *Proceedings Creativity & Cognition* 6. Washington, DC. https://eprints.qut.edu.au/6623/1/6623.pdf

Center for Open Educational Resources and Language Learning (COERLL) (2012) *Voices for Openness in Language Learning.* University of Texas.

Chik, A. and Ho, J. (2017) Learn a language for free: Recreational learning among adults. *System* 69, 162–171.

Collier, A. and Ross, J. (2017) For whom, and for what? Not-yetness and thinking beyond open content. *Open Praxis* 9 (1), 7–16. https://openpraxis.org/index.php/OpenPraxis/article/view/406

Conole, G.C. and Ehlers, U.D. (2010) Open educational practices: Unleashing the power of OER. UNESCO Workshop on OER in Namibia. Windhoek. https://oerknowledgecloud.org/sites/oerknowledgecloud.org/files/OEP_Unleashing-the-power-of-OER.pdf

Cronin, C. and MacLaren, I. (2018) Conceptualising OEP: A review of theoretical and empirical literature in Open Educational Practices. *Open Praxis* 10 (2), 127–143. https://openpraxis.org/index.php/OpenPraxis/article/view/825

De Langen, F.H.T. (2013) Strategies for sustainable business models for open educational resources. *The International Review of Research in Open and Distributed Learning* 14 (2), 53–66. http://www.irrodl.org/index.php/irrodl/article/view/1533/2485

Dressman, M. and Sadler, R.W. (eds) (2020) *The Handbook of Informal Language Learning.* Chichester: John Wiley & Sons.

Elo, S. and Kyngäs, H. (2008) The qualitative content analysis process. *Journal of Advanced Nursing* 62 (1), 107–115.

Farrow, R. (2015) Open education and critical pedagogy. *Learning, Media and Technology* 42 (2), 130–146. http://doi.org/10.1080/17439884.2016.1113991

Howe, J. (2006) The rise of crowdsourcing. *Wired.* https://www.wired.com/2006/06/crowds/

Jones, C. (2015) Openness, technologies, business models and austerity. *Learning, Media and Technology* 40 (3), 328–349.

Knox, J. (2013) The limitations of access alone: Moving towards open processes in education technology. *Open Praxis* 5 (1), 21–29. https://openpraxis.org/index.php/OpenPraxis/article/view/36

Kurek, M. and Skowron, A. (2015) Going Open with LangOER: A Teacher's Handbook. http://langoer.eun.org/c/document_library/get_file?uuid=3647b9db-836b-45cb-8140-6dff1b310fad&groupId=395028

Liu, M., Abe, K., Cao, M.W., Liu, S., Ok, D.U., Park, J., Parrish, C. and Sardegna, V.G. (2015) An analysis of social network websites for language learning: Implications for teaching and learning English as a second language. *Computer Assisted Language Instruction Consortium* 32, 113–152.

Loiseau, M., Potolia, A. and Zourou, K. (2011) Communautés Web 2.0 d'apprenants de langue avec parcours d'apprentissage: rôles, pédagogie et rapports au contenu. *Proceedings of EIAH Conference.* Belgium. 111–123. https://hal.archives-ouvertes.fr/hal-00598762v3

Ma, Q. (2017) A multi-case study of university students' language-learning experience mediated by mobile technologies: A socio-cultural perspective. *Computer Assisted Language Learning* 30 (3), 183–203.

Mucchielli, R. (2006) *L'analyse de contenu: Des documents et des communications* (9th edn). Paris: ESF (original work published in 1984).

Orsini-Jones, M., Brick, B. and Pibworth, L. (2013) Practicing language interaction via social networking sites: The 'expert student's' perspective on personalized language learning. In B. Zou, M. Xing, Y. Wang, M. Sun and C.H. Xiang (eds)

Computer-Assisted Foreign Language Teaching and Learning: Technological Advances (pp. 40–53). Philadelphia: IGI Global. https://curve.coventry.ac.uk/open/file/de4f060b-0838-8069-b72f-669063bb5571/1/brickcomb2.pdf

Osipov, I., Volinsky, A., Nikulchev, E. and Plokhov, D. (2015) Study of monetization as a way of motivating freemium service users. *Contemporary Engineering Sciences* 8 (20), 911–918.

Paulin, D. and Haythornthwaite, C. (2016) Crowdsourcing the curriculum: Redefining e-learning practices through peer-generated approaches. *The Information Society* 32 (2), 130–142.

Pomerantz, J. and Peek, R. (2016) Fifty shades of open. *First Monday* 21 (5). http://firstmonday.org/article/view/6360/5460

Potolia, A. and Zourou, K. (2019) Penser son accompagnement dans une communauté d'apprentissage des langues en ligne: Intérêts et limites pour les enseignants du français langue étrangère. *Distances et Médiation des Savoirs* 26. https://journals.openedition.org/dms/3499.

Reinhardt, J. (2017) Social network sites and language education. In S. Thorne and S. May (eds) *Language, Education and Technology* (pp. 1–12). New York: Springer International Publishing.

Reinders, H. and Benson, P. (2017) Research agenda: Language learning beyond the classroom. *Language Teaching* 50 (4), 1–8.

S. Sauro, and K. Zourou (2019) What are the digital wilds? Introduction to special issue. In S. Sauro and K. Zourou (eds) *Computer Assisted Language Learning in the Digital Wilds. Language Learning and Technology* 23 (1). https://www.lltjournal.org/item/3090

Schreier, M. (2014) Qualitative content analysis. In U. Flick (ed.) *The SAGE Handbook of Qualitative Data Analysis* (pp. 170–183). London: Sage.

Selwyn, N. (2014) *Distrusting Educational Technology: Critical Questions for Changing Times*. London: Routledge.

Stevenson, M.P. and Liu, M. (2010) Learning a language with Web 2.0: Exploring the use of social networking features of foreign language learning websites. *CALICO Journal* 27 (2), 233–259.

Thomas, M. and Evans, M. (2014) Open educational resources in language learning. *Computer Assisted Language Learning* 27 (2), 107–108.

Thorne, S.L. (2010) The 'intercultural turn' and language learning in the crucible of new media. In F. Helm and S. Guth (eds) *Telecollaboration 2.0 for Language and Intercultural Learning* (pp. 139–164). Bern: Peter Lang.

UNESCO (2012) *2012 Paris OER Declaration*. Paris: World OER Congress. http://www.unesco.org/new/fileadmin/MULTIMEDIA/HQ/CI/CI/pdf/Events/Paris%20OER%20Declaration_01.pdf

Watters, A. (2014) *From 'Open' To Justice*, Blog, 16 November. http://hackeducation.com/2014/11/16/from-open-to-justice

Weller, M. (2014) *The Battle for Open*. London: Ubiquity Press.

Whyte, S. (2016) From 'solitary thinkers' to 'social actors': OER in multilingual CALL teacher education. *Alsic* 19 (1). https://doi.org/10.4000/alsic.2906

Wiley, D. (2014) *The Access Compromise and the 5th R,* Blog, 5 March. http://opencontent.org/blog/archives/3221

Zourou, K. (2016) *Social Dynamics in Open Educational Language Practice*. Alsic, 19 (1). https://journals.openedition.org/alsic/2983

Zourou, K. and Lamy, M.N. (2013) Social networked game dynamics in web 2.0 language learning communities. *Alsic* 16. https://journals.openedition.org/alsic/2642?lang=en

Zourou, K., Potolia, A. and Zourou, F. (2017) Informal social networking for language learning: Insights into autonomy stances. In M. Cappellini, T. Lewis and A. Rivens Mompean (eds) *Learner Autonomy and Web 2.0* (pp. 141–167). Sheffield: Equinox Publishing Ltd.

Part 2

The Mesosystem: Developing Knowledge in L2 Teacher Education

5 Second Language Teachers and the Open Education Movement in the United States: A National Survey

Joshua J. Thoms and Frederick Poole

The open education movement has resulted in the creation and sharing of copyright-free content – also referred to as open educational resources (OER) – by instructors working in a number of disciplines throughout the world. In addition, the 'open turn' has also ushered in new approaches to engaging students in the processes of locating, creating and/or curating open content – part of which constitutes open educational practices (OEP). However, little is known about how and why language teachers in the United States (US) are embracing (or not) open education. This study reports on the survey responses of 1484 language teachers working in various US educational contexts. Results indicate that 52% of respondents reported that they are aware of OER. Language instructors teaching in blended and fully online environments, those working in K-12 and community college contexts and those teaching English as a Second Language are more aware of OER than their colleagues for a variety of reasons. Survey respondents' primary reason for using/incorporating OER in their language courses is that open materials address aspects of their courses that are not adequately covered elsewhere; the main deterrent to using OER relates to the notion that OER are not comprehensive in nature. Finally, of those respondents who indicated that they make use of and/or create OER for their language courses, 79% indicated that OER have changed their teaching practice(s) in various positive ways.

Introduction

Over the past two decades, the open education movement has affected all levels of education in a number of different countries (de los Arcos & Weller, 2018; Jhangiani & Biswas-Diener, 2017). The Open Education Consortium (n.d.) defines open education as encompassing 'resources, tools and practices that employ a framework of open sharing to improve educational access and effectiveness worldwide.' Many open education efforts to date have centered on the creation, adaptation, and/or use of open educational resources (OER), which are defined as resources 'that are openly available for use by educators and students, without an accompanying need to pay royalties or license fees' (Butcher, 2011: 5). OER are typically shared via Creative Commons licenses that allow educators to revise, remix, reuse and/or redistribute content without dealing with restrictive copyright. Recent work in open education has begun to research the open educational practices (OEP) of educators (Blyth, 2017; Jhangiani & DeRosa, 2017), which encompass 'all activities that open up access to educational opportunity, in a context where freely available online content and services ... are taken as the norm' (Beetham *et al.*, 2012: 1). Both OER and OEP often draw upon 'open technologies that facilitate collaborative, flexible learning and the open sharing of teaching practices' (Cape Town Open Education Declaration, 2008: 1).

The open education movement is considered by some in the second language (L2) field to be disruptive in that it is creating new knowledge ecologies involving students, instructors and researchers in response, in part, to the overall increasing cost of textbooks (Weller *et al.*, 2017; 'Open Education,' 2017), inadequate funding for K-16 education in various states in the US (Center on Budget and Policy Priorities, 2016), and the proliferation of technology-mediated L2 content available on the web (Cummings *et al.*, 2017; Kessler, 2018). However, when compared to the science, technology, engineering and mathematics (STEM) disciplines, the field of L2 education has only tepidly embraced open education initiatives. Specifically, STEM educators are the more prominent users of OER given that OER repositories such as Openstax (https://cnx.org/), Merlot (https://www.merlot.org/merlot/index.htm) and OER Commons (https://www.oercommons.org/) show two to three times as many entries/resources for STEM categories when compared to the arts, humanities and social sciences. One reason why language educators have been hesitant to participate in the open education movement relates to a lack of research investigating the benefits and challenges of language learning and teaching in open environments and via open materials, how OER compare to publisher-produced content with respect to learning outcomes and the reasons why and how language educators engage in OEP at their institutions (Thoms & Thoms, 2014).

Although work has begun to explore aspects of OER and OEP in foreign language (FL) education contexts in various parts of the world (e.g. de los Arcos *et al.*, 2017; Whyte, 2016; Zourou, 2016), a critical need remains for research that investigates (a) the variables that affect how language educators are aware and/or perceive and make use of OER in their classrooms, (b) reasons why language educators create, adapt, or use OER, (c) the kinds of OER most commonly used by language educators and (d) if the proliferation of OER affects language educators' teaching practice(s). In response to the paucity of research related to OER and OEP in FL education in the US, coupled with growing efforts to increase access to education and knowledge via various open-access initiatives (Herb & Schöpfel, 2018), a rising number of massive open online courses (Rubio *et al.*, 2016), and efforts around open pedagogy (Jhangiani & DeRosa, 2017), this study reports on the results of the first wide-scale survey administered to language educators with the overarching goal of understanding the current state of open education and language teaching and learning in the US.

Researching OER and OEP in the US

While language educators working in contexts outside of North America (e.g. Europe) have created and made use of OER in FL curricula since the early 2000s (Beaven *et al.*, 2013), OER have only recently begun to affect FL education in the US. Few empirical studies exist that investigate how the open education movement is affecting FL educators working in K-16 contexts in the US. The first project (Thoms & Thoms, 2014) involves a small-scale study that surveyed 155 university-level FL program directors. Results of the study indicated that only 33% of respondents were familiar with the term OER. Those who had created and/or used OER in their FL programs stated that they were primarily motivated to do so due to inadequacies of their adopted publisher-produced textbook and that OER were perceived to be more current, engaging and authentic when compared to publisher-produced materials. In addition, survey respondents stated that one of the primary reasons for interest in OER was the growing number of blended and fully online courses offered at their institutions. The study also investigated the challenges to creating and/or using OER in FL programs. Respondents stated that they refrained from adopting OER given that it was difficult to identify skill-appropriate OER for their students' and FL programs' needs, issues related to the quality of OER content and not knowing where to look for OER for their courses. Finally, a majority of the language program directors indicated that their FL programs' instructors lacked sufficient time and technological knowledge to create and/or adapt OER.

A second and more recent survey-based study (Thoms *et al.*, 2018) involved researchers analyzing the responses of 310 English as a Second Language (ESL) instructors working in K-16 environments across the US to understand how these instructors either made use of and/or created OER in their courses and if OER had affected their teaching practice in any way. Results indicated that 59% of the ESL instructors were either aware or very aware of OER and that those instructors who had less teaching experience (i.e. less than 10 years) were two times as likely of being aware of OER versus those who had spent more time in the profession (i.e. more than 10 years of experience). In addition, ESL instructors working in K-12 settings were more likely to use OER than those teaching in community colleges and universities. ESL instructors' main reason for using OER included the ease of adapting and/or incorporating OER in their courses while also signaling that their primary reason for not using OER involved difficulty in locating OER. Finally, respondents indicated that the main way in which OER have impacted their teaching is that they make their teaching more interesting/dynamic for both themselves and their students.

While the aforementioned studies shed some initial light on how a small segment of the FL education community in the US is beginning to take part in the open education movement, various issues related to OER and OEP have yet to be fully investigated. For example, discussions about how OER can be best utilized in traditional face-to-face, blended and fully online FL courses have still not sufficiently addressed the issue of effectively mixing open and closed materials, tools and practices (Blyth, 2013). In addition, little is known about how a number of variables (the teaching experience of FL educators, the FL being taught, aspects of one's teaching context, etc.) affect how aware US-based FL educators are of OER. Furthermore, there is a scant amount of information in the research literature regarding why (or why not) US-based FL educators teaching in K-12 contexts make use of OER in their classrooms. As a result of numerous voids in the research literature, this survey study investigates the following research questions: (1) what demographic variables affect how aware language instructors are of OER and the ways in which OER are used in their classes?; (2a) what are the main reasons why language instructors use OER in their courses?; (2b) what are the main reasons why language instructors refrain from using OER in their courses?; and (3) have OER changed language instructors' teaching practices?

Methods

Participants and procedures

The data analyzed for this study come from an anonymous survey sent to language educators in Summer 2015 who either taught FL or ESL courses and were working in K-12, community college, and four-year university and college settings across all 50 states in the US. The survey used to collect data for this study (see Appendix 5.1) was adapted from one used by Allen and Seaman (2014). To seek out research participants for this current project, one of the researchers carried out an online search for language instructors teaching in K-16 contexts. Given that the email addresses of instructors teaching in higher education were more accessible when compared to those FL instructors teaching in K-12 environments, a majority of survey respondents for this study comes from language educators teaching in community colleges and four-year universities and colleges in the US.

Once a database of names was established, the other researcher sent out emails to the instructors on the contact list and explained the research project and invited them to take the anonymous survey. As such, completing the survey was done on a volunteer basis. However, some respondents opted to enter a drawing that awarded a $50 Amazon gift certificate to ten randomly selected survey respondents in appreciation for their time and insights.

In all, 1674 teachers began the survey, but only 1484 participants answered all of the questions. As such, the data that we report on here come from those 1484 language educators who completed the survey. While all geographic locations in the US are represented in the data, the majority of respondents came from the Midwestern (25.4%), Mid-Atlantic (19.8%) and Southeastern (18.4%) regions. Respondents' ages were distributed as follows: under 25 (3.3%); 25–34 (22.9%); 35–44 (27.1%); 45–54 (23.8%); and 55 or older (22.9%). A majority of respondents (51.5%) indicated that they possessed a Master's degree, 35.7% held a PhD, 10.5% had a Bachelor's degree, and 2.3% reported that they held some other kind of degree. Regarding years of experience teaching language, 20.7% of respondents had 0–5 years of experience, 36.7% had taught between 6 and 15 years, and 42.6% had taught for 16 or more years.

Table 5.1 indicates the contexts in which the language instructors worked. As can be seen, an overwhelming majority taught in face-to-face environments. In addition, 72% of respondents worked in a community college or a four-year university or college setting. Again, this disproportion in the data stemmed from the difficulty of locating reliable contact information online for language educators working in K-12 environments, a detail we have noted in the limitations section of this paper. Finally, the majority of survey respondents taught Spanish (35.4%), followed by ESL (17.6%), French (16.5%), German (9.3%), Italian (4.0%) and various other languages (see Appendix 5.2 for the other languages mentioned by respondents).

Table 5.1 Educational contexts of language educators

Format of language class

Face-to-face	85.7%
Blended/hybrid	13.5%
Fully online	0.8%

Educational context(s)

Primary school	0.5%
Middle school	0.8%
High school	25.4%
Community College	6.7%
4-year university or college	65.3%
Other (e.g. independent language center)	1.3%

Operationalization of OER in survey

Given that one of the research questions investigated in this study looks at possible factors/variables that affect how aware language educators are of OER and reasons as to why they do (or do not) make use of OER in their courses, the following definition of OER was provided early on in the survey:

> ...any educational resources (including curriculum maps, course materials, textbooks, streaming videos, multimedia applications, podcasts, and any other materials that have been designed for use in teaching and learning) that are openly available for use by educators and students, without an accompanying need to pay royalties or license fees. (Butcher, 2011: 5)

Immediately following the definition, the survey underscored the idea that when compared to traditional copyrighted language materials and tools, OER are open and can often be shared, edited, modified, remixed and/or reused depending on one's specific educational context and need(s). By providing information about OER near the beginning of the survey, this ensured that all survey respondents were working with the same definition when responding to questions in the latter part of the survey.

Quantitative data collection/analysis procedures

In addition to background information (e.g. age, degree, educational context, teaching experience, teaching format and target language taught) we also asked a series of questions related to (a) awareness of OER, (b) use of OER (e.g. as a primary or supplementary source), (c) reasons for using OER (e.g. cost, current nature of materials), (d) types of OER used (e.g. handouts, videos), (e) how OER compares to traditional, publisher-produced resources and (f) deterrents to using OER.

To answer our first research question regarding demographic variables that affect awareness and use of OER, we used both Chi-square analysis and Classification and Regression (CART) analysis.[1] Given that our data contained multiple responses for each category, we needed to reduce some of the categories for data analysis/statistical purposes. For example, participants were given seven response options in the survey for indicating their length of teaching experience; ranging from less than 1 year to more than 20 years. The seven possible response categories were reduced to two: less than 10 years and more than 10 years. For teaching context, participants were given three options; face-to-face, blended/hybrid and online. The final two categories (blended/hybrid and online) were collapsed into one category. The language that teachers taught were collected via open-ended response and then coded as either ESL or a non-ESL language. For OER awareness, participants were given a four-point Likert scale ranging from not aware to very aware. This was reduced to two categories, aware and not aware. Finally, use of OER also had a four-point Likert scale ranging from never use to regularly use. This category was also reduced to two categories: use and not use.

Qualitative data collection/analysis procedures

To answer research question 2, descriptive statistics and bar charts were used to explore the main reasons why (or why not) language instructors used OER in their courses. For the third research question, qualitative analyses of instructors' free responses to a survey question were carried out based on the principles of grounded theory (Charmaz, 2006). This approach involves raters making multiple passes through the data to determine if any possible patterns emerge. For this study, one of the researchers first read through the responses for the following survey question: *If you have incorporated OER in your language course(s), briefly explain how it has changed your teaching.* That initial pass through respondents' answers to the aforementioned open-ended question resulted in the creation of categories for the responses and a description of each category was determined. The researcher then discussed the categories with another rater and agreed on how each one was defined based on the first pass of the data. The second rater then read and coded all comments for the survey question based on the categories established by the researcher. The inter-rater reliability between the researcher and secondary rater for the responses was then calculated and determined to be Kappa = 0.948. More information about the various categories is provided in the Results section.

Results

The results are organized and presented based on the three research questions investigated in this study.

Research Question 1. What demographic variables affect how aware language instructors are of OER and the ways in which OER are used in their classes?

To explore potential background factors that may affect (a) awareness of OER and (b) the use of OER as either a primary or supplementary source, we used chi-square analysis to compare percentages of those who reported being aware of and/or using OER in their classrooms by the degree one holds (e.g. Bachelors, Masters, or Doctorate), teaching experience (e.g. more or less than 10 years), teaching format (e.g. face-to-face or blended/online), teaching context (e.g. K-12, Community College, University) and language taught (e.g. ESL or Non-ESL Language).

In terms of degree (see Table 5.2), we did not find a significant statistical difference between those who reported being aware of OER when compared to those who reported not being aware, (χ^2 (2, N = 1484) = 0.85, p = 0.654). However, we did find significant differences for both use of

Table 5.2 OER awareness and use by degree

	Awareness		χ^2 (p value)	Primary source		χ^2 (p value)	Supp. source		χ^2 (p value)
	Yes	No		Yes	No		Yes	No	
Degree									
Bachelors	76 49%	78 51%		54 41%	77 59%		98 65%	52 35%	
Masters	418 53%	367 47%	$\chi^2 = 0.85$ p = 0.654	283 40%	430 60%	$\chi^2 = 11.89$ p = .002*	519 68%	243 32%	$\chi^2 = 18.68$ p < .001*
Doctorate	283 52%	262 48%		151 31%	343 69%		299 56%	231 44%	

Note: All percentages are rounded to the nearest whole number.

OER as a primary source, (χ^2 (2, N = 1338) = 11.89, $p = 0.002$), and as a supplementary source, (χ^2 (2, N = 1442) = 18.68, $p < 0.001$), between those who held different levels of degree. Most notable was that those who held a doctorate degree reported using OER as primary source (31%) and supplementary source (56%) less than those with either a Bachelor's or Master's degree.

As for teaching experience (see Table 5.3), we did not find a significant difference between awareness (χ^2 (1, N = 1484) = 0.31, $p = 0.579$) or use of OER as a primary (χ^2 (1, N = 1338) = 2.30, $p = 0.129$) or supplementary source (χ^2 (1, N = 1442) = 0.81, $p = 0.368$) by those who had more or less than ten years of teaching experience. In other words, according to the chi-square analysis, teaching experience does not appear to be a determining factor of OER awareness or use.

In terms of teaching context (see Table 5.4) we found a few interesting findings. First, there was a significant difference in the number of teachers who reported being aware of OER between the two contexts,

Table 5.3 OER awareness and use by teaching experience

	Awareness		χ^2 (p value)	Primary source		χ^2 (p value)	Supp. source		χ^2 (p value)
	Yes	No		Yes	No		Yes	No	
Experience									
Less than 10 Years	263 51%	249 49%	$\chi^2 = 0.31$ p = 0.579	189 39%	294 61%	$\chi^2 = 2.30$ p = 0.129	328 65%	176 35%	$\chi^2 = 0.810$ p = 0.368
More than 10 Years	514 53%	458 47%		299 35%	556 65%		588 63%	350 37%	

Note: All percentages are rounded to the nearest whole number.

Table 5.4 OER awareness and use by teaching format

	Awareness		χ^2 (p value)	Primary Source		χ^2 (p value)	Supp. Source		χ^2 (p value)
	Yes	No		Yes	No		Yes	No	
Format									
Blended/Online	125 59%	88 41%	$\chi^2 = 3.99$ $p = 0.045*$	78 42%	108 58%	$\chi^2 = 4.97$ $p = 0.095$	148 71%	30 29%	$\chi^2 = 6.11$ $p = 0.013*$
Face-to-Face	652 51%	619 49%		410 36%	742 64%		768 62%	466 38%	

Note: All percentages are rounded to the nearest whole number.

(χ^2 (1, N = 1484) = 3.99, $p = 0.045$); more teachers who were working in blended/online teaching formats reported being aware (59%) of OER than those who were in traditional face-to-face environments (51%). A similar trend is seen in terms of use of OER as both a primary and supplementary source. However, only use of OER as a supplementary source was significantly different, (χ^2 (1, N = 1442) = 6.11, $p = 0.013$). These findings suggest that teachers in a blended/online format are generally more aware of OER and tend to use OER more.

When comparing differences in OER awareness and use by context (see Table 5.5), we found that the use of OER as both primary (χ^2 (2, N = 1338) = 53.12, $p < 0.001$) and supplementary (χ^2 (2, N = 1442) = 16.18, $p < 0.001$) source yielded a significant difference between teaching context. The findings suggest that K-12 teachers and community college teachers use OER as primary and supplementary sources more than university teachers. Awareness of OER appears to follow a similar trend, but this difference was not significantly different, (χ^2 (2, N = 1484) = 2.38, $p = 0.303$).

Table 5.5 OER awareness and use by teaching context

	Awareness		χ^2 (p value)	Primary source		χ^2 (p value)	Supp. source		χ^2 (p value)
	Yes	No		Yes	No		Yes	No	
Context									
K-12	215 55%	174 45%		185 48%	168 52%		271 71%	109 29%	
Community College	55 55%	45 45%	$\chi^2 = 2.38$ $p = 0.303$	30 34%	57 66%	$\chi^2 = 53.12$ $p < .001*$	65 68%	30 42%	$\chi^2 = 16.18$ $p < 0.001*$
University	507 51%	488 49%		273 30%	625 70%		580 60%	387 40%	

Note: All percentages are rounded to the nearest whole number.

Table 5.6 OER awareness and use by language

	Awareness		χ^2 (p value)	Primary source		χ^2 (p value)	Supp. source		χ^2 (p value)
	Yes	No		Yes	No		Yes	No	
Language									
ESL	161 58%	116 42%	$\chi^2 = 4.54$ $p = 0.033*$	82 33%	167 67%	$\chi^2 = 1.65$ $p = 0.198$	181 67%	90 33%	$\chi^2 = 1.54$ $p = 0.215$
Non-ESL Language	616 51%	591 49%		406 37%	683 63%		735 63%	436 37%	

Note: All percentages are rounded to the nearest whole number.

Finally, when looking at the effect of languages taught on awareness and use of OER (see Table 5.6), we found that more ESL teachers (58%) reported being aware than non-ESL language teachers (51%). This finding is statistically significant, (χ^2 (1, N = 1484) = 4.54, p = 0.033). The use of OER as a primary source (χ^2 (2, N = 1388) = 1.65, p = 0.198) and supplementary source (χ^2 (1, N = 1442) = 1.54, p = 0.215), however, was not significantly different.

Classification and regression tree analysis

Although the chi-squares analyses are informative, they do not provide information on how the variables interact. In other words, although we did not find a significant difference in OER awareness or use when comparing those with more or less than 10 years teaching experience, there may have been a difference in teaching experience among those who taught in the university setting compared to those in a K-12 setting. While there are analysis techniques that would allow us to test this hypothesis (path analysis, multiple linear regression, etc.), such techniques assume that the hypotheses are generated by theory. Furthermore, although interactions can be tested by linear regression analyses, such analyses are limited in the number of interactions that can be tested at once (Strobl et al., 2009). Given that research on OER is relatively new and, in particular, research concerning L2 practitioners' familiarity with OER, we decided to use a classification and regression tree (CART) analysis approach[1] to explore the data. Data mining approaches such as CART analysis do not focus on generalizability and statistical significance. Rather, the goal is to make complex data sets and patterns within data sets more understandable and interpretable (Han & Kamber, 2006). To further explore possible factors that lead to awareness of OER, we created a decision tree with awareness as the outcome variable and teaching context, teaching experience, language taught and teaching format as predictors. Figure 5.1 below illustrates the output for this analysis.

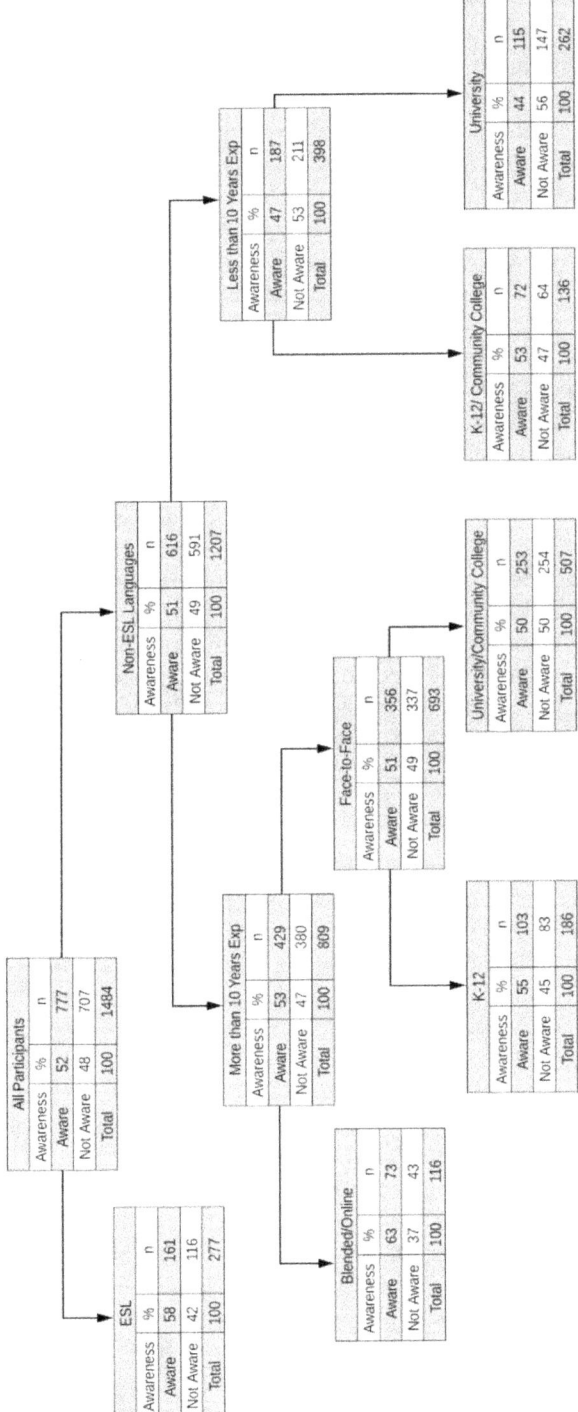

Figure 5.1 Classification and regression tree analysis

The first node labeled 'All Participants' shows that of all the participants who completed our survey, 52% reported being aware of OER compared to 48% who reported not being aware. This CART analysis split this first node by language. Of the survey respondents who teach ESL, 58% reported being aware compared to only 51% of those who teach a non-ESL language. The next split occurred within the non-ESL languages and was by teaching experience. Of those with more than 10 years of teaching experience, 53% reported being aware compared to only 47% of those with less than 10 years of experience. Those who taught a non-ESL language and had less than 10 years teaching experience were further split by teaching context. Of those in a K-12 or community college context, 53% reported being aware of OER compared to 44% of those in a university context. For those who teach a non-ESL language and have more than 10 years of experience, they were further divided by teaching format. Of those in a blended or online environment, 63% reported being aware of OER compared to only 51% in a face-to-face environment. The final split was by teaching context and occurred among those who taught a language other than ESL, who had more than 10 years teaching experience and taught in a face-to-face environment. In these final nodes, of the participants teaching in K-12 settings, 55% reported being aware of OER compared to 50% in a university or community college setting. The implications of these findings, in addition to the findings from the chi-squares analyses, will be further discussed in the Discussion and Conclusion section below.

Research Question 2a. What are the main reasons why language instructors use OER in their courses?

When asked why they choose to use OER in their courses, the FL instructors indicated a number of reasons. The primary reason (35%) for using OER related to the fact that OER addressed aspects of their courses that were not adequately covered elsewhere (e.g. via publisher-produced textbooks). Second most common reason why FL instructors use OER (34%) reflected the idea that OER are more current than publisher-produced materials. The third reason indicated by survey respondents (31%) as to why they use OER in their courses had to do with the fact that OER are easy to find/locate. Figure 5.2 shows the various other reasons why FL instructors use OER in their courses.

To better understand the nature of the OER used by survey respondents, a related survey question asked about the types of OER used by the FL instructors. As can be seen in Figure 5.3, a range of different OER are used. The most common type of OER used were videos (74%), followed by images (72%) and then homework exercises/activities (48%). Other popular types of OER mentioned by the respondents included slides/class presentations, interactive games or simulations, video lectures, assessment resources, among other materials.

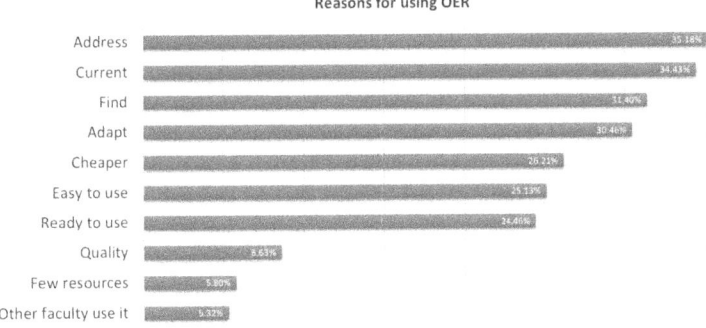

Figure 5.2 Reasons for using OER

Research Question 2b. What are the main reasons why language instructors refrain from using OER in their courses?

Figure 5.4 shows the various reasons why survey respondents do not opt to use OER in their FL courses. The primary deterrent related to the idea that OER are not comprehensive enough compared to publisher-produced materials (39%). That is, given that FL OER oftentimes target one particular aspect of FL learning and teaching (e.g. an activity about a specific cultural or linguistic phenomenon) versus entire FL OER textbooks, this is most likely the reason why respondents saw this as a challenge to using OER in the FL classroom. The second most common deterrent related to the idea that OER are too hard to find (32%). This finding differs with one of the findings in research question 2a. We will explore this seemingly contradictory issue in the Discussion/Conclusion section below. Finally, the third most common deterrent focused on the issue of FL instructors not being sure if they have permission to use the materials that they do find (25%). Various other deterrents were also mentioned.

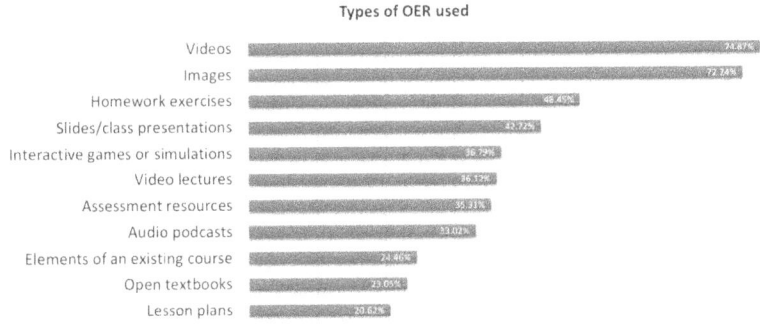

Figure 5.3 Types of OER used by language instructors

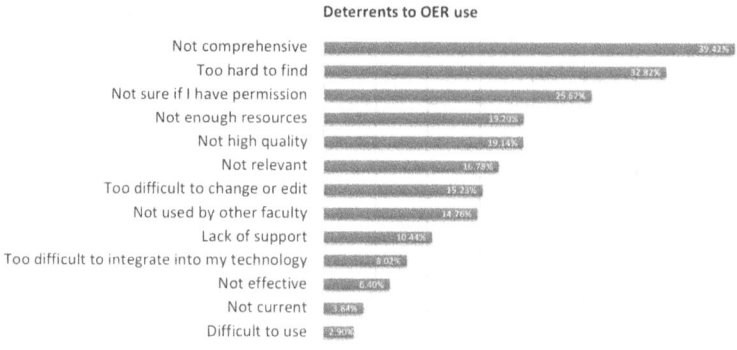

Figure 5.4 Reasons for not using OER

Research Question 3. Have OER changed language instructors' teaching practices?

Data for research question 3 came from the answers of those FL instructors who indicated that they make use of OER in their classes. The specific open-ended survey question was the following: *If you have incorporated OER in your FL or ESL course(s), briefly explain how it has changed your teaching.* Overall, 79% of respondents indicated that the use of OER had indeed changed their teaching, 16% stated that OER have not changed their teaching practices, while 5% of the responses to this question were either off target or did not fit into the aforementioned categories.

Of the 79% who indicated that OER had changed their teaching in some way, the most common type of change mentioned related to the idea that OER are more current, relevant and/or authentic when compared to traditional/publisher-produced materials. One survey respondent summarized this particular kind of change by stating:

> OER have helped me develop a curriculum based on authentic sources. I can also incorporate current events/issues into the curriculum. I teach at the high school level and our text dates back to 1998. I use the textbook for grammar and OER for reading, listening and essay writing. Orals can also be based on a reaction to a current news article or a video.

The second most common theme that emerged in the responses of those FL instructors who indicated that OER have changed their teaching reflected the notion that OER makes their teaching more interesting, engaging and/or interactive for both the FL instructor and their students. One respondent indicated this kind of change when she stated 'Students tend to respond positively to things such as TED talks or other YouTube videos. OER can make my teaching more interesting and dynamic than it would be if I just stuck to the textbook.' The other three types of teaching changes indicated by the FL instructors focused on the issue that OER make teaching more flexible (with many respondents indicating that they use OER when teaching in flipped contexts/classrooms), the ability to use OER to provide for differentiated instruction which, in turn, can more effectively target students' learning outcomes/objectives, as well as the idea that finding and adapting OER can save FL instructors time when prepping for their courses.

Of the 16% who said that OER have not changed their teaching, two primary themes emerged in respondents' answers. First, the most common theme in this category reflected the idea that OER are only viewed and used as supplementary materials and/or tools. One respondent stated 'It has not changed my teaching. These materials have merely augmented the visual or audio materials I use in courses. They add illustrative value, often entertaining, but never the core material.' The second theme from this subset of data focused on the idea that OER are poor quality. It is important to note here that out of the 915 responses to this survey question, only 6 respondents (i.e. less than 1% of responses to this question) indicated that OER did not change their teaching due to poor-quality OER. In sum, an overwhelming majority of FL instructors indicate that OER have changed their teaching practices in positive/helpful ways.

Discussion and Conclusion

The primary purpose of this survey-based study was to gain a better understanding about how the open education movement, as reflected in the development and/or use of OER and the embrace of OEP, is affecting language instructors in the US. In terms of overall awareness, just over half of respondents (52%) indicated that they are aware of OER. This figure is an improvement from a previous survey study (Thoms & Thoms, 2014) that looked at the awareness issue among FL language program directors; only 33% of respondents in that study stated that they knew what OER were and/or used it in their university-level language programs. While the results related to the OER awareness question investigated in this survey project are encouraging, in that they indicate that more language instructors are becoming aware of an important aspect of the open education movement, there are still some segments of language instructors in the US who are more aware than others. The most important variable in determining awareness of OER in our study was related to whether or not a language instructor taught ESL. That is, ESL instructors are more aware of OER when compared to non-ESL language instructors. While respondents' survey responses shed some light on why ESL instructors make use (or not) of OER (see Thoms *et al.*, 2018 for more), a possible reason why ESL instructors are more aware of OER could be related to the fact that there are simply more English-related OER available when compared to non-ESL language OER. However, more research is needed to fully explore if this factor is indeed contributing to ESL instructors being more aware of OER versus their non-ESL counterparts.

Our data also suggest that instructors teaching blended and/or fully online language courses are more aware of OER when compared to their colleagues teaching in traditional face-to-face course contexts. This particular finding is not surprising given the fact that language instructors teaching blended and online courses typically encounter or deal with copyright issues when sharing content with students in a virtual environment. That is, the nature of blended and/or fully online courses are more likely to push instructors to consider a wider variety of teaching materials and tools (Thoms, 2020), many of which are open and don't carry restrictive copyrights thereby making it easier to share with students.

Yet another interesting finding associated with teaching context and its connection to awareness of OER in our data related do the fact that a majority of language instructors working in K-12 and community college contexts are more aware of OER than their colleagues working in universities. In many ways, this result is not surprising due to the fact that many state legislatures across the US have increasingly cut funding to K-12 public schools over the last decade, which means that many K-12 public school districts have fewer resources to dedicate to purchasing current textbooks/ teaching materials for their students (Allen & Seaman, 2017; Bureau of Labor Statistics, 2019). Another possible reason why K-12 language instructors are more aware of OER versus their colleagues working in higher education could be related to efforts such as the *Go Open* initiative supported by the US Department of Education (South *et al*., 2017). *Go Open* is an outreach program for teachers and administrators working in public school districts across the country with an aim to provide training and resources related to OER and to encourage instructors to engage in OEP with their colleagues in their schools/school districts. In sum, the economic realities of working in K-12 and community college environments, coupled with more training opportunities (e.g. via *Go Open*), may result in language instructors working in those contexts to become more aware of OER and embrace various other aspects of the open movement.

Our study has also provided insights about the reasons why (or why not) language instructors make use of OER in their courses along with how OER have changed their teaching practices. One contradictory finding was the fact that respondents indicated that locating OER was both a top reason why language instructors make use of OER in their courses and why they didn't. This unexpected survey result may reflect the wide range of OER and perhaps how different instructors perceive what constitutes OER. Given that some of the most common types of OER used by respondents in this study included videos and images (i.e. multimedia-based OER), it's possible that some language instructors may perceive OER as primarily consisting of videos that are easily found on YouTube and/or images located via various popular repositories of open images (e.g. Flickr, Pixabay). However, some language instructors looking for 'big OER', such as full-length OER textbooks, complete sets of lesson plans, exams or PowerPoint presentations to teach various lexical, grammatical, or culture topics, may experience more difficulty in locating these kinds of text-based materials and therefore may conclude that finding OER is a major deterrent for them. However, no distinction was made in our survey regarding what constitutes as 'big OER' and 'little OER' (Weller, 2010), and therefore it is difficult to fully know why the issue of locating/finding OER was simultaneously viewed as both a reason to use OER and to view that aspect as a deterrent.

Finally, this study has a number of limitations. First, regarding some of the quantitative data analyses, the CART analyses were not used for predictive purposes and thus no other validation measures in regard to the classification tree were run. The findings from this analysis should be seen as hypothesis-generating rather than inferential. Second, it was challenging for the researchers to recruit language instructors working in K-12 educational contexts, as the bulk of survey respondents who participated in the study worked in various post-secondary settings. As such, more research is needed that specifically targets how the open education movement is affecting language instructors working in primary, middle school and high school environments across the US. Third, additional qualitative data via post-survey interviews would have helped to provide more in-depth information about some of the respondents' answers to the various open-ended questions. However, despite these limitations, this survey project has attempted to provide a clearer picture about how open education is affecting language instructors working in a variety of contexts in the US. Hopefully it can serve to spur future research in this area.

Note

(1) CARTs are a nonparametric approach that create a feature space containing all predictor variables and then recursively partitions the space so that observations that have similar values are grouped together (see Strobl *et al.*, 2009 for an introduction to CART analysis).

References

Allen, E. and Seaman, J. (2014) Opening the curriculum: Open educational resources in U.S. higher education. Babson Park, MA: Babson Survey Research Group. See http://onlinelearningsurvey.com/reports/openingthecurriculum2014.pdf

Allen, E. and Seaman, J. (2017) What we teach: K-12 school district curriculum adoption process, 2017. Babson Survey Research Group. See http://onlinelearningsurvey.com/reports/k12oer2017/whatweteach_2017.pdf

Beaven, A., Comas-Quinn, A. and Sawhill, B. (eds) (2013) *Case Studies of Openness in the Language Classroom*. Research-publishing.net. https://research-publishing.net/book?10.14705/rpnet.2013.9781908416100

Beetham, H., Falconer, I., McGill, L. and Littlejohn, A. (2012) Open practices: Briefing paper. *JISC*. See https://oersynth.pbworks.com/w/page/51668352/OpenPractices Briefing

Blyth, C. (2013) Opening up foreign language education with OER: The case of *Français interactif*. In F. Rubio and J. Thoms (eds) *Hybrid Language Teaching and Learning: Exploring Theoretical, Pedagogical and Curricular Issues* (pp. 196–218). Boston: Heinle Cengage.

Blyth, C. (2017) Open educational resources (OERs) for language learning. In S. Thorne and S. May (eds) *Language, Education and Technology* (pp. 169–180). Cham, Switzerland: Springer.

Bureau of Labor Statistics. (2019, January 2) U.S. Department of Labor. See https://www.bls.gov/opub/ted/2016/college-tuition-and-fees-increase-63-percent-since-january-2006.htm

Butcher, N. (2011) *A Basic Guide to Open Educational Resources (OER)*. Vancouver: Commonwealth of Learning.

Cape Town Open Education Declaration (2008) See http://www.capetowndeclaration.org/read-the-declaration

Center on Budget and Policy Priorities (2016, January) Most states have cut school funding, and some continue cutting. See https://www.cbpp.org/research/state-budget-and-tax/most-states-have-cut-school-funding-and-some-continue-cutting

Charmaz, K. (2006) *Constructing Grounded Theory: A Practical Guide Through Qualitative Analysis*. Thousand Oaks, CA: SAGE. See https://www.cbpp.org/research/state-budget-and-tax/most-states-have-cut-school-funding-and-some-continue-cutting

Cummings, A., Conroy, K. and Hildebrandt, S. (2017) Student teachers and CALL: Personal and pedagogical uses and beliefs. *Calico* (34) 3, 336–354.

de los Arcos, B. and Weller, M. (2018) A tale of two globes: Exploring the north/south divide in engagement with OER. In U. Herb and J. Schöpfel (eds) *Open Divide: Critical Studies on Open Access* (pp. 147–156). Sacramento, CA: Litwin Books.

De los Arcos, B., Faems, B., Comas-Quinn, A. and Pulker, H. (2017) Teachers' use and acceptance of gamification and social networking features of an open repository. *European Journal of Open, Distance and E-learning* 20 (1), 126–137.

Han, J. and Kamber, M. (2006) *Data Mining: Concepts and Techniques*. New York: Morgan Kaufman.

Herb, U. and Schöpfel, J. (2018) *Open Divide: Critical Studies on Open Access*. Sacramento, CA: Library Juice Press.

Jhangiani, R. and Biswas-Diener, R. (eds) (2017) *Open: The Philosophy and Practices that are Revolutionizing Education and Science*. London: Ubiquity Press.

Jhangiani, R. and DeRosa, R. (2017) Open pedagogy. In E. Mays (ed.) *A Guide to Making Open Textbooks with Students* (pp. 6–21). Montreal: The Rebus Community for Open Textbook Creation.

Kessler, G. (2018) Technology and the future of language teaching. *Foreign Language Annals* 51, 205–218.

Open Education (2017, October 13) See https://sparcopen.org/open-education/

Open Education Consortium (n.d.) About the open education consortium. See https://www.oeconsortium.org/about-oec/

Rubio, F., Fuchs, C. and Dixon, E. (2016) Language MOOCs: Better by design. In E. Martín-Monje (ed.) *Technology-Enhanced Language Learning for Specialized Domains: Practical Applications and Mobility*. London: Routledge.

South, J., Stevens, K. and Peters, K. (2017) #GoOpen district launch packet. Washington, D.C.: U.S. Department of Education, Office of Educational Technology. See https://tech.ed.gov/open/districts/launch/

Strobl, C., Malley, J. and Tutz, G. (2009) An introduction to recursive partitioning: Rationale, application, and characteristics of classification and regression trees, bagging, and random forests. *Psychological Methods* 14 (4), 323–348.

Thoms, J. (2020) Re-envisioning L2 hybrid and online courses as digital open learning and teaching environments: Responding to a changing world. *Second Language Research and Practice* 1, 86–98.

Thoms, J. and Thoms, B. (2014) Open educational resources in the United States: Insights from university foreign language directors. *System* 45, 138–146.

Thoms, J., Arshavskaya, E. and Poole, F. (2018) Open educational resources and ESL education: Insights from educators in the United States, *Teaching English as a Second Language (TESL-EJ)* 22 (2), 1–24.

Weller, M. (2010) Big and little OER. In: OpenED2010: Seventh Annual Open Education Conference, 2–4 Nov 2010, Barcelona, Spain. See http://oro.open.ac.uk/24702/2/926FFABC.pdf

Weller, M., de los Arcos, B., Farrow, R., Pitt, R. and McAndrew, P. (2017) What can OER do for me? Evaluating the claims for OER. In R. Jhangiani and R. Biswas-Diener (eds) *Open: The Philosophy and Practices that are Revolutionizing Education and Science* (pp. 67–77). London: Ubiquity Press. DOI: https://doi.org/10.5334/bbc.e.

Whyte, S. (2016) From 'solitary thinkers' to 'social actors': OER in multilingual CALL teacher education. *ALSIC Revue* 19 (1). See https://alsic.revues.org/2906

Zourou, K. (2016) Social networking affordances for open educational practice. *ALSIC Revue* 19 (1). https://journals.openedition.org/alsic/2903

Appendix 5.1: Survey Questions

NOTE: Some of the questions in the survey were adapted/used from Allen and Seaman (2014).

Background information

(1) What is your gender?
(2) What is your age?
(3) In what state is your primary academic institution located? NOTE: If you work for a multi-state or virtual/online institution, please select the state from which you most often work.
(4) What language do you currently teach?
(5) What is the highest degree that you possess?
(6) How many years have you been teaching foreign language(s) or ESL?
(7) Considering the three different teaching environments described below (i.e. face-to-face, blended/hybrid, and online), which one best describes the context in which you have taught your FL or ESL during the most recent academic year?
(8) From the options below, choose the one that best describes the educational context where you teach your FL or ESL. If you teach in more than one context (e.g. in a high school AND at a local community college or university), choose the one where you teach most often.
(9) Do you/your students use a traditional, publisher-produced text in the FL or ESL course(s) that you teach at your institution?

Open educational resources (OER)

The following questions focus on open educational resources (OER). OER have been defined as 'any educational resources (including curriculum maps, course materials, textbooks, streaming videos, multimedia applications, podcasts and any other materials that have been designed for use in teaching and learning) that are openly available for use by educators and students, without an accompanying need to pay royalties or license fees' (Butcher, 2011). Compared to traditional copyrighted materials/tools, OER are open in that they typically can be shared, edited, modified or remixed depending on one's specific educational context/needs.

(10) How aware are you of OER?
(11) In thinking about the FL or ESL course(s) you teach, indicate how often you have used OER as (a) primary course material, and (b) supplementary material?
(12) What are the top three reasons why you use OER resources in your class(es)?
(13) Indicate whether or not you have used any of the following types of OER resources in your FL or ESL class(es): videos; audio podcasts; images; interactive games or simulations; video lectures/tutorials; assessment resources (e.g. texts or quizzes); open textbooks or chapters from textbooks; homework exercises; slides and class presentations; elements of an existing course (e.g. a module/unit); lesson plans; any other type.
(14) How would you compare the quality of open resources to that of traditional (i.e. publisher-produced/copyrighted) resources on the following dimensions: cost; proven to improve student performance; includes all the materials I need; high-quality and factually correct; covers my FL sufficiently; mapped to learning outcomes; current and up-to-date; easy to use; materials are rated/reviewed by faculty or editors; adaptable/editable.
(15) How would you rate the ease of searching for educational resources for your FL or ESL class(es)?
(16) What are the three most important deterrents to using OER in your classes?
(17) If you have incorporated OER in your FL or ESL course(s), briefly explain how it has changed your teaching.
(18) Do you think you will use/rely on OER more than traditional, publisher-produced content/texts in the next three years in the course(s) that you teach? Why or why not?
(19) Would you like to be re-directed to a page where you can provide your contact information in order to be entered into a drawing to receive one of ten $50 Amazon gift certificates for having completed this survey?

Appendix 5.2: Languages Taught by Survey Respondents

Spanish: 35.4%
English as a Second Language: 17.6%
French: 16.5%
German: 9.3%
Italian: 4.0%
Chinese: 3.9%
Japanese: 2.8%
Russian: 2.4%
Other (various languages): 1.9%
Arabic: 1.8%
Portuguese: 1.5%
Latin: 1.1%
Korean: 0.7%
Hindi: 0.3%
Polish: 0.2%
Danish: 0.1%
Finnish: 0.1%
Greek: 0.1%
Hebrew: 0.1%
Swahili: 0.1%
Vietnamese: 0.1%

6 Raising the Curtain on OER/OEP: Opening Pathways from Awareness to Engagement in a Graduate Course on Foreign Language Program Direction

Beatrice Dupuy

Thoms and Thoms (2014) reported that many Language Program Directors (LPDs) were unfamiliar with the term 'open educational resources' (OER) and unclear about how to find and use them. They suggested that education and active engagement could trigger change. This chapter reports the findings of a study conducted in an online graduate course focused on language program direction. The goals of this study were to examine the potential impact of a course unit on OER/OEP and an OER-based project on increasing both awareness and knowledge about these materials and practices in graduate students. Findings indicate that while study participants had heard about OER prior to the start of the study, levels of use, authoring and sharing ranged from non-existent to extensive. Completing coursework on OER/OEP contributed to increase all study participants' awareness about OER/OEP and the final project, by allowing them to engage in the design of an OER-based resource for LPDs that they shared publicly and helped them realize that they too can be actors in the OER/OEP movement. However, the findings also reveal the need for more education and hands-on experience with OER/OEP among future LPDs if we want to see the proverbial needle move in the direction of embracing and actively using OER and engaging in OEP in foreign language programs. The chapter concludes by suggesting ways in which L2 researchers and educators can build on the results presented.

Introduction

Open educational resources (OER) awareness and adoption levels among faculty in higher education have steadily increased over the past decade. While this is certainly cause for optimism, these levels still remain relatively low. According to the Babson Research Group Report (Seaman & Seaman, 2017), only 30% of US faculty indicate that they are 'very aware' to 'aware' of OER and 47% report that they are 'very aware' to 'aware' of Creative Commons licensing. Surveyed faculty underscore that affordances such as low cost and flexibility make OER particularly appealing. However, the effort it takes to find materials and evaluate their suitability and quality continue to be major roadblocks to higher levels of OER adoption and implementation. Similar results were reported three years earlier by Thoms and Thoms in their 2014 study in which they investigated OER awareness and adoption levels in a more targeted group, namely collegiate foreign language (FL) program directors (LPD) in the US. To remedy the situation and promote OER and open educational practices (OEP), open education advocates call for sustained education, active engagement and appropriate support in OEP as the way forward to attract new adopters (Blyth & Dalola, 2016; Kurek, 2016; MacKinnon *et al.*, 2016; Whyte, 2016; Zourou, 2016). With increased OER experience, it is hypothesized that new adopters will start to create their own materials, by possibly remixing several OER initially, and sharing them with colleagues using an appropriate Creative Commons license (Weller *et al.*, 2015). Open education advocates also recognize the power of social networks to sustain increased user participation through OER adoption and repurposing which is considered central for OEP expansion (Zourou, 2016). Among the many questions left to answer is how teacher education coursework and professional development experiences should be structured to establish connections between knowledge and practice to increase adoption and integration of OER and engagement in OEP by future LPDs.

Literature Review

Materials in foreign language education

Although LPDs frequently lament language textbooks' shortcomings, namely that 'they are conservative and generic and thus ill fitted to a given institution's particular (and actual) needs' (Blyth & Davis, 2007: 177), textbooks remain central to instruction and learning in US collegiate FL programs. Whether it is a lack of time on the part of LPDs, the need for consistency in large, lower-level multi-section courses which are often taught by graduate student instructors (GSIs) who juggle the demands of graduate study and teaching, or the sense that the textbooks' content defines what is 'legitimate knowledge' (e.g. Nunan, 1991; Ghosn, 2003; Guerrettaz & Johnston, 2013) that can best explain the status quo, it remains that textbooks hold unique authority and power in FL programs and have a tremendous impact on what happens in the FL classroom. For example, Guerrettaz and Johnston's article (2013) provides insight into the deterministic role textbooks have on actual practice: the content taught, the activities selected, the discourse of the classroom, the pace of the class, the completion of quizzes and tests as a measure of success and progress, and the instructional choices made in the classroom. In other words, textbooks shape programmatic curricular goals, provide the content to be taught and recommend the ways it ought to be taught and assessed (Byrnes, 1998). As they consider the current FL teaching and learning landscape, Rossomondo and Lord (2018) ask the following question: 'The world is not flat, so why are our textbooks?'. Blyth and Davis (2007: 177) argue that 'the structure of commercial academic publishing actually inhibits innovation and results in materials that are not particularly learner-centered or user-friendly' and that 'locally produced digital materials' are one way in which innovation can be brought about. Friss (2018) echoes Blyth and Davis and suggests that 'to transform the focus, design and medium of "flat textbooks" is, ironically, for instructors to just slow down by adopting the principles of the Slow Movement and authoring "well-rounded" digital teaching materials either individually or, ideally, by teaming up' (2018: 258). He further underscores the benefits of this approach for novice GSIs whose professional learning cannot just be left 'to distant editorial teams at publishing houses' (2018: 258). Although Friss does not mention OER specifically, his advocacy for growing 'local, seasonal, sustainable, non-corporate and organic' (2018: 259) materials seems to align well with the core values of the OER/OEP movement and those of education as a whole.

Affordances of OER and Foreign Language Education

The bulk of the literature on the affordances of OER has primarily focused on their phenomenal cost-saving potential in the face of the rising costs of textbooks. Access to cheaper or no-cost materials can be of tremendous benefit to students, parents, instructors and institutions. It is reported that in the 2017–2018 academic year, undergraduate students spent about $1200 on books and supplies, with new and used textbooks costing respectively $80 and $50 on average (College Board, 2018). Evidence shows that adopting OER can cut the amount students spend on books and supplies substantially if not eliminate costs completely. In the current US context where soaring college tuition and student debt are making the headlines, it is easy to understand why the cost savings of OER have captured the attention of many stakeholders.

Another key benefit of OER for both instructors and students is the flexibility that open materials offer when compared to traditional copyrighted materials produced by an increasingly small group of very large publishers and the promise they hold for a power shift. Masuhara (2011) describes two trends that have recently contributed to increasing the power of commercial textbooks, namely the widening gap between producers and consumers, and the increasing reliance on these materials to give shape and direction to language programs and courses. She argues for the need to empower FL educators so that they can be in a better position to counter these trends. OER that carry Creative Commons licenses allow users to engage in the '5R' activities (Figure 6.1) which represent the affordances, practices and possibilities of working with OER and offer a framework for OEP.

What the '5R' activities mean for LPDs and FL instructors is that they do not have to settle for a one size fits all approach to instruction. Instead, these activities give them the option to use and author materials that meet the specific needs of their educational context and replace the 'flat' learning experience offered by textbook materials. OER present a real opportunity for instructors to become active and visible participants in the construction of user-generated materials. Such locally produced materials often incorporate textual content that goes beyond students' immediate world with the goal of engaging them in critical analysis while facilitating their linguistic development (Allen & Paesani, 2010; Byrnes, 1998, 2001; Kern, 2000; Paesani et al., 2016; Swaffar & Arens, 2005). OER not only make it possible for recent applied linguistic research to inform the development of instructional materials, they can also support long-term professional learning within a community of practice where faculty members, GSIs, undergraduate students co-design pedagogical content and share it openly online. Blyth (2017) provides two concrete examples in the US context. One is *Français interactif*, an online first-year French program grounded in the notion of language as communicative practice, which was developed by more than 30 developers: faculty members, GSIs and

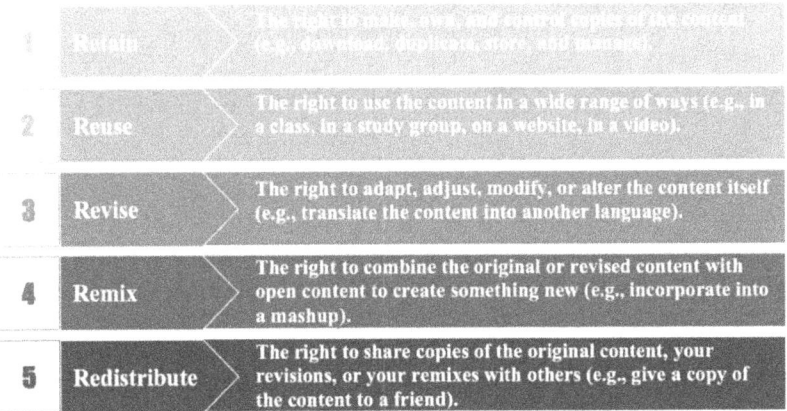

Figure 6.1 '5R' activities (Wiley, 2015)

undergraduate students from the Department of French & Italian at the University of Texas at Austin. Contributing to curriculum development by designing new materials and testing them in the classes they teach provided GSIs with useful professional learning. Another example is *Acceso*, a second-year Spanish program designed at the University of Kansas to foster the development of translingual and transcultural competence as recommended by the 2007 Modern Language Association (MLA) report, also involved faculty members and GSIs (Rossomondo, 2011). Through supervised experience in curriculum and materials design, *Acceso* contributed to the professional learning of the GSIs who overwhelmingly (94%) reported a positive impact on their teaching. More recently, Zapata (2020) examined an OER faculty–graduate student collaboration in a book sprint experience and found that GSIs had an overall positive experience and benefitted in the following ways: they learned more about OER; they reviewed and applied knowledge developed in previous coursework; they became authors; and they enhanced their teaching practices. Such collaborations, and the shared resources that result from them, have the potential to break long-standing barriers between various constituencies within foreign language and literature departments, unify and strengthen the curriculum and approaches to teaching, and foster a sense of ownership by all stakeholders (Allen & Paesani, 2010; Byrnes, 2001).

While evidence of innovation on multiple levels can be found in the projects briefly described above, Thoms and Thoms (2014: 140) underscore the fact that science, technology, engineering and mathematics (STEM) faculty continue to be the leaders in OER use and that there are two to three times more entries for the STEM categories in popular OER repositories than there are for the arts, humanities and social sciences. Lack of OER awareness, unfamiliarity with the open Creative Commons license, and time constraints were three of the main roadblocks identified by their study participants and could explain why fewer OER are available in these disciplines.

In light of these study results, more information is needed to find out what FL GSIs, the next generation of FL faculty members, including LPDs, know and believe about OER and OEP and how they might use OER and engage in OEP. Conducted in an online graduate course on language program direction, this study aimed to examine what new knowledge future LPDs enrolled in an online course on FL program direction developed after completing a course unit on OER/OEP and how they applied their new knowledge to shape a final class project whose goal was to develop a digital OER-based resource site meant to support the programmatic needs of LPDs.

Conceptual Frameworks

Two conceptual frameworks guided this study: sociocultural theory and pedagogical content knowledge.

As a framework, sociocultural theory (SCT) has not only been used for investigating language-learning processes but also for studying teacher cognition and professional development in a variety of contexts (e.g. Johnson & Golombek, 2011). SCT-based perspectives on teacher learning and professional development underscore that knowledge building is situated, is inherently a dynamic process of social interaction, and is co-constructed through mediational tools, which can be best understood as 'signs and symbols, interpersonal relations and individual activities' (Kozulin, 1995: 120). Johnson (2009) explained that teacher learning is highly dependent on the availability of 'multiple and sustained opportunities for dialogic mediation, scaffolded learning and assisted performance as they participate in and learn about relevant aspects of their professional worlds' (2009: 4–5).

Teachers' underlying knowledge base of teaching, broadly conceived as all profession-related insights relevant to their activities, includes not only both subject matter (content) knowledge and general knowledge of instructional approaches (pedagogical knowledge) as core elements but also specific subject matter teaching knowledge which is referred to as pedagogical content knowledge (PCK). PCK has been used as a framework to design teacher education programs and professional development opportunities. It includes curricular knowledge, knowledge and beliefs about learning and learners, knowledge of general and specific contexts and knowledge of instructional strategies for teaching particular topics and achieving particular goals (Grossman, 1989, 1990; Shulman, 1986, 1987; Shulman & Shulman, 2004). It can be acquired from a range of sources including subject matter knowledge, models for teaching specific topics teachers experienced as learners (Lortie, 1975), and subject-specific teacher education courses like the one in which the participants in this study were enrolled. According to Shulman (1987), PCK 'represents the blending of content and pedagogy into an understanding of how particular topics, problems, or issues are organized, represented and adapted to the diverse interests and abilities of learners, and presented for instruction' (1987: 8). As such, subject-matter teacher education coursework that fosters connection and integration can play a central role in helping learners acquire pedagogical content knowledge, a core element of the knowledge base of teaching.

Context and Methods

Research questions

This study sought answers to the following questions:

(1) What did study participants know about OER/OEP before completing a course unit on OER/OEP? Had they used OER and engaged in OEP? If so, what benefits and challenges did they report about these materials and practices?

(2) What new knowledge about OER/OEP did study participants develop as a result of completing a course unit on OER/OEP?
(3) How did study participants approach the creation of their OER-based LPD resource sites? How did their newly developed knowledge help them shape these? What kinds of resources did they select and/or author?
(4) What new practices did study participants engage in while creating their OER-based LPD resource sites? What new realizations about OER and OEP did they come to and what challenges did they encounter while creating their OER-based LPD resource site?

Study Site

This study was conducted at a large, public research university in the Southwestern US in a semester-long online graduate course focused on directing collegiate FL programs which is part of an online graduate certificate in language program direction and evaluation. The course started with a general introduction to language program direction (Week 1) followed by four sequential thematic modules: (1) LPD work and issues in language program direction (Weeks 2 & 3); (2) Program development and evaluation (Weeks 4, 5, 6, 7 & 8); (3) Course Development (Weeks 9, 10, 11 & 12); (4) TA professional learning (Weeks 13 & 15); and concluded with LPDs as agents of innovation (Week 16). Each module was divided into pertinent weekly topical units. The core text for the course was Lord's *Language Program Direction: Theory and Practice* (2014) which was supplemented by recent professional literature, webinars and other web resources. Unit assignments to be completed either individually or in groups using digital platforms and tools included: a statement of language program administration leadership which was peer-reviewed, weekly readings which students discussed online, bi-weekly 'Dilemmas: Got Solutions' scenarios to which students responded drawing from both course content and professional experience, end of module reflective blog posts, a LPD interview report and a final class project which consisted of the creation of a digital OER-based resource site to support LPD work and supplement the core text used in the course, and a reflective essay. Recent teacher education research demonstrates that courses that encourage knowledge integration by engaging students in solving real educational problems can produce the kinds of deep understandings they need to become adept users of particular tools and strategies in their teaching (Comas-Quinn & Fitzgerald, 2013; Whyte, 2016). The following prompt was provided to guide students as they planned their final class project:

> Based on the readings you did this semester and the information you gathered during your interviews with LPDs, you will develop an OER-based resource site to assist LPDs and GSIs with their work and supplement the core text for this course. For this resource site you will redistribute, revise, remix and/or author OER that they could potentially

use for program development, program evaluation, or GSI professional learning and provide guidelines on how the OER could potentially be used. Please make sure to license the OER you author. The requirements for this resource site include: 1) a targeted collection of at least 20 OER including brief descriptions and 'how to use' guidelines for each, 2) a companion 10-reference annotated bibliography built on open access literature that LPDs could use to develop expertise in the chosen focus of the resource site and 3) a 2-page reflective essay on your experience putting this resource site together and the value you see in OER/OEP.

Before students started planning and creating their digital OER-based LPD resource site, they completed Module 3 on Course Development which included four units presented in this sequence: *Course Syllabi, Choosing instructional materials for the lower-level FL program, OER and digital technology in language teaching and learning, and Supporting language teaching and learning with technology.* Table 6.1 provides an

Table 6.1 Course materials and schedule of assignments

Week 11	*OER and digital technology in language teaching and learning*
Webinar	• Joshua Thoms – How to equip language teachers with updated and effective textbooks? (https://www.youtube.com/watch?v=2_AHu4N5T3w&feature=emb_logo)
Core Readings	• Blyth, C. (2009) From textbook to online materials: The changing ecology of foreign language publishing in the era of digital technology. In M. Evans (ed.) *Foreign Language Learning with Digital Technology* (pp. 179–202). London: Continuum. • Borthwick, K. and Gallagher-Brett, A. (2014) Inspiration, ideas, encouragement: Teacher development and improved use of technology in language teaching through open educational practice. *Computer Assisted Language Learning* 27, 163–183.
Additional Readings	• Blyth, C. (2013) LCTLs and technology: The promise of open education. *Language Learning & Technology* 17, 1–6. • Dixon, E. and Hondo, J. (2014) Re-purposing an OER for the online language course: A case study of Deutsch Interaktiv by the Deutsche Welle. *Computer Assisted Language Learning* 27, 109–121.
Assignments	• OER/OEP survey (completed Week 10) • Reading discussion forum post (completed Week 11) • End of module blog post (completed Week 11) • Dilemma! Got solutions? (completed Week 12) *It is often the case that instructors will be reluctant to share with other instructors, resources that they have created. They may feel that they have put in a lot of thought and energy into a resource and want to keep the fruit of their work for themselves; they may be concerned that they might not be recognized for their work; they may not want to be criticized; they may be protective of the resource they created and do not want it to be changed. How could introducing instructors to OER help mitigate some of these issues and convince instructors in your program of the benefits of open education?* • Final class project and reflective essay (completed Week 16)
Resources	After students had responded to the OER/OEP survey, various resources selected on the basis of students' responses, were linked to in the LMS used in the course. For example: LRC portal; MERLOT II; LORO; OER Commons; Creative Commons, etc.

overview of the course materials for the *OER and digital technology in language teaching and learning* unit, the assignments students completed before, during and after this unit, and a timeline of their completion dates.

Participants

Six students were enrolled in the course and were consented by a third party via email since the researcher was also the course instructor. Three students (Javier, Maia and Veronika, all pseudonyms) gave permission to have their survey responses and written work (reading discussion forum posts, end of module blog posts, reflective essays) included in this study. It is unknown to the researcher why the other three students did not give consent. It is surmised that email checking habits and attitude toward research might have played a role. Sending out a pre-notification email and especially a reminder might have increased participation in the study.

They were all in their late 20s (Javier and Maia) to early 30s (Veronika), were all international and had some experience teaching a FL at the post-secondary level. They were also very well versed in their subject matter. Javier was in the second and final year of a MA in applied linguistics, Maia was a first-year PhD student in applied linguistics and Veronika was a PhD candidate in language and literacy education. Although all study participants indicated they had heard the term OER prior to the beginning of the study, only one had heard the term OEP. Furthermore, their level of OER use and authoring, and OEP experience varied greatly. A summary of the participant demographics is provided in Table 6.2.

Data Collection

SCT principles informed this mixed methods study (Creswell, 2015). Five data sources were collected sequentially over a period of four weeks during the second half of the course in which study participants were enrolled in Spring 2018 and were used to answer the four main research questions investigated in this study (see Table 6.3). The five data sources

Table 6.2 Participant demographics

Participants	Have language teaching experience	Self-reported knowledge of OER and OEP		Self-reported use of OER and OEP		
		Heard of OER	Heard of OEP	Use OER	Author OER	Use OEP
Javier	Yes	x				
Maia	Yes	x	X	x	x	x
Veronika	Yes	x		x		

Table 6.3 Summary research questions and data collected

	Research questions	Data set
RQ1	What did study participants know about OER/OEP before completing a course unit on OER/OEP? Had they used OER and engaged in OEP? If so, what benefits and challenges did they report about these materials and practices?	Closed and open-ended survey questions
RQ2	What new knowledge about OER/OEP did study participants develop as a result of completing a course unit on OER/OEP?	Reading discussion forum posts; 'Dilemmas: Got Solutions' scenarios, end of module reflective blog posts
RQ3	How did study participants approach the creation of their OER-based LPD resource sites? How did their newly developed knowledge help them shape these? What kinds of resources did they select and/or author?	LPD resource sites; reflective essays
RQ4	What new practices did study participants engage in while creating their OER-based LPD resource site? What new realizations about OER and OEP did they come to and what challenges did they encounter while creating their OER-based LPD resource site??	LPD resource sites; reflective essays

included: (1) responses to closed and open-ended questions in an online survey which was distributed to students before the start of the unit on *OER and digital technology in language teaching and learning* as a way of ascertaining whether they knew or not the terms OER and OEP and had used OER and engaged in OEP, and if they had, what benefits and challenges they experienced with each; (2) reading discussion forum posts related to the literature that had been selected for this course unit; (3) recommendations made to the 'Dilemmas: Got Solutions' scenario; (4) end-of-module reflective blog posts; and (5) reflective essays on the process of creating the digital OER-based LPD resource site, including the challenges they had encountered in the process.

Data Analysis

Given the small size of the participant pool, only raw numbers were reported in the quantitative data analysis. For the qualitative data analysis, once the extraction of data segments in which study participants discussed OER and OEP was completed, the researcher read them through to develop a coding scheme which reflected the focus of the study's research questions. Code definitions (see Appendix 6.1) and sample data segments were then identified to exemplify each one. To ensure intra-rater reliability, the researcher carried out a second read through three months later, coding the qualitative data using the established coding scheme one more time. Both sets of coded segments were then compared and cross-referenced to check for any discrepancies which were few (Cohen's Kappa coefficient: 0.93). Triangulation among the various data sources was used to strengthen the findings.

Working Definitions of OER and OEP

In the survey, students were initially asked whether they had heard of OER and OEP and if so, to define them as a way to ascertain their knowledge levels but also to find out what aspects were most salient to them. Subsequently, a working definition for both OER and OEP was provided to ensure that all respondents would have a common understanding of both terms before continuing on with the OER/OEP-specific questions included in the rest of the survey. While the term was adopted and defined at a UNESCO meeting in 2002, the definition provided by Butcher (2015) was chosen for its specificity and clarity. OER are 'any educational resources (including curriculum maps, course materials, textbooks, streaming videos, multimedia applications, podcasts and any other materials that have been designed for use in teaching and learning) that are openly available for use by educators and students, without an accompanying need to pay royalties or license fees' (2015: 5). OEP was defined as 'the range of practices around the creation, use and management of open educational resources with the intent to improve quality and innovate in education' (Andrade *et al.*, 2011: 4).

Findings

Study results are presented in the order the research questions were presented in Table 6.3.

A starting point: Study participants' knowledge about and experience with OER and OEP (RQ1)

The survey distributed before students started the unit on *OER and digital technology in language teaching and learning* allowed the researcher to gauge their knowledge of OER and level of engagement in OEP and gauge the level and nature of the support they might need for their final project. When asked whether they had heard of the terms open educational resources and open educational practices, all three participants indicated that they had. They had heard these terms in courses they had taken (Maia and Veronika), at conferences/workshops they had attended (Maia and Veronika) and/or through colleagues (Javier and Veronika). As a follow-up and a way to gauge study participants' knowledge level about these two terms, OER/OEP-aware respondents were given the opportunity to define both terms. Javier defined OER as 'resources instructors and students can access for free', explaining further that OER are 'not private, subject to a fee, published and administered by a publisher' (*survey response*). Veronika stated that OER are 'free resources available via the internet', further specifying that 'these resources are not based on one existing set of materials, but rather adopt various activities and materials for a group of students and a specific context' (*survey response*). Maia's more expert knowledge about OER came through her technical definition in which she explained that OER are 'educational resources usually covered by a Creative Commons (CC) license (or a similar one). Depending on the type of the CC license applied to the resource, an individual might be able to modify the material, distribute it or use it for commercial or non-commercial purposes' (*survey response*). Only Maia was familiar with OEP, Javier and Veronika indicated they were not. Javier surmised that 'it must have to do with the practice of using OER' (*survey response*).

Indicating familiarity with the term OER, however, does not necessarily lead to active use or authoring. In the survey, two study participants (Maia and Veronika) reported that they use OER in the courses they teach and that their chosen OER are used as supplementary materials to the coursebook in use rather than primary materials. The most common types of OER Maia and Veronika reported using were lesson plans, slides, images and videos. They both explained that what influences them to select an OER over another is that (1) the content can be easily adapted, closely followed by and in this order, (2) it is up-to-date, (3) it promotes interaction, (4) it meets student needs better (Maia and Veronika) and (5) aligns with program learning outcomes. When asked to compare the value and usefulness of OER to textbook materials for L2 teaching and learning, the following four aspects were highlighted: (1) OER are more authentic (Maia); (2) they provide more current, interesting and interactive content (Maia and Veronika); (3) they allow to expand the range of topics typically found in coursebooks (Maia).

Using and sharing OER depends largely on the degree of familiarity and experience one has with OER societies and organizations and the licensing structure. In the survey, two study participants (Maia and Veronika) reported that they were familiar with Creative Commons, MERLOT II, MIT OpenCourseware and Open Learning Initiative among others. Two study participants (Maia and Javier) indicated that they had considered their university library as a resource for finding or authoring OER, however, only one (Maia) was aware of the OER-related outreach done by her university library. The unit on *OER and digital technology in language teaching and learning* happened to overlap with Open Education Week and a number of campus events had been scheduled.

Two study participants (Maia and Veronika) mentioned authoring OER and one (Maia) reported that she had shared a number of them on MERLOT II. The top three motivating factors for authoring OER reported by these study participants included: (1) a strong belief in the OER movement and the need to support it not only through use but also authoring and sharing (Maia); (2) a desire to better meet student needs (Maia and Veronika); (3) a focus on reducing the cost of education for students (Maia).

While highlighting the benefits of OER, Maia and Veronika also commented that finding quality OER that meet their particular course(s) needs often proves challenging. One other challenge with OER noted by Maia is related to 'finding out whether such digital materials are really open to use' (*survey response*). Maia explained that 'some of the resources found on websites like MERLOT are uploaded by random people. Therefore, you need to be careful in selecting those materials that can actually be reused' (*survey response*). Not only could finding quality OER be challenging, but Maia and Veronika also reported that authoring OER could be challenging as well. Among the challenges mentioned by these study participants were (1) lack of time (Maia and Veronika), (2) uncertainty about licensing (Veronika) and (3) lack of feedback (Veronika). Veronika indicated that receiving feedback on her authored OER, namely their quality and effectiveness, would let her know whether her contributions are of value and would prompt her to make further contributions. The open license structure was also not entirely clear to Veronika. Javier indicated that his lack of awareness about OER repositories and understanding of the open license structure were barriers to using and authoring OER. He further reported that if it were not the case he would definitely use and author OER. All three participants admitted that they wish they knew more about OER and OEP, even Maia, and Javier expressed the desire 'to have more hands-on opportunities' (*survey response*).

Study participants' responses to the survey give us a good indication of what they knew and thought about OER and OEP at the start of the study and whether they were actively using or authoring OER and engaging in OEP. Interestingly many of their responses were not that different from those reported by LPDs in Thoms and Thoms' study (2014) in that the participants in this study also indicated that their use of OER was largely motivated by the fact that they are more up to date, more authentic, more relevant and as such, are better able to serve the needs of the learners they teach. In this study too, participants reported that finding and creating appropriate OER are challenging and time consuming.

On course: Study participants' development of new knowledge after completing a unit on OER/OEP (RQ2)

As indicated by its name, OEP is at its core a social activity embedded in its local context and mediated by tools with OER being created, (re) used in innovative ways for the purpose of cutting the cost of education and raising the quality of instruction, and shared through an open structure. In the spaces (forum, Dilemmas: Got Solutions and blog) where OER and OEP were discussed during the unit on *OER and digital technology in language teaching and learning*, study participants engaged with several of these dimensions which they either only touched on briefly (e.g. cost savings) or did not bring up at all (e.g. empowerment of teachers and learners) in their survey responses.

All three participants actively discussed the cost-saving nature of OER and the opportunity for teachers to have greater involvement in materials creation. For example, Javier wrote the following comment:

> When I think about my context, public education in a developing country, I realize – and well, I know this firsthand – how expensive textbooks can be. Many of my students did not have the financial resources to pay for a book that is extremely expensive. Knowing that these students could use resources for free for their courses makes me feel confident that it could lessen their stress. In fact, they could even play a meaningful role in creating such materials. *(reading discussion forum post)*

In this post Javier is starting to realize how OER/OEP could play a role in the drive to democratize tertiary education in his home country and to see how student-teachers in his program could become social actors. In a post in that same reading discussion forum, Maia embedded a photo of a large white board placed at the entrance of her institutional library which she had taken during Open Education Week. It invited students to finish the following sentence posted at the top: 'If I didn't have to buy textbooks, I could …' (Figure 6.2). With the photo, Maia included the

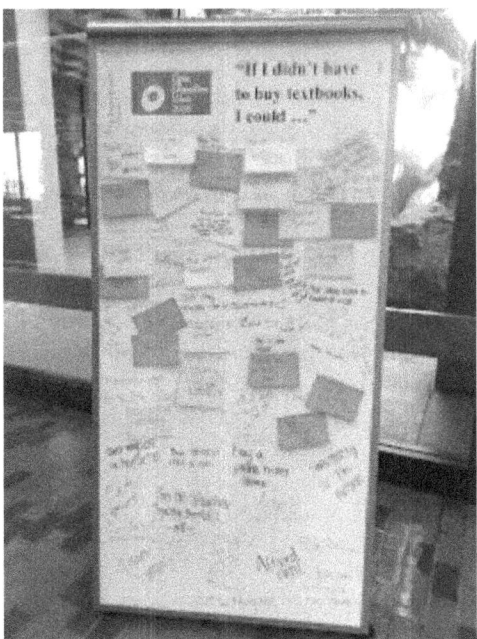

Figure 6.2 If they didn't have to buy textbooks, students could...

following comment: 'Some of the answers are certainly interesting and important: "eat food", "pay rent on time", "not work until 3 a.m. before school", "buy a plane ticket home"... I think the cost advantage is one of the greatest aspects of using OERs in the educational context' (*reading discussion forum post*). In this post, Maia connects the comments that her peers had made when thinking about the value of OER, mostly economic, with comments from students in the wider campus community, and informs her peers in this way that Open Education Week is taking place on their campus and that she is taking part in ongoing events scheduled at their institutional library. Maia noted that not only teachers but also 'learners are becoming more involved in the development of materials.'

Study participants also learned about and discussed the shared and dynamic aspects of OER, one aspect that they had not considered in full before the start of the unit. For example, Maia discussed the value of having materials 'produced locally by those who are directly involved in teaching' and concluded that OEP 'is fostering innovation and a more open process' (*reading discussion forum post*). Sharing Maia's view, Javier reflects on OEP and sees 'a way to empower teachers as they engage in the practice of creating materials and participate of and in a world-wide community that has the same purpose' (*reading discussion forum post*).

The practical dimension of OER was also noticed by study participants. For example, Maia appreciated how OER give 'the ability to adapt content for our own courses and purposes' (*reading discussion forum post*). They also acknowledged the capacity of social networks to increase access and support distribution of OER. On a related note, Maia explained that 'with the spread of technology, instructors are not constrained to the language textbook anymore; on the web they can find updated materials related to current issues to support language learners' (*reading discussion forum post*). She further highlighted how sharing resources on the web under an open CC license makes it possible for 'instructors across the world [to] use them, adapt them to their needs and reduce the cost of textbooks for their students' (*reading discussion forum post*). Veronika underscored how social networks are 'redistributing power and control from publishers to the end users' (*reading discussion forum post*).

While study participants lauded the practice of sharing resources openly, the fact remains that the practice is still far from being mainstream. Lack of knowledge about OER repositories, and the open license structure are all explanations that study participants mentioned after viewing the webinar and reading scholarly literature, but professional identity is another. The *Dilemma: Got Solutions* scenario for the unit on *OER and digital technology in language teaching and learning* prompted study participants to consider the reluctance that teachers might have to share their materials with others and suggest solutions that they, as future LPDs, might implement in their program in order to promote the use of

OER in FL teaching but most importantly foster OEP. Upon reading the *Dilemma: Got Solutions* scenario, Maia confessed,

> I once did not like to share my own resources with other instructors. The main reason was that I put in so much time and effort that it did not seem fair that others could just have the finished polished product. Once I learned about OER my perspective on material sharing changed.

Not surprisingly, Maia advocated for emphasizing the benefits of OER/OEP and sharing information about the open CC license. In her recommendation to the *Dilemma: Got Solutions* scenario, she explained how as a LPD she would engage all GSIs under her supervision into authoring and sharing OER and encourage them to spread the word about their authored OER so they would see themselves 'as contributors to a bigger purpose' and 'not just to their program.' In her end of module reflective blog post Maia wrote that,

> to embrace OER and OEP, I think teachers, language program directors and administrators need to be informed. They need to attend workshops and meetings where they can discuss OER and learn about best practices and strategies to implement open resources in their own courses.

Along the same line, Javier and Veronika recommended a series of workshops wherein teachers would develop materials for the courses they teach that they would later share after trying them out. They underscored the need to create a community of practice. Javier even contemplated the possibility of 'gamifying large curricular projects' (*end of module blog post*) as a way to make them more meaningful and increase engagement among the GSIs that he would supervise. In an earlier reading discussion forum post written in response to Blyth (2009), both Veronika and Javier had indicated that as LPDs they would hesitate to use OER as primary materials in a language program. Veronika explained that she,

> would consider perhaps starting off with 'partial' OER, somewhat similar to the process described in Blyth (2009), and then modifying and adding to the materials based on ongoing student feedback and evaluation of the materials. I feel I need more experience using/creating OER without any textbook use/support.' (*reading discussion forum post*)

Although Javier had previously discussed the burden of costly commercial instructional materials on students and the inadequacy of their content for teaching and learning, he yet volunteered that he was not ready to abandon textbooks completely as they offer structure and support to novice teachers, an indication of their continued stronghold on language instruction, instructors and LPDs.

> I do not think I would consider going exclusively with OER as textbooks somehow lessen the burden for some of the instructors in a FLP (Foreign Language Program) such as TAs and non-tenure-track faculty. Knowing that a textbook can aid these instructors in their teaching is an aspect I cannot ignore; therefore, I think that going exclusively with OER is not realistic nor completely beneficial. (*reading discussion forum post*)

By the time they had completed the unit on *OER and digital technology in language teaching and learning*, study participants demonstrated a much more substantial level of understanding of the potential of OER and OEP and came to realize that they mean much more than just open access to free materials but that they give agency to teachers and students and afford them increased control over content and delivery. Study participants started imagining and formulating ways in which they, as LPDs, could support their programs and students and the GSIs who teach them by using OER and engaging in OEP. They grasped the ways in which OER have the potential to support contemporary approaches to teaching and learning languages and meet teacher and learner needs, although both Veronica and Javier were still reluctant to completely forgo textbooks which they viewed as useful support for more novice instructors. They started to understand the possibilities and rewards that come for teachers and learners with joining this community of practice. In the reading discussion and end of module reflective posts, what also emerged is how study participants also started grappling with broader questions that revolve around the meaning of education and access, the power relations that exist with commercial materials adoption versus OER, the meaning of authorial authority and credibility, and the fears that come with change in education models. Maia, who was already involved in the movement before the start of the unit, became much more of an activist. Open education advocates call for sustained education to raise awareness and attract new adopters (Blyth & Dalola, 2016; Kurek, 2016; MacKinnon *et al.*, 2016; Whyte, 2016; Zourou, 2016). This course unit while only being a start seems to have done that and more for both Javier and Veronika and has allowed Maia to take on a stronger stance. In addition to sustained education, open education advocates also call for active engagement and appropriate support in OEP, which was the goal of the final OER-based final class project.

Putting it all together: Study participants' knowledge, beliefs and experiences shaped their OER-based LPD resource sites (RQ3)

The final class project consisted of the creation of an OER-based resource site which could support LPD work. To complete this project, study participants could draw from the readings, discussions and webinars that they had completed/participated in/viewed in this course, the LPD interviews they had conducted earlier in the semester, and their own past and current professional experiences to inform the selection of both focus, content and materials organization for their sites.

All study participants chose *Padlet*, a collaborative digital pin board widely used by teachers and teacher educators, to create their LPD resource sites. When a Padlet is public, anyone can freely access it, further contribute to it either by commenting or pinning a new note with a link to a document, slideshow, video, or image and rate the contributions made.

It thus has the potential for the making of a truly socially constructed digital repository.

Veronika had, for several years, led technology workshops for GSIs, LPDs and other faculty members in one of the colleges at her institution. In her reflective essay, she reported that her first-hand knowledge of the difficulties they faced in using technology for teaching and the technology needs her interviewees had expressed, greatly influenced her choice of topic for her LPD resource site (technology) and OER selection. For example, her site included resources on technology enhanced language learning and digital applications useful for language teaching and learning accompanied by recommended best practices. All these were selected with the purpose of supporting LPDs interested in incorporating more technology tools to support language teaching and learning in the courses they oversee. In anticipation of his future LPD role in his home country, Javier chose 'to focus on grouping resources relevant to train novice language teachers on language teaching methods' and since 'These can also serve for ongoing professional development. I also decided to include non-traditional topics such as technology, intercultural communication and literacies' (*reflective essay*). These three topics were discussed in the course but are not always, especially the last two, included in language teaching methods coursebooks which generally tend to focus on the teaching of the four skills. Javier underscored that these topics needed to be included in a resource site focused on language teaching methods for novice language teachers. On his site, he included recorded webinars on topics relevant for the professional development of novice teachers, an OER on technology he had authored, and articles in open-access scholarly journals for example. Maia, aware of the results of Thoms and Thoms' study (2014), chose to focus on OER development and technology hoping that it would not only educate but also potentially support LPDs and the GSIs they supervise in using and developing OER for their programs and engaging in OEP. For example, Maia provided on her site links to recorded webinars and talks that discuss open textbook initiatives and she included a link to LOERN as an incentive for LPDs and GSIs to author OER and get recognized for their contributions. Table 6.4 provides an overview of the kinds of resources study participants selected for their LPD resource sites.

Study participants brought their knowledge of and beliefs about second language teaching and learning, their insights in language program direction and the challenges LPDs face, their former and present professional experiences, their knowledge of their targeted audience and their new understandings of OER/OEP to bear on the focus, content and materials organization of their individual OER-based LPD resource site. All showed growth in their sensitivity to the web of complex interactions that exist between content, pedagogy and OER/OEP for language learning and teaching and teacher professional development.

148 Part 2: The Mesosystem: Developing Knowledge in L2 Teacher Education

Table 6.4 Overview of the content linked to in the LPD resource sites

LPD resource sites	Javier: *Language teaching methods and approaches*	Veronika: *Technology in and for language teaching and learning*	Maia: *OER development and technology*	Total
Videos (TED talks, video recordings of presentations at universities, etc.)	10	5	6	21
Digital application		6	1	7
Digital application evaluation (authored)	1			1
Teacher / Educator blogs		6		6
Teacher / educator presentations (Prezi, PPT, webinar, etc.)		1	1	2
Guidelines / handbooks			1	1
Teaching / learning materials				20
National educational organization website	1		7	8
Local educational organization website		1		1
Language teacher / educator / organization website		1		1
Module	1		1	2
Textbook / Workbook	3			3
Open-access journal articles	2		3	5

Safe driving or choosing the road more taken: Study participants' practices with and new realizations about OER and OEP while developing their OER-based LPD resource site (RQ4)

Although students had been encouraged to revise, remix and/or author OER, study participants primarily reused and redistributed. Veronika indicated that she 'discovered that there were so many resources available on the internet that I hadn't explored yet and that didn't even know existed' (*reflective essay*). She further reported that 'there were more resources available on how to use tools, not necessarily why these tools were important or how to integrate them for teaching in effective ways' (*reflective essay*) which meant that she had to do extra research to find what she needed. Similarly impressed by the wealth of available resources, Javier, however, shared in his reflective essay that he felt overwhelmed by 'the vast amount of open resources on the web' and stated that 'this can actually complicate one's efforts in choosing resources since there are so many resources to choose from.' He further explained that it took time to sift through them to find those he thought would be most appropriate for the purpose and audience of his LPD resource site. He also indicated that ensuring that OER are of quality also takes time. As a result, he confessed that he tended to gravitate towards OER which had institutional backing (e.g. national and local educational organizations, including national Language Resource Centers and universities) rather than those posted by individuals whose work did not have this kind of endorsement and other study participants did too as Table 6.4 shows.

Besides the time required to sift through numerous OER, another constraining factor was the audience they were targeting with their resource sites, i.e. LPDs, and the focus they chose. Used to search for language teaching OER to implement in their classes, this project asked students to put on an LPD cap and search for OER that would contribute to program development, program evaluation and/or GSI professional learning by providing guidelines on how the OER could be used. For example, Maia reported in her reflective essay that 'it is much simpler to find materials that are solely created for the language classroom' and indicated that she knew several websites and platforms where she could find open materials for the language classes she teaches. She further observed that OER relevant for LPD work are not as plentiful and she surmised that 'the development of materials designed for LPDs might need specific knowledge that few people have' (*reflexive essay*). Although study participants had just completed a graduate course on language program direction, their lack of on-the-ground LPD experience often played a role in choosing not to author OER as Maia's comments suggest. Javier was the only study participant who authored one OER for the final project. In the process of creating his LPD resource site, he came to realize that

> Some of the previous work I have done can become OER. For example, I wrote 6 digital tools/resources evaluations as part of a course on technology and foreign language teaching I took. I used those 6 evaluations as resources for my resource web page (*reflective essay*)

Understanding the open license structure was another constraining factor when it comes to revising, remixing or authoring OER for this project. Maia, the most knowledgeable about OER of the study participants and a strong advocate of OEP, indicated that one needs to 'check thoroughly whether the document/activity/image […] is really open source and to use it the way intended by the creator' (*end of module blog post*). Javier, who turned in six evaluations of digital tools/resources he had authored, admitted in his reflective essay that it took him time to understand how to go about licensing these resources.

In this situated learning opportunity, study participants expanded and refined their knowledge base about OER and engaged in OEP in very concrete ways by re-investing and repurposing content for a specific audience. Study participants got to actively search OER repositories and discover some in the process, select OER that would best support the goal of their sites, realize what is available and what is not (Maia and Veronika), author and license OER (Javier), share their sites so that LPDs could use them and further contribute, and engage in OEP.

Although a few uncertainties regarding the open CC licensing structure indicated in the survey remained for Javier, he did come to realize that work that he had previously done could become an OER and worked through the process of licensing it so he could include it on his site. The unit on *OER and digital technology in language teaching and learning* and this final project provided a way for Javier and Veronika to spread their wings and for Maia to soar as she came to this with some already solid knowledge and practice.

Discussion and Conclusion

In the discussion of their findings, Thoms and Thoms (2014) underscored that the level of knowledge and integration of OER and participation in OEP among LPDs was low and that basic education about OER/OEP and the ways in which they can be used might contribute significantly to improving this situation. They called for a renewed effort to educate LPDs and make them aware of 'the plethora of OER-based materials and tools that are available to be used, remixed, and incorporated' (2014: 144) in the courses they supervise.

Another and related effort would be to educate and provide hands-on use and participation to GSIs who have language program direction as a professional goal and thus engage them in OER and OEP before they enter the profession which was the focus of this study.

Findings in this study indicate that the unit on *OER and digital technology in language teaching and learning* and final project contributed to increase study participants' PCK about teaching with OER and engaging in OEP and as such demonstrate that teacher education coursework can be a powerful influence and shape what teachers learn from experience.

The final class project, a situated learning opportunity embedded in the course structure, allowed students to engage first-hand in the design of an OER-based resource for LPDs which they shared publicly and contributed to the realization that they too can be actors in the OER/OEP movement. In planning an OER-based resource for LPDs, the curricular choices made by study participants reflect not only the grounds upon which they made their decisions but also the different contexts they were considering. In addition to their recently developed knowledge about OER/OEP, their knowledge and beliefs about second language learning and teaching, their knowledge about their audience's needs and interests and teaching contexts, and their previous and current professional experiences also influenced the foci of their OER-based resource sites as well as their selection and organization of the materials for them. All these elements worked intricately together and informed study participants' curricular planning.

Maia was already an OER/OEP active user at the beginning of the course. The term OER had meaning for her, she was well versed in issues around open education, was aware of and had used open licenses and was a strong advocate for OER/OEP. The course unit and the final project however made her realize that OER are not only 'materials for language learning and teaching languages, thus for teachers and students' but can also be used 'for the professional development of language teachers' (*reflective essay*) and led her to outline what she would do as a LPD to help GSIs embrace open education based on what she had learned through course and her personal and professional experiences. Although Maia had already created materials which she had licensed, she did not for her final class project. Time but most likely the fact that 'the development of materials designated for LPDs require specific knowledge' (*reflective essay*), might indicate that she believed that she did not have the authority or credibility to do so yet. Such beliefs might also have played a role in Veronika choosing not to author OER although she had years of experience leading workshops for language faculty. Rather than drawing from her professional experiences to author an OER on how to make meaningful use of select technology tools in language teaching and learning, Veronika chose to look for relevant OER for reuse and redistribution. Javier was the only one who authored OER. Since he had already received feedback on them, we can surmise that it had for Javier the kind of authority and credibility which guided his selection of other OER. Javier and Veronika were OER aware at the start of the course but moved towards being OER consumers (Javier and Veronika) and OER producers (Javier) towards the end of the course.

By participating in this final class project, study participants not only discovered new resources but also new ways of using them, better understood the licensing structure and used it (Javier) to cater to the learning and teaching needs of their audience: LPDs. More broadly, for study participants the course unit and final class project brought to the surface questions about the meaning of education and equity, the nature of power in education, the meaning of credible expertise, and the risks associated with educational change.

Several practical implications emerge from this study's findings in relation to teacher education and professional development practices for future LPDs. The course unit on *OER and digital technology in language teaching and learning* served as an introduction to OER/OEP and the hands-on final class project was highly valued by the study participants who recognized its contributions to their own professional development. However, the main findings also underscore the need for more education and extended hands-on experience with OER/OEP among GSIs, and future LPDs, if we want to see the proverbial needle move in the direction of embracing and actively using OER and engaging in OEP in FL programs.

In this online graduate seminar on FL program direction, although all study participants indicated in the survey that they had heard of OER, only Maia was an active OER user. Maia was also the only one who reported having heard of OEP and had already authored and shared her work under an open CC license. Veronika, an advanced PhD candidate, was less so, and for Javier, a MA student in his final semester of coursework, it was the first opportunity he had. In the reflective essay Javier wrote after completing his final project, he indicated that creating the LPD resource site had opened 'a new world,' 'had strengthened my understanding of OER,' and made him realize that 'some of the previous work I have done can become OER.' He further explained that creating the LPD resource site by curating OER was 'an enriching task' that made him consider which resources would be 'relevant, meaningful and up to date' to support the professional learning of novice GSIs in his program and left him 'feel empowered' (*reflective essay*). At this time, it is unclear whether Javier or Veronika continued to engage with OER/OEP beyond the work they did for their LPD resource sites, a graded assignment for a course in which they were enrolled. Comas-Quinn and Fitzgerald (2013) underscore that 'constant communication, encouragement and training for active users and those who show an interest helps grow the core group of contributors and might in due time encourage content consumers to become more active in the community' (2013: 5–6). Based on their LORO project experience, they suggest that 'a discipline-oriented approach to OER' with 'a ready-made community with common interests, expectations and needs' (2013: 5–6) could more readily promote the sharing of resources.

Teacher education coursework with built-in activities that engage students with openness as they solve real educational problems can foster OER use and participation in OEP and make a difference. For Maia, it was a course in her MA program that introduced her to the concept of openness. It picked her interest and she sought opportunities on her own to learn more once her course had ended. In this second course, she developed new knowledge about OER/OEP as tools for teacher professional development and took on an advocacy role. However, one course in itself is often not enough and longer-term and more sustained experiences in teacher education have to be thoughtfully and systematically built in along the way (Comas-Quinn & Fitzgerald, 2013). Interestingly, departmental professional development opportunities were not given by study participants as a source where they had learned about OER and how to reuse or author them. Thoms and Thoms (2014) found that the majority of the LPDs they interviewed were not aware of the wealth of open resources available or understood how they could be reused, revised or remixed to benefit their program and support the professional learning of the GSIs they supervise. For example, Blyth (2017), Rossomondo (2011) and Zapata (2020) show how involving GSIs in the development of first-year textbooks in French and Spanish not only had a tremendous impact on their professional and personal learning but also allowed the LPDs to bring innovation in their teaching and learning contexts and do away with textbooks that were not meeting the needs of their programs and students. Thoms and Thoms highlight that other campus entities beyond the FL department, such as libraries, could play a role in supporting LPDs and GSIs in using and authoring OER. Librarians could facilitate locating and evaluating OER, which several students reported as challenging. They could promote understanding and alleviate concerns about the open CC license structure which was not clear to two of the three participants in this study. The unit on *OER and digital technology in language teaching and learning* overlapped with Open Education Week. Emails which advertised a week-long series of events went out to the campus community, yet only one study participant, Maia, was aware of it. Comas-Quinn and Fitzgerald (2013) argue that

> in order to reach out to those who do not have an initial interest in OER and OEP, open resources and practices should become part of other projects and activities. Fostering understanding of open practices and open resources needs to become part of teachers' regular professional development activities. (2013: 6)

Practical concerns about OER were also reported by study participants, namely time, quality and sharing/licensing. As suggested by Thoms and Thoms, Blyth, Rossomondo and the study participants themselves in the recommendations they made to resolve the *Dilemma: Got Solutions* scenario, using weekly meetings to involve GSIs in locating, vetting, revising or remixing OER for the courses they teach, would not only give them a useful professional learning opportunity as previously suggested but also cut the time they spend planning lessons. Quality was a concern all three study participants brought up. For their LPD resource sites they mostly curated OER produced by academic institutions which take on a leading role in the vetting of these resources by adopting the traditional peer review practices familiar to academia (Blyth, 2017). Blyth (2017) mentions that crowdsourcing is another approach to quality control by users for users and that 'OER developers have begun combining elements of peer review with [these] newer crowdsourcing approaches' (2017: 176). As quality control processes become more standardized, concerns such as those expressed by Javier, Veronika and Maia should recede and confidence in the quality of resources found under an open CC license should increase. Sharing one's work can bring concerns of having it appropriated without due recognition or fears of being challenged and negatively evaluated by peers. Maia indicated that in the past she was reluctant to share her work before she became more knowledgeable about OER. Explaining and having opportunities to use the open CC license structure could help ease the former, and as suggested by Zourou (2016), 'approaching OER as work in progress and not polished content off the shelf, as happens to other successful, social network enabled communities of practice, can increase participation and user engagement, and situate OEP in a more socially sustained environment' (2016: 14) could help address the latter. Zourou underscores that issues of professional identity cannot be ignored since they could hold users back in sharing which is central to OEP. Comas-Quinn and Fitzgerald further suggest that professional learning opportunities should carve out time for instructors to reflect so that they can 'work through the implications of open [educational] practices for their work, their identity as teachers and their role in relation to learners' (2013: 6).

Limitations and Future Research

Several limitations impact this study. The small number of participants and the participant status of the author, who combined instructor and research roles in this study and thus 'influenced' the ways and means by which the data were collected cannot be overlooked. The background of the participants who are all graduate students in applied linguistics or language education and literacy is another limitation. Graduate students in literature, cultural studies or linguistics often become LPDs as well (see VanPatten, 2015). Including graduate students in these areas of specialization would provide a more accurate picture. Follow-up interviews with study participants would have provided richer and more detailed answers.

It seems clear that FL teacher education must include more emphasis on OER and OEP to help future LPDs and GSIs become better acquainted with these important pedagogical innovations. Research has shown that GSIs require sustained professional development that includes extensive coursework and supervised classroom experience in order for them to transform their praxis (e.g. Allen & Paesani, 2010; Dupuy & Allen, 2012; Menke, 2018). Future research should focus on determining what exactly new LPDs and GSIs need to know in order to become more active participants in the open education movement. A large-scale research study of FL GSIs representing the variety of specializations typically found in language and literature departments should be conducted in order to get a better understanding of what they already know about OER and the extent to which they already engage in OEP. Future research should also examine how FL GSIs who are OER adopters use these materials in conjunction with the assigned textbook for the courses they teach, and how they engage in OEP and with whom. In brief, we call for more research to investigate how learning about open education – its practices, its products and its values – affects the professional development of future FL LPDs and GSIs.

References

Allen, H. and Paesani, K. (2010) Exploring the feasibility of a pedagogy of multiliteracies in introductory foreign language courses. *L2 Journal* 2, 119–142.

Andrade, A., Ehlers, U.-D., Caine, A., Carneiro, R., Conole, G., Kairamo, A.-K. ... Holmberg, C. (2011) *Beyond OER: Shifting Focus to Open Educational Practices*, OPAL Report 2011. See https://oerknowledgecloud.org/sites/oerknowledgecloud.org/files/OPAL2011.pdf (accessed July 1, 2018).

Blyth, C. (2009) From textbook to online materials: The changing ecology of foreign language publishing in the era of digital technology. In M. Evans (ed.) *Foreign Language Learning with Digital Technology* (pp. 179–202). London: Continuum.

Blyth, C. (2013) LCTLs and technology: The promise of open education. *Language Learning & Technology* 17, 1–6.

Blyth, C. (2017) Open educational resources (OERs) for language learning. In S.L. Thorne and S. May (eds) *Language, Education and Technology, Encyclopedia of Language and Education* (pp. 169–179). Berlin: Springer International Publishing.

Blyth, C. and Davis, J. (2007) Using formative evaluation in the development of learner-centered materials. *CALICO Journal* 25, 48–68.

Blyth, C. and Dalola, A. (2016) Translingualism as an open educational practice: Raising critical language awareness on Facebook. *Apprentissage des Langues et Systèmes D'information et de Communication (ALSIC)*, 19. See https://alsic.revues.org/2962 (accessed July 1 2018).

Butcher, N. (2015) *A Basic Guide to Open Educational Resources (OER)*. Vancouver: Commonwealth of Learning. See http://oasis.col.org/handle/11599/36 (accessed July 1 2018).

Byrnes, H. (1998) Constructing curricula in collegiate foreign language departments. In H. Byrnes (ed.) *Learning Foreign and Second Languages: Perspectives in Research and Scholarship* (pp. 262–95). New York, NY: MLA.

Byrnes, H. (2001) Articulating foreign language programs: The need for new, curricular bases. In C.G. Lally (ed.) *Foreign Language Program Articulation: Current Practice and Future Prospects* (pp. 63–77). Westport, CT: Bergin & Garvey.

College Board. (2018) *Average Estimated Undergraduate Budgets, 2017–18*. See https://trends.collegeboard.org/college-pricing/figures-tables/average-estimated-undergraduate-budgets-2017-18 (accessed July 1 2018).

Comas-Quinn, A. and Fitzgerald, A. (2013) *Open Educational Resources in Language Teaching and Learning. Open Educational Resources Case Study: Pedagogical development from OER practice*. United Kingdom: Higher Education Academy (HEA) and the Joint Information Systems Committee (JISC).

Creswell, J.W. (2015) *A Concise Introduction to Mixed Methods Research*. Thousand Oaks, CA: Sage.

Dixon, E. and Hondo, J. (2014) Re-purposing an OER for the online language course a case study of Deutsch Interaktiv by the Deutsche Welle. *Computer Assisted Language Learning* 27, 109–121.

Dupuy, B. and Allen, H.W. (2012) Appropriating conceptual and pedagogical tools of literacy: A qualitative study of two novice foreign language teaching assistants. In G. Gorsuch (ed.) *Working Theories for Teaching Assistant and International Teaching Assistant Development* (pp. 275–315). Stillwater, OK: New Forums Press.

Friss, R. (2018) The next course: The slow textbook. *Hispania* 100, 258–259.

Ghosn, I.K. (2003) Talking like texts and talking about texts: How some primary school coursebook tasks are realized in the classroom. In B. Tomlinson (ed.) *Developing Materials for Language Teaching* (pp. 291–305). London: Continuum.

Grossman, P. (1989) A study in contrast: Sources of pedagogical content knowledge for secondary English. *Journal of Teacher Education* 40, 24–31.

Grossman, P. (1990) *The Making of a Teacher*. New York, NY: Teachers College Press.
Guerrettaz, A.M. and Johnston, B. (2013) Materials in the classroom ecology. *Modern Language Journal* 97, 779–796.
Johnson, K.E. (2009) *Second Language Teacher Education: A Sociocultural Perspective*. New York: Routledge.
Johnson, K.E. and Golombek, P. (2011) The transformative power of narrative in second language teaching education. *TESOL Quarterly* 45 (3), 486–509.
Kern, R. (2000) *Literacy and Language Teaching*. Oxford: Oxford University Press.
Kozulin, A. (1995) The learning process: Vygotsky's theory in the mirror of its interpretations. *School Psychology International* 16, 117–129.
Kurek, M. (2016) Addressing cultural diversity in preparing teachers for openness: Culturally sensitive appropriation of open content. *Apprentissage des Langues et Systèmes D'information et de Communication (ALSIC)* 19. See http://alsic.revues.org/2904 (accessed July 1, 2018).
Lord, G. (2014) *Language Program Direction: Theory and Practice*. Upper Saddle River, NJ: Pearson.
Lortie, D. (1975) *Schoolteacher: A Sociological Study*. Chicago, IL: University of Chicago Press.
Mackey, A. and Gass, S.M. (2015) *Second Language Research: Methodology and Design*. Abingdon: Routledge.
MacKinnon, T., Pasfield-Neofitou, S., Manns, H. and Grant, S. (2016) A meta-analysis of open educational communities of practice and sustainability in higher educational practice. *Apprentissage des Langues et Systèmes D'information et de Communication (ALSIC)* 19. See https://alsic.revues.org/2908 (accessed July 1, 2018).
Masuhara, H. (2011) What do teachers really want from coursebooks? In B. Tomlinson (ed.) *Materials Development in Language Teaching* (pp. 236–266). Cambridge: Cambridge University Press.
Menke, M. (2018) Literacy-based curricula in university foreign language instruction: Perceptions from non-tenure track faculty. *L2 Journal* 10, 111–133.
Modern Language Association (2007) Foreign languages and higher education: New structures for a changed world: MLA ad hoc committee on foreign languages. *Profession*, 234–45.
Nunan, D. (1991) *Language Teaching Methodology*. Harlow: Longman.
Paesani, K., Allen, H.W. and Dupuy, B. (2016) *A Multiliteracies Framework for Collegiate Foreign Language Teaching*. Upper Saddle River, NJ: Pearson.
Rossomondo, A. (2011) The Acceso project and FL graduate student professional development. In H.W. Allen and H.H. Maxim (eds) *Educating the Future FL Professoriate for the 21st Century* (pp. 128–148). Boston, MA: Heinle Cengage.
Rossomondo, A. and Lord, G. (2018) The world is not flat, so why are our textbooks? *Hispania* 100, 251–257.
Seaman, J. and Seaman, J. (2017) *Opening the Textbook: Educational Resources in U.S. Higher Education, 2017*. Babson Survey Research Group. See https://www.onlinelearningsurvey.com/reports/openingthetextbook2017.pdf (accessed July 1, 2018).
Shulman, L.S. (1986) Those who understand: Knowledge growth in teaching. *Educational Researcher* 15, 4–14.
Shulman, L.S. (1987) Knowledge and teaching: Foundations of the new reform. *Harvard Educational Review* 57, 1–22.
Shulman, L.S. and Shulman, J.H. (2004) How and what teachers learn: A shifting perspective. *Journal of Curriculum Studies* 36, 257–271.
Swaffar, J. and Arens, K. (2005) *Remapping the Foreign Language Curriculum: An Approach Through Multiple Literacies*. New York, NY: MLA.
Thoms, J. and Thoms, B. (2014) Open educational resources in the United States: Insights from university foreign language directors. *System* 45, 138–146.
VanPatten, B. (2015) Where are the experts? *Hispania* 98 1, 2–13.

Weller, M., de los Arcos, B., Farrow, R., Pitt, B. and McAndrew, P. (2015) The impact of OER on teaching and learning practice. *Open Praxis,* 7. See https://www.openpraxis.org/index.php/OpenPraxis/article/view/227/179 (accessed July 1, 2018).

Wiley, D. (2015) Defining the Open in Open Content. See http://opencontent.org/definition/ (accessed July 1 2018).

Wiley, D. (2017) The evolving economics of educational materials and open educational resources: Toward closer alignment with the core values of education. In R.A. Reiser and J.V. Dempsey (eds) *Trends and Issues in Instructional Design and Technology* (4th edn). New York, NY: Pearson Education.

Whyte, S. (2016) From 'solitary thinkers' to 'social actors': OER in multilingual CALL teacher education. *Apprentissage des Langues et Systèmes D'information et de Communication (ALSIC),* 19. See https://alsic.revues.org/2906 (accessed July 1, 2018).

Zapata, G. (2020) Sprinting to the finish line: the benefits and challenges of book sprints in OER Faculty-graduate student collaborations. *International Review of Research in Open and Distributed Learning* 21 (2), 1–17. https://doi.org/10.19173/irrodl.v21i2.4607

Zourou, K. (2016) Social networking affordances for open educational language practice. *Apprentissage des Langues et Systèmes D'information et de Communication (ALSIC),* 19. See https://journals.openedition.org/alsic/2903 (accessed July 1, 2018).

Appendix 6.1

Descriptive codes

Code	Definition
Challenges with OER	Frustration with locating OER, understanding of open license structure and permission level, time cost in searching, authoring, and sharing
Issues with OER	Concern with quality of OER, fear of sharing and not getting recognition
Motivation for OER selection and use	Ease of adaptation, interactivity, feasibility with program learning outcomes, match with student needs
Strategies to increase OER adoption, creation and sharing	Workshops, conferences, hand-on professional development opportunities, meetings, mentoring
Value of OEP	Innovative instruction, empowerment of teachers, empowerment of learning, learners, community of practice, increase access, redistribution of power and control
Value of OER	Authentic, up-to-date, wide range of topics, cost-saving

7 The Role of OER in Promoting Critical Reflection and Professional Development: The Foreign Languages and the Literary in the Everyday Project

Carl S. Blyth, Chantelle Warner and Joanna Luks

This chapter describes the Foreign Languages and the Literary in the Everyday (FLLITE) project, a joint initiative of two national foreign language resource centers (US Department of Education). The FLLITE project seeks to provide tools and professional development resources for L2 teachers to learn how to create their own open educational resources (OER), which incorporate literary language, i.e. playful and creative uses of the target linguistic system. The FLLITE project has two interconnecting goals: (1) the creation of a professional learning community whose members (university-level faculty, language program directors and graduate students of language, literary and/or cultural studies) create L2 literacy-based materials in the form of open lessons for copyrighted or open texts (written, oral, visual); and (2) the development of an ecology of professional learning based on the OER life cycle (Gurell, 2008). The OER life cycle refers to the phases involved in OER development: finding content for the OER, composing the OER, adapting the OER, using the OER in class and sharing the results with the community. Importantly, the OER life cycle not only changes the OER, but also the developer. In brief, the FLLITE project is guided by a hypothesis from the OER Hub's OER Evidence Report 2013–2014: 'Use of OER leads to critical reflection by educators, with evidence of improvement in their practice' (http://oerhub.net/research-outputs/reports/). In this chapter, case studies of two FLLITE participants, a graduate student instructor of Spanish and a graduate student instructor of German, suggest that the creation of OER exposed them to new ways of thinking about language and led them to reconceptualize their language teaching practices.

Introduction

In a seminal article on open educational resources (OER) development, Nathan Yergler, former Chief Technology Officer at Creative Commons, claimed that the benefits of open design 'are based on the supposition that educators and learners will discover existing resources, improve them, and share the results, resulting in a virtuous cycle of improvement and re-use' (2010: 1). In other words, the perceived benefits of OER depend on a set of assumptions about their developmental process referred to as a 'loop' or 'cycle', or increasingly, a 'life cycle' (Gurell, 2008). The metaphor of 'the life cycle' construes OER development as an incremental, evolutionary process driven by the contributions of many community members who adapt the resource to their local contexts. While descriptions of the OER life cycle such as Gurell (2008) typically focus on the product – that is, the open resource itself – in this chapter, we focus on the process, or more precisely, how teachers change as a result of developing their own OER. In particular, we analyze how two L2 teachers were able to reflect on their teaching practices through different forms of engagement with OER.

These two case studies derive from the Foreign Languages and the Literary in the Everyday project (FLLITE), a teacher development project jointly sponsored by the Center for Educational Resources in Culture, Language and Literacy (CERCLL) at the University of Arizona and the Center for Open Educational Resources in Language Learning (COERLL) at the University of Texas at Austin. Both CERCLL and COERLL are National Foreign Language Resource Centers sponsored by the US Department of Education (http://nflrc.org/). Inspired by multiliteracies approaches in contemporary language teaching and learning (e.g. Kalantzis & Cope, 2015; Kern, 2000; New London Group, 1996; Paesani *et al.*, 2016), the project provides tools and professional development resources for L2 teachers to learn how to create their own OER that incorporate literary language; that is, playful and creative uses of the target linguistic system. Through this emphasis on the literary, the FLLITE project aligns with the multiliteracies framework by taking a reflective approach to understanding how textual meaning is designed by language users in situated contexts. These two case studies indicate that the process of OER development provides the kinds of sustained opportunities for professional learning (e.g. Allen & Dupuy, 2012) that have been shown to lead to paradigm change, by allowing teachers to critically reflect on their teaching practices and to make significant shifts in their conceptualization of second language learning and teaching.

The chapter begins with the origins and development of the FLLITE project, followed by a general discussion of the conceptual framework of the project, namely, the multiliteracies approach to language instruction and the key concept of language play. Next, the chapter describes the development of two OER created by graduate students from different foreign language departments. Both students participated in a FLLITE workshop that led to the creation of their OERs. The chapter ends with a discussion of how the OER life cycle helped the two students to further their conceptual development related to multiliteracies pedagogy and to see themselves as active designers of learning.

Origins and Development of the FLLITE Project

The story of FLLITE begins with Joanna Luks, who was the coordinator of the first-year French curriculum in a two-tiered foreign language department at Cornell University. Inspired by the 2007 Modern Language Association (MLA) report's suggestions to teach foreign languages in ways that fostered translingual and transcultural competence, Luks decided to look for an alternative to standard communicative French textbooks. After perusing both commercial and open materials, she settled on *Français interactif*, an open program developed by French faculty and graduate students at the University of Texas at Austin. *Français interactif* may be accessed at https://www.laits.utexas.edu/fi/home.

Luks was generally pleased with the open design of *Français interactif* but worried that she would be unable to foster the kind of textual engagement and critical reflection in her classes that the 2007 MLA report had recommended. As a result, Luks decided to adapt the open materials to her local context by customizing some of the open textbook's content and by creating her own literacy-based activities aimed at bridging the well-known language/literature divide prevalent in foreign language departments. Early on in the process, Luks contacted COERLL at the University of Texas at Austin, the publisher of *Français interactif*, to discuss her efforts to adapt the materials. Discussions with the COERLL staff helped Luks realize that many of her plans were not in keeping with open educational practices (OEP). For example, she discovered that some of her newly created activities could not be published as OER because they violated copyright law.

With assistance from the COERLL staff, Luks revised her original lessons and replaced all copyrighted material with openly licensed content. Thus, by developing her own materials, Luks learned important OEP such as how to search and find open content on the internet as well as how to understand and select appropriate copyright licenses for OER. In addition to these important OEP, Luks learned new ways to engage her students with a wider variety of French texts. In 2013, COERLL published Luks' materials as an OER entitled *Le littéraire dans le quotidien* (The Literary in the Everyday). The OER was made available on Google Drive to allow French teachers to download separate lessons as editable Word documents. In addition, Luks' open lessons were published collectively as a print-on-demand textbook for teachers who wanted to use the OER as a supplement to their introductory French textbook.

While Luks' OER is notable for its use of open technologies, its true innovation lies in the conceit of 'the literary in the everyday,' a phrase that Luks coined to capture her novel approach to literary ways of meaning-making in everyday discourse. In the preface of her OER, Luks criticizes current foreign language materials for taking a reductionist approach to language by emphasizing the literal while downplaying the importance of 'the literary.' Following scholars such as Claire Kramsch who argue for the importance of the literary imagination in language learning, Luks claims that the literary is not a marginal feature of language but rather central to all human meaning-making. In brief, Luks envisions the literary as any creative use of the linguistic system that is not an exception to a grammatical rule per se, but rather an extension of conventional linguistic patterning. Luks points out that such creative uses of language may be absent from pedagogical grammars but are nonetheless more frequent and more systematic than many teachers realize. Finally, Luks frames 'the literary' in terms of the individual who construes reality based on lived experience.

In line with other multiliteracies approaches (e.g. Cope & Kalantzis, 2009, 2015; Paesani *et al*., 2016), Luks' approach to text-based language learning broadens the notion of *text* to include written, oral and visual forms, and reframes reading/viewing/listening as interpreting, and writing as designing. Furthermore, Luks calls for different ways of knowing and analyzing language that are usually associated with different disciplines: '…[students] must develop the deductive skills of a linguist, the honed intuitions of an anthropologist, and the playful bent of a poet' (Luks, 2013: 2). Despite arguing for the literary as an important part of L2 literacy, Luks acknowledges that foreign language literature often proves inaccessible to beginning learners who know little about the texts' cultural and historical contexts. As a compromise, Luks proposes a focus on the creative uses of the foreign language ('the literary') found in texts whose ordinary contexts are widely accessible ('the everyday'). In other words, in Luks' approach, *the everyday* refers to quotidian texts and contexts, the usual content of lower division language classes. The notion of 'the literary in the everyday' encompasses many kinds of texts: non-literary texts that one encounters in everyday life such as letters or emails or public signage, texts that belong to the literary genre of realism and texts that index a speaker's personal life such as fan fiction, a genre in which fans write themselves into a pre-existing storyline (Sauro & Sundmark, 2016). Luk's approach to the study of everyday language aligns well with current research in 'linguistic landscapes,' a new field described by Landry and Bourhis (1997: 23) as the 'visibility and salience of languages on public and commercial signs in a given territory or region.' Primarily anchored in the fields of sociolinguistics and social semiotics, the study of linguistic landscapes has recently attracted the interest of SLA scholars who are exploring the affordances of public signage as a rich source of authentic input for language learners (Malinowski & Dubreil, 2019). In summary, the literacy lessons in Luks' OER are based on the premise that 'the literary' is not a special, marginal kind of language, but rather, part of ordinary discourse that literally surrounds us in our everyday environments.

When *Le littéraire dans le quotidien* first appeared, the reactions of French teachers were somewhat mixed. For example, many teachers lauded its diverse selection of texts and its pedagogical scaffolding to promote deeper textual engagement. However, other teachers appeared puzzled by Luks' use of English for critical framing activities, a practice that violated their beliefs about the exclusive use of the target language in communicative language teaching. Still other teachers seemed unsure how to align their grammatical syllabi with Luks' unconventional treatment of grammar as a resource for textual meaning. It became clear to Luks and to Carl Blyth, director of COERLL, that many French teachers were simply too unfamiliar with multiliteracies pedagogy and the practices of open education to take full advantage of Luks' OER.

At this point, Luks and Blyth contacted Chantelle Warner, co-director of CERCLL at the University of Arizona, to discuss how to address the conceptual difficulties experienced by teachers, as they tried to implement 'the literary in the everyday' into their own teaching practices. The result of these discussions was the professional development project FLLITE, a joint project of CERCLL and COERLL. Much like the COERLL staff who had assisted Luks during the development of her own OER, the FLLITE project aimed to assist foreign language instructors, including preservice teachers such as graduate students, with the development of open lessons to promote foreign language literacy. In order to accomplish this goal, the project inaugurated a series of summer workshops for foreign language teachers and created a website with resources about multiliteracies and open education.

In the first year of the project, it became evident that many teachers overlooked the literary potential of their chosen texts. Instead, they focused mainly on their texts' literal meanings that were closely tied to the grammatical agenda of the courses they taught. In other words, many teachers had been trained to think of reading as an activity whose primary goal was to review structures and vocabulary. In brief, teachers needed a more expansive view of reading as semiotic activity and more guidance in the critical analysis of literary meaning-making. It also became evident that L2 teachers, even those trained in literary analysis, lacked a metalanguage for helping their students engage with textual meaning. As a consequence, the FLLITE project directors devised a list of language play categories to assist learners and teachers in their analysis of a text's

'Designs of Meaning,' that is, the creative uses of a language as instantiated in a given text. Central to the pedagogy of Multiliteracies, 'Designs of Meaning' refers to three components (e.g. Available Designs, Designing, the Redesigned) that constitute the production and interpretation of textual meaning (New London Group, 1996). The FLLITE language play list is best understood as a heuristic aimed at demystifying the process of close reading:

- Culture Play (e.g. practices, values, schemas of products, societal multilingualism)
- Genre Play (e.g. hybrid genres such as modern fairy tales or prose poems)
- Grammar Play (e.g. nouns used as adjectives, non-standard grammar in poetry)
- Narrative Play (e.g. storylines, narrative structures, modes of storytelling)
- Perspective Play (e.g. point of view, characterization, mood, evaluation, judgment)
- Pragmatic Play (e.g. register, politeness, forms of address, functional language)
- Sound Play (e.g. rhyming, homophones, alliteration)
- Symbolic Play (e.g. metaphor, metonymy, digression, oppositions, juxtapositions)
- Visual Play (e.g. punctuation, formatting, visual symbolism, media intertextuality, cinematography, multimodality)
- Word Play (e.g. puns, spelling, capitalization, lexical semantics)

The adoption of 'language play' as a key concept frames language as a flexible semiotic system rather than a structural system based on rules. It also signals to teachers and learners that all speakers and writers, native or non-native, take creative liberties with the linguistic system when designing their texts. The concept of language play is meant to highlight important textual functions, for example, to soften or intentionally obscure meanings, to express new or unique meanings, to differentiate or obscure perspectives, to invoke aesthetic and affective responses, to develop themes and to create textual coherence. On the FLLITE website (fllite.org), the categories of language play are exemplified using texts from different languages and cultures. In addition, in the FLLITE framework, an 'authentic text' is not simply a text produced by a native user for a native audience, but rather, a text that plays literary dimensions of meanings off literal norms and conventions for intended rhetorical effects.

Finally, the FLLITE project created an editorial board of L2 faculty at various American colleges and universities who agreed to give developers feedback on their lessons. When a lesson is submitted for review, the author is paired with an editorial board member who is a specialist in the relevant language. Following guidelines, the board member evaluates the lesson and sends feedback to the developer via email. Next, the developer is encouraged to make changes in keeping with the feedback and to resubmit the lesson for publication. Unlike most editorial board members who do their work in private, an academic practice known as 'blind peer review,' FLLITE board members work in an open, collaborative fashion with developers. As such, the editorial board functions more as an online community of practice in which L2 professionals collaborate with developers to explore the pedagogical potential of the literary as manifested in the developer's chosen text. Currently, these professionals represent nine languages (e.g. Arabic, Chinese, English, French, German, Portuguese, Persian, Russian and Spanish). Today, the FLLITE project represents a community of L2 professionals committed to the development of OER for L2 learning.

The FLLITE Project and the Multiliteracies Framework

It is important to understand the FLLITE project in terms of the debates about curriculum and pedagogy that are currently occurring in the field of L2 education. Within the North American context, the concept of *literacy* has become closely associated with the call for curricular reform, which has been motivated by the mounting critiques of traditional two-tiered language programs and the need for 'a broader and more coherent curriculum in which language, culture and literature are taught as a continuous whole…' (MLA Report 2007 n.p.). While the MLA report brought visibility to curricular disjunctions that are familiar to many departments of foreign languages, literatures and cultures, scholars in L2 education and applied linguistics have long argued that 'literacy,' often appearing in the expanded sense that is captured by the term 'multiliteracies,' provides a conceptual frame for realizing this vision for more articulated curricula in which language and culture are deeply interconnected (e.g. Byrnes *et al*., 2006; Kern, 2000; Kramsch, 1994; Swaffar *et al*., 1991; Swaffar & Arens, 2006; see also Warner & Dupuy, 2018 for a historical view). In recent years, these discussions have coalesced into a coherent set of calls for paradigm change within university-level L2 education (e.g. Dupuy & Michelson, 2019; Maxim, 2006; Paesani & Allen, 2012; Paesani *et al*., 2016).

In these discussions, literacy is understood as extending beyond reading and writing to include ways of knowing (e.g. Cope & Kalantzis, 2009, 2015) and ways of being in the world (e.g. Gee, 2012). Literacy in this sense entails much more than encoding and decoding information through reading and writing (i.e. comprehension); it also involves forms of *invisible semiotic mediation* (e.g. Hasan, 2002), that is, the ways in which everyday discourse mediates our dispositions, including how we tend to respond to particular situations, our beliefs about the world around us and our sense of our place within it. In short, literacy is at the intersection of language and culture. For this reason, discussions of literacy and language learning often emphasize the importance of pedagogies that deliberately foster critical awareness raising and self-reflection (e.g. Kern, 2000, 2015; Kramsch, 2011; Warner, 2011).

Multiliteracies approaches are also associated with a renewed interest in literature and the literary in language and culture teaching. While this has been motivated by discussions of curricular integration, in which literature is treated as an inevitability of the upper-level curriculum, many scholars have also recognized that literary reading is well-suited for language learning because poetic and playful literacy practices make *invisible semiotic mediation* more visible (e.g. Blyth, 2018; Gramling & Warner, 2012, 2016; Kramsch, 2006; Nance, 2010; Warner, 2011; Warner & Gramling, 2014). By emphasizing the potential of literary discourse as a form of critical framing, contemporary discussions of literacy and literature return to the lessons of earlier scholars such as Widdowson (1975), who argued that because readers cannot rely on literal meaning and schematic background knowledge in the same ways as with many other forms of communication, reading literature can encourage an attention to linguistic style that would foster language awareness and learning in turn.

At the same time, scholars such as Blyth (2018), Gramling and Warner (2012, 2016) and Warner and Gramling (2014) also argue that literature is a valuable site for intercultural reflection. This work is in part inspired by the work of Kramsch (and her associates), who has argued that literature can play a key role in the development of what she has recently theorized as symbolic competence, namely...

> the ability to shape the multilingual game in which one invests – the ability to manipulate the conventional categories and societal norms of truthfulness, legitimacy, seriousness, originality – and to reframe human thought and action. (Kramsch & Whiteside, 2008: 667)

Kramsch has argued that this form of symbolic competence has to be 'nourished by literary imagination at all levels of the language curriculum' (2006: 251), because it is through the literary that students are able to not only reflect on the forms of semiotic mediation described above, but also to experience alternate realities, including other possible selves.

Attention to the literary within a multiliteracies framework thus enables learners the space to reflect on form and meaning connections, but also on language use as a form of social practice within fields of play. This view of literacy and language learning aligns with existing research on language play in key ways. Research in second language acquisition has suggested that play functions in the acquisition of new forms (e.g. Broner & Tarone, 2001; Lantolf, 1997; Tarone, 2000, 2019). Other studies have also considered the ways in which play can help learners to negotiate their emerging sense of self as multilingual language users (e.g. Belz, 2002; Warner, 2004). Of relevance to multiliteracies approaches, scholars such as Guy Cook (2000) have argued that function does not unidirectionally determine form, but that new meanings and alternate realities can emerge through playful language use. Play – in both its more fun and more serious instantiations – can thus enable L2 learners to explore and expand their sense of the everyday forms of semiotic mediation, while also enabling them to participate in the transformation of language systems and their place within them.

The OER Life Cycle as a Template for the Professional Development of L2 Teachers

In recognition of the kinds of deep conceptual knowledge needed to bring about paradigmatic change, scholarship and advocacy for multiliteracies approaches to collegiate L2 teaching have developed in tandem with discussions of teacher education. Given the particular structure of many language, literature and culture departments, the focus of much of this work has been on graduate student education (e.g. Allen, 2011; Allen & Dupuy, 2011; Dupuy & Allen, 2012). Based on case studies of graduate student instructors in French, Allen and Dupuy (2011) and Dupuy and Allen (2012) argue that the typical approach to graduate student teacher education, whereby students participate in a single methods course at the start of their program, is ill-suited to the kind of sustained, targeted professional learning needed to 'overcome the inertia of FL teachers' everyday concepts' (Allen & Dupuy, 2011: 279). This is of particular importance when introducing new pedagogical paradigms because, as these scholars note, areas of tension often exist and persist between innovative pedagogies and traditional materials still in use in many language programs. Furthermore, the two studies from Allen and Dupuy suggest that even the availability of new pedagogical methods and materials may not be enough to shift teachers' conceptual understanding of language and language teaching.

> It is not enough to attempt to 'reprogram' TAs with new techniques and strategies; rather, dialogic mediation and explicit discussion of the need to align one's conceptual and pedagogical tools are necessary to encourage TAs to evolve in their teaching practices beyond how they learned languages themselves in the past. (Dupuy & Allen, 2012: 305)

Recognizing that innovative methods and materials may only lead to superficial changes, discussions of multiliteracies and teacher education have drawn support from sociocultural approaches to teacher education (e.g. Johnson & Golombek, 2011) and have emphasized teacher reflexivity (see Byrd Clark & Dervin, 2014; Crane, 2015). As noted by Gramling and Warner, reflection as a process 'requires reflective socio-cognitive spaces and surfaces to prompt the activity of reflection' (2016: 83).

The FLLITE project was created to help teachers understand the principles behind multiliteracies pedagogy and, in so doing, to promote a more reflective approach to teacher education and professional development. As such, it takes the OER life cycle as a template for professional development. In his OER handbook created under the auspices of the Center for Open and Sustainable Learning at Utah State University and published online by Lulu.com, Seth Gurell claims that the OER life cycle represents a sequence of five actions in the development of open materials: find, compose, adapt, use and share (Gurell, 2008). According to Gurell (2008), an OER begins when an educator searches for a resource to meet a perceived need. For example, an instructor may perceive a textbook to be lacking in a particular area and wish to supplement the textbook or replace it altogether as in the previously cited case of Joanna Luks. Educators looking for resources typically turn to search engines such as Google or OER repositories such as OER Commons. Once the instructor has found promising resources, they must combine those resources into a coherent set of materials. As part of the process, instructors tend to think deeply about the local needs of their classrooms and, as a consequence, they often change the materials to reflect their students' life worlds. When the instructor has finished the materials, the next step is to test them in the classroom. Feedback from students often uncovers problems with the content or the pedagogical sequence. Once the OER has been revised in light of the feedback, it is ready to be shared online with other educators and students who will hopefully continue the life cycle of adaptation and improvement.

In this study, the use of Gurell's description of the OER life cycle as a template for teacher development is based on the hypothesis that engaging in OER creation and use is likely to have a positive effect on teacher reflexivity. According to the OER Hub's OER Evidence Report 2013–2014, preliminary research suggests that when teachers use an existing OER or when they develop a new OER, they become more reflective about their own teaching practices (OER Evidence Report: 21). For example, a handful of studies have shown that teachers who engage with OER discover new pedagogical approaches and share their discoveries with colleagues (Haßler et al., 2015; Karunanayaka et al., 2015; Tosata & Bodi, 2011). However, these studies were based on science, technology, engineering and mathematics (STEM) fields and did not address the beliefs and practices of language teachers per se.

The FLLITE project challenges language teachers to design lessons that bridge the divide between lower-level language courses and upper-level literature courses, a curricular divide that has received widespread criticism from foreign language educators (e.g. Byrnes, 2002; MLA Report, 2007; Swaffar & Arens, 2006), by engaging in the development and dissemination of open, user-generated materials based on authentic L2 texts. In the FLLITE life cycle (see Figure 7.1), an OER begins when an educator finds an appropriate foreign language text for use as the basis of a literacy lesson. Next, the educator reflects on the text's 'design' and

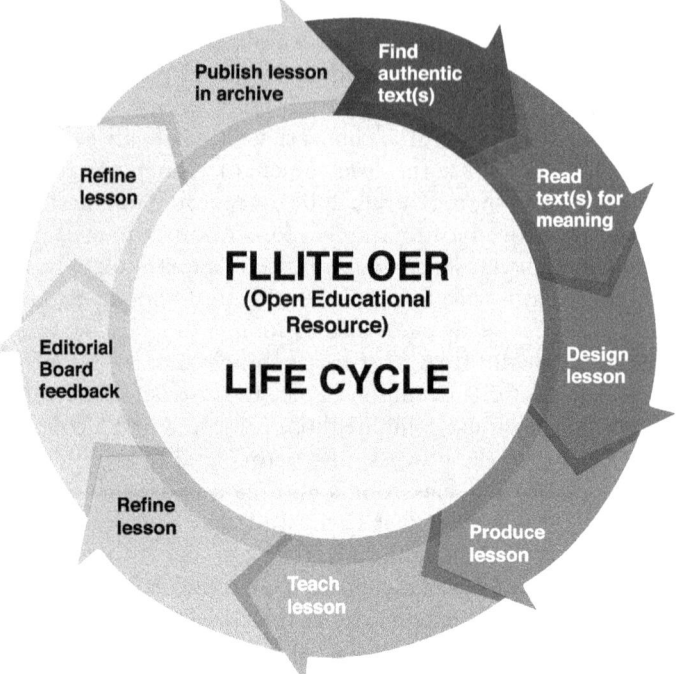

Figure 7.1 The life cycle of a FLLITE lesson

decides how the text should be didacticized. The design of a text refers to its identifiable features, such as the use of particular grammatical constructions or rhetorical tropes, that communicate particular literal and non-literal meanings. Didacticizing a text means turning it into a well-designed lesson following the FLLITE principles of language play. When the educator has created a copy of the FLLITE lesson, they are ready to teach the lesson in their classroom. Based on student feedback, the educator makes editorial changes to the original lesson and submits the revised OER for editorial review. Editorial board members serve as mentors, offering constructive feedback so that developers can revise their OER. Developers are encouraged to publish their OER lessons in the archive in order to make them publicly available. The published OER then becomes a resource for foreign language teachers, who may continue the cycle by accessing the published OER and adapting it to their local contexts.

Analyzing the Impact of the OER Life Cycle on Teachers

In the FLLITE project, the publication and dissemination of an OER is not only the culminating step in the OER life cycle, but the point at which developers begin to see themselves as members of an open, professional community committed to sharing their materials and ideas with each other. Unfortunately, studies of the OER life cycle have shown that teachers who use OER and who develop their own materials do not always share them online with others (OER Hub 2014 Evidence Report). To understand the effect of the FLLITE project on the professional development of foreign language educators, the project directors conducted interviews with two FLLITE authors – Devon and Marcelo – who had completed the entire OER life cycle. To a large extent, the interviews focused on the nature of the revisions that Devon and Marcelo made during the OER life cycle.

Devon and Marcelo were selected for further study for several reasons. First, they represented different disciplines; Devon came from applied linguistics and Marcelo from literary studies. Second, they taught different languages; Devon taught German, and Marcelo taught Spanish. Finally, after publishing their OER in the FLLITE archive, both engaged in the promotion of OER and FLLITE principles. Devon co-authored an article about the creation of literacy-based materials for language teaching that was published in *Die Unterrichtspraxis*, an academic journal for German teachers (Benjamin et al., 2020). Marcelo and Carol Ready, a colleague from the Department of Spanish and Portuguese Studies at the University of Minnesota who had also published a FLLITE lesson, gave a co-presentation about the FLLITE project at the Center for Advanced Research on Language Acquisition (CARLA) (Ready & Fuentes, 2018). For these reasons, it appeared that the FLLITE project had had a profound impact on both Devon and Marcelo, and thus, the FLLITE project directors decided that these two FLLITE authors would make excellent candidates for in-depth interviews. The interviews took place during the summer of 2018 and were conducted by telephone and by email.

Devon's German Lesson

Devon, a doctoral candidate in Foreign Language Education at the University of Texas at Austin, learned about the FLLITE project as part of an in-service workshop for German instructors at her university. Following the workshop, Devon and her fellow instructors were asked to brainstorm potential texts for a possible FLLITE lesson for the beginning German curriculum. Devon immediately thought of a viral video on YouTube that she had recently watched called *Is mir egal* ('I don't care'). In the two-minute video, the Turkish-German rapper Kazim Akboga portrays an employee of a Berlin public transportation company, the Berliner Verkehrsbetriebe Gesellschaft. Rapping about the different people he encounters on the subway, Akboga states that he doesn't care what the riders do on the transit system as long as they are respectful to the subway employees as well as to the other riders. The video intentionally blends genres – part music video, part advertisement – in order to convey the message that Berliners, including those who work for the municipal public transportation system, not only tolerate but celebrate diversity. When Devon shared the quirky video with her fellow German instructors at the workshop, they enthusiastically agreed to collaborate with her on the development of a FLLITE lesson.

In her interview, Devon said that her scholarly focus on language pedagogy distinguished her from her graduate student peers whom she characterized as specialists in literature, linguistics and culture studies. Devon characterized herself as energetic and extroverted, someone unafraid to try new ideas in her German classes. At the time of her introduction to FLLITE, Devon had already begun her dissertation on drama-based pedagogy, an improvisational form of drama in which students are guided by their teacher to imagine and reflect upon their learning experiences (Lee *et al.*, 2016). Devon noted that the FLLITE approach resonated with her because it was similar to drama-based pedagogy: '… the notion of the literary and the everyday was an extension of my work with drama-based pedagogy. I was trying to get students to play with the language, to be interactive and to explore and to work with the language in fun and creative ways. And so, I really liked how FLLITE extended that to everyday texts or finding literary texts and bringing them into the everyday.' Despite the perceived similarities between the two approaches, Devon claimed that FLLITE had provided her with some new 'tools' to overcome the long-standing curricular divisions between beginning 'language' courses and more advanced 'literature' courses: '…we have this sense that lower division is supposed to be about daily life and upper division is reserved for the canon, you know, very important literary works. And I liked that FLLITE questions that division…I know that the MLA report was one of the things that sparked the whole FLLITE project. The concept of [studying] literature even at the early levels and continuing language study even at the upper levels.'

After teaching the lesson to her beginning German students, Devon submitted it to the editorial board for review. The reviewers' feedback criticized the lesson for assuming a proficiency level well beyond that of a beginning German student and proposed several ways to simplify the instructional language. Devon and her co-authors responded to this feedback by amplifying the introductory parts of the lesson in order to guide the textual analysis in a step-by-step manner. The reviewers also questioned some of the 'language play' objectives of the original version of the lesson. For instance, the reviewers pointed out that some types of literary play that were listed in the table of contents did not actually appear in the lesson. Moreover, both reviewers challenged the lesson's treatment of the dative case, a grammar point that the authors had singled out as important for understanding the text. One reviewer commented that the treatment of the dative case was nothing more than a decontextualized grammatical explanation and therefore did not meet the criteria of

FLLITE's category of 'grammar play.' The reviewers suggested that the co-authors approach the dative case in terms of its impact on the overall meaning of the text. One reviewer suggested the students be asked at the outset of the lesson who exactly the 'mir' was in the title. *Mir* is the German first-person dative pronoun that means 'to me.'

In the revised version of the lesson, the authors decided to eliminate the grammatical discussion of the dative case altogether and focus instead on the rhyming couplets. Another significant revision concerned the use of English to discuss the cultural significance of the video. In the video, the protagonist sometimes employs English loanwords to describe things that he does or doesn't care about. The use of English by a German speaker as well as the general theme of multiculturalism seemed to give the students tacit permission to mix English and German in their responses. Furthermore, Devon argued for the use of code switching in parts of the lesson due to the students' minimal linguistic proficiency: '… some of the students were approaching the novice-high level on the American Council on the Teaching of Foreign Languages (ACTFL) standards. And so, we realized that to have a fruitful conversation about meaning making in the text, we would need to allow for some code switching.'

When asked how her participation in the FLLITE project had impacted her teaching, Devon noted that she had gained new ideas for using literary texts in the language curriculum, especially ideas about how to choose non-canonical texts: '…it doesn't have to be Goethe or Schiller…. You can find really beautiful language and very simple language for your students.' She also credited the FLLITE emphasis on language play as giving her the ability to frame textual interpretation in a way that led to 'more fruitful discussions' about language. In particular, Devon contended that FLLITE had helped her to get students to interpret 'different texts as well as different messages from the same text.' In addition, Devon highlighted the importance of the integration of language and culture when analyzing texts with her students, something that she had become more aware of through the development of her FLLITE lesson. Finally, Devon mentioned that the pedagogical applications of open media, a central feature of the FLLITE project, was something that she wanted to explore further.

In their *Die Unterrichtspraxis* article describing the development and teaching of their FLLITE lesson, Devon and her co-authors extolled the importance of adaptation that lies at the heart of the OER movement, demonstrating an understanding of the open-ended nature of OER development. In fact, the authors purposely refused to refer to their published lesson as a 'final draft' so as not to discourage others from adapting it (Benjamin *et al.*, 2020). Along similar lines, Devon mentioned during her interview that she wished the FLLITE archive included a space where authors could communicate with each other about how to adapt their FLLITE lessons to different local contexts. In essence, she wanted to make the phases of the OER life cycle even more apparent to members of the community.

Marcelo's Spanish Lesson

At the time of his collaboration in the FLLITE project, Marcelo was a doctoral student in Spanish literature at the University of Minnesota-Twin Cities. In 2017, Marcelo participated in the FLLITE summer workshop during which he refined a draft of a lesson entitled 'Una carta para Dios (A letter for God).' The lesson focused on a piece of found literature, a short, handwritten letter to God, which Marcelo had stumbled upon in his exploration of a church on the Chilean island of Chiloé. In the interview a year later, Marcelo recounted that his language program director had encouraged him to attend the workshop and that he had found the notion of the literary in the everyday particularly attractive because he felt that it was something he had 'intuitively already been doing.'

Marcelo explained that he often integrated authentic materials into his language classes, including everyday literary texts; however, this was not directly supported by his prior pedagogical training, which had been framed as communicative, but relied heavily on audiolingual methods. Marcelo's prior experience with more formal approaches to language teaching and learning is apparent in the original draft of his lesson. In the original draft, for the category 'Language Use & Language Play,' he focused almost exclusively on the accuracy of the letter, noting, 'Because the letter was written by a child or a teenager in a very spontaneous way, the writing offers several problems that intermediate or advanced students can detect and correct.' He went on to identify the salience of the subjunctive form, which 'the writer uses effortlessly' and 'even advanced learners still need to practice.' Already in the tension suggested in this early draft, Marcelo was beginning to recognize a constraint of formal approaches which privilege idealized notions of 'correctness' over contextual sensitivity, i.e. that the writer was young and the letter written spontaneously. In fact, Marcelo stated that his objective for using this text was 'to emphasize the precarious and spontaneous quality in the design of all the materials we will use.' However, the formal paradigms of his training had reduced this quality to linguistic 'problems.'

After completing the FLLITE workshop, Marcelo revised the draft of his lesson to focus more closely on the meaning design of the letter. In the final version of the lesson, the letter is framed in terms of two learning objectives: (1) *Manifestations of popular religiosity as part of Latin American culture,* and (2) *Personal letters as cultural and personal expressions of needs and wishes.* In particular, Marcelo's newly revised focus on linguistic expressions of needs and wishes seemed to evidence a shift in his pedagogical approach to the letter. In the revised lesson, the letter no longer serves primarily as an example of grammatical structures, but as an artifact from a social world in which it partakes and playfully engages with expectations of religiosity, one's relationship with God, and the genre of the personal letter. It appears that this revision resulted from feedback from the two reviewers who had noted the sociolinguistic factors that may have shaped the particular language used in the letter.

The revisions to the 'Cultural knowledge and perspectives' section also points to another aspect of Marcelo's conceptual development, which can be seen across the different versions of the lesson. In the original version of the lesson, the emphasis is on the material. But in the revised lesson, Marcelo wrote:

> Central to the activity are all the images, which show important cultural elements of southern Chile, and particularly the letter, written by hand over a sheet of paper torn from a school copybook. Since the activity's topic is popular religiosity and the central material is an anonymous handwritten letter, I want to emphasize the precarious and spontaneous quality in the design of all the materials we will use.

In this revised version, the text has been reframed in terms of the kinds of learning it affords. The linguistic learning objectives in the lesson plans created after the workshop more clearly connect to the cultural aspects of the letter. For example, the draft versions cited the opportunities afforded by the letter to practice difficult grammatical structures, notably the subjunctive, and yet, the grammatical goal seemed largely disconnected from the lesson's cultural focus. The cultural context of Chiloé and the popular religiosity of the churches remain a central focus in all versions of the lesson, but the final, revised version gives a more active role to the students in terms of 'Reading and analyzing letters as cultural and personal forms of expression.' This is linked to the more literacy-oriented objective of 'Personal letters as cultural and personal expressions of needs and wishes,' which is also reflected in the new emphasis on 'Grammar choices (verb tenses and mood) related to requests and wishes.'

The concept of language play, as conceptualized within the FLLITE project, seems to have enabled Marcelo to consider the 'message structure' (Swaffar, 2004) of the text, that is, the ways in which the letter organizes a perspective through choices in grammar and style that are shaped by social activity. The move away from language-as-structure toward language-as-meaning-potential allowed Marcelo to articulate the connections between the style of the letter and the compelling expression of desire enacted by the letter, the very connections that had drawn him to the text in the first place. In Marcelo's words, through the apprenticeship and participation in the OER community around FLLITE, he became more 'methodical.' He went on to explain that he had always taught in a learner-centered way and had 'let the students do the work,' but that he had not previously thought to consider the ways in which students might need different kinds of scaffolding in order to interpret the text themselves.

In the interview, Marcelo attributed his initial pedagogical choices to a tendency to 'focus on the ideas and sweep the language under the carpet,' which he viewed as common in foreign language literature courses. He also commented that he had never thought to make the feelings evoked by the text a core part of the lesson, because such a practice is generally avoided in literary studies and dismissed as 'touchy feely.' The notion that affective elements could be connected to language learning in a deliberate and integrated way was something new for Marcelo. When asked about his impressions looking back on his experience across the stages of developing a FLLITE lesson, Marcelo cited this as his most valuable lesson learned from the workshop: 'This has become an ethical thing for me.'

Marcelo's description of his experience echoes discussions in the field about the difficulty literary scholars have in teaching literature for language-learning purposes (e.g. Bernhardt, 2018). Near the end of the interview, Marcelo stated there are still things he wishes to 'polish,' a comment that highlights how the OER life cycle is in actuality more of a spiral. Through the acts of designing, revising, dialoguing around, reflecting on and revising again a text-based lesson, Marcelo initiated a transformational process of professional learning that – by his account – did not end with the publication of the revised FLLITE lesson.

Discussion

Both Devon and Marcelo embraced the FLLITE framework due in large part to their prior interests in literariness and language play. For Devon, this was shaped by an interest in drama-based pedagogy and for Marcelo, a desire to bring his expertise as a literary scholar to bear in the language classroom. Despite choosing texts that clearly captured the notion of the literary in the everyday, both of their original lessons missed the mark in their decontextualized treatments of grammatical features that were at odds with FLLITE's multiliteracies-inspired approach to grammar as a resource for textual meaning-making. Through their careful engagement with feedback from the editorial reviewers and their students, Devon and her co-authors and Marcelo were able to revise their lessons to include better scaffolding, a greater emphasis on language play, and a richer attention to the ways in which linguistic forms are meaningful within these texts. Having published their lessons, both also exemplified the OER life cycle where the development of one OER prompts the development of a derivative. In the case of Devon and her colleagues, this took the form of a scholarly publication, which provided space for further reflection. For Marcelo, this was expressed as a need to continue to 'polish things,' which captured the transformational orientation of OER (in contrast to the more static feel of other educational materials and products).

The most striking impact of the FLLITE OER life cycle on teacher cognition in these case studies was how the teacher-developers moved away from structuralist conceptions of language and began to embrace post-structuralist conceptions of language as social semiotic and situated practice (e.g. Allen, 2011; Dupuy & Allen, 2012). This shift in new ways of conceptualizing language seemed to be in part related to the categories of language play adopted by the FLLITE project, which offered a meta-language that was relatively intuitive and not the providence of a particular discipline. But at the same time, the ecological model of professional development provided through the OER life cycle created an opportunity for responsive mediation (e.g. Johnson & Golombek, 2011) from the mentors on the editorial board. Thus, the OER life cycle allowed the participants to discover new dimensions of literacy, which in turn enabled them to consider new ways of teaching language.

When integrated within a formal training program, the professional development model of FLLITE is an example of social pedagogy in which student work does not comprise one-off assignments that only the professor-of-record will see but 'real' products to be evaluated by a community. As such, the social orientation towards peer review and publication was a key element of the collaborative process for these FLLITE authors. In their reflections of the FLLITE OER life cycle, Devon and Marcelo mentioned the importance of receiving meaningful feedback and advice from a professional in the field who was neither their professor nor their mentor. At the same time, and perhaps more importantly, the practice of creating an OER seemed to foster openness to new pedagogies. Both Devon and Marcelo seemed to already identify strongly as foreign language educators, which is why they were motivated to take part in the workshops in the first place, and why they agreed to be interviewed a year later. But their participation in the FLLITE project repositioned them as 'open' foreign language educators. One of the strongest indicators of this is that they both emphasized the open-ended nature of what they had produced at the end of their testimonies. Rather than focusing on their OER as a finished product, they were thinking more about OER development as a continuous cycle of revision and improvement.

In addition, Devon and Marcelo were also thinking of their teaching and OER development in terms of a wider community. As noted, studies show that teachers who are new to the open education movement tend to treat OER like commercial products that do not allow for editorial change. As they become more aware of OER and the affordances of open licenses, teachers slowly begin to create their own derivatives. However, even after several years of developing OER for their own classrooms, many teachers never take the final step of sharing their OER with others. For some, online publication is too face-threatening since it makes one vulnerable to public criticism. For others, the development and dissemination of pedagogical materials is the role of commercial publishers, not of the classroom teacher. Or, it may simply be that teachers who develop their own OER are still unclear how to share their materials online with their colleagues. Whatever the case may be, the public sharing of one's OER is a turning point, the moment when a teacher fully embraces the new professional identity of an 'open educator.' This new identity is grounded in the value system of open education that emphasizes the importance of sharing one's ideas and products with members of one's community of practice (Bonk, 2009; Iiyoshi & Kumar, 2010; Jhangiani & Biswas-Diener, 2017). In summary, based on the OER life cycle, the FLLITE project created the requisite conditions for changes in teacher cognition and behavior. Through their participation in the FLLITE project, Devon and Marcelo not only became more aware of their pedagogical beliefs and practices, but they received the much-needed guidance and encouragement to change those beliefs and practices.

Conclusion

The concept of the OER life cycle has traditionally been invoked in the research literature to highlight professional practices implicated in the development and dissemination of OER (Gurell, 2008). As shown in this chapter, however, the OER life cycle can also be employed to highlight how the process changes the developer. In similar fashion, in the multiliteracies framework, literacy is viewed as an active process of designing a text that inevitably affects the designer: 'The act of designing leaves the designer redesigned' (Kalantzis *et al.*, 2016: 224). Thus, the development of open pedagogical materials guides L2 professionals to reflect more deeply on the classroom ecology. It is shown that such reflection may lead L2 teachers to examine their tacit conceptions of the second language itself. That said, the OER life cycle should not be seen as a panacea for the problems of professional development. For example, as discussed, the majority of FLLITE participants who created OER never published their work. Given the benefits that the case studies of Devon and Marcelo suggest, future studies of L2 teacher development will need to explore the obstacles that keep graduate students as well as teachers in the field from sharing their pedagogical materials with others. In addition, future studies should explore how the OER life cycle facilitates L2 teacher development by promoting the growth of a more open and collaborative knowledge ecology in the field of L2 education.

References

Allen, H.W. (2011) Embracing literacy-based teaching. A longitudinal study of the conceptual development of novice foreign language teachers. In K.E. Johnson and P.R. Golombek (eds) *Research on Second Language Teacher Education. A Sociocultural Perspective on Professional Development* (pp. 86–101). New York: Routledge.
Allen, H.W. and Dupuy, B. (2011) Evolving notions of literacy-based foreign language teaching: A qualitative study of graduate student instructors. In H.W. Allen and H.H. Maxim (eds) *Educating the Future Foreign Language Professoriate for the 21st Century* (pp. 171–191). Boston: Heinle Cengage.

Belz, J. (2002) Second language play as a representation of the multicompetent self in language study. *Journal of Language, Identity, and Education* 1 (1), 13–39.
Benjamin, J., Donohue-Bergeler, D., Fuchs, K. and Lorenz, A. (2020) 'Is nicht egal': Guided multimodal reading of a music video advertisement. *Die Unterrichtspraxis* 53 (1), 55–65.
Bernhardt, E. (2018) The chimera of curricular integration. *ADFL Bulletin* 44 (2), 107–110.
Blyth, C. (2018) Designing meaning and identity in multiliteracies pedagogy: From multilingual subjects to authentic speakers. *L2 Journal* 10 (2), 62–86.
Bonk, C. (2009) *The World is Open: How Web Technology is Revolutionizing Education*. San Francisco: Jossey Bass.
Broner, M. and Tarone, E. (2001) 'Is it fun?' Language play in a fifth grade Spanish immersion classroom. *Modern Language Journal* 85 (3), 363–379.
Byrd Clark, J. and Dervin, F. (2014) *Reflexivity in Language and Intercultural Education: Rethinking Multilingualism and Interculturality*. London: Routledge.
Byrnes, H., Crane, C., Maxim, H.H. and Sprang, K.A. (2006) Taking text to task: Issues and choices in curriculum instruction. *International Journal of Applied Linguistics* 152, 85–110.
Crane, C. (2015) Exploratory practice in the FL teaching methods course: A case study of three graduate student instructors' experiences. *L2 Journal* 7 (2), 1–23.
Cook, G. (2000) *Language Play, Language Learning*. Oxford: Oxford University Press.
Cope, B. and Kalantzis, M. (2009) 'Multiliteracies': New literacies, new learning. *Pedagogies* 4 (3), 164–194.
Cope, B. and Kalantzis, M. (eds) (2015) *A Pedagogy of Multiliteracies: Learning by Design*. London: Palgrave.
Dupuy, B. and Allen, H.W. (2012) Appropriating conceptual and pedagogical tools of literacy: A qualitative study of graduate student instructors. In G. Gorsuch and C. Davis (eds) *Working Theories for Teaching Assistant and International Teaching Assistant Development* (pp. 267–310). Stillwater, OK: New Forums Press.
Dupuy, B. and Michelson, K. (eds) (2019) *Pathways to Paradigm Change: Critical Examinations of Prevailing Discourses and Ideologies in Second Language Education. AAUSC Issues in Language Program Direction*. Boston: Cengage Thomson.
Gee, J.P. (2012) *Social Linguistics and Literacies: Ideology in Discourses* (4th edn). New York: Routledge.
Gramling, D. and Warner, C. (2016) 'Whose 'crisis in language'? Translating and the futurity of foreign language learning.' *L2 Journal* 8 (4), 76–90.
Gramling, D. and Warner, C. (2012) 'Toward a contact pragmatics of literature: Habitus, text, and the advanced L2 classroom.' In G. Levine and A. Phipps (eds) *Critical and Intercultural Theory and Language Pedagogy. AAUSC Issues in Language Program Direction* (pp. 57–75). Boston, MA: Heinle.
Gurell, S. (2008) *Open Educational Resources Handbook 1.0 for Educators*. Center for Open and Sustainable Learning, Utah State University. https://www.lulu.com/content/3597933.
Hasan, R. (2002) Semiotic mediation and mental development in pluralistic societies: Some implications for tomorrow's schooling. In G. Wells and G. Claxton (eds) *Learning for Life in the 21st Century: Socio-cultural Perspectives on the Future of Education* (pp. 112–126). Oxford: Blackwell.
Haßler, B., Hennessey, S., Cross, A., Chileshe, E. and Machiko, B. (2015) School-based professional development in a developing context: Lessons learnt from a case study in Zambia. *Journal of Professional Development in Education* 41 (5), 806–825.
Iiyoshi, T. and Kumar, V. (2010) *Opening Up Education: The Collective Advancement of Education Through Open Technology, Open Content and Open Knowledge*. Boston: MIT Press.

Jhangiani, R. and Biswas-Diener, R. (2017) *Open: The Philosophies and Practices that are Revolutionizing Education and Science*. London: Ubiquity Press.

Johnson, K.E. and Golombek, P.R. (2011) The transformative power of narrative in second language teacher education. *TESOL Quarterly* 45 (3), 486–509.

Kalantzis, M., Cope, B., Chan, E. and Dalley-Trim, L. (2016) *Literacies* (2nd edn). Cambridge: Cambridge University Press.

Karunanayaka, S., Naidu, S., Rajendra, J. and Ratnayake, H. (2015) From OER to OEP: Shifting practitioner perspectives and practices with innovative learning experience design. *Open Praxis* 7 (4), 339–350. See https://www.learntechlib.org/p/161991/ (accessed February 13, 2019).

Kern, R. (2000) *Literacy and Language Teaching*. Oxford: Oxford University Press.

Kern, R. (2015) *Language, Literacy, and Technology*. Cambridge: Cambridge University Press.

Kramsch, C. (2011) The symbolic dimensions of the intercultural. *Language Teaching* 44, 354–367.

Kramsch, C. (2006) From communicative competence to symbolic competence. *The Modern Language Journal* 90 (2), 249–252.

Kramsch, C. (1994) *Context and Culture in Language Teaching*. Oxford: Oxford University Press.

Kramsch, C. and Whiteside, A. (2008) Language ecology in multilingual settings. Towards a theory of symbolic competence. *Applied Linguistics* 29 (4), 645–671.

Landry, R. and Bourhis, R. (1997) Linguistic landscape and ethnolinguistic vitality. *Journal of Language and Social Psychology* 16 (1), 23–49.

Lantolf, J.P. (1997) The function of language play in the acquisition of L2 Spanish. In A. Pérez-Leroux and W.R. Glass (eds) *Contemporary Perspectives on the Acquisition of Spanish* (pp. 3–24). Somerville, MA: Cascadilla Press.

Lee, B., Cawthon, S. and Dawson, K. (2016) What happens when the apprentice is also the master? A qualitative analysis of graduate students in a cognitive apprenticeship. *International Journal of Teaching and Learning in Higher Education* 28 (3), 347–360.

Luks, J. (2013) *Le Littéraire dans le quotidien: Resources for a transdisciplinary approach to reading/writing at the first and second year levels of college French*. Austin, TX: Center for Open Educational Resources and Language Learning.

Malinowski, D. and Dubreil, S. (2019) Linguistic landscape and language learning. In C. Chapelle (ed.) *Encyclopedia of Applied Linguistics*. New York: John Wiley and Sons.

Maxim, H. (2006) Integrating textual thinking into the introductory college-level foreign language classroom. *The Modern Language Journal* 90, 19–32.

Nance, K.A. (2010) *Teaching Literature in the Languages: Expanding the Literary Circle Through Student Engagement*. Upper Saddle River: Pearson.

New London Group (1996) A pedagogy of multiliteracies: Designing social futures. *Harvard Educational Review* 66 (1), 60–92.

OER Evidence Report 2013–2014: Building Understanding of Open Education (2014) See https://oerresearchhub.files.wordpress.com/2014/11/oerrh-evidence-report-2014.pdf (accessed August 12, 2019).

Paesani, K., Allen, H.W. and Dupuy, B. (2016) *A Multiliteracies Framework for Collegiate Foreign Language Teaching*. Upper Saddle River, NJ: Pearson.

Paesani, K. and Allen, H.W. (2012) Beyond the language-content divide: A review of research on advanced collegiate foreign language teaching and learning. *Foreign Language Annals* 45, 54–75.

Ready, C. and Fuentes, M. (2018) Incorporating the literary and the everyday in the foreign language classroom. Presentation given at the CARLA Presentation Series, University of Minnesota, Minneapolis, MN. See https://z.umn.edu/2018_ReadyFuentes (accessed on July 20, 2019).

Sauro, S. and Sundmark, B. (2016) Report from middle earth: Fan fiction tasks in the EFL classroom. *ELT Journal* 70 (4), 414–423.
Swaffar, J., Arens, K. and Byrnes, H. (2005) *Reading for Meaning: An Integrated Approach to Language Learning.* Englewood Cliffs: Prentice Hall.
Swaffar, J. and Arens, K. (2005) *Remapping the Foreign Language Curriculum: An Approach Through Multiple Literacies.* New York: MLA.
Swaffar, J. (2004) A template for advanced learner tasks: Staging genre reading and cultural literacy through the précis. In H. Byrnes and H. Maxim (eds) *Advanced Foreign Language Learning: A Challenge to College Programs* (pp. 19–45). Boston: Thompson and Heinle.
Tarone, E. (2000) Getting serious about language play: Language play, interlanguage variation and second language acquisition. In B. Swierzbin, F. Morris, M. Anderson, C. Klee and E. Tarone (eds) *Social and Cognitive Factors in SLA: Proceedings of the 1999 Second Language Research Forum* (pp. 31–54). Somerville, MA: Cascadilla Press.
Tarone, E. (2019) Language play and double voicing in second language acquisition and use. In M. Haneda and H. Nassaji (eds) *Perspectives on Language as Action* (pp. 177–192). Bristol: Multilingual Matters.
Tosata, P. and Bodi, G. (2011) Collaborative environments to foster creativity, reuse and sharing of OER. *European Journal of Open, Distance and E-learning.* See http://www.eurodl.org/?p=special&sp=articles&article=461&abstract=456 (accessed February 19, 2019).
Warner, C. (2004) It's just a game, right?: Types of play in foreign language CMC. *Language Learning and Technology* 8 (2), 69–87.
Warner, C. (2011) Rethinking the role of language study in internationalizing higher education. *L2 Journal* 3 (1), 1–21.
Warner, C. and Dupuy, B. (2018) Moving toward multiliteracies in foreign language teaching: Past and present perspectives ... and beyond. *Foreign Language Annals* 51 (1), 116–128.
Warner, C. and Gramling, D. (2014) Kontaktpragmatik: fremdsprachliche Literatur und symbolische Beweglichkeit. *Jahrbuch Deutsch als Fremdsprache* 51, 67–76.
Widdowson, H.G. (1975) *Stylistics and the Teaching of Literature.* London: Longman.
Yergler, N.R. (2010) Search and discovery: OER's open loop. In *Open Ed 2010 Proceedings. Barcelona: UOC, OU, BYU.* See http://hdl.handle.net/10609/4852 (accessed October 18, 2018).

Part 3
The Exosystem: Developing Knowledge in the Field of L2 Education

8 The Affordances and Challenges of Open-access Journals: The Case of an Applied Linguistics Journal

Dorothy Chun and Trude Heift

This chapter addresses the role of open-access journals in a 'knowledge ecology' as the main theme of this volume and an approach to scholarship in foreign language teaching. As Editors-in-Chief of *Language Learning & Technology* (*LLT*), we provide a brief history of *LLT* since its inception in 1997 and discuss the affordances and the challenges faced by an online, open-access journal in applied linguistics. In 2010, Chun and Thompson reported on the advantages and disadvantages of open-access journals for the first 13 years of *LLT*'s existence. Some of the affordances cited that continue to this day include the wide dissemination and access on the internet, ease of tracking authorship and readership, and the speed and lower costs of publication as compared with print journals. The main challenges that *LLT* initially faced concerned the perception in the profession that online journals were of lower quality. That perception is changing. *LLT's* high-impact factors have remained steady, and researchers have been able to publish their work without paying author processing fees while also retaining copyright of their publication. Although the future seems bright for this new knowledge ecology, the major challenge of financial security to ensure longevity of the journal remains.

Initial Concept

Language Learning & Technology (*LLT*) was the first Computer-Assisted Language Learning (CALL) journal that was entirely online and open access from its inception in 1997. The founding editor, Mark Warschauer, was prescient in predicting and implementing an open knowledge ecology with a cutting-edge journal that would be available to everyone in the world. The journal was initially supported by two Language Resource Centers (LRCs) funded by US Department of Education Title VI grants: the National Foreign Language Resource Center (NFLRC) at the University of Hawai'i at Mānoa and the Center for Language Education and Research (CLEAR) at Michigan State University. NFLRC funding supported the hiring of a graduate student to serve as Managing Editor, and CLEAR funding hosted the website and supported employment of a webmaster. Despite the fact that the initial sponsors were US federal grantees, the vision was that readers anywhere in the world, in particular those in developing countries, would have access to the journal. In 2019, CLEAR withdrew as a sponsor but another LRC, the Center for Open Educational Resources & Language Learning (COERLL) began their sponsorship. It may be pertinent to note the founding some two decades later of Open Access 2020 (https://oa2020.org), which 'is a global alliance committed to accelerating the transition to open access' for all academic publishing.

Brief History

The first issue of *Language Learning & Technology* appeared in July 1997. For the first four years, two issues per year were published. In order to ensure a strong start to the journal, special issues were commissioned for half of the issues, starting with the inaugural special issue 'Defining the Research Agenda.' The editors in chief first identified important topics in the field of Computer-Assisted Language Learning then approached leading scholars in the field to serve as guest editors for these special issues. Calls for Papers were disseminated widely, with the guest editors also pro-actively inviting top scholars working on the topic to submit papers. Of course, all submissions to the journal, then and now, including those invited by guest editors, undergo blind peer review by 2–4 expert reviewers. The alternation of special issues with regular issues was successful in attracting quality submissions that were eventually published.

After a solid first four years, it became necessary to increase the number of issues per year from two to three. We persisted in publishing half of the issues as regular issues and half as special issues with specific topics, and this continues to the present day. It has been a good model, as identifying themes that are on the cutting edge brings together current work on that topic in one dedicated issue and provides a stimulating synergy. Having intentional clusters of articles emphasizes the 'hot topics' at a given point in time and soliciting contributions from top scholars ensures greater international readership.

In addition to regular research articles, *LLT* has published a variety of other columns, starting with reviews of books, software, websites and apps. The 'Emerging Technologies' column has been an integral and popular column since *LLT*'s inception, and other columns include 'Commentaries' (brief observations about published articles in *LLT*), 'On the Net' (in Volumes 1–12, descriptions of websites that were useful for language learning), 'Action Research' (Volumes 15:2–20:1) and 'Language

Learning and Technology Forum' (starting with Volume 21:1). These columns are intended to complement the research articles and to provide practicing teachers with the latest information on available technologies and pedagogical applications.

Affordances and Challenges of Online, Open Access

Chun and Thompson (2010) discussed the advantages and disadvantages of online, open access journals in applied linguistics as experienced by *LLT* from 1997–2009. The primary affordances over traditional print journals in the first decade or so, and ones that have continued to be the case for our journal, include:

- broad dissemination and access;
- ability to track readership, quantitatively and geographically;
- unlimited virtual space for content and ease of hyperlinks;
- relatively lower cost of production;
- relatively shorter length of time between submission of manuscript and acceptance/publication;
- ease of access and its influence on journal impact.

Each of the above will be discussed below, based on the statistics that have been gathered over the last 22 years.

Broad dissemination and *LLT*'s readership

Online, open-access journals allow scholarly research to become freely and permanently available without restrictions, not only to scholars and practitioners in developed countries without access to university libraries, but also to those in developing countries who personally or through their institutional libraries cannot afford journal subscriptions. Over the past two decades, *LLT* has increasingly been able to reach a broad audience including researchers in developing countries and small or specialized research institutions. Due to online tracking capabilities, we are also able to readily collect data on *LLT*'s readership.

Table 8.1 shows the total number of visitors to the *LLT* site along with the total number of unique IP addresses at five-year intervals from 2007 to 2017. *Total visitors* includes human visitors, but excludes search engine

Table 8.1 Number of *LLT* site visitors

Year	Total visitors	Total unique IPs / unique visitors
2007	753,611	257,446
2012	687,892	372,640
2017	1,264,648	611,632

robots and other automated systems. Visitors are tracked by the IP address of the computer they are using. If the same IP address returns to view the site, that will not increase the number of unique visitors. Note that the number of unique visitors, however, is only a rough estimate: the IP address of some visitors could change between visits (depending on their type of network connection), and different visitors can sometimes appear to share the same IP address if they are behind a 'proxy server' at a large company or ISP.

The data provided in Table 8.1 further show that the total number of visitors has increased by roughly 68% from 2007 to 2017. By now, *LLT* has over 1 million visitors to its site. While there were slightly more visitors in 2007 compared to 2012 (65,719), the number of total unique IPs increased by roughly 45% from 2007 to 2012 indicating that there were more unique visitors as opposed to people revisiting the *LLT* site. Over the past 10 years, *LLT* has seen an increase of 138% of unique visitors to its website with a total of 611,632 visitors in 2017.

The number of visitors of the top 10 countries for 2012 and 2017 is presented in Table 8.2. These data act as a metric for active users and readership. They reveal that in the United States and China there is a stable, core readership that actively visits the *LLT* website year after year. The visitors for the United States and China show an increase of 69.83% and 91.3% over the past five years, respectively. Russia broke into the top three countries for the first time in 2017, with a total of 69,263 active visitors. India continued its steady growth with an increase of 115.29% from 2012 to 2017, as did most of the previously lower-ranking countries such as Brazil and others which are not presented in Table 8.2. The UK and Canada fell in their rankings of the top 10 visitors but they, nevertheless, record an increase in visitors over the last five years of 22.02% and 96.47%, respectively. Vietnam, Indonesia and Switzerland are no longer

Table 8.2 Visitors for 2012 and 2017 by country

2012	Count	2017	Count	% Increase
1. US	193,952	1. US	329,381	69.83
2. China	76,239	2. China	145,844	91.3
3. UK	38,677	3. Russia	69,263	N/A
4. Vietnam	37,997	4. Philippines	49,558	329.63
5. Germany	20,080	5. UK	47,192	22.02
6. India	17,111	6. Brazil	37,633	N/A
7. Indonesia	16,749	7. India	36,839	115.29
8. Canada	13,079	8. Germany	32,038	59.55
9. Switzerland	12,305	9. France	30,182	N/A
10. Philippines	11,535	10. Canada	25,696	96.47
TOTAL visitors	437,724		803,626	

Table 8.3 Number of *LLT* subscribers

LLT subscribers	1997	2002	2007	2012	2017
Total	1,076	3,944	10,681	20,766	24,114

in the top 10 in 2017 but France joined the top 10 visitor's list for the first time in 2017. It is, however, exciting to see countries such as Vietnam, India, Indonesia, Philippines and Brazil even in the top 10, as this suggests that the journal is reaching developing countries. It is plausible that *LLT*, as a small niche journal, has gone global in two decades due to being open access from the very start.

In contrast to data on website visitors, Table 8.3 displays the number of *LLT* subscribers at five-year intervals from the inception of the journal in 1997 to 2017. In 1997, *LLT* recorded a total of 1,076 subscribers. This number has been steadily increasing over the past 20 years and reached a total of 24,114 subscribers in 2017. Subscriptions are free but require readers to fill out an online subscription form. Subscribers are then notified when each new issue is published. Information about subscribers provides important demographic data for *LLT*'s sponsors.

Unlimited virtual space and production costs

One of the advantages of being published entirely and exclusively online is that there are no page limits in terms of physical space limitations. The number of pages of *LLT* issues has been increasing steadily, and the main limitation is the workload for the editors and the editorial staff.

As indicated in Table 8.4, the number of articles and total page numbers per issue and year remained fairly steady from 2004–2012. Starting in 2013, however, these numbers have nearly doubled, peaking at 22

Table 8.4 Number of articles and page numbers

Year	Number of articles	Number of pages	Year	Number of articles	Number of pages
2004	12	351	*2011*	12	409
2005	14	410	*2012*	11	380
2006	12	402	*2013*	19*	611
2007	13	442	*2014*	19	613
2008	12	374	*2015*	19	558
2009	12	350	*2016*	24	624
2010	10	293	*2017*	22	659

Note: *One article from one of the issues in 2013 includes a 75-page annotated bibliography, which is equivalent to about three articles.

articles with a total of 659 pages in 2017. Instead of *LLT*'s historical average in publishing around four articles per issue, now it is not uncommon that an issue contains up to eight articles in addition to other columns.

Clearly, such an increase in journal size is not possible with a print journal without a considerable increase in cost. For *LLT*, this has resulted in engaging additional editorial staff such as copy-editors. Yet, no additional production costs have been incurred, as the journal has relied on the expertise and goodwill of professionals in the field, including graduate students. The fact that none of the *LLT* editorial staff, however, has to reside in the same location is a small, yet not insignificant advantage of online journals. Editorial assistants (or managing editors) of many journals often live and work in the same place as the journal editors or webmasters, though this is changing as everyone is becoming accustomed to digital communications. This ability to scale up without significant cost increases is in line with the Open Access 2020 goal of ensuring 'that research articles are published immediately open access and that the costs associated with their dissemination are transparent, equitable and economically sustainable' (https://oa2020.org/progress-report/).

Despite the fact that online publishing can accommodate including multimedia with articles much more readily than print media, it has been disappointing that more *LLT* authors have not taken advantage of this capability. The irony of course is that authors are often use cutting edge technologies in their research and teaching but somehow do not think to link these rich resources to their scholarly publications even when there are few restrictions for doing so. Perhaps *LLT*'s editors will need to be more pro-active in the future and strongly encourage authors to add multimedia links to their articles.

In addition, online journals do not have to be constrained by the same structure as print journals, namely publishing set annual volumes and any number of issues per volume. However, *LLT* has not yet converted to a 'rolling' publication schedule because of a lack of funding to cover the additional personnel cost. But we are striving to implement a system of publishing articles when they are ready that does not require added personnel.

Publication times

Online journals have the advantage of being able to pre-publish an article before the issue in which it appears is published. *LLT* has not followed this model in the past, mainly due to the fact that *LLT*'s webpages were created manually. As a result, the pre-publication of manuscripts would have increased the workload for its Managing Editor and Webmaster significantly thus requiring additional resources. *LLT*'s new website, however, is a part of ScholarSpace at the University of Hawai'i, an open-access, digital institutional repository which will make it less onerous for *LLT*'s editorial staff to display manuscripts on its website as soon as they are accepted (see later section).

Table 8.5 displays the mean and median length of time between submission and acceptance of research articles. On average, it took roughly 270 days between submission and acceptance of an article with an average median of 275 days. While the means for 2013–2017 are comparable, there is a slight increase in the mean length of time of submission to acceptance in 2017 while the median time shows a small decrease in 2017 compared to 2013. The fact that these numbers have not changed drastically over the past five years is a reflection of the overall review process of *LLT*. Clearly, the numbers are not affected by the fact that *LLT* is an online, open-access journal. Instead, *LLT* articles which pass the internal review process are additionally reviewed by 2–4 external expert reviewers and it is not uncommon that several iterations of corrections are required for an article to be accepted. Accordingly, the processing time of submission to acceptance of an article has remained fairly constant over the years. Note, however, that the processing times displayed in Table 8.5 apply to research articles only and other column contributions (e.g. book reviews, commentaries) are processed significantly faster due to a less lengthy and rigorous review process.

Table 8.5 further shows the mean and median length of time between submission and publication of research articles. Note that in odd years, *LLT* publishes only one special issue while in even years, there are two special issues per volume. These special issues have a fixed time frame of 15 months from the time of manuscript submission to publication. Table 8.5 indicates that the length of time between submission and publication of articles is longer in years where *LLT* publishes two special issues (526.16 in 2014, 616.70 in 2016) suggesting that the research articles that appear in regular issues are generally processed faster than those in special issues.

A final point is that since there are no space limitations, the journal does not have the same kind of 'backlog' that a print journal might incur. This means that there is no limit to the number of articles that can be

Table 8.5 Mean and median number of days between *LLT* submissions and their acceptance and publication

Year	Submission to acceptance		Submission to publication	
	M	Med	M	Med
2013	260.95	265.00	401.58	441.00
2014	276.74	315.00	526.16	529.00
2015	249.90	271.00	459.81	457.00
2016	263.04	268.00	616.70	675.00
2017	295.59	256.00	571.45	457.00

published in a given issue. The quality of the article is the only factor determining when and in which issue it appears.

Does ease of access result in greater numbers of citations and in turn greater impact?

Some studies conducted at the turn of the millennium, shortly after *LLT* commenced publication, indicated that academic articles published online received substantially more citations than those published in print journals (e.g. Curti *et al.*, 2001 for medicine; Lawrence, 2001, for computer science). However, a critical review of the literature by Craig *et al.* (2007) found no evidence to support a *causal* relationship between the Open Access status of a given article and higher citation count, but rather showed a more complex set of contributors to the effect itself. A study by McCabe and Snyder (2015) of economics and business journals determined that the huge difference in citations found previously for online vs. print articles was reduced to nothing due to the fact that quality of the publications was not controlled. They found substantial heterogeneity across platforms, but did find that some platforms, including Elsevier's ScienceDirect, exhibited no online effects, whereas JSTOR showed significantly positive effects, namely a 10% increase in citations (2015: 162).

Table 8.6 displays *LLT*'s impact factors from 2010–2018 which have been steadily increasing and peaking in 2016 with a 2-year impact factor of 2.29 and a 5-year impact factor of 3.31. In 2019 *LLT* ranked 14th out of 181 journals in Linguistics and 47th out of 238 journals in Education, according to Journal Citation Reports (JCR), one of the most widely used resources for determining journal impact, based on the Web of Science database. If sorted by Open-access Journals, *LLT* was ranked #1 in the world among Open-Access journals in Linguistics and #3 in the world among Open-access journals in Education in 2017.

Table 8.6 *LLT*'s impact factors 2010–2018

Year	Impact factor	5-year	Linguistics	Education
2018	2.57	3.30	11 out of 184	32 out of 243
2017	2.11	3.01	14 out of 181	47 out of 238
2016	2.29	3.31	8 out of 180	26 out of 235
2015	1.38	2.42	14 out of 179	30 out of 230
2014	1.13	2.10	13 out of 171	30 out of 224
2013	1.93	2.36	10 out of 169	26 out of 219
2012	1.38	2.21	12 out of 160	19 out of 216
2011	1.74	2.47	7 out of 162	15 out of 206
2010	1.69	2.46	8 out of 141	15 out of 177

The ability to access these impact factors is a result of an Open Education Practice of using open-access databases to track journal rankings. The JCR database contains more than 12,000 journals and is accessible via one's institution, e.g. a university library, so is free to anyone at the institution but not to the general public. Alternative databases and journal ranking sources that are truly free and open access, include, e.g. Google Scholar Metrics, where *LLT* is ranked #10 of all Educational Technology journals; Eigenfactor (http://eigenfactor.org), where *LLT* has an Eigenfactor of 36 and an Article Influence score of 72 in 2019; SCImago Journal and Country Rank (SJC), where *LLT* had index of 1.08 in 2017 and an h-index of 57. These calculations of journal impact factors are more open and more transparent to readers than ever before, an important tenet of the open knowledge ecology.

Challenges of Online, Open-access Journals

In addition to the many affordances of online, open-access journals described above, there are, however, a number of challenges which will be discussed below. Chun and Thompson (2010) had presented the following:

- perception in the profession of online journals being of lower quality;
- impact of the perception in the profession on tenure and promotion decisions;
- financial uncertainty.

Perception of online publications: Changing from challenge to affordance

In the field of applied linguistics, electronic publications were initially often viewed as less rigorous than publications in print media (Magnan, 2007). CALL researchers, however, expressed positive views of online journals and believed that a rigorous peer-review process resulting in quality content is the main criterion for all publications, both online or in print (Smith & Lafford, 2009).

In 2015, the American Association of Applied Linguistics approved an extensive set of Promotion and Tenure Guidelines for the field of applied linguistics (https://www.aaal.org/promotion-and-tenure-guidlines). Inasmuch as peer-reviewed journal articles are the expected venue for publication in the field, one of the most significant recommendations was 'that peer reviewed online journals should be treated similarly to traditional print journals.' This is significant because in the early years of *LLT*'s existence, there was a perception that online, open-access journals might not be as rigorous in their publication standards as print journals, despite the fact that submissions to the journal would undergo the same

Table 8.7 *LLT's* acceptance rates 1997–2017

Year	Total submissions	Published	Acceptance rate
1997	25	8	32%
2002	71	8	11%
2007	147	15	10%
2012	225	19	11.7%
2017	211	22	10.4%

rigorous peer review process as print journals. It is now widely accepted that the advantages of traditional print journals (double-blind peer-review, copyright protection) do not have to be sacrificed in free online journals (Suber, 2002).

Table 8.7 provides the acceptance rates of *LLT*'s manuscript submissions at five-year intervals since its inception in 1997 to 2017. While *LLT*'s acceptance rate during its first year of operation was 32%, for the following 20 years, the acceptance rates are at least as rigorous as a highly competitive print journal. On average, *LLT* has published roughly 10% of its total submissions during the past 20 years.

Financial challenges to open access

One of the most challenging dilemmas faced to date is whether to remain free and open access or to be acquired by and published by a traditional press. During its existence thus far, there have been a number of instances when consideration was given to the latter option, primarily to ensure the stability and longevity of the journal. Traditional publishers have contacted us, proposing their publishing services, generally touting their ability to market the journal more widely and to take advantage of their existing infrastructures for copyediting and production. We have entered into sometimes lengthy negotiations with different publishers. In earlier years, publishers wanted to adhere to their traditional models of charging subscription fees to libraries and individuals. More recently, as the publishing industry has been evolving and changing, proposals for article processing charges (APCs) for authors were put forth.

Despite the fact that funding for the journal has until now been completely reliant on US Department of Education Title VI grants to national Language Resource Centers (LRCs) – whose continuance is by no means guaranteed – and since 2014 on the Center for Language and Technology (CLT) at the University of Hawai'i at Mānoa, *LLT* continues its commitment to remain open access. Support from LRCs and the CLT is naturally greatly appreciated. The journal continues to operate on a minimal budget, with the only paid position being that of the Managing Editor, usually a graduate student in Applied Linguistics, and with modest stipends to the Editors-in-Chief that began in 2010. As with print journals or those published by commercial or university presses, Associate Editors, column editors and peer reviewers are providing valuable professional service to the journal without receiving monetary compensation. As noted above, *LLT* relies primarily on graduate student volunteers to assist with copyediting.

For a number of years (2010–2018), we subscribed to ScholarOne Manuscripts (previously known as Manuscript Central, now owned by Clarivate Analytics), to facilitate online manuscript submission and the peer review process. Support for this subscription was provided by NFLRC and CLEAR, and most recently, CLT. In an effort to trim costs, we have transitioned to the Open Journal Systems, an open-source software for the management of peer-reviewed academic journals, created by the Public Knowledge Project at Simon Fraser University. Using OJS aligns with our mission to keep the journal economically sustainable.

Over the years, the *LLT* website has required updating, to stay abreast of the latest web functionalities (e.g. back end databases, digital repositories) and appearance (e.g. web design). Website updates have not occurred as frequently as might be desirable due to financial constraints, but we are pleased and gratified to have received support from the CLT from 2017–18 to inaugurate *LLT*'s new website (www.lltjournal.org), now a part of ScholarSpace at the University of Hawai'i, an open-access, digital institutional repository. ScholarSpace provides a *permanent* web location for access to all volumes of the journal.

Diversity of *LLT* Authors and Quality of Submissions

Ideally, journal publications represent a wide geographical diversity of scholars, especially as it allows authors to share and disseminate their research projects around the world. The quality of submissions, however, has not allowed *LLT* to achieve a very high level of diversity although its author demographics have certainly shifted over the past 20 years.

Table 8.8 provides data on the location of our authors' academic affiliations by displaying their journal contributions at five-year intervals from 1997 to 2017. In considering the totals of those years, 52% of *LLT* authors are affiliated with a US institution, followed by European institutions with 22%. In those past 20 years, *LLT* has also recorded an increasing number of authors from the Asia/Pacific countries (20%) as well as from Canada (5%). Unfortunately, due to a much more limited number and the general quality of submissions, *LLT* has not been able to publish research during those years from Latin American countries, the Middle East and Africa with the exception of a co-authored publication in 2012.

As a way of raising the level of submissions from developing countries, the Editors of *LLT* offered workshops on conducting and publishing CALL research at the annual CALICO Conference (from 2010–2013).

Table 8.8 Authors' demographics

Countries of authors' institutions	1997	2002	2007	2012	2017	Total	% of Authors
Asia/Pacific		3	8	7	9	27	20%
Canada		3	1		2	6	5%
Europe		5	4	9	12	30	22%
Latin America						0	0%
Middle East/Africa				1		1	1%
US	9	22	11	8	20	70	52%
Total*	9	33	24	25	43	134	100%

Note. *In the case of a co-authored publication, each author's institution was considered.

The hope was that students and scholars, in particular those from developing countries, would participate in these workshops so that they could better understand how to conduct CALL research and write up their research findings. The PowerPoint slides used in these workshops were posted on the *LLT* website and were updated in 2017, easily accessible on the website under 'Research Guidelines.' At our annual *LLT* Editorial Board meetings, a topic of discussion is perennially how to encourage and attract submissions from less developed nations.

In one of the annual meetings, the Editors and Editorial Board of *LLT* discussed the possibility of publishing articles in languages other than English to promote a wider geographical diversity of scholars but decided against it for practical reasons. Not only would a much larger pool of reviewers be needed but also *LLT's* editorial staff would need to cover a fairly wide range of languages to be fully inclusive of all language submissions and to ensure appropriate fit and standards of the journal.

Integration with Other Entities in the 'Knowledge Ecology'

Since 2003, the journal has been listed in the Directory of Open-access Journals. Open access means that readers are allowed to download, copy, distribute, print, or link to the full texts of the articles, or use them for any other lawful purpose, without asking prior permission from the publisher or the author, as long as *Language Learning & Technology* is cited as the source of the content. Furthermore, authors are not charged (and have never been charged) APC for submitting articles or for publication of their accepted articles. From the start, authors have always maintained copyright over their individual articles and are the ones to be contacted regarding any questions about or permission to republish parts or all of their articles. Starting in 2020, everything published in *LLT* is under an Attribution-NonCommercial-NoDerivs Creative Commons license, or CC-BY-NC-ND, which permits users to download and share the original work (provided they credit the original source), without any alterations or commercial use.

This direct open access allows college and university instructors to include *LLT* articles in their course readers without obtaining prior permission or paying royalties. It is also becoming increasingly common for institutions of higher education to make it mandatory for faculty to deposit copies of their research into open-access repositories in order to make their scholarship available to anyone in the world. This type of access is sometimes termed 'green' open access and allows authors to make final versions of their article openly available, either after being accepted for publication or immediately upon publication. In the case of *LLT*, authors can deposit the actual published article into the repository, not just the final draft.

As another way of supporting an open knowledge ecology, since 2013, *LLT* has been encouraging its authors to consider uploading their data collection materials to the IRIS database, an online digital repository for data collection materials used for second language research (see Marsden et al., 2016). Whenever an article is accepted for publication in *LLT*, the letter of acceptance includes a link to our website (https://www.lltjournal.org/submission-guidelines/), which states '*LLT* encourages authors to consider uploading their data collection materials to the IRIS database. IRIS is an online repository for data collection materials used for second language research. This includes data elicitation instruments such as interview and observation schedules, language tests and stimuli, pictures, questionnaires, software scripts, URL links, word lists, teaching intervention activities, amongst many other types of materials used to elicit data. Please see http://www.iris-database.org for more information and to upload. Any questions, or the materials themselves, may be sent to iris@iris-database.org. When your article has been formally accepted for publication, your instrument(s) can be uploaded to the IRIS database with an "in press" reference. The IRIS team will add page numbers to the reference once they are available.'

In addition, the same team that initiated the IRIS database has introduced another open resource, OASIS, the Open Accessible Summaries In Language Studies initiative (https://oasis-database.org), which aims to make research findings on language learning and teaching available and accessible to a wide audience. *LLT* fully and heartily supports this endeavor with links to the database and direct emails to journal article authors encouraging them to submit one-page summaries of their work that would make their research accessible to teachers, language policy makers and the general public outside of academia. Specifically, OASIS requested that we submit a short list of *LLT* articles for their staff to summarize, and all of the articles we suggested have been summarized. We will start providing links to these summaries at the top of every article that has been summarized. We also contacted authors of the most recent issues of *LLT* and requested a one-page summary of their article. In all of our acceptance letters, we are including a request for a summary as we feel strongly that a significant aspect of the open knowledge ecology is that the general public have access to the results of academic research, particularly in such an important global issue as language and culture learning.

SPARC (the Scholarly Publishing and Academic Resources Coalition) advocates the adoption of policies and practices that advance Open Access, Open Data and Open Education. The fact that *LLT* is and always will be Open Access, combined with actively encouraging authors to contribute their empirical data to IRIS (Open Data) and to summarize their research findings succinctly into one-page synopses accessible to the general, world-wide public (Open Education), positions our journal well in the new knowledge ecology.

In comparing *LLT* with other CALL journals (e.g. *ReCALL*, *CALL*, *CALICO* journal, *System*), the initial goal and concept of an open knowledge ecology with a cutting-edge journal that would be available to everyone in the world still sets *LLT* apart from other CALL journals. Since *LLT's* inception, other CALL journals with high impact factors have gone online and some of them provide albeit limited open access in the form of pre-publication of articles, for instance. Yet, *LLT* with its truly free and open access fills a different niche in that it is and, likely remains, the only highly ranked CALL journal without any APC or journal/membership subscription fees. *LLT* therefore is in a position to reach a broad audience including researchers in developing countries and small or specialized institutions.

Summary

This chapter provided an overview of the affordances and challenges faced by an online, open-access applied linguistics journal. After more than 20 years of operation, *LLT* has become exemplary for this new knowledge ecology and by now, the affordances certainly outweigh the challenges the journal has faced since its inception in 1997. The only challenge that remains for any open-access model including *LLT* is the financial security to ensure the longevity of the journal. *LLT* has been extremely fortunate to have academic sponsors and volunteers who enabled the operation of the journal over the past 20 years.

More generally speaking, however, this new knowledge ecology requires a shift in thinking and allocation of resources in that subscription and publication fees are no longer carried by each individual academic institution or authors. Instead, it takes a fraction of the monies currently paid to publishers to support the open-access model. Academic institutions, especially those who are in the position to receive public funding can support the model from which all researchers will benefit. In the case of *LLT*, this has allowed for research to reach a broad audience including researchers in developing countries and small or specialized research institutions. This is clearly not possible under the traditional model of a publisher who charges steep subscription fees to each subscriber by, in addition, also retaining copyright of the author's work. *LLT* takes pride in the fact that it has been in a position to provide free access to its readership and authorship all over the world and the retention of authors' copyright for more than 20 years.

Acknowledgements

We gratefully acknowledge the support of Julio Rodriguez, the Director of the National Foreign Language Resource Center and the Center for Language and Technology at the University of Hawai'i at Mānoa; Susan Gass, the Director of the former Center for Language Education and Research at Michigan State University; and Carl Blyth, the Director of the Center for Open Educational Resources and Language Learning at the University of Texas at Austin. We also thank Ivan Banov, former Managing Editor of *Language Learning & Technology*, who helped compile some of the data in this chapter.

References

Chun, D.M. and Thompson, I. (2010) Issues in publishing an online, open-access CALL journal. *The Modern Language Journal* 94 (4), 648–651.

Craig, I., Plume, A., McVeigh, M., Pringle, J. and Amin, M. (2007) Do open access articles have greater citation impact? A critical review of the literature. *Journal of Informetrics* 1 (3), 239–248.

Curti, M., Pistotti, V., Gabutti, G. and Klersy, C. (2001) Impact factor and electronic versions of biomedical scientific journals. *Haematologica* 86, 1015–1020.

Lawrence, S. (2001) Free online availability substantially increases a paper's impact. *Nature* 411, 521.

Magnan, S.S. (2007) Commentary: The promise of digital scholarship in SLA research and language pedagogy. *Language Learning & Technology* 11 (3), 152–155.

Marsden, E., Mackey, A. and Plonsky, L. (2016) The IRIS Repository: Advancing research practice and methodology. In A. Mackey and E. Marsden (eds) *Advancing Methodology and Practice: The IRIS Repository of Instruments for Research into Second Languages* (pp. 1–21). New York: Routledge.

McCabe, M.J. and Snyder, C.M. (2015) Does online availability increase citations? Theory and evidence from a panel of economics and business journals. *The Review of Economics and Statistics* 97 (1), 144–165.

Smith, B. and Lafford, B.A. (2009) The evaluation of scholarly activity in Computer-Assisted Language Learning. *The Modern Language Journal* 93, 868–883.

Suber, P. (2002) Open access to the scientific journal literature. *Journal of Biology* 3.

9 Analysing Teachers' Tacit Professional Knowledge of OER: The Case of Languages Open Resources Online (LORO)

Tita Beaven

This chapter is based on the idea that open educational resources (OER) 'have the potential to enhance teaching and learning practices by facilitating communities of teachers who collaborate, share, discuss, critique, use, reuse and continuously improve educational content and practice' (Petrides *et al.*, 2010: 390). Iiyoshi and Kumar (2008) point out that most pedagogic practical knowledge tends to remain tacit because it is notoriously difficult to make it visible. They argue that open educational practices (OEP) can play a crucial role in transforming teachers' tacit knowledge into 'commonly usable knowledge' that can be shared and therefore used to improve the quality of teaching and learning.

This chapter focuses on a case study of OER engagement from a specific OER collection, LORO (Languages Open Resources Online), among language teachers at a distance university. Through the thematic analysis of data gathered through professional conversations with the participants, the study sought to understand the practices of language teachers when engaging with OER from the repository. The study's unique contribution is to elicit and make explicit the often tacit cognitive, affective and systemic knowledge, skills and competences (Tait, 2000) that teachers use when working through the OER lifecycle (Gurell, 2008).

Introduction: OER and OEP from the Teacher's Perspective

Open educational resources (OER) are educational materials (such as textbooks, audio and video, lecture notes or other resources) that are in the public domain or have been published under an open license, so they can be legally and freely copied, used, adapted and reshared (UNESCO, n.d.). OER, therefore, go hand in hand with a series of practices that are made possible because of their open licenses, and which Wiley (2007, 2014) summarised as the 5 Rs: reuse, rework, remix, redistribute and retain. A number of authors (Clements & Pawlowski, 2012; Glahn *et al.*, 2010; Pawlowski & Zimmermann, 2007; Santally, 2011) have built on Wiley's framework to define the OER cycle. One of the earliest and best known is Gurrell's (2008), who characterised the OER lifecycle as comprising the following steps: find, compose, adapt, use and share. What these models have in common is that they attempt to characterise the practices that users of OER engage in, and indeed, in the past 15 years, there has been a growing interest in the research literature in open educational practices (OEP) (e.g. the OLCOS project 2006–2007), the Open Educational Practice Landscape (OPAL) initiative (OPAL, 2011a); see also Cronin & MacLaren, 2018, for an overview of definitions of OEP.

The Cape Town Open Education Declaration (2007) explains how:

> open education is not limited to just open educational resources. It also draws upon open technologies that facilitate collaborative, flexible learning and the open sharing of teaching practices that empower educators to benefit from the best ideas of their colleagues. It may also grow to include new approaches to assessment, accreditation and collaborative learning.

OEP have been defined as 'a collaborative practice in which resources are shared by making them openly available, and pedagogical practices are employed which rely on social interaction, knowledge creation, peer learning and shared learning practices' (OPAL, 2011a: 4) with 'the intent to improve quality and innovate education' (OPAL, 2011b).

Although definitions of OEP have expanded to include a multitude of actors and practices, this chapter focuses on the practices of teachers. It is a case study of language teachers' engagement with OER, which aimed at understanding how teachers engage (or not) with the different steps of the OER lifecycle, and the professional knowledge that they use in doing so. The research was prompted by the general consensus expressed in the literature about low level of adoption of OER (Abeywardena, 2012; Cox & Trotter, 2017; Dimitriadis *et al.*, 2009; Wiley, 2009). A wide range of reasons have been suggested for the lack of OER adoption, ranging from lack of awareness of OER, issues around licencing, quality, interest, time and recognition at institutional level, and, in the global South 'infrastructural access deficits, technical capacity issues and socially and pedagogically related challenges' (Cox & Trotter, 2017). I am particularly interested in the pedagogical challenges related to teacher knowledge, which include:

- teachers not understanding the resources and therefore not being able to reuse them effectively (Dimitriadis *et al.*, 2009);
- teachers lacking the necessary skills to make informed choices about technology, and being bewildered by the possibilities (this goes beyond

the context of OER, and relates to technology adoption in general) (Conole, 2010);
- and teachers lacking the technical skills to re-purpose OER in effective and meaningful ways (Abeywardena, 2012).

My experience of working with, training and providing academic leadership for language teachers at my institution did not align with the reasons put forward in the literature quoted above to justify lack of engagement with OER. Indeed, since setting up a repository of OER in 2009, which all language teachers at the institution started using in 2010 (Beaven, 2018; Comas-Quinn, 2013), we had run a number of workshops around OER and OEP, and teachers seemed to understand the resources, and how to find, use and adapt them (see, for instance, Alvarez *et al.*, 2013). To ascertain whether there were any issues around the teachers' lack of understanding or skills to engage with OER seemed particularly important because, as McAndrew (2011) has pointed out, while OER are becoming established as learning materials available for teaching and learning, it is the 'methods and practices that enable learners, teachers and institutions to best engage with OER' that 'may well be more important in enabling change in education systems than the availability of the resources themselves' (McAndrew, 2011: 1).

Indeed, after the initial emphasis on the creation of OER collections, in the second and current phase of the OER movement the emphasis is moving from resources to practices, or 'using OER in a way that improves learning experiences and [innovative] educational scenarios' (Camilleri *et al.*, 2014: 12). As Ehlers explained, 'OER usage, re-usage, sharing and creation are not an end in itself' but engaging with them has to result in better teaching practices and learning experiences (Ehlers, 2011: 7).

According to Conole (2010), learning activities are made up of different components, including 'the type of pedagogy being used, the context in which the learning activity will be enacted, the types of intended learning outcomes associated with the activity, the nature and number of tasks to be undertaken by the learner, the associated tools and resources they will use and any formative or summative assessment' (Conole, 2010: 483). Conole goes on to explain that these subcomponents are interdependent – pedagogical choices will influence task selection, different tools will have different affordances, and all these factors will influence the learning experience. I would argue that in engaging with OER, teachers have to make complex pedagogical decisions which engage them in reflection, develop their professional knowledge and enhance their professional practice.

Indeed, the literature on OEP seems to indicate that one of the key aspects of open educational practices is that they have the potential to improve the quality of teaching (West & Victor, 2011). According to Petrides *et al.* (2010), OER 'have the potential to enhance teaching and learning practices by facilitating communities of teachers who collaborate, share, discuss, critique, use, reuse and continuously improve educational content and practice' (Petrides *et al.*, 2010: 390). This close engagement with OER is what defines open educational practices and, in their seminal edited book, *Opening Up Education* (2008), Iiyoshi and Kumar suggested that OER have the potential to 'iteratively and continuously [improve] the quality of teaching and learning through effective development and sharing of educational innovations and pedagogical knowledge' (Iiyoshi & Kumar, 2008: 5). Indeed, they argued that OER collections can enable teachers to better understand how others create and reuse resources and thus build upon one another's experience and practical knowledge precisely because such collections facilitate the finding, reuse, adaptation and public sharing of resources (Iiyoshi & Kumar, 2008).

Dalziel (2008), writing in the same volume, was more critical and, while acknowledging the successes of the OER movement in developing and sharing resources through OER collections, considered there had been little progress when it came to sharing what he called 'pedagogical know-how' among teachers. He went on to explain that 'what we lack is an agreed way to describe and share the teaching process [...]. If we could share descriptions of educational processes together with advice on the reasons for their design, then not only could a novice educator benefit from the work of experts, but all educators could collectively adapt and improve each other's work, leading to improved quality overall' (Dalziel, 2008: 376). Dalziel advocated the use of the then emerging field of learning design, and expressed the hope that 'if we can combine the great ideas and reflections of educators with exemplars of good practice in the form of "runnable" learning designs, and share these in a way that they can be easily adopted and adapted by any educator, then we will make new progress towards the goal of transforming education through the dissemination of pedagogical know-how' (Dalziel, 2008: 389), something which had already been advocated in the OLCOS roadmap (OLCOS, 2007) the previous year.

Iiyoshi and Kumar (2008) went on to make a number of recommendations, including that practice and knowledge should be made visible and shareable. They pointed out that most pedagogic practical knowledge 'is notoriously hard to make visible and portable', as it usually 'remains tacit and invisible'. Open educational practices, they argued, are about building the 'intellectual and technical capacity for transforming "tacit knowledge" into "commonly usable knowledge"' (Iyoshi & Kumar, 2008: 435).

There is, of course, an extensive literature about teacher cognition dating back more than 30 years (Clark & Peterson, 1986) whose original aim was to understand what private, invisible work was taking place in the minds of teachers as they conducted the very public work of teaching. These conceptualisations have often been influenced by constructs from the broader educational research such as Lave and Wenger's (1991) notion of situated cognition, Lantolf's (2000) sociocultural theory, or the conceptualisation of language learning from the perspective of complexity theory by Larsen-Freeman (2002) and Larsen-Freeman and Cameron (2008), and have drawn on individualist, social and socio-historical ontologies, and on complexity theory to shed light on teacher decisions and beliefs, on how meaning-making is situated in a social context, on how thinking always occurs in interaction and negotiation with social and historical contexts, and on how teacher learning is dynamic, non-linear, unpredictable and chaotic (for an overview of research on language teacher cognition, see Burns *et al.*, 2015).

However, a key issue in the literature about professional learning is the development of professional, personal or tacit knowledge, which can take place in the formal, informal and non-formal learning contexts. Eraut (2000: 114) refers to two types of knowledge: codified knowledge, or public or propositional knowledge, which is '(1) subject to quality control by editors, peer review and debate and (2) given status by incorporation into educational programs, examinations and courses'; and personal knowledge, or 'the cognitive resource which a person brings to a situation that enables them to think and perform.' This includes both codified knowledge that has been personalised, as well as 'procedural knowledge and process knowledge, experiential knowledge and impressions in episodic memory', and skills. Whereas codified knowledge is explicit by its very nature, personal knowledge can be either explicit or tacit and is 'constructed through experience and its nature depends on the cumulative acquisition, selection and interpretation of that experience' (Eraut, 1994: 20). According to Polanyi (1958), professional practice is grounded on personal knowledge, the 'vast repertoire of experiential knowledge that [people] draw on for making any one of the split-second decisions that are a feature of everyday practice.' It is this tacit professional knowledge on which professional practice is grounded that I sought to access in this study.

Research Question

In this chapter, I draw on a wider study into language teachers' engagement with OER from a languages repository in relation to the OER life cycle (Beaven, 2018; Blyth *et al.*, this volume), and focus on how the study also sought to understand the often tacit professional knowledge that teachers draw on when engaging with the OER lifecycle, as it has been argued that, through open educational practices, this tacit knowledge can be made explicit, and therefore usable and shareable, and thus contribute to enhancing the quality of teaching and learning.

The aim of the research was to understand how teachers used OER and the tacit professional knowledge that guided their engagement with the OER lifecycle, that is, their selection, adaptation and use of the OER.

The specific research question that this chapter focuses on, therefore is: What tacit professional knowledge do teachers draw on when working with OER?

Methodology

The study explored how a group of teachers on two blended beginners' language courses at The Open University (OU), a distance teaching university in the UK, engaged with a specific OER collection, Languages Open Resources Online (LORO). The participants in the study were 12 language teachers of French and Spanish for beginners at the OU (eight teachers of Spanish and four of French, which I refer to as S1 to S8 and F1 to F4, respectively, in the data). They were Associate Lecturers (AL) i.e. part-time lecturers for the OU, who often also work at other institutions; they all had at least five years' previous language teaching experience; all had taught for the OU for a minimum of three years, and many had taught for the OU for much longer. The youngest teacher was in her 30s and the older was in her late 60s. All of them had several years' experience of teaching online, as that is the mode that has been operating in the Languages Department at the OU since 2002, when audiographic tutorials were first introduced. The OU provides a series of continuous professional development events on aspects of language learning pedagogy online and at a distance, which ALs attend, and they also hold a Bachelor's degree in a relevant subject, and usually a Masters in language teaching, or some other post-graduate teaching qualification.

Invitation to participate in the study was sent to all 72 Spanish and French tutors teaching the beginners' course, so the 12 (eight Spanish and four French) that responded represented 16% of the total. Whether the participants of my study constituted a representative sample is open to question. They were, after all, self-selected, and therefore probably more interested than most in OER or in their own professional development. The case itself in a case study, however, is made up of the data generated in interaction with those particular individuals, and in that sense, the large amount of rich data generated, and the thick descriptions (Geertz, 1973) provided, will help the reader 'to understand the processes, cultures, decision-making and so on within the research site. The findings and, in turn, the validity, will rest on these descriptions' (The Open University, 2013, n.p.).

In the OU pedagogic model, students receive learning materials (in the form of books or online, audio and video resources, assignments and an online course website with additional resources and forums), which have all been produced by a team of central academics such as the one I worked in at the time of the study. The teachers are responsible for marking the work of a group of about 20 students, giving them feedback on their progress, providing support and advice, and running regular language classes, which take place online in a videoconferencing setting. The resources for the online language classes are available through LORO, our institutional open repository of languages OER. Traditionally, language teachers tend to produce or find online some of their own materials for classes, and OU ALs are no exception. One of the participants said she never did this for her tutorials, preferring to use only the resources the OU provided, but all the others regularly sourced resources for their lessons by looking for images or activities online, or designing their own.

The study addresses the lack of 'real world' research into OER use (Duncan, 2009; Robson, 2011), by situating the research around specific learning events, namely the preparation of and subsequent reflection on specific language classes that the teachers had with their students.

Data were generated through professional conversations with 12 participants, who shared with me the resources they were using for their classes and discussed the reasons for the selection, adaptation and use of these resources. To ensure the learning events were comparable, the teachers were drawn from the staff who taught on the French and Spanish beginners' courses at the OU and all discussed with me a similar teaching event (i.e. tutorial 3 and/or 4 in the course).

The rationale for using professional conversations in the data generation for this study is that, through professional conversations, teachers can engage in professional learning and develop a deep understanding of what they do (Britt *et al.*, 2001: 31). Indeed, these 'learning conversations' enable teachers to 'negotiate their understandings of practice' (Schuck *et al.*, 2008: 216) and to reflect on it, as they aim to 'maximize thoughtfulness on the part of the teacher' (Danielson, 2009); they are, as Senge (2006: 8) describes them, 'learningful conversations that balance inquiry and advocacy, where people expose their own thinking effectively and make that thinking open to the influence of others'. According to Danielson (2015), professional conversations are useful because they extend beyond the particular context in which they take place; she argues that by taking part in such exchanges, teachers develop the 'habits of mind' that enable them to become autonomous thinkers and evaluators of their practice, and that therefore professional conversation are a very powerful 'vehicle for learning' (Danielson, 2015: 5). To that extent, then, professional conversations provide a useful framework to try to understand the professional practices of teachers as they engage with OER, and to facilitate the articulation of their professional knowledge that otherwise tends to remain tacit.

The data generation took place on the same online conferencing system teachers used for their classes (Elluminate at the time of the research). The professional conversations, conducted before and after two tutorials (tutorials 3 and 4), lasted between 45 minutes and one hour each. They were recorded and transcribed, and the data set also included the resources used for each tutorial that the teachers discussed in the conversations. These were used in particular to triangulate the data from the conversations by checking if the issues discussed around knowledge, affective issues and adaptations to the resources resulted in changes to the resources themselves or to how they were used. The data were imported into NVivo9 and analysed using applied thematic analysis (Guest *et al.*, 2012), using an exploratory approach. The analysis was inductive, involving therefore a bottom-up, data-driven approach which resulted in the coding of the data into 50 nodes in total, which were then organised around two overarching themes and three subthemes:

- OER lifecycle (nodes in this theme included e.g. provenance of resources, changes made to resources, rationale for choice, composing, sharing)
- Professional knowledge, encompassing:
  - Pedagogical and technical issues (e.g. knowledge about grammar, teaching methodology, Elluminate)
  - Affective issues (e.g. empathy with students, teacher vulnerability)
  - Contingencies to deal with unexpected events (relating to the notion of teacher vulnerability)

The analysis of how the use, adaptation and reuse of the resources related to the OER lifecycle has been reported elsewhere (Beaven, 2018), so in this chapter I am focusing on the results relating to professional knowledge. As I discuss below, the codes were then mapped onto Tait's (2000, 2003) conceptual framework of the primary functions of student support in Open and Distance Learning.

Professional Learning

There have been a number of studies of the professional learning of part-time teachers at a distance (Knight *et al.*, 2006), and specifically of language teachers' professional learning in the context of OER engagement (Alvarez *et al.*, 2013; Borthwick & Dickens, 2013; Comas-Quinn & Borthwick, 2015; Daniels, 2019). Although it is sometimes possible for part-time staff or staff working at a distance or online to take part in formal staff development activities, it is more likely that such professional learning takes place informally (Stickler & Emke, 2015); indeed as Knight (1998) points out, it is informal or non-formal learning, which is often life-long, that is key to helping part-time teachers confront what he calls 'professional obsolescence' (Knight, 1998).

Professional practice is grounded on personal knowledge, the 'vast repertoire of experiential knowledge that [people] draw on for making any one of the split-second decisions that are a feature of everyday practice' (Polanyi, 1958). An example of this are the seamless decisions made by teachers during a lesson, which appear to be made almost unthinkingly, but which are grounded in their extensive, tacit professional experience.

The development of professional, personal or tacit knowledge has been widely discussed in the literature about professional learning. As mentioned above, as opposed to the controlled and high-status codified knowledge, or public or propositional knowledge, personal knowledge is the cognitive resource that enables one to think and perform. It can be either explicit or tacit and is developed through experience. Moreover, by having to use one's personal knowledge of specific concepts in new and different contexts, that personal knowledge is enriched, and the understanding of the concepts strengthened (Eraut, 1994, 2000).

Eraut (2000) advises that, while tacit knowledge is important in understanding professional knowledge, eliciting tacit or near-tacit knowledge is not without difficulties, and warns researchers to be both inventive and modest with their aspirations when investigating it. Other researchers have suggested ways of bringing out tacit professional knowledge through collaborative professional learning engendered through discussion with peers, co-teaching, peer coaching, peer observation, or joint discussion of resource implementation (Duncombe & Armour, 2004). For Schuck *et al.* (2008), peer observation, and the ensuing professional learning conversations, are a way to question one's own practice rather than just operating routinely using an 'unthinking repertoire'. These practices force practitioners 'to re-examine that tacit knowledge and question the ways [they] have been doing things', and thus to 'rethink the taken-for-granted in our teaching' (Schuck *et al.*, 2008: 223). Kahn *et al.* (2006) point out that dialogue is the most prominent form of social interaction in the studies they reviewed, and that it is considered to be central to the reflective process as it helps those involved to problematise practice and supports ongoing engagement in a supportive atmosphere. They also remind us that the social dimension is central to the reflective process (Kahn *et al.*, 2006). Knight *et al.* (2006) emphasise the fact that professional development that takes place within situated social practices can help to unlock implicit knowledge from the specific settings in which it is 'hidden' and enable teachers and researchers to capture it and share it.

From the above literature, one could surmise that, in engaging with the OER lifecycle of locating, adapting, reusing and sharing resources, teachers might be engaging with the pedagogic knowledge necessary to reuse those resources effectively by reflecting on what is required in the lesson they are preparing, finding relevant OER and adapting them so that they are more appropriate to the context of their lesson, and integrating that knowledge with other professional knowledge in the planning and implementation of their teaching. In addition, reusing and adapting OER might enhance the teachers' capacity to think and act, and enrich their personal knowledge by engaging them in resituating teaching resources into new contexts.

To sum up, then, it appears that teachers ground much of their practice in their professional, personal or tacit knowledge, which they might have acquired through formal, non-formal or informal learning opportunities. This knowledge is what enables experienced practitioners to deal with the demands of everyday practice. Collaborative, situated social practices and dialogue, as well as reflection, enable practitioners to examine their tacit knowledge and question practices they might take for granted, and engage in a process of continuous learning that enables them to deal with the dilemmas of classroom practice. Understanding teachers' tacit knowledge when engaging with OER – especially in non-formal and informal settings – is important because it enables this knowledge to become shareable, thus providing opportunities to enhance teaching quality.

Conceptual Framework

Central to the role of the teacher in Open and Distance Learning is student support which, according to Tait (2000, 2003) has the following primary functions:

(1) cognitive: supporting and developing learning through the mediation of the standard and uniform elements of course materials and learning resources for individual students;
(2) affective: providing an environment which supports students, creates commitment and enhances self-esteem; and
(3) systemic: establishing administrative processes and information management systems which are effective, transparent and overall student-friendly (Tait, 2000).

Baumann and colleagues (Baumann *et al.*, 2008; Murphy *et al.*, 2011) researched the role of the distance language teacher and identified eight broad categories of the tutor role, which they mapped onto Tait's (2000) functions (see Table 9.1).

Table 9.1 The tutor's role: categories mapped onto Tait's (2000) functions, based on Bauman *et al.* (2008: 384)

Knowledge, skills, and competences (from Bauman *et al.*, 2008)	Functions of student support (from Tait, 2000)		
	Cognitive	Affective	Systematic
Qualities and affective orientation		x	
Pedagogical expertise	x		
Subject matter expertise	x		
IT skills	x		x
One-to-one interactive support skills		x	
Self-management		x	x
Group support and management	x	x	x
Professional skills and responsibilities	x		x

There have been other important contributions to the growing literature about the skills and expertise or knowledge required by language teachers working online (Adnan, 2018; Comas-Quinn, 2011; Compton, 2009; Guichon, 2009; Hampel & Stickler, 2005) in which the roles of online teachers have been mainly categorised as pedagogical, managerial, social, technical and instructional (Adnan, 2018). Researching the changing roles of online tutors in the Chinese open and distance education context, Li *et al.* (2017) also identified similar roles: instructional designer, manager/administrator, social and pedagogical roles.

Based on an analysis of the literature on teaching skills for online and distance language learning, I would argue that engagement with OER necessitates the exercise of some of the cognitive, affective and systemic (including ICT) knowledge, skills and competences identified above, as well as, presumably, reflection, flexibility and openness to the ideas of others, and that engagement with OER can therefore be a useful tool in enhancing the professional practices of teachers and the quality of teaching.

Findings and Discussion

After the professional conversations with the 12 teachers in the study as they were preparing their lessons and after they had delivered them, the teachers' engagement with a total of 151 resources (or an average of 12 per lesson) was analysed and mapped onto the OER lifecycle. Of the resources used, more than 40% came from LORO, the institutional OER repository, just over 30% were created by the individual teachers, and nearly 16% had been created by other teachers and shared. The analysis demonstrated that teachers' practices followed the OER lifecycle, and that they engaged in locating, composing, adapting, reusing and sharing the resources with others (Beaven, 2018).

The transcripts of the conversations with the participants were also analysed for evidence of professional knowledge, and the key themes are summarised in Table 9.2.

A second key theme that emerged from the data was the issue of the affective support for students that teachers incorporated into their teaching, summarised in Table 9.3.

As can be seen from some of the subthemes in the two tables below, some of the cognitive and affective knowledge, skills and competences deployed by teachers overlap with systemic issues, such as building the students' confidence with using the online conferencing platform, or being *au fait* with the specific details of the course structure and the resources and systems available for supporting students.

In terms of professional knowledge, another theme that emerged from the conversations was the flexibility that teachers demonstrate in their planning of the language lessons, when they make contingency plans to

Table 9.2 Knowledge used when preparing language lessons

Theme: Knowledge used by teachers when preparing language lessons
Research Question: What tacit professional knowledge do teachers draw on when working with OER?

Subthemes	Instances	Number of teachers
Communicative language teaching pedagogy and resources	12	5
Language/linguistics and how to teach it	11	7
Functionality of online conferencing system and how to use it for teaching languages	11	7
What students have covered in previous tutorials, what they need more practice with	10	6
The course, the course calendar, the students' progress within the course	9	8
Their own experience of teaching the course in previous years	9	6
Their own experience as language learners	6	4
Teaching languages in other settings/contexts	6	4
The resources in LORO	4	4
Technical issues about how to make/adapt resources on the online conference platform	4	3
The students' needs	3	2
Their long language teaching experience	2	2

Table 9.3 Affective issues mentioned in discussion of OER use

Theme: Affective issues relating to teaching mentioned during discussion of OER used
Research Question: What tacit professional knowledge do teachers draw on when working with OER?

Subthemes	Instances	Number of teachers
Boost the students' confidence and provide reassurance	16	9
Cater to different students' needs	9	6
Build a sense of community amongst students	5	5
Make lessons/activities enjoyable	5	4
Keep students engaged	3	3
Provide help and advice to those students that have fallen behind	3	3
Build up confidence in using the online conferencing platform	2	2
Find out how students are doing	1	1
Be responsive to students' mood (e.g. if they are getting tired)	1	1

deal with different eventualities or are able to cope with issues 'on the hoof'. The main themes are illustrated in Table 9.4.

The data show that teachers made use of their cognitive, affective and systemic knowledge, skills and competences during all the phases of their engagement with the OER lifecycle. When locating and selecting resources

Table 9.4 Contingency plans/spontaneous changes to use of OER

Theme: Contingency plans/spontaneous changes to use of OER
Research Question: What tacit professional knowledge do teachers draw on when working with OER?

Subthemes: Professional knowledge about:	Changes / reasons	Instances	Number of teachers
Students	Depending on numbers attending, nature of the group, students' confidence and abilities	30	9
Activities	More planned than needed (in case there is time left at the end, in case students need additional help or more practice, etc.)	21	10
	Depending on how activity is going	5	4
	Flexibility, responding to students ('going off at a tangent', 'thinking on your feet', etc.)	4	4
Time	Running out of time. activity takes less time than planned, difficult to estimate timing of activity	15	7
Technical issues	Set up/use breakout rooms if needed (e.g. for pairwork)	9	6
	Technical problems during the class (e.g. student mike not working, uploading the wrong slide, student with poor connectivity, etc.)	4	4

for their tutorial, teachers used their cognitive knowledge, such as their knowledge of language and linguistics and how to teach it, and their knowledge of what students had already covered or needed more help with. They drew on their own experience of teaching in other contexts, and of having taught the course in previous years. They also used their knowledge of the course materials and resources in LORO, and of their students.

The following example shows the cognitive, pedagogic knowledge that one of the teachers deploys when selecting resources from LORO:

Researcher: How do you decide which activities to use from LORO?
S5: Since the aim of the tutorial is just to enable students to use Spanish, to use the language, the main selling point for me is: is that activity going to be useful in terms of communication? Can I exploit it, can I adapt it, can I enlarge it, you know? So that's the main thing. In this one, you can do… some vocabulary, the prepositions, describing things… you can do a follow-up activity maybe on pronunciation maybe if there is a particular sound…. the most important thing is that the students can use the language meaningfully with the resources.

In terms of understanding affective issues, when selecting resources teachers tried to cater to different students' needs, to find activities that would make tutorials fun, and to build a sense of community amongst students. For instance, when looking for activities to use in her tutorial, S1 explained that sometimes she worried that her lessons are not good fun:

> S1: You know we practise what we have to practise, and sometimes I try to think of how this could be made a bit more good fun, a bit more a bit of a game, which is perhaps the thing that I'm less confident with [...] Sometimes I fear I'm a bit too academic and I have to... I try to do something sometimes a bit more fun, more like games.

From a systemic point of view, when discussing their selection of resources, teachers demonstrated their understanding of the functionality of the online conferencing platform, the function of LORO, the role the course calendar plays in informing students what they should be studying, the aims and objectives of the course, and their role in student support.

In terms of the next stages of the OER lifecycle, composing, adapting and reusing resources, teachers also demonstrated their cognitive, affective and systemic knowledge, skills and competences. When composing a teaching sequence, teachers use their pedagogical knowledge of language teaching and learning methodology to produce a sequence of activities that follows the traditional communicative approach of moving from more controlled to freer practice in a lesson. They also use their understanding of affective issues, for instance by introducing a fairly simple activity after a particularly challenging sequence, so that students have time to relax and build up their confidence again before the next sequence. In terms of systemic issues, they use their technical skills to organise the resources in the most appropriate sequence, by adding, removing or adapting slides in the resources they use.

For instance, when organising his slides, S6 gave them all a uniform look in terms of headings, design and font used. He explained why this was important:

> S6: I like things to be well presented, organised, and everything looking the same – consistent. [...] I think it helps the students to feel more comfortable because everything is in order and it possibly [makes them feel more] secure.

He went on to explain that when using the online conferencing system it was important to get students to feel secure and comfortable using the different tools.

When adapting a resource before the session, teachers again make use of their pedagogical knowledge, for instance to extend an activity from its original intended purpose so that it fulfils another need they have identified. One example of this was provided by S5, who explained how when using a particular OER form LORO that focused on describing and locating furniture in a room through a communicative game, he also added a further step to the activity to practise the pronunciation of a difficult sound that appeared in some of the vocabulary. In this stage of the OER lifecycle, teachers also engaged with affective issues, for instance by adding to a resource a list of key phrases that would be needed in the activity in order to provide affective support for their student:

> S2: It's quite early on [...] so their confidence is not as great in general; so that's why I do that. I think it's more like a comfort blanket for them, in fact, that's the idea.

Similarly, when adapting a resource, teachers are clear about the systemic knowledge, especially related to technology, that they need to draw on, such as the technical issues using a resource might entail (for instance, whether a resource needs to be used in a break-out room in pairs or whether it can be done in plenary).

When composing their tutorial, and after they had used the resources with their students, several teachers explained that they engage in reflection, either when preparing a lesson plan, by making notes during or after the lesson, or by saving the resources they have adapted for future reference, all of which help them when preparing their lessons next time they teach the course.

Although teachers did not usually share the resources they had developed or adapted with colleagues, they certainly shared them with students after the lesson, often adapting them further by including additional explanatory notes and by changing their format into one that was more easily useable by students. This practice again demonstrates their cognitive knowledge (the importance of reviewing and recapping in language learning), their awareness of affective issues (the need to support students who were not able to attend the tutorial, for instance), and of systems (the technical skills to record and share online classes with students, or to adapt and save resources into PDF, which can be shared on the tutor group forum).

Several teachers discussed the fact that the resources are fairly versatile, and that it is not difficult to think of ways of exploiting them. In all the lessons, teachers had to make some changes to how they had planned to use the resources because of the numbers of students who attended being fewer than anticipated, because students had technical problems, or for a variety of other reasons.

Sometimes, teachers had already anticipated different eventualities and built contingency plans into their lesson which they discussed in the planning stages. In this first example, when preparing the lesson, the teacher is articulating her understanding of cognitive issues, and in particular of communicative language teaching when planning for possible eventualities of how she would use a specific resource in her forthcoming lesson:

> F3: So this one is really open production where people will have to be in smaller groups. Maybe we'll do a chain, depending on the number of people again, where we'll be asking and answering questions about their real or imagined family.

In this second example, the teacher discusses her contingency plans in the context of affective and systemic issues:

F2: If I can… you know, if numbers allow and so on, I will group the students depending on their confidence and ability for this because […] some are really quite well ahead and they could get a lot out of this and have a lot of fun with it and, if there's a weaker student or a quieter student, I will go and join that group and work with them.

At other times, teachers had to adapt their resources and their approach 'on the hoof'; for instance, they may have planned a group activity and only one student attended the session, a student might have sound problems and only be able to intervene in writing through the chat box, or the students attending might be able to cope with the activities better than anticipated. In these unforeseen situations, teachers use their cognitive, affective and systemic knowledge together with their ability to reflect 'in action' (Schön, 1983) and their resilience in situations of vulnerability (Kelchtermans, 2009). In the following example, F1 explains why she made some changes to the planned activity during the lesson:

Researcher: These changes… was it just with the fact that you had those particular students in the group and you decided to do it like that during the lesson, or had you already thought of this variation of the activity beforehand?
F1: No, I didn't think about this beforehand […]. It also depends on how confident the students are with the original dialogue, then, we expand a little bit more, make it more relevant to them, make it more personal. I think it makes it more enjoyable as well.

The fact that teachers were undaunted by having to adapt to different eventualities and simply adjusted to the circumstances indicates that they felt confident using the resources and that they understood how to use them even in changing and challenging situations. In fact, they seemed quite sanguine about embracing the paradoxes of teacher vulnerability (Kelchtermans, 2009) and being able to engage in thoughtful lesson planning, while at the same time preparing for and allowing the unexpected to happen.

It would seem, then, that the rationale for the disappointing level of adoption and adaptation of OER discussed in the literature which points to pedagogical challenges experienced by the teachers as the reasons for poor levels of engagement with OER (i.e. that teachers lack the necessary understanding or skills to be able to engage with OER in an effective and meaningful way, as suggested by Abeywardena, 2012; Conole, 2010; Dimitriadis *et al.*, 2009), does not seem to hold true in this study. This may be because it is a repository of resources that are very closely tailored to the needs of the OU teachers that use them and that follow a pedagogical approach – communicative language teaching – that is familiar to them, so they understand the types of activities used in the resources. It might also be that the wealth of the teachers' professional knowledge enables them to understand the different components of the learning activities they use (Conole, 2010), such as pedagogy, context, associated learning outcomes, tools and resources.

Conclusion

This chapter discussed the findings of a case study of a group of language teachers' engagement with OER. It aimed at making teachers articulate the tacit professional knowledge they access when finding, adapting, using and sharing OER, as it had been proposed that, although making tacit professional knowledge explicit might be complex (Eraut, 2000), it is a first step towards making that knowledge shareable, and thus transformed into commonly usable knowledge that can improve the quality of teaching and learning (Iiyoshi & Kumar, 2008). If it is possible to make tacit professional knowledge explicit and shareable, it could then be used to discuss practice among teachers and enhance the quality of teaching. In that sense, this study answers the call of this volume, namely, to achieve a better understanding of how language teachers engage in OEP at their institutions.

The study also demonstrated that teachers make use of cognitive, affective and systemic knowledge, skills and competences (Tait, 2000) when engaging in the different stages of the OER lifecycle (locating, composing, adapting, reusing and sharing resources). It found that teachers make contingency plans before the lessons in case of unforeseen circumstances or adapt the resources or the way they use them 'on the hoof' during the lesson, therefore demonstrating reflection and flexibility in dealing with the inherent vulnerability of teaching (Kelchtermans, 2009). In that sense, the study contributes to our understanding of how to achieve the open sharing of teaching practices advocated by the Cape Town Open Education Declaration (2008).

The study has a number of limitations, as the number of participants, 12 in total, was relatively small (16% of the total of 72 staff teaching the two French and Spanish beginner courses at the time of the study). The usefulness of a case study, however, rests on the large amount of rich data generated, which helps to understand key aspects of the research site. Where possible, data were triangulated by checking if practice was consistent across the two teaching sessions discussed with each teacher, and by cross-referencing the reported provenance and adaptation of OER with the data from the repository and the teachers' resources. In order to ascertain how typical the practices observed are, further studies would need to be conducted in other settings and institutions. From a methodological point of view, the unique contribution of this study is the use of professional conversations before and after specific learning events not only to understand the teachers' engagement with the OER lifecycle, but more specifically to capture the teachers' tacit professional knowledge when looking for, using, adapting and sharing OER.

Indeed, by engaging in professional conversations with teachers around the OER lifecycle both before and after a class, we can draw out their tacit professional knowledge and understand the complex pedagogical, affective and systemic rationale for their specific use and adaptation of resources. This appears to be a promising professional development activity, and future research should address how this tacit pedagogical know-how, once made explicit, can be harnessed in the professional development of teachers so that they can build on one another's experience and contribute to the enhancement of teaching quality.

References

Abeywardena, I. (2012) *A Report on the Re-use and Adaptation of Open Educational Resources (OER): An Exploration of Technologies Available.* See http://oasis.col.org/handle/11599/233 (accessed 25 July 2018).

Adnan, M. (2018) Professional development in the transition to online teaching: The voice of entrant online instructors. *ReCALL* 30 (1), 88–111.

Alvarez, I., Beaven, T. and Comas-Quinn, A. (2013) Performing languages: An example of integrating open practices in staff development for language teachers. *Journal of e-Learning and Knowledge Society* 9 (1), 85–92.

Baumann, U., Shelley, M., Murphy, L. and White, C. (2008) New challenges, the role of the tutor in the teaching of languages at a distance. *Distances et Savoirs* 6 (3), 365–392.

Beaven, T. (2018) 'Dark reuse': An empirical study of teachers' OER engagement. *Open Praxis* 10 (4), 377–391.

Blyth, C.S., Warner, C. and Luks, J. (2021) The role of OER in promoting critical reflection and professional development: The foreign languages and the literary in the everyday project. In C.S. Blyth and J. Thoms (eds) *Open Education and Second Language Learning and Teaching: The Rise of a New Knowledge Ecology* (pp. 158–180). Bristol: Multilingual Matters.

Borthwick, K. and Dickens, A. (2013) The Community Café: Creating and sharing open educational resources with community-based language teachers. *Journal of e-Learning and Knowledge Society* 9 (1), 73–83.

Britt, M.S., Irwin, K.C. and Ritchie, G. (2001) Professional conversations and professional growth. *Journal of Mathematics Teacher Education* 4 (1), 29–53.

Burns, A., *et al.* (2015) Theorizing and studying the language-teaching mind: Mapping research on language teacher cognition. *Modern Language Journal* 99 (3), 585–601.

Camilleri, A.F., Ehlers, U.D. and Pawlowski, J. (2014) *State of the Art Review of Quality Issues Related to Open Educational Resources (OER).* Publications Office of the European Union. See http://publications.jrc.ec.europa.eu/repository/handle/JRC88304 (accessed 25 July 2018).

Cape Town Open Education Declaration (2007) *Cape Town Open Education Declaration: Unlocking the Promise of Open Educational Resources* See http://www.capetowndeclaration.org/read-the-declaration (accessed 25 July 2018).

Clark, C.M. and Peterson, P.L. (1986) Teachers' thought processes. In M.C. Wittrock (ed.) *Handbook of Research on Teaching* (3rd edn) (pp. 255–296). New York: Macmillan.

Clements, K.I. and Pawlowski, J.M. (2012) User-oriented quality for OER: Understanding teachers' views on re-use, quality, and trust. *Journal of Computer Assisted Learning* 28 (1), 4–14.

Comas-Quinn, A. (2011) Learning to teach online or learning to become an online teacher: An exploration of teachers' experiences in a blended learning course. *ReCALL* 23 (3), 218–232.

Comas-Quinn, A. and Fitzgerald, A. (2013) *Open Educational Resources in Language Teaching and Learning*. Higher Education Academy (HEA), York. See http://oro.open.ac.uk/37550/ (accessed 10 May 2019).

Comas-Quinn, A. and Borthwick, K. (2015) Sharing: Open educational resources for language teachers. In R. Hampel and U. Stickler (eds) *Developing Online Language Teaching: Research-based Pedagogies and Reflective Practices*. Basingstoke: Palgrave Macmillan.

Compton, L.K. (2009) Preparing language teachers to teach language online: A look at skills, roles, and responsibilities. *Computer Assisted Language Learning* 22 (1), 73–99.

Conole, G. (2010) An overview of design representations. In L. Dirckinck-Holmfeld, V. Hodgson, C. Jones, M. de Laat, D. McConnel and T. Ryberg (eds) *Proceedings of the 7th International Conference on Networked Learning*. Lancaster: Lancaster University.

Cox, G. and Trotter, H. (2017) An OER framework, heuristic and lens: Tools for understanding lecturers' adoption of OER. *Open Praxis* 9 (2), 151–171.

Cronin, C. and MacLaren, I. (2018) Conceptualising OEP: A review of theoretical and empirical literature in open educational practices. *Open Praxis* 10 (2), 127–143.

Dalziel, J. (2008) Learning design: Sharing pedagogical know-how. In T. Iiyoshi and M.S. Kumar (eds) *Opening Up Education – The Collective Advancement of Education Through Open Technology, Open Content, and Open Knowledge*. Cambridge Massachusetts: MIT Press.

Daniels, P. (2019) Open practices as a catalyst for language teachers' professional development. In A. Comas-Quinn, A. Beaven and B. Sawhill (eds) *New Case Studies of Openness in and Beyond the Language Classroom* (pp. 159–171). Research-publishing.net. https://doi.org/10.14705/rpnet.2019.37.973

Danielson, C. (2009) *The Handbook for Enhancing Professional Practice: Using the Framework for Teaching in your School*. Moorabbin, Australia: Hawker Brownlow Education.

Danielson, C. (2019 and 2015) *Talk About Teaching! Leading Professional Conversations* (1st and 2nd edn). Thousand Oaks, CA: Corwin Press (SAGE).

Dimitriadis, Y., McAndrew, P., Conole, G. and Makriyannis, E. (2009) New design approaches to repurposing open educational resources for collaborative learning using mediating artefacts. In R.J. Atkinson and C. McBeath (eds) *Ascilite 2009: Same Places, Different Spaces*, 6–9 December 2009, Auckland, New Zealand, The University of Auckland, Auckland University of Technology, and Australasian Society for Computers in Learning in Tertiary Education (ascilite).

Duncan, S. (2009) Patterns of learning object reuse in the connexions repository. PhD thesis, Utah State University.

Duncombe, R. and Armour, K.M. (2004) Collaborative professional learning: From theory to practice. *Journal of In-Service Education* 30 (1), 141–166.

Ehlers, U.-D. (2011) From open educational resources to open educational practices. *eLearning Papers* 23 (March), 1–8.

Eraut, M. (1994) *Developing Professional Knowledge and Competence*. Falmer: Routledge.

Eraut, M. (2000) Non-formal learning and tacit knowledge in professional work. *British Journal of Educational Psychology* 70 (1), 113–136.

Geertz, C. (1973) Thick description: Toward an interpretive theory of culture. In *The Interpretation of Cultures – Selected Essays* (pp. 3–32). New York: Basic Books, Inc.

See http://chairoflogicphiloscult.files.wordpress.com/2013/02/clifford-geertz-the-interpretation-of-cultures.pdf (accessed 25 April 2019).

Glahn, C., Kalz, M., Gruber, M. and Specht, M. (2010) Supporting the reuse of open educational resources through open standards. In T. Hirashima, A.F. Mohd Ayub, L.F. Kwok, L. Wong, S.C. Kong and F.Y. Yu (eds) *Workshop Proceedings of the 18th International Conference on Computers in Education: ICCE2010*. Faculty of Educational Studies, Universiti Putra Malaysia.

Guest, G., MacQueen, K. and Namey, E. (2012) *Applied Thematic Analysis*. London: Sage.

Guichon, N. (2009) Training future language teachers to develop online tutors' competence through reflective analysis. *ReCALL* 21 (2), 166–185.

Gurell, S. (2008) *Open Educational Resources Handbook 1.0 for Educators*. Utah: Center for Open and Sustainable Learning.

Hampel, R. and Stickler, U. (2005) New skills for new classrooms: Training tutors to teach languages online. *Computer Assisted Language Learning* 18 (4), 311–326.

Iiyoshi, T. and Kumar, M.S.V. (2008) *Opening Up Education – The Collective Advancement of Education through Open Technology, Open Content, and Open Knowledge*. Cambridge, MA: MIT Press.

Kahn, P., Young, R., Grace, S., Pilkington, R., Rush, L., Bland, T. and Willis, I. (2006) *The Role and Effectiveness of Reflective Practices in Programmes for New Academic Staff: A Grounded Practitioner Review of the Research Literature*. London: Higher Education Academy.

Kelchtermans, G. (2009) Who I am in how I teach is the message: Self-understanding, vulnerability and reflection. *Teachers and Teaching* 15 (2), 257–272.

Knight, P. (1998) Professional obsolescence and continuing professional development in higher education. *Innovations in Education and Training International* 35 (3), 248–256.

Knight, P., Tait, J. and Yorke, M. (2006) The professional learning of teachers in higher education. *Studies in Higher Education* 31 (3), 319–339.

Lantolf, J.P. (2000) *Sociocultural Theory and Second Language Learning*. Oxford: Oxford University Press.

Larsen–Freeman, D. (2002) Language acquisition and language use from a chaos/complexity theory perspective. In C. Kramsch (ed.) *Language Acquisition and Language Socialization* (pp. 33–46). London: Continuum.

Larsen–Freeman, D. and Cameron, L. (2008) *Complex Systems and Applied Linguistics*. Oxford: Oxford University Press.

Lave, J. and Wenger, E. (1991) *Situated Learning: Legitimate Peripheral Participation*. Cambridge: Cambridge University Press.

Li, S., Zhang, J., Yu, C. and Chen, L. (2017) Rethinking distance tutoring in e-learning environments: A study of the priority of roles and competencies of Open University tutors in China. *The International Review of Research in Open and Distributed Learning* 18 (2).

McAndrew, P. (2011) Fostering open educational practices. *eLearning Papers* 23.

Murphy, L.M., Shelley, M.A., White, C.J. and Baumann, U. (2011) Tutor and student perceptions of what makes an effective distance language teacher. *Distance Education* 32 (3), 397–419.

OLCOS (2007) *Open Educational Practices and Resources – OLCOS Roadmap 2012*, Austria. See http://www.esode.com/downloadable files/OLCOS Project/olcos_roadmap (accessed 6 July 2018).

OPAL (2011a) *OEP Scape: The Open Educational Practice Landscape*. See http://www.oer-quality.org/wp-content/uploads/2011/03/OEP-Scape-final.pdf (no longer online).

OPAL (2011b) *What Constitutes Good Open Educational Practices?* See http://www.oer-quality.org/wp-content/uploads/2011/03/OEP-const-elements.pdf (no longer online).

Pawlowski, J.M. and Zimmermann, V. (2007) Open Content: A concept for the future of e-learning and knowledge management? *Knowtech 2007 Frankfurt*. See http://users.jyu.fi/~japawlow/knowtech_20070907finalwithcitation.pdf

Petrides, L., Jimes, C., Middleton-Detzner, C. and Holly Howell (2010) OER as a model for enhanced teaching and learning. In Universitat Oberta de Catalunya (ed.) *Barcelona Open Ed 2010 The Seventh Annual Open Education Conference November 2–4 2010* (pp. 389–398). Barcelona: Universitat Oberta de Catalunya.

Polanyi, M. (1958) *Personal Knowledge*. London: Routledge and Kegan Paul.

Robson, C. (2011) *Real World Research: A Resource for Social Scientists and Practitioner-Researchers*. Oxford: Blackwell.

Santally, M. (2011) OERs in context: Case study of innovation and sustainability of educational practices at the University of Mauritius. *European Journal of Online and Distance Learning* 1.

Schön, D. (1983) *The Reflective Practitioner – How Professionals Think in Action*. Farnham: Ashgate.

Schuck, S., Aubusson, P. and Buchanan, J. (2008) Enhancing teacher education practice through professional learning conversations. *European Journal of Teacher Education* 31 (2), 215–227.

Senge, P. (2006) *The Fifth Discipline: The Art and Practice of Learning Organizations*. New York: Random House.

Stickler, U. and Emke, M. (2015) Part-time and freelance language teachers and their ICT training needs. In R. Hampel and U. Stickler (eds) *Developing Online Language Teaching: Research-Based Pedagogies and Reflective Practices*. Houndmills: Palgrave Macmillan.

Tait, A. (2000) Planning student support for open and distance learning. *Open Learning: The Journal of Open and Distance Learning* 15 (3), 287–299.

Tait, A. (2003) Reflections on student support in open and distance learning, *International Review of Research in Open and Distance Learning in Open and Distance Learning* 4 (1). Retrieved from: https://doi.org/10.19173/irrodl.v4i1.134

The Open University (2013) *E891 Educational Enquiry Study Guide*. The Open University. See https://learn2.open.ac.uk/course/view.php?id=201970 (accessed 1 May 2019).

UNESCO. *What are Open Educational Resources (OERs)?* See http://www.unesco.org/new/en/communication-and-information/access-to-knowledge/open-educational-resources/what-are-open-educational-resources-oers (accessed 6 July 2018).

West, P.G. and Victor, L. (2011) *Background and Action Paper on OER – A Background and Action Paper for Staff of Bilateral and Multilateral Organizations at the Strategic Institutional Education Sector Level*. See http://www.paulwest.org/public/Background_and_action_paper_on_OER.pdf (accessed 6 July 2018).

Wiley, D. (2014) 'The Access Compromise and the 5th R', *Iterating Toward Openness*, blog post, 5 March. See http://opencontent.org/blog/archives/3221 (accessed 6 July 2018).

Wiley, D. (2009) Impediments to learning object reuse and openness as a potential solution. *Revista Brasileira de Informática na Educação* 17 (3), 17–19.

Wiley, D. (2007) 'Open Education License Draft', *Iterating Toward Openness*, blog post, 8 August. See http://opencontent.org/blog/archives/355 (accessed 6 July 2018).

10 Towards a Pedagogy of Openness: Bridging English-language and Foreign-language Digital Humanities

Rebecca F. Davis and Carl S. Blyth

Openness, a key value underlying the English-language and foreign-language (FL) communities within the digital humanities (DH), is expressed in production and use of open educational resources (OER), teaching and learning in the open, open knowledge production, creation of infrastructure to support open knowledge production, transparency about teaching and learning and open acceptance of the learner as an equal into the community. Models of the use of OER, open educational practices (OEP) and open knowledge production demonstrate the potential benefits to student learning in terms of agency and efficacy, as well as the challenges of open education. The challenges include using open source software tools, negotiating student privacy, concerns about student labor, eliciting learning from authentic experiences, finding resources, tools and opportunities for student open knowledge production and ensuring the quality of that production. Strategies for addressing those challenges, open sharing of assignments and transparency about teaching, including failures, make up a pedagogy of openness. This mature development of open education thrives in the English-language DH community and increasingly in the foreign-language DH community and promises an avenue for bridging divides between these communities, as well as other silos in FL education.

Introduction

Foreign language (FL) instructors looking to engage in open educational practices should look to the digital humanities (DH) community, which already includes FL specialists and has grown up along with the open education movement. An exploration of how open educational resources (OER) and open educational practices (OEP) have impacted teaching and learning in this community provides insights into the benefits and challenges of open education, as well as the motivations driving its adoption. Beyond production and use of OER, OEP include open teaching and learning, open scholarship, open sharing of teaching ideas and use of open technologies (Beetham *et al.*, 2012). This chapter will begin by exploring why open education flourishes in DH as practiced in American institutions of higher education, before turning to concrete examples of how OEP are expressed in DH teaching and learning. While many examples come from English and History, two fields that have dominated DH, examples of FL projects will also be highlighted. We will also explore the teaching strategies that have arisen to facilitate open education and how instructors, too, openly share their teaching materials and practices. Taken together, these examples of OER and OEP make up a 'pedagogy of openness in the digital humanities,' a phrase we use to refer to the practice of open education within DH. Ultimately, we hope to show that FL scholars are an important part of the DH community and that a pedagogy of openness is increasingly relevant to FL education.

While we draw lessons for FL educators, we will also highlight the tensions and gaps in the DH community that might be hidden by an overly rosy examination of openness. It is important to recognize the heterogeneity of this community; silos based on disciplinary boundaries still remain. Thus, relevant knowledge produced by those practicing DH in FL departments may often be missed by specialists in departments, like History or English. In effect, even though many FL educators are DH scholars, their work may be somewhat marginalized within the larger DH community because of the dominance of the English language in the American academy and because of the different needs of their pedagogy. For example, in 2016 the editors of *Digital Pedagogy in the Humanities* found it necessary to add the keyword, 'Language Learning' (Davis *et al.*, 2020a; Oskoz, 2020) to the project in response to critiques raised by FL educators during a roundtable at the Modern Language Association (MLA) convention that the project had hitherto left out FL examples. Like that keyword, our chapter aims to bridge such gaps by showing the many links and parallel developments between English-language and foreign-language DH. We use the term 'bridge' intentionally building on Granovetter's (1973) concept of bridging weak ties that facilitate the passing of information between separate networks defined by strong ties. In our case, we are authors who have strong ties to our home professional networks – the DH community (Davis) and the FL community (Blyth) – and weak ties to each other's network. Together we are uniquely positioned to build bridges that can further the development of OEP in both communities. Such bridges fulfill the promise of a pedagogy of openness by facilitating that open exchange.

Openness and the Digital Humanities

Fitzpatrick (2010) encapsulates the methodological approaches of DH as 'a nexus of fields within which scholars use computing technologies to investigate the kinds of questions that are traditional to the humanities, or . . . who ask traditional kinds of humanities-oriented questions about computing technologies.' That nexus includes scholars of English, History, Rhetoric, Media Studies, Classical Studies and foreign languages to name just a few. Spiro (2012) defines the DH community by the shared values of openness, collaboration, collegiality and connectedness, diversity and experimentation (2012: 23–31).

The core value of openness in the DH community offers a path for FL instructors to engage with that community as well as a model to sustain their pedagogy of openness. Spiro (2012) traces this value back to the influence of the internet on DH culture as it leverages 'networked technologies to exchange ideas, create communities of practice, and build knowledge.' (2012: 21). Openness sustains the connections within the DH community, as well as its knowledge production, through the open sharing of content across networks. Kirschenbaum (2010) explains DH for English faculty as follows:

> the digital humanities today is about a scholarship (and a pedagogy) that is publicly visible in ways to which we are generally unaccustomed, a scholarship and pedagogy that are bound up with infrastructure in ways that are deeper and more explicit than we are generally accustomed to, a scholarship and pedagogy that are collaborative and depend on networks of people and that live an active, 24-7 life online. (2010: 6)

Open communication and sharing of tools and content in this networked community allow for collaborative knowledge production and depend on network ties for dissemination. The three values – openness, connectedness and collaboration – are intertwined and undergird the pedagogy of openness. Thus, McCarthy and Witmer (2016) identify the values of critical thinking, collaboration, production and openness as central to their perspective of DH pedagogy. They used these values to build community in a multi-disciplinary institute on Digital Humanities and Social Sciences at James Madison University and celebrate how 'Political scientists and foreign language instructors swapped strategies for improving assignments' (McCarthy & Witmer, 2016). This institute illustrates the promise of DH openness in building community across disciplinary boundaries based on a shared interest in pedagogy. By networking beyond the FL community, FL instructors can access the models and lessons learned from the broader community.

Nevertheless, it is worth noting that while pedagogy is part of this community, it is often secondary – as Hirsch (2013) observes about the parentheses used by Kirschenbaum – to the production of publicly visible online scholarship, 'such as in open-source software tools, freely accessible digital collections, and open-access journals and books' (Spiro, 2012: 24). The necessary focus of FL educators on teaching basic language skills before such knowledge production can occur, explains, in part, how the work of FL scholars in DH may not receive as much attention as those from more dominant fields.

A FL pedagogy of openness could also benefit from the DH practice of openly sharing online innovative assignments, tools and resources, such as those collected in the web companion – published under a Creative Commons license and using Scalar, an open source web-publishing tool – to a recent book on DH pedagogy (Battershill & Ross, 2017a, 2017b). Pointing to 'Open-Access Introductions to the Digital Humanities,' Battershill and Ross (2017c) explain, 'Many digital humanists are passionate about providing and disseminating open access works'. Clearly, Battershill and Ross are no different. Their book offers beginners an easy way into the DH community, and this, too, is part of openness, or as Spiro puts it, collegiality. Spiro (2012) explains the passion for open sharing in terms of social justice: 'For the digital humanities, information is not a commodity to be controlled but a social good to be shared and reused' (2012: 22). Openness for the DH community implies connectedness, collaboration, knowledge production, collegiality and social justice.

OER in Digital Humanities Pedagogy

In the DH community the production and open sharing of OER sustains OEP. Consider how the Salem Witch Trials assignment, developed by historian Elizabeth Matelski (2018a), illustrates this practice and is itself openly shared as part of a repository of DH assignments (Alice, n.d.). Students drew data from the trial transcripts made available as part of the *Salem Witch Trials Documentary Archive and Transcription Project*, a digital edition produced by the Scholar's Lab at the University of Virginia (Ray, 2002). This early DH project represents the first wave of OER, making its material available 'freely for non-commercial educational purposes' (Ray, 2002). Matelski's students used up to three different open source tools to extract and analyze data from the transcripts. They first annotated transcripts using Annotation Studio, a suite of collaborative web-based annotation tools, to identify data in the texts, and then manipulated the data by using Palladio, a tool for visualizing complex historical data, and Gephi, a network analysis tool. Matelski (2018b) has already used this assignment in two successive semesters and plans for each new group of students to add to a growing database until all 162 transcripts are done. In this way, earlier students will provide data to fuel the analysis of later students, who will in turn be expanding the analysis in that earlier work.

If the Salem Witch Trials Documentary Archive and Transcription Project represents the first wave of OER, the tools employed by Matelski's students represent more recent efforts, especially in the DH community, to move beyond sharing content alone to making available the tools used to create that content. While Gephi comes from the community built around the academic field of network science, both Palladio and Annotation Studio come from centers with DH funding from the National Endowment for the Humanities (NEH). To create Palladio, the Humanities + Design Research Lab at Stanford University (whose mission is to build open source tools for research) repurposed visualization and analysis tools developed for the Mapping the Republic of Letters Project ('Palladio,' n.d.). MIT's HyperStudio used NEH funding to create Annotation Studio, a collaborative tool for marking up digital texts ('Funders,' 2017). Palladio and Annotation Studio are both products of interdisciplinary collaborations between humanists and computer scientists that typify DH projects.

Akin to Annotation Studio, eComma has been used in FL programs to facilitate the social reading of FL texts (Blyth, 2014; Law et al., 2020). Originally designed by faculty and graduate students from the Department of English at the University of Texas at Austin with NEH funds, the tool was adapted to the FL environment by the Center for Open Educational Resources and Language Learning (http://www.coerll.utexas.edu/coerll/). Thus, early in its history, eComma represents a successful bridging between English-language and foreign-language DH enabled by a shared institutional home. eComma is an open-source Drupal module for digital annotation that is optimized for multilingual use. For instance, eComma allows users to annotate and discuss a text in a synchronous or asynchronous format in multiple languages, including non-Roman alphabetic languages such as Arabic, Chinese, Hindi and Russian. In addition to multilingual annotations, eComma allows users to tag a text with digital images or sounds. In other words, with digital tools such as eComma or Annotation Studio, textual interpretation becomes a multimodal as well as a multilingual experience.

Researchers in FL education have recently begun to explore the affordances of digital social reading and digital annotation to enhance the textual engagement of language learners. Thoms et al. (2017) conducted a qualitative study of the use of eComma by American learners enrolled in a second-semester Chinese course at the university level. The learners in the study were asked to annotate Chinese texts using eComma as homework assignments. Thoms et al. (2017) found that, under such asynchronous conditions, the learners mainly used eComma to query each other about the meaning of unknown Chinese characters. In a similar study, Thoms and Poole (2017) examined the use of a commercial Digital Annotation Tool (DAT) called Hylighter by college students enrolled in an advanced Spanish literature course. During the semester, the students employed Hylighter to analyze and discuss 18 different Spanish poems. Thoms and Poole (2017) found that, unlike the beginning students of Chinese, the advanced Spanish learners rarely asked each other about grammar or vocabulary. Rather, they used Hylighter to comment on various literary features of the poems. In a follow-up study, Thoms and Poole (2018) reanalyzed the same set of textual annotations produced by the advanced Spanish learners, but this time, they categorized the poems according to 'level of difficulty' as measured by tests of lexical density and syntactic complexity. The goal of the follow-up study was to explore the relationship between text difficulty and the types of annotations that learners produce. In brief, their results showed an inverse relationship between text difficulty and literary annotation. In other words, the more difficult the poem, the less likely the learners were to annotate the literary features of the text. Based on their findings, Thoms and Poole (2018) suggest that instructors who use DAT to teach literary texts as part of a foreign/second language course should 'highlight and define some of the more difficult words upfront (i.e. either outside of or within the virtual environment), before having students interact with each other in the DAT' (2018: 54).

Law *et al*. (2020) investigated how the use of the DAT eComma varied across time, across texts, and across different groups of beginning L2 French learners. To investigate the pragmatic patterns of peer interaction during six social reading activities, the authors conducted a quantitative analysis of 5065 annotation tokens produced during the semester. Following Thoms and Poole (2017), the annotations were classified according to their primary function (linguistic, literary or social). The results showed that the majority of the annotations drew on the texts' literary affordances, followed closely by the texts' linguistic affordances. In short, Law *et al*. (2020) found that their L2 French learners did not use eComma to engage in dialogic interaction with each other as had been expected but rather to post personal comments about the text that elicited few responses from other readers. Nevertheless, qualitative analyses of different groups of learners showed significant differences in the patterns of peer collaboration. For instance, some learners co-constructed meaning in a highly collaborative fashion without using the DAT's reply function. In summary, DAT has been explored by FL educators to increase learner engagement with difficult texts. To date, most of these studies have focused on the affordances of DAT for improving basic reading comprehension. By contrast, Matelski's history students used the DAT Annotation Studio to extract data from English-language texts as part of a larger data analysis workflow, a use made possible by the students' native proficiency.

It is interesting to note that Annotation Studio and eComma, similar tools developed contemporaneously at different institutions, have been embraced by very different DH subcommunities. Annotation Studio was developed at MIT's HyperStudio as a general annotation tool with a strong emphasis on visualization. Digital humanists from several different fields were involved in its development. Not surprisingly, the case studies featured on the Annotation Studio website reflect its origins in English-language textual analysis. For example, there is only one FL case study (Spanish) among the seven case studies featured (https://www.annotationstudio.org/pedagogy/case-studies/). In contrast, eComma was explicitly developed for use in FL classrooms and, as a result, was marketed to FL instructors. As such, all six case studies reported on the eComma website feature its use in FL settings such as lower-division language classes in French, German, Hebrew and Spanish (https://ecomma.coerll.utexas.edu/research/). This development points to an unfortunate phenomenon in DH as a new and heterogenous field; the knowledge associated with the use of a specific digital tool is often confined to the tool's community of practice and, as a consequence, may escape the notice of other communities of practice employing different but related tools.

Furthermore, the case of Annotation Studio and eComma highlights the important differences between the practices of DH scholars in English departments and those in FL departments. While the two academic disciplines overlap significantly, they still comprise relatively discrete communities with different interests and different foci. For example, FL instructors who employ DAT are typically more concerned with their students' variable linguistic and cultural proficiency than English instructors whose students have native or near-native proficiency in the target language and culture. Therefore, literature courses in FL focus to some degree on issues of basic grammar and vocabulary. Of course, the same is true for literature courses in Classics as well as English literature courses on writers such as Chaucer or Shakespeare, whose texts prove difficult for native speakers of modern English. In an effort to take advantage of the 'strength of weak ties' (Granovetter, 1973: 1360) and help users escape their silos, the developers of eComma included a webpage that provides links to different social reading tools (https://ecomma.coerll.utexas.edu/social-reading-tools/). The hope is that FL instructors interested in using eComma will be exposed to a variety of annotation practices and pedagogical applications beyond those associated with their home community of practice.

Projects like Annotation Studio, eComma and Palladio, received NEH funding in part because they promise to create an infrastructure that would enable knowledge production within the DH community and beyond. In a similar manner, the Alliance for Visual Culture at the University of Southern California first supported the creation of individual works of multimedia scholarship through a series of NEH-funded workshops (Ethington & McPherson, 2011; Goldberg & McPherson, 2009; Willis & McPherson, 2008) before moving to NEH-funded infrastructure creation in the form of Scalar, 'a free, open source authoring and publishing platform that's designed to make it easy for authors to write long-form, born-digital scholarship online' ('About Scalar Overview,' n.d.; Ethington *et al.*, 2015) as Battershill and Ross (2017b) did in their open-access web companion. The use of community peer review for NEH grants indicates community support for the marked change in strategy from supporting the creation of individual scholarly works alone to the creation of infrastructure in the form of open source tools that can support such knowledge creation. While various DH communities have created a range of tools to enable further digital production, this heterogeneous ecosystem of tools faces challenges in ensuring not just their wide availability but also their wide dissemination and adoption across all fields beyond their initial communities of practice. While tools and other OER created for the FL community offer the benefits of being designed for that community's needs, the overlap in functionality in annotation tools suggests that there may be other OER created by the wider DH community that similarly would benefit FL instruction.

Tools made available as OER play a special role in advancing OEP. Ayers (2013) characterizes early efforts of digital scholarship as digitization and digital publication heavily influenced by the standardized format of monographic culture, and challenges digital scholarship to break out of this conservative format and innovate 'more aggressively' (2013: 29) Ayers (2013) lays out a vision for what he terms 'generative scholarship – scholarship that builds ongoing, ever-growing digital environments even as it is used' (2013: 34). For Ayers (2013), generative scholarship broadens scholarly perspectives by inviting collaborators at all levels from undergraduates to scholars to the general public. While Ayers (2013) cites the public history project, Visualizing Emancipation, produced by the Digital Scholarship Lab at the University of Richmond as his example ('Visualizing Emancipation,' n.d.) – one that combines an archive and tools for exploring it – tools like Gephi, Palladio, Annotation Studio, eComma and Scalar all perform a similar function of opening up digital scholarship beyond traditional academics to students and others. They democratize knowledge production.

FL instructors who practice DH similarly engage their students in producing generative scholarship. Italian Professor Clarissa Cló (2020) of San Diego State University invites her students to build digital projects from existing archives in the form of a story map generated from a collection of the 1990s Italian magazine Aelle/AL 'to trace the history of Italian youth and music subcultures' (2020: 1). Thus, the project Hip Hop Italiano (n.d.), combines language learning with a geospatial methodology aimed at cultural exploration (Berens, 2020). This story map builds on the work of earlier students to create an online archive of Italian Hip-Hop materials ('About,' SDSU Italian Hip-Hop, n.d.). Because this is a language class, however, Cló (2020) also gives her students the caveat, 'Since the goals of the course include the incremental development of your intermediate-mid to advanced-low proficiency in Italian (in reading, writing, listening, speaking and cultural competency), you are not expected to produce a "superior" or "native" level Italian' (2020: 2). This project unites multimodal, geospatial methodologies and DH interests in open knowledge production with a recognition of the limitations of intermediate to advanced language students.

Many FL projects of generative scholarship support classroom instruction. For example, the Charlie Archive offers a collection of digital artifacts related to the 2015 terrorist attacks on the French satirical magazine Charlie Hebdo in Paris (http://cahl.io/). A collaboration between the French language program at Harvard and the Harvard Libraries, the Charlie Archive curates digital artifacts uploaded by people from all over the world: cartoons, essays, paintings, personal stories, posters, street art and videotaped interviews. Also included in the archive are thousands of individual web pages that represent different, often contradictory perspectives within contemporary French society. In their recent book on FL teaching and curriculum development, Bourns *et al.* (2020) discuss how the French language program at Harvard mines the archival content to enrich its language courses. One of the many activities the authors discuss is a social media exercise that obliges students to analyze a set of Twitter hashtags, such as

#Jesuischarlie (#Iamcharlie)
#Jenesuispascharlie (#Iamnotcharlie)

As part of this exercise, students examine and categorize the associated tweets and images. According to Bourns *et al.* (2020), this exercise is part of a longer lesson that carefully guides students to understand the diversity of viewpoints surrounding the 2015 terrorist attacks.

Another crowdsourced digital archive used for FL instruction is the Cityscape Project. Created by the Language Resource Center at Columbia University, this project allows New York residents and visitors to document the city's rich linguistic landscape by uploading, geotagging and commenting on personal digital photos of signage and other forms of written language in the public environment (http://cityscape.lrc.columbia.edu/). The photos can be sorted according to language as well as neighborhood. In addition to the photo archive, the project's website includes a link to a Zotero bibliography and Diigo user group devoted to exploring the concept of the 'linguistic landscape' for language teaching and linguistic research. Both the Charlie Archive and the Cityscape Project are excellent examples of generative scholarship, enabled by open practices like crowdsourcing and open publication, in which FL students learn a new language and culture while contributing to an open, scholarly archive, which can in turn facilitate language learning for other students. Such projects represent an evolution in student interaction with OER from consumption to further production

OEP in Digital Humanities Pedagogy

The OEP of networked learning, already well-established in FL pedagogy, offers another pillar to support an FL pedagogy of openness. In the DH community the 'active, 24–7 life online' (Kirschenbaum, 2010) that holds the community together through digital connections supports this OEP. The data set used for a recent social network analysis of the DH community comprised 3160 unique users with nearly 6 million tweets from March 2006 to May 2017 (Gao *et al.*, 2018). While this digitally networked community creates opportunities for open sharing and learning, it might also hinder the dissemination of information between various communities of practice within the larger DH community if those communities are strong networks without bridging ties between them, as Granovetter (1973) explains. *Digital Humanities Now* (2018), *DHNow* for short, was created in 2009 to capture the DH community's conversation and informally published scholarship and resources on the open web. The publication works by aggregating online content from blogs and other feeds, which are vetted by volunteer Editors-at-Large on a weekly basis, with the Editor-in-Chief then selecting pieces that drive the field forward as 'Editor's Choices' to be featured, while jobs, calls for papers, conference and funding announcements, reports, and recently-released resources are shared as news. At the end of 2017, *DHNow* reported 33,000 users and just over 26,500 followers on Twitter, with 104 items for Editor's Choice and 311 news items (Crossley, 2017). By rotating Editors-at-Large and aggregating online content, this publication can help bridge the gaps between strong networks, such as those based around disciplines, and encourage the dissemination of information and innovation across the DH community, as long as members of those disparate networks opt in as Editors-at-Large and submit their online outlets to the list of sources followed by *DHNow*.

Professional learning within the DH community happens across social media networks and through the open sharing of content online just as much if not more than through print publications and face-to-face conferences. DH pedagogy shares in many of the same OEP as DH scholarship and professional learning, inviting students to tweet and blog, to engage in open online conversations, and to share the products of their learning in ways that are familiar to many language instructors. For example, in #TvZ, students play a game of tag across Twitter that builds networked learning communities by requiring virtual collaboration with strangers over an intense 3-day period (Bali & Zamora, 2020). First developed by Pete Rorabaugh and Jesse Stommel, the game has gone through multiple iterations, with the 2015 version led by six administrators located across Canada, Egypt and the US (Rorabaugh, 2015). Such global networks offer opportunities for language students to practice their communication skills, enhance their cultural knowledge, and have the kind of Twitter experience common in the DH community – meeting and collaborating over social media.

Likewise, the Exquisite Engendering Remix assignment uses open practices to engage students at Penn State and the University of Helsinki in cross-cultural dialogue by networking across open social media (Lino and VoiceThread), openly producing knowledge in the form of an exhibition of remix videos, and situating this networking in the context of the larger FemTechNet Distributed Open Collaborative Course (DOCC) (Eagle *et al.*, 2016; Keifer-Boyd, 2017; Middleton, 2020). The FemTechNet Collaborative, a community dedicated to a shared interest in feminism and technology, has created a set of common assignments and activities that extend the boundaries of the classroom, as well as OER that each participating class or student can choose to use or not depending on the course, learning goals and preference ('the Network', *FemTechNet*, 2018). These activities support a range of network engagements at different levels, moving from an individual classroom (Object Making and Exchange) to a network of classrooms (Exquisite Engendering Video Remix) to creating resources for the entire FemTechNet community (Keyword Videos) to completely open exchange and knowledge production for the public (Wiki Storming, Feminist Mapping and Community Participation via Blog Commenting) ('Key Learning Projects,' 2018). The levels of engagement and openness available in the key learning projects help students develop their skills of network engagement as they move from smaller to larger and more open networked communities and demonstrate an evolving approach to open practices conditioned by contemporary political realities that have caused the collective to make some formerly open online activities private ('femtechnet on social media,' 2018; Kim, 2018). For example, the Feminist Mapping activity, which uses an open Google map, includes the option of contributing under a pseudonym. It is important to consider students' right to privacy and anonymity, not just based on their personal preference but also to shield them from potential attack when they are dealing with divisive issues.

While the above examples are based on English-language communities, the use of multilingual networks in open pedagogy is on the rise. Applied linguists Thorne and Ivkovic (2015: 169) point out that sociolinguists have increasingly emphasized '…a changing world in which interpersonal, professional and recreational life activities have come to involve intercultural and plurilingual communication.' Characterizing popular social networking sites such as YouTube as 'language contact zones,' the authors claim that the internet's participatory culture (Jenkins, 2009) transcends national and linguistic borders and allows speakers of different languages from different cultures to communicate and share digital content with each other (2009: 187). It is no surprise then that FL educators have been early adopters of social networking to promote language and culture learning. A prime example is 'online intercultural exchange' (O'Dowd, 2007), the activity of engaging learners in collaborative project work with partners from other cultures using online communication technology. One of the oldest and most popular examples of this form of open pedagogy is the *Cultura* Project (Furstenberg *et al.*, 2001; See also the chapter by Levet & Tschudi in this volume for an in-depth description of

Cultura's open design). The brainchild of French instructors at MIT who partnered with English instructors at Ecole Polytechnique in Paris, *Cultura* represents an online dialogue between two connected classrooms. Through a series of guided assignments, the students in both classrooms conduct collaborative linguistic and cultural analyses. More than 20 years old, *Cultura* has grown to include exchanges between different classrooms in many different languages. Furthermore, the original curriculum that focused on college-age learners has been adapted for high school students. Finally, as part of its open design, *Cultura* archives past dialogues for further research and analysis.

Twitter has also been used as a tool in FL education to foster awareness of cross-cultural pragmatics, the cultural norms governing the use of different languages in different social contexts. Blattner *et al.* (2016) asked intermediate and advanced French learners to analyze data from Twitter as a means of enhancing their grasp of formal and informal contexts of language use. Students selected three personalities from a list of preselected French native speakers to follow for 10 weeks. Next, the students were led through a series of activities that helped them understand how different sociolinguistic factors such as topic and interlocutor condition the variation apparent in the use of the French language. In a similar study, Blyth and Dalola (2016) examined how French language educators extended an OER entitled *Français interactif* (Blyth, 2012) by creating an accompanying Facebook page where students and teachers interacted with native and non-native French speakers from around the world. The researchers found that linguistic practices such as code switching and lexical borrowing that are proscribed in traditional classroom settings were not only accepted but encouraged by the francophones on the Facebook site. The authors conclude that open, translingual 'affinity spaces' (Gee, 2005) such as Facebook provide an ideal environment for raising learners' critical language awareness.

Beyond developing language and cultural skills, learning in online communities prepares students for learning and work in an emerging digital ecosystem 'shaped by networks, which are fundamentally social; characterized by horizontal access to creation and production; and increasingly driven by data, algorithms and artificial intelligence' (Bass & Eynon, 2016). In this context, students must learn to partner with technology to solve problems, requiring twenty-first century skills like critical thinking, creativity, communication and collaboration (P21, 2016), as well as mentored practice working across networks, creating knowledge, manipulating data and participating in this digital ecosystem (Levy & Murnane, 2013). Such participation depends on learners developing 'the skills, knowledge, ethical frameworks and self-confidence needed to be full participants in contemporary culture' (Jenkins, 2009: 7). The openness of the internet provides alternatives to the closed environment of the learning management system, with their 'architectures that prioritize user management, rigidly defined and restricted user roles, automated assessments and hierarchical, top-down administration' (Groom & Lamb, 2014). Likewise, Mozilla (2017) measures internet health by the degree of openness, a key environment for students to develop creativity. In this way, the networked learning practiced by foreign-language and the English-language DH communities responds to the needs of students to develop skills for thriving in the current digital knowledge ecosystem.

Open Knowledge Production

Open knowledge production offers another pillar for a pedagogy of openness in both the foreign-language and English-language DH communities. A good example is *Antología abierta de literatura hispana*, a Spanish-language project that aims to make knowledge more openly available and accessible via the collaborative contribution of a number of different participants, in this case, to enable the study of Hispanic literary texts. A specialist in modern Latin American literature, Ward (2017a) created her DH project as a collaboration between third-year students from her Fall 2016 Introduction to Hispanic Literature and Culture, librarians at the University of Oklahoma, a graduate student research guide for the students, and two undergraduate research students, who helped finalize the work for publication. Ward (2017a) derives her use of open pedagogy and collaborative open knowledge production from her commitment to broad accessibility. Ward (2017b) included Hispanic literary texts in the public domain on her course's reading list, and assigned groups of 4–5 students to select a text and create a critical edition, which she describes in the assignment for her students as a 'scholarly, annotated edition of an Hispanic literary text . . . [that] will allow future readers to understand allusions and references, literary structures and socio-historical context' (2017b: 1). While scholarly publication can be a challenge for language students who must master issues of grammar and style in addition to content and literary theory, the introductory critical edition falls within the range of students at this level and gives them additional motivation to develop their understanding of the text.

The *Antología abierta de literatura hispana* project demonstrates how DH offers opportunities to engage students in the practice of undergraduate research, one of ten high-impact practices identified by George Kuh (2008) as engaging students and positively affecting learning, especially for underserved students (Finley & McNair, 2013). Schantz (2008) concedes that traditional humanities scholarship discourages collaboration and that expertise barriers prevent undergraduate engagement in such scholarship. Knowledge production projects, however, open up opportunities to involve undergraduates. In particular, Blackwell and Martin (2009) propose that students play a role in translating humanities scholarship for broader audiences.

The *Antología abierta de literatura hispana* models student–faculty collaborative undergraduate research as students in partnership with their instructor use primary source documents to produce new knowledge. Such open knowledge production assignments represent authentic learning experiences for these students. Lombardi (2007) explains that authentic learning engages students in solving complex problems for which there is no clear answer. These experiences develop students in the conative domain, 'which determines whether a student has the necessary will, desire, commitment, mental energy and self-determination to actually perform at the highest disciplinary standards' (Lombardi, 2007: 9). For example, a case study of the project reports that Alice Barrett, one of Ward's students who was funded by the OU Office of Undergraduate Research to continue preparation of the text for publication, 'feels more confident about taking on big projects as well as writing in Spanish' (Mays, 2017b). In designing this project for her students, Ward paid special attention to scaffolding the role of the professional scholar, as well as the skills of collaboration and project management, two common features of DH work (Spiro, 2012; Siemens, 2020). In 'Teaching Guide: Expand an Open Textbook' Ward (2017d) shares her week-by-week lesson plans for the project; they include examples and readings about assignments, teamwork analysis and peer review. Students developed agency by learning how to accomplish a number of tasks on their own, for example, how to analyze a genre, how to find works in the public domain and how to choose a Creative Commons license. All contributors, including the students, are credited on the information page of the text with their project roles, such as drafting or copyediting, clearly listed (Ward, 2017c). Essentially, Ward professionalizes her students, treating them as working scholars. Having an open audience is important because students attach more importance to the potential impact of their work. Projects like these can impact the student's identity as they undergo a consequential transition where they reinterpret their sense of self in relation to the community within which they produce this knowledge, as well as the community they benefit, thereby ultimately gaining a sense of agency and efficacy (Davis, 2017).

Multiple communities enabled the *Antología abierta de literatura hispana*, including the University of Oklahoma (which funded the project with institutional grants supporting alternative textbooks and undergraduate research) and the open education community. The *Antología* is published through the Rebus Community, 'a platform for creating and publishing open textbooks,' ('About', Rebus Community, n.d.) which provides guidance and support for producing OER projects including *A Guide to Making Open Textbooks with Students* (Mays, 2017a). The Rebus Community uses Pressbooks, a platform built on top of WordPress that is itself available as open source software to support open source book publishing (McKenzie, 2012; Wagstaff, 2017). In return, Ward (2017b) openly shares her lesson plans, assignments, checklists and rubrics for the project under a Creative Commons license and calls for others to add to the *Antología* or create their own. Since the Rebus Community is interdisciplinary, supporting projects ranging from Finance to History of Science to Education, Ward can also be a bridging tie connecting the network of FL educators to the open textbook community.

Pedagogical Strategies to Address the Challenges of Open Education

While OER and OEP promise benefits for student engagement, learning and the development of agency, they come with their share of concerns, as well. FL instructors can leapfrog these challenges by taking advantage of strategies developed by both foreign-language and English-language members of the DH community. A common challenge for OER is locating appropriate and reliable resources. Because open, online scholarship is a norm in the DH community, finding reliable quality resources is not so much of a challenge as using them. For example, Rockwell (2012) offers several criteria for ensuring quality resources in a special issue of the *Journal of Digital Humanities* which is dedicated to evaluating digital work. While digital editions or digitized archives might be relatively straightforward to use, digital tools may present more of an issue. As noted above, there are multiple tools that serve similar functions and are not always disseminated to the same communities. Once a tool is selected, other challenges remain. For example, in reporting the results of her Salem Witch Trial assignment, Matelski (2018a) delineates several challenges around tool usage, including usability and the number of tools. Reducing the number of different tools used for one assignment can help reduce the cognitive load for students (Miller, 2014: 82), so that they can focus instead on the analysis of their data, an area of challenge for students in this assignment (Matelski, 2018a).

A second challenge for open education is negotiating laws that govern student privacy such as the Family Educational Rights and Privacy Act (FERPA) in the US and the General Data Protection Regulation (GDPR) in the European Union ('What is FERPA?', n.d.; Grama, 2018). Practice in this area is well established in the DH and open education communities and beyond. Guidelines circulated in the DH community for complying with FERPA and encouraging public student work include informing students early of any public assignments, allowing the use of a pseudonym, reminding students not to post private information and offering alternative assignments (Smith, 2012). Keralis (2017) created a form to operationalize these guidelines, by specifying technology to be used, sharing assignment learning goals, laying out choices of participation (contribution with attribution, anonymous contribution, or offline contribution only for the purposes of the assignment), and requiring a student signature. While Smith's guidelines speak to blog posts, Keralis' form is adapted to the needs of the

DH community with students making public contributions to larger digital projects.

Concerns about student labor pose a third challenge for open education. Keralis (2016) argues that not only are students who contribute to faculty projects as part of classwork laboring for free, they may even be paying for the privilege in the form of tuition. In addition, there is a power inequity in the classroom that puts a student at a disadvantage in this situation. In response, the *Student Collaborators' Bill of Rights* (Di Pressi *et al.*, 2015) created by the UCLA DH program articulates principles to ensure fairness to student labor on digital projects including fair pay, credit for their contribution, right to mentorship and instruction, rights to be a project team member and present on the work, but also the right to alternative assignments, and the need for project preservation so students can point back to this work in the future. This manifesto builds on the *Collaborators' Bill of Rights* (Clement *et al.*, 2011), which was produced by participants in a workshop on professionalization in DH centers. Since collaboration is a key value underlying the DH community, as the community matures, we see professional practices being developed in support of scholarship and then being transferred to pedagogical practice. Ward (2017b) shares a Faculty-Student MOU that enacts these principles by defining terms of work on the project, Creative Commons licensing for content, and the student's right to remove their name, work, or change licensing at any point prior to publication. By working on digital knowledge production projects, not only should students gain experience transferring and applying their knowledge to new contexts and digital skills, they should also gain insight into the world of work and implications for their future careers.

A fourth open education challenge is presented by the need to elicit learning from authentic experiences rather than labor alone. Instructors in the DH community have developed a number of process-based and reflection assignments to support metacognitive understanding. In his course entitled 'Crafting Digital History,' Graham (2018) adapts McDaniel's (2013) model of open notebook history (itself modeled on open science notebooks and open source software) to the 'Fail Log and Open Notebook' assignment that requires students to keep their research notes in a GitHub repository to document successes and failures, encourage learning from failure and provide a trail when students return to the project at a later date. For large digital projects Graham (2014) also assigns a paradata document which explains design decisions with references to theoretical readings and historical sources. Ward (2017b) provides several opportunities for her students to reflect on and discuss their collaborative process in creating critical editions. The fail logs, reflections, open history notebooks and paradata documents all work to ensure that students learn from their projects rather than just performing tasks or providing unpaid labor.

A fifth challenge for open education is that of finding projects where students can contribute to knowledge production. Several of the DH projects discussed above depend on local contexts to provide opportunities for students to do original research or contribute to the publication of hitherto unpublished material. Often local projects also have the advantage of offering material outside of the dominant historical narrative as well as connecting to the student's lived experience in their community (Shannon & Galle, 2017). Davis (2012) suggests that crowdsourcing projects (like the Charlie Archive and the Cityscape Project), where the general public is engaged in performing tasks, also provide 'opportunities out there for motivated students to engage in the process of digitizing, preserving, and studying collective resources and data.' For example, the Smithsonian runs a Transcription Center for digital volunteers to transcribe things like 'field notes, diaries, ledgers, logbooks, currency proof sheets, photo albums, manuscripts, biodiversity specimen labels' ('Smithsonian Digital Volunteers,' 2018). The Zooniverse platform for crowdsourced research offers both opportunities for volunteers to contribute and the capacity to partner with researchers looking for such help ('Zooniverse,' n.d.). Davis (2012) recommends making such crowdsourcing experiences meaningful for students by linking them to course learning outcomes, examining the goals of the larger project and encouraging students to reflect on their contribution.

Beyond public crowdsourcing projects, a number of DH projects open up opportunities for student contributions to support open knowledge production. For example, the *Map of Early Modern London (MOEML)* project offers a pedagogical partnership program whereby an instructor can act as a guest editor on the project while students act as contributors, providing entries into the project's encyclopedia (Jenstad & McLean-Fiander, n.d.). Similarly, the Perseids project (Beaulieu, 2014), spun off from the well-established Perseus Project, offers 'an integrated platform on which students will collaboratively transcribe, edit and translate Latin and Greek texts, creating vetted open source digital editions.' The larger goal is 'a convergent, collaborative effort to use abstract skills and training to add to the sum of human knowledge' (Beaulieu, 2014). Perseids also offers an infrastructure that can be connected to different archive partners, such as a target language archive, so that disciplines beyond classical studies might take advantage of the tool. Likewise, the Rebus community offers opportunities for making open textbooks with students (Mays, 2017a). Language projects might consider ways to find audiences beyond the target language community. This might be as simple as adding an English translation, as in the case of the Charlie Archive at Harvard, which would offer more opportunities for applied work.

A sixth challenge for open digital projects comes in ensuring project quality. The aforementioned MOEML project tackles this challenge by providing extensive documentation of their standards, including an editorial style guide, typographical conventions, a checklist for submissions, as well as advice for students on research, writing for the web, and using disciplinary sources (Jenstad & McLean-Fiander, n.d.). As a final safety net, they have the instructor act as guest editor to vet the work of student contributors. Students who participate in this program take on the identity of a professional scholar developing a sense of efficacy as they are able to transfer their knowledge to a professional setting, write for the standards of the project rather than a grade, and write for the general public rather than their instructor (Davis, 2017).

Ward ensured quality in the *Antología abierta de literatura hispana* by providing extensive guidelines, examples of critical editions, the support of a graduate student as research guide, and hiring two undergraduates to copy edit and prepare the manuscript for publication. Projects like the *Antología abierta de literatura hispana* also depend on funding and collaboration with other offices on campus and beyond. Ward found opportunities for institutional support in an alternative textbook grant from OU libraries and support for undergraduate research from the Undergraduate Research office and the Honors College. Collaboration with the Rebus community provided additional support. Instructors interested in pursuing such projects can benefit from the models of those who have gone before and openly shared their process, as Ward (2017d) does in her 'Teaching Guide: Expand an Open Textbook.'

Quality is complicated even further in collaborative student projects, where two or more students are responsible for the same work. Ward (2017d) tackled this challenge by making teamwork a subject of study in her class and using peer evaluations. Taylor (2014) mentors her students in developing equitable group contracts to govern the work they will do on public digital projects. A group contract developed by students contributing to the White Violence/Black Resistance project lays out the goals of the project, tools to be used, scheduled project milestones, and norms of behavior for the group. By requiring that students develop their own contract, Taylor encourages them to take ownership of the project and be responsible for its quality.

Towards a Pedagogy of Openness

The use of OER and OEP coupled with the strategies to negotiate the challenges in open education combine to form a pedagogy of openness. DH adds another dimension to this pedagogy because not only does learning happen in the open, community members are also open about their pedagogy. The values of openness, connectedness and collaboration underlie the practice of pedagogy in the English-language as well as the foreign-language DH communities and result in a well-developed culture of pedagogical sharing. A search for 'teaching' on *DHNow* returns 416 results. Teaching resources, assignments, student work, syllabi, course sites and reflections are shared across the community. Some take the form of open course sites like Keifer-Boyd's (2018) Visual Culture & Educational Technologies class (home to the Exquisite Engendering Remix project) or assignment banks like Alice (n.d.) at Endicott College which hosts the Salem Witchcraft Assignment. Others publish model assignments (Ward, 2017d), make available online courses and the student work produced in them (Graham, 2018), or blog about their own teaching and pedagogical choices they make (Sample, 2013).

An important category of openness about teaching comes with transparency about failure. The *Journal of Interactive Technology and Pedagogy* includes a section of teaching fails, which publishes assignments that did not work out as a way of thinking through what went wrong and a lesson for others (Kane, n.d.). Other instructors include reflections about teaching fails on their blogs, like Davis's (2013) 'Reflections on a Text Analysis Assignment.' In a study of where physics faculty leave the pedagogical innovation process, Henderson *et al.* (2012) found that a third of faculty who had tried a new Research Based Instructional Strategy (RBIS), had discontinued the innovation. The authors suggest that this departure occurs because these innovations are often presented in an 'overly rosy' manner that does not match with the implementation experience (Henderson *et al.*, 2012: 11). The open sharing of teaching fails and other challenges along with pedagogical innovations can provide a valuable corrective narrative to over-enthusiastic selling of innovation.

The open sharing of assignments has led to the phenomenon of the forked assignment where one instructor uses an assignment, and another instructor is inspired to use it with slight adaptation. The forking metaphor comes from software engineering where one developer takes source code in a different direction than the original code, which may also continue development (Croxall, 2012). This phenomenon happens whenever teachers see a great idea and borrow it for their courses. Unfortunately, the evidence of such OER adaptation is not always visible since it largely goes on behind closed classroom doors. The DH community has partially adopted open publishing practices to make this practice more visible. For example, in the *Digital Pedagogy in the Humanities* collection of artifacts, 28% of the 589 artifacts have some form of Creative Commons license openly posted where the artifact was originally published online (Davis *et al.*, 2020b). The use of an open license makes clear the creator's granting of permission to copy and use an assignment, permission that was only implicit through posting assignments openly online. The natural response is to grant attribution when reusing an assignment. This practice of licensing and attribution represents a mature – if unevenly applied – development of openness in and about DH pedagogy and treats pedagogical production as scholarship. In addition to adding a Creative Commons license and acknowledging pedagogical sources, Lawson (2014) also recommends including year and semester as a version number, uploading syllabi to a stable online repository, adding metadata that can be harvested, and including a changelog with some explanation.

The culture of openness in DH scholarship makes the adoption of OER and OEP easier for DH pedagogy as practice transfers from open scholarly communication to teaching and learning rather than needing to be established ex nihilo. Thus, Ward collaborates with students and others to openly publish *Antología abierta de literatura hispana* under a Creative Commons license then does the same for her lesson plans for the production of the anthology. As the DH community has matured in its open practices, it has evolved conventions, guidelines and strategies to mitigate the challenges presented by OER and OEP, with many of these built on models from DH scholarship. Maturity has also brought a more nuanced approach to openness, recognizing the need to scaffold open practices for students, to mentor them in networked engagement and to focus on the learning just as much as the knowledge production. With this pedagogy of openness comes new roles for faculty as editors, project managers, supervisors, mentors, co-creators and peers. As students gain in efficacy and agency, they ultimately become not students but equal members of the DH community. The pedagogy of openness in the DH community in the end means production and use of OER, teaching and learning in the open, open knowledge production, creation of infrastructure to support open knowledge production, transparency about teaching and learning and acceptance of the learner as an equal member of the community. In summary, OEP are successful in the DH community because, as a shared community value, openness pervades both scholarship and pedagogy.

Conclusion

In this chapter, we have demonstrated how a pedagogy of openness benefits both the English-language DH community as well as the foreign-language DH community. Following Ward's model, more FL educators might wish to combine open scholarship and open education. Each community has much to learn from each other and both communities should intentionally build bridging ties between their communities rather than merely co-existing in separate networks defined by strong ties. We contend that a pedagogy of openness can bridge differences between the foreign-language and English-language DH communities, as well as bridge long-standing divisions within language-specific fields. For instance, as noted in the 2007 MLA report on foreign languages (Modern Language Association, 2007), foreign language departments have traditionally divided their curricula into lower division courses focused on 'language learning' and upper division courses focused on 'literary and cultural content,' a phenomenon commonly referred to as the 'bifurcated language department.' A similar division of labor exists in English departments where lower division composition courses are typically taught by non-tenure track instructors (graduate students, lecturers or adjuncts) and upper division literature courses are taught by tenured or tenure-track professors. A pedagogy of openness as practiced by DH scholars holds the very real possibility of reconciling the language/literature divide by allowing instructors in both foreign language departments and English departments to integrate the development of language and literacy skills with the development of various types of content-based knowledge rooted in cultural and literary studies.

References

'About', *SDSU Italian Hip-Hop,* online archive (n.d.) See http://godfathersofhiphop.weebly.com/about.html (accessed 13 June 2019).
'About', *Rebus Community,* website (n.d.) See https://about.rebus.community/ (accessed 20 June 2019).
'About Scalar, Overview' *The Alliance for Networking Visual Culture,* website (n.d.) See https://scalar.me/anvc/scalar/ (accessed 3 September 2018).
Alice (n.d.) database. See https://alice.endicott.edu/ (accessed 7 September 2018).
Ayers, E.L. (2013) Does digital scholarship have a future? *EDUCAUSE Review* 48 (4), 24–34. See http://er.educause.edu/articles/2013/8/does-digital-scholarship-have-a-future
Bali, M. and Zamora, M. (2020) Network. In R.F. Davis, M.K. Gold, K.D. Harris and J Sayers (eds) *Digital Pedagogy in the Humanities: Concepts, Models, and Experiments.* New York: Modern Language Association of America. See https://digitalpedagogy.hcommons.org/keyword/Network
Bass, R. and Eynon, B. (2016) *Open and Integrative: Designing Liberal Education for the New Digital Ecosystem.* Association of American Colleges and Universities. See https://www.aacu.org/publications-research/publications/open-and-integrative-designing-liberal-education-new-digital
Battershill, C. and Ross, S. (2017a) *Using Digital Humanities in the Classroom: A Practical Introduction for Teachers, Lecturers, and Students.* London: Bloomsbury Publishing.
Battershill, C. and Ross, S. (2017b) 'Introduction'. *Using Digital Humanities in the Classroom,* web companion. See http://scalar.usc.edu/works/digital-humanities-in-the-classroom-a-practical-introduction/introduction (accessed 30 May 2018).
Battershill, C. and Ross, S. (2017c) 'About', *Using Digital Humanities in the Classroom,* web companion. See http://scalar.usc.edu/works/digital-humanities-in-the-classroom-a-practical-introduction/about (accessed 7 September 2018).
Beaulieu, M.-C. (2014) *Digital Humanities in the Classroom: Bridging the Gap between Teaching and Research* (Final Performance Report No. HD-51548–12).
Beetham, H., Falconer, I., McGill, L. and Littlejohn, A. (2012) *Open Practices: A Briefing Paper.* JISC. See https://oersynth.pbworks.com/w/page/51668352/OpenPracticesBriefing
Berens, K.I. (2020) Interface. In R.F. Davis, Matthew K. Gold, Katherine D. Harris and J. Sayers (eds) *Digital Pedagogy in the Humanities: Concepts, Models, and Experiments.* New York: Modern Language Association of America. See https://digitalpedagogy.hcommons.org/keyword/Interface
Blackwell, C. and Martin, T.R. (2009) Technology, collaboration, and undergraduate research. *Digital Humanities Quarterly* 3 (1). See http://www.digitalhumanities.org/dhq/vol/3/1/000024/000024.html
Blattner, G., Dalola, A. and Lomicka, L. (2016) Mind your hashtags: A sociopragmatic study of student interpretations of French native speakers' tweets. In C. Wang and L. Winstead (eds) *Handbook of Research on Foreign Language Education in the Digital Age* (pp. 33–58). Hershey, PA: IGI Global.

Blyth, C. (2012) Opening up FL education with open educational resources: The case of *Français interactif*. In F. Rubio and J. Thoms (eds) *Hybrid Language Teaching and Learning: Exploring Theoretical, Pedagogical and Curricular Issues* (pp. 196–218). Boston, MA: Heinle Thomson.

Blyth, C. (2014) Exploring the affordances of digital social reading for L2 literacy: The case of *eComma*. In J. Pettes Guikema and L. Williams (eds) *Digital Literacies in Foreign and Second Language Education* (pp. 201–226). San Marcos, TX: CALICO.

Blyth, C. and Dalola, A. (2016) Translingualism as an open educational language practice: Raising critical language awareness on Facebook. *Apprentissage des Langues et Systèmes d'Information et de Communication*, 19. See https://journals.openedition.org/alsic/2962; DOI: https://doi.org/10.4000/alsic.2962

Bourns, S., Krueger, C. and Mills, N. (2020) *Perspectives on Teaching Language and Content*. New Haven, CT: Yale University Press.

Clement, T., Croxall, B., Flanders, J., Fraistat, N., Jones, S., Kirschenbaum, M., Lodatto, S., Mandell, L., Marty, P., Nowviskie, B., Olsen, S., Reside, D., Scheinfeldt, T., Seaman, D., Tebeau, M. and Walter, K. (2011) 'Collaborators' Bill of Rights', *Media Commons Press*. See http://mcpress.media-commons.org/offthetracks/part-one-models-for-collaboration-career-paths-acquiring-institutional-support-and-transformation-in-the-field/a-collaboration/collaborators%e2%80%99-bill-of-rights/

Cló, C. (2020) *Italian-Language Study Using Geospatial Methodology*. Assignment. See https://hcommons.org/deposits/item/hc:31047/

Crossley, L. (2017) 'DHNow: 2017 in Review'. *Digital Humanities Now*. See http://digitalhumanitiesnow.org/2017/12/dhnow-2017-in-review/

Croxall, B. (2012) 'Forking your syllabus'. *The Chronicle of Higher Education Blogs: ProfHacker,* blog post, 22 March. See https://www.chronicle.com/blogs/profhacker/forking-your-syllabus/39137 (accessed 20 June 2019).

Davis, R.F. (2017) Pedagogy and learning in a digital ecosystem. In J. Moore and R. Bass (eds) *Understanding Writing Transfer and its Implications for Higher Education*. (pp. 27–38). Sterling, VA: Stylus Publishing.

Davis, R.F. (2012) Crowdsourcing, undergraduates, and digital humanities projects. *Rebecca Frost Davis: Liberal Education in a Networked World,* blog post, 3 September. See http://rebeccafrostdavis.wordpress.com/2012/09/03/crowdsourcing-undergraduates-and-digital-humanities-projects/ (accessed 12 October 2012).

Davis, R.F. (2013) Reflections on a text analysis assignment. *Rebecca Frost Davis: Liberal Education in a Networked World,* blog post, 12 November. See http://rebeccafrostdavis.wordpress.com/2013/11/12/reflections-on-a-text-analysis-assignment/ (accessed 11 December 2013).

Davis, R.F., Gold, M.K. and Harris, K.D. (2020a) Keywords | Curating digital pedagogy in the humanities. In R.F. Davis, M.K. Gold, K.D. Harris and J. Sayers (eds) *Digital Pedagogy in the Humanities: Concepts, Models, and Experiments.* New York: Modern Language Association of America. See https://digitalpedagogy.hcommons.org/introduction/intro-keywords

Davis, R.F., Gold, M.K. and Harris, K.D. (2020b) Pedagogical materials as scholarship | Curating digital pedagogy in the humanities. In R.F. Davis, M.K. Gold, K.D. Harris and J. Sayers (eds) *Digital Pedagogy in the Humanities: Concepts, Models, and Experiments.* New York: Modern Language Association of America. See https://digitalpedagogy.hcommons.org/introduction/pedagogical-materials-as-scholarship

Di Pressi, H. (2015) A Student collaborators' bill of rights'. *Center for Digital Humanities – UCLA*. See https://cdh.ucla.edu/news/a-student-collaborators-bill-of-rights/ (accessed 3 September 2018).

Digital Humanities Now (2018) See http://digitalhumanitiesnow.org/ (accessed 7 September 2018).

Eagle, E., Finamore, A., Geiple, J., Johson, L., Kirby, Z., Long, J. and Stamm, K. (2016) Exquisite Engendering Remix Exhibition, Spring. See http://cyberhouse.arted.psu.edu/811/2016.html (accessed 3 June 2019).

'femtechnet on social media', *Femtechnet* (2018) See https://femtechnet.org/get-involved/social-media/ (accessed 5 September 2018).

Ethington, P., Anderson, S., McPherson, T. and Fletcher, C. (2015) NEH grant details: Implementing scalar for digital humanities multimodal online publishing: Editorial and authorial workflow in collaboration. See https://securegrants.neh.gov/publicquery/main.aspx?f=1&gn=HK-230970-15 (accessed 21 July 2019).

Ethington, P. and McPherson, T. (2011) NEH grant details: Broadening the digital humanities: The Vectors-CTS summer institute on digital approaches to American studies. See https://securegrants.neh.gov/publicquery/main.aspx?f=1&gn=HT-50036-10 (accessed 21 July 2019).

Finley, A.P. and McNair, T. (2013) *Assessing Underserved Students' Engagement in High-Impact Practices*. Association of American Colleges and Universities.

Fitzpatrick, K. (2010) Reporting from the digital humanities 2010 conference. *The Chronicle of Higher Education Blogs: Profhacker*, blog post. See http://chronicle.com/blogs/profhacker/reporting-from-the-digital-humanities-2010-conference/25473 (accessed 21 July 2011).

Funders (2017) *Annotation Studio*, web application. See https://www.annotationstudio.org/community/funders/ (accessed 7 September 2018).

Furstenberg, G., Levet, S., English, K. and Maillet, K. (2001) Giving a virtual voice to the silent language of culture: The Cultura project. *Language Learning & Technology* 5 (1), 55–102. See http://dx.doi.org/10125/25113

Gao, J., Nyhan, J., Duke-Williams, O. and Mahony, S. (2018) Visualising the digital humanities community: A comparison study between citation network and social network. Presented at the Digital Humanities 2018 Conference, Mexico City: Alliance of Digital Humanities Organizations. See https://dh2018.adho.org/en/visualising-the-digital-humanities-community-a-comparison-study-between-citation-network-and-social-network/

Gee, J. (2005) Semiotic social spaces and affinity spaces: From the age of mythology to today's schools. In D. Barton and K. Tusting (eds) *Beyond Communities of Practice: Language, Power and Social Context*. (pp. 214–232). Cambridge: Cambridge University Press.

Gephi – The Open Graph Viz Platform (2017), web application. See https://gephi.org/ (accessed 7 September 2018).

Goldberg, D.T. and McPherson, T. (2009) NEH grant details: Broadening the digital humanities: The Vectors-IML/UC-HRI summer institute on multimodal scholarship. See https://securegrants.neh.gov/publicquery/main.aspx?f=1&gn=HT-50022-09 (accessed 21 July 2019).

Graham, S. (2014) Minecrafted history, website. See https://github.com/shawngraham/hist3812a (accessed 8 July 2016).

Graham, S. (2018) *Course Manual for Crafting Digital History HIST3814o|DIGH3814o @ Carleton U Summer 2018*. See http://site.craftingdigitalhistory.ca/rubric-and-assessment.html#weekly-work

Grama, J. (2018, May 1). *7 Things You Should Know About GDPR*. Educause Learning Initiative. See https://library.educause.edu/resources/2018/5/7-things-you-should-know-about-gdpr

Granovetter, M. (1973) The strength of weak ties. *American Journal of Sociology* 78 (6), 1360–1380.

Groom, J. and Lamb, B. (2014) Reclaiming Innovation. *EDUCAUSE Review* 49 (3). See https://www.educause.edu/visuals/shared/er/extras/2014/ReclaimingInnovation/default.html

Henderson, C., Dancy, M. and Niewiadomska-Bugaj, M. (2012) Use of research-based instructional strategies in introductory physics: Where do faculty leave the innovation-decision process? *Physical Review Special Topics – Physics Education Research*, 8 (020104), 1–15. See http://prst-per.aps.org/pdf/PRSTPER/v8/i2/e020104

Hip Hop Italiano (n.d.), online archive. See https://www.arcgis.com/apps/MapJournal/index.html?appid=36d80c623d9a4b4291eea52c9ae279ac (accessed 12 June 2019).

Hirsch, B. (2013) Digital Humanities and the Place of Pedagogy. In B. Hirsch (ed.) *Digital Humanities Pedagogy: Practices, Principles and Politics* (pp. 3–30). Open Book Publishers. http://www.openbookpublishers.com/reader/161

Jenkins, H. (2009) *Confronting the Challenges of Participatory Culture: Media Education for the 21st Century* (John D. and Catherine T. MacArthur Foundation Reports on Digital Media and Learning). Cambridge, MA: MIT Press.

Jenstad, J. and McLean-Fiander, K. (n.d.) 'Pedagogical Partners' Welcome Package'. *The Map of Early Modern London,* digital project. See https://mapoflondon.uvic.ca/ppp_welcome.htm

Kane, L. (n.d.) Call For Submissions, webpage. See http://jitp.commons.gc.cuny.edu/call-for-submissions/ (accessed 5 September 2018).

Keifer-Boyd, K. (2017) Exquisite engendering video ReMIX, MIXed reality art project: In & out of place, art exhibit, *AED 322 Visual Culture & Educational Technologies*, Spring. See http://cyberhouse.arted.psu.edu/322/projects/4_ExquisiteEngendering.html (accessed 17 June 2019).

Keifer-Boyd, K. (2018) A ED 322 Visual culture & educational technologies, course website. See http://cyberhouse.arted.psu.edu/322/index.html (accessed 20 June 2019).

Keralis, S. (2016) Milking the deficit internship. In *Disrupting the Digital Humanities*. See http://www.disruptingdh.com/milking-the-deficit-internship/

Keralis, S. (2017) Consent of Disclosure of Education Record. See https://hcommons.org/deposits/item/hc:31087/

'Key learning projects', *Femtechnet* (2018), website. See https://femtechnet.org/get-involved/self-directed-learners/key-learning-project/ (accessed 5 September 2018).

Kim, D. (2018) Medieval studies since Charlottesville. *Inside Higher Ed*, 30 August. See https://www.insidehighered.com/views/2018/08/30/scholar-describes-being-conditionally-accepted-medieval-studies-opinion

Kirschenbaum, M.G. (2010) What is digital humanities and what's it doing in English departments? *ADE Bulletin* (150). See http://mkirschenbaum.files.wordpress.com/2011/01/kirschenbaum_ade150.pdf

Kuh, G.D. (2008) *High-Impact Educational Practices: What They Are, Who Has Access to Them, and Why They Matter.* Association of American Colleges and Universities. See https://www.aacu.org/leap/hips

Law, J., Barny, D. and Poulin, R. (2020) Patterns of peer interaction in multimodal L2 digital reading. *Language Learning & Technology* 24 (2), 70–85. See https://www.lltjournal.org/item/3150

Lawson, K.M. (2014) 'Citing syllabi'. *The Chronicle of Higher Education Blogs: ProfHacker*, blog post, 21 August. See https://www.chronicle.com/blogs/profhacker/citing-syllabi/57893 (accessed 23 July 2019).

Levy, F. and Murnane, R. (2013) *Dancing with Robots: Human Skills for Computerized Work.* third way. See http://www.thirdway.org/publications/714

Lombardi, M.M. (2007) *Authentic Learning for the 21st Century: An Overview* (ELI White Papers). Educause Learning Initiative. See http://www.educause.edu/library/resources/authentic-learning-21st-century-overview

Matelski, E. (2018a) 'Assignment result – What makes a witch? a Salem witch trials network analysis', *Alice*. See https://alice.endicott.edu/assignment_groups/63 (accessed 7 September 2018).

Matelski, E. (2018b) Personal Interview. By Rebecca Frost Davis.

Mays, E.E. (2017a) *A Guide to Making Open Textbooks with Students*. See https://press. rebus.community/makingopentextbookswithstudents/

Mays, E.E. (2017b) Case study: Antología Abierta de Literatura Hispánica. In *A Guide to Making Open Textbooks with Students*. See https://press.rebus.community/ makingopentextbookswithstudents/chapter/case-study-antologia-abierta-de-literatura-hispanica/

McCarthy, S. and Witmer, A. (2016) Notes toward a values-driven framework for digital humanities pedagogy. *Hybrid Pedagogy*. See http://hybridpedagogy.org/values-driven-framework-digital-humanities-pedagogy/

McDaniel, C. (2013) 'Open Notebook History', blog post. See http://wcm1.web.rice.edu/open-notebook-history.html (accessed 4 September 2018).

McKenzie, H. (2012) What does an open-source book publishing platform look like? We're about to find out, *Pando*, website, 20 December. See https://pando.com/2012/12/20/what-does-an-open-source-book-publishing-platform-look-like-were-about-to-find-out/ (accessed 20 June 2019).

Middleton, K. (2020) Remix. In R.F. Davis, M.K. Gold, K.D. Harris and J. Sayers (eds) *Digital Pedagogy in the Humanities: Concepts, Models, and Experiments*. New York: Modern Language Association of America. See https://digitalpedagoy.hcommons.org/keyword/Remix

Miller, M.D. (2014) *Minds Online: Teaching Effectively with Technology*. Cambridge: Harvard University Press.

Modern Language Association Report (2007) Foreign languages and higher education: New structures for a changed world. See http://www.mla.org/flreport (accessed 10 July 2019).

Mozilla (n.d.) Protect internet health and privacy with Mozilla. *Mozilla*, website. See https://www.mozilla.org/en-US/internet-health/ (accessed 15 October 2017).

'the Network', *FemTechNet*, webpage (2018). See https://femtechnet.org/about/the-network/ (accessed 5 September 2018).

O'Dowd, R. (2007) *Online Intercultural Exchange: An Introduction for Foreign Language Teachers*. Clevedon: Multilingual Matters.

Oskoz, A. (2020) Language learning. In R.F. Davis, M.K. Gold, K.D. Harris and J. Sayers (eds) *Digital Pedagogy in the Humanities: Concepts, Models, and Experiments*. New York: Modern Language Association of America. See https://digitalpedagogy.hcommons.org/keyword/Language-Learning

P21 (2016) Framework for 21st Century Learning. See http://www.p21.org/storage/documents/docs/P21_framework_0816.pdf (accessed 15 October 2017).

Palladio (n.d.), web application. See http://hdlab.stanford.edu (accessed 7 September 2018).

Ray, B. (2002) Salem witch trials documentary archive, archive. See http://salem.lib.virginia.edu/home.html (accessed 2 September 2018).

Rockwell, G. (2012) Short guide to evaluation of digital work. *Journal of Digital Humanities*, 1 (4). See http://journalofdigitalhumanities.org/1-4/short-guide-to-evaluation-of-digital-work-by-geoffrey-rockwell/

Rorabaugh, P. (2015) 'The Evolution of #TvsZ', *Pete Rorabaugh: All is Telling*, blog post, 19 February. See http://peterorabaugh.org/tvsz/the-evolution-of-tvsz/ (accessed 5 September 2018).

Sample, M. (2013) 'Flogging reflection', *DIG 401: Hacking Remixing Design*, course website. See http://web.archive.org/web/20150822212436/sites.davidson.edu/hacking/course-guidelines/flogging-reflection (accessed 7 September 2018).

Schantz, M. (2008) Undergraduate research in the humanities: Challenges and prospects. *Council on Undergraduate Research Quarterly* 29 (2), 26–30.

Shannon, D. and Galle, J. (eds) (2017) *Interdisciplinary Approaches to Pedagogy and Place-Based Education – From Abstract to the Quotidian*. Cham, Switzerland: Palgrave Macmillan.

Siemens, L. (2020) Project Management. In R.F. Davis, M.K. Gold, K.D. Harris and J. Sayers (eds) *Digital Pedagogy in the Humanities: Concepts, Models, and Experiments*. New York: Modern Language Association of America. See https://digitalpedagogy.hcommons.org/keyword/Project-Management

Smith, K. (2012) 'Guidelines for public, student class blogs: ethics, legalities, FERPA and more' HASTAC, blog post, 30 November. See http://www.hastac.org/blogs/cathy-davidson/2012/11/30/guidelines-public-student-class-blogs-ethics-legalities-ferpa-and-mo (accessed 20 May 2015).

Smithsonian Digital Volunteers (2018) See https://transcription.si.edu/ (accessed 7 September 2018).

Spiro, L. (2012) 'This is why we fight': Defining the values of the digital humanities. In M.K. Gold (ed.) *Debates in the Digital Humanities* (pp. 16–35). Minneapolis: University of Minnesota Press. See http://dhdebates.gc.cuny.edu/debates/text/13

Taylor, T. (2014) Group Contract (COMM 4543). See https://hcommons.org/deposits/item/hc:31225/

Thoms, J. and Poole, F. (2017) Investigating linguistic, literary, and social affordances of L2 collaborative reading. *Language Learning & Technology* 21 (2), 139–156. See https://www.lltjournal.org/item/3004

Thoms, J. and Poole, F. (2018) Exploring digital literacy practices via L2 social reading. *L2 Journal* 10 (2), 36–61. See https://escholarship.org/uc/item/0fk329vn

Thoms, J., Sung, K.-Y. and Poole, F. (2017) Investigating the linguistic and pedagogical affordances of an L2 open reading environment via eComma: An exploratory study in a Chinese language course' *System* 69, 38–53.

Thorne, S. and Ivkovic, D. (2015) Multilingual *Eurovision* meets plurilingual *YouTube*: Linguascaping discursive ideologies. In D. Koike and C. Blyth (eds) *Dialogue in Multilingual and Multimodal Communities* (pp. 167–192). Amsterdam/Philadelphia: John Benjamins.

Visualizing Emancipation (n.d.), digital project. See https://dsl.richmond.edu/emancipation/ (accessed 3 September 2018).

Wagstaff, S. (2017) 'Getting started with pressbooks', *Steel Wagstaff*, blog post, 9 November. See https://medium.com/@steelwagstaff/getting-started-with-pressbooks-ee3e5f07f4d2 (accessed 20 June 2019).

Ward, J.A. (2017a) 'Antología abierta de literatura hispana'. *Julie Ann Ward, PhD*, web page. See http://julieannward.com/home/portfolio/student-projects/work-in-progress-antologia-abierta-de-literatura-hispana/ (accessed 18 June 2019).

Ward, J.A. (2017b) Edición Crítica, SPAN 3853: Introduction to Hispanic Literature and Culture. *Julie Ann Ward, PhD*, assignment. See http://julieannward.com/home/portfolio/student-projects/work-in-progress-antologia-abierta-de-literatura-hispana/

Ward, J.A. (2017c) Información. *Antología Abierta de Literatura Hispana.*, digital edition. See https://press.rebus.community/aalh/front-matter/informacion/

Ward, J.A. (2017d) Teaching guide: Expand an open textbook. In a *Guide to Making Open Textbooks with Students*. See https://press.rebus.community/makingopentextbookswithstudents/chapter/teaching-assignment-expand-an-open-textbook/

'What is FERPA?', *Protecting Student Privacy* (n.d.), website. See https://studentprivacy.ed.gov/faq/what-ferpa (accessed 22 July 2019).

Willis, H. and McPherson, T. (2008) NEH grant details: Broadening the digital humanities: The vectors-IML summer institute on multimodal scholarship. See https://securegrants.neh.gov/publicquery/main.aspx?f=1&gn=HT-50010-08 (accessed 21 July 2019).

Zooniverse (n.d.), crowdsourcing platform. See https://www.zooniverse.org/about (accessed 4 September 2018).

11 Finding and Using the Good Stuff: Open Educational Practices for Developing Open Educational Resources

Christian Hilchey

Open educational resources (OER) are the concrete products of various open educational practices (OEP). As such, OER are typically more visible and better understood than OEP. Thus, the goal of this chapter is to make the hidden, tacit knowledge of OEP more apparent to L2 specialists who may wish to design their own OER. In particular, this chapter seeks to describe and demonstrate two OEP that are central to the development of OER: (1) how to find high-quality open content; and (2) how to adapt open content for the creation of user-generated materials. The chapter begins by demonstrating effective methods for finding rich and usable open media. This section summarizes the affordances of different search engines and media repositories (e.g. Google, Flickr, Forvo, Pixabay, YouTube, Vimeo). Next, useful strategies for developing elements of a language curriculum based on openly licensed content are described. The chapter ends with a discussion of the pros and cons of technologies for the creation of OER content, such as freely available programs for editing texts (Google Docs) and creating quizzes (Quizlet).

Introduction

From the initial conception of an open educational resources (OER) project to its completion, an open educator must answer many questions: Which open media should I use? Should I employ only homegrown content, or should I incorporate various types of openly licensed texts and media? How should I organize my materials into a coherent whole? The answer to these questions implicate open educational practices (OEP), a term that refers to the many ways that educators create coherent materials and pedagogies based on open content and open technologies. This raises a larger question: How do educators develop knowledge of OEP? In response to this question about tacit professional knowledge, this chapter is based on my personal experiences of learning how to create a foreign language OER. More specifically, this chapter describes the various OEP that I learned through trial and error during the development of *Reality Czech*, an OER developed at the University of Texas at Austin under the auspices of the Center for Open Educational Resources and Language Learning (COERLL).

The use of open materials has been instrumental in my own evolution as a foreign language (FL) instructor and as an open educator. My personal narrative recounted in this chapter focuses on the moments that impacted my conceptualization of effective language pedagogy. Working with OER transformed many of my professional practices, for instance, the amount and types of media I use in class, the designs of my materials and even the grammatical and thematic topics I cover. It is my hope that through sharing my personal experiences, I will be able to demonstrate how FL instructors new to open education can pick up many OEP by a similar process of learning by doing. Today, after several years of working on my OER project, I have developed important professional know-how, including strategies for finding high-quality open content and for incorporating openly licensed images, video and texts into coherent pedagogical materials. Given the ethos of the open source and open education movements, it is only fitting that I share some of the concrete strategies that I have learned as a way of promoting OEP and furthering the mission of delivering high-quality OER.

OER is reaching a critical point of acceptance among faculty and educational institutions. While commercial textbooks remain the default choice for many FL instructors, the popularity of OER is on the rise. According to recent studies such as D'Antoni (2009), Nichols (2009) and Florida Virtual Campus (2016), language instructors are increasingly adopting OER to offset the high cost of pedagogical materials. In addition to their lower costs, OER have proven to be as pedagogically effective as commercial textbooks (Hilton, 2016). Given such encouraging news, one can expect a continued increase in OER adoption. While open textbooks and open curricula exist for many world languages, there are still considerable gaps in the availability of open FL materials, especially for less commonly taught languages (LCTLs). Belikov and Bodily (2016) contend that the lack of appropriate OER in many disciplines still constitutes one of the greatest impediments to the open education movement. Currently, many LCTL instructors are compelled to cobble together materials from various sources or to create their own OER from scratch. Until the internet era, the idea of creating one's own materials and sharing them with the public was barely thinkable. As a result, many LCTL educators know little about the practical aspects of user-generated content such as how to read a copyright license or how to use a search engine to find open content. This chapter begins where I began in late 2014 as I came to terms with the fact that there were no open materials available for Czech and, that I would need to build my own course materials from scratch. At the time, I was a complete newcomer to open education and had no prior knowledge of OER and/or OEP.

Reality Czech

Begun in 2014, the *Reality Czech Project* aims to create an openly licensed beginning Czech textbook and curriculum. Licensed under a Creative Commons Attribution-Share Alike license (CC-BY-SA), the goal of the project is to address the lack of high-quality pedagogical materials for university students who want to learn the Czech language and culture. After an extensive review of existing Czech materials, it was decided that commercial Czech textbooks presented multiple problems; they were either too expensive, too difficult to obtain, too out of date, or too limited in the requisite technology that students and teachers expect from modern pedagogical materials. The name of the textbook – *Reality Czech* – is a playful reference to the reality-style videos that accompany the themes of the textbook. Each chapter contains original videos of unscripted interviews with native Czech speakers who respond in a natural, unrehearsed manner to various questions about their daily lives. These responses are edited together into videos that illustrate naturally occurring Czech discourse on everyday topics.

I began the project with a vision of a homegrown textbook that included scripted videos and a storyline based on Czech and American characters who would navigate their way through various circumstances and events. In a very real sense, my content began to converge around the structure of existing textbooks in the field. After reviewing pedagogical materials, I noticed that most chapters in Czech textbooks were organized around a grammar item, such as the genitive case or verbs of motion. Moreover, these chapters were full of exercises largely focused on grammatical accuracy. In short, it became clear to me that grammar was the central organizing principle behind commercial Czech textbooks. Such a grammar-driven pedagogical approach to language teaching is deeply rooted in Czech society. For example, in the Czech Republic, children spend many years learning how to navigate the intricacies of orthography and grammar in written Czech that diverges from the spoken vernacular. In much of the same way that Czech children are instructed in their native language, Czech foreign language pedagogy is largely based on getting the endings right. Blyth (2013: 1) states that 'Open Education is particularly relevant to the LCTL context because it represents a promising alternative to traditional conceptualizations of foreign language publishing associated with the values and praxis of the commonly taught European languages.' Not surprisingly, my initial attempts at conceptualizing a Czech textbook reflected the traditional pedagogies that had been passed along to me during my own studies of Czech as a foreign language. Without realizing it, I had been socialized to think of the Czech language and of FL teaching in ways that reflected long-standing prescriptivist ideologies.

After shooting the initial interview videos in the Czech Republic, it became clear to me that I would need to incorporate more authentic content beyond that which I could produce myself. I had come to realize that my scope and sequence of the textbook reflected a rather outdated and normative vision of 'Czech reality.' In addition, I was disappointed by my students' reactions when I had pilot tested the materials in the classroom. I was forced to admit that my materials were boring and stilted and had failed to excite my students. Moreover, classroom testing revealed that the materials lacked the necessary connection between the communicative goals I was hoping to achieve and my grammar-based scope and sequence.

As the lead faculty author of *Reality Czech*, I began to grapple with the pedagogical implications of the word *reality*. What exactly does it mean to focus on reality? Besides, whose reality was I trying to capture in these materials? I began to wonder how I could reconcile the fact that unscripted speech rarely aligned with traditional pedagogies that relied heavily on samples of scripted language that no native speaker would ever say. In search of answers, I turned to openly licensed videos and was shocked to find a large amount of content directly related to the thematic topics I had initially chosen for the textbook. However, these videos packaged the grammar and vocabulary in ways that defied my preordained grammatical and lexical syllabus. In a previous life, I would have probably dismissed these videos as being too difficult for beginners, but they were *too good* not to use. They were not only entertaining, but they also provided a more interesting picture of contemporary Czech society. They were, in a word, real.

What does the reality of a Czech speaker look like in today's global era where languages and cultures flow across national boundaries? Czechs don't only read Czech literature, and drink only Czech beer, and eat only Czech food. So, how could I avoid presenting a caricature of the Czech language and culture in *Reality Czech*? Risager (2006, 2007) criticizes language and culture pedagogies that rely on 'convergent' scenarios in which monolingual speakers of a target language discuss stereotypical topics associated with the imagined target culture. Risager (2006, 2007) contends that such scenes in which language, topic and place 'converge' (e.g. Czech speakers in Prague discussing stereotypical Czech topics) are the result of a longstanding nationalist paradigm in world language education that focuses on a single nation-state, typically the so-called mother country. In place of such an approach, Risager advocates for a transnational paradigm that entails the use of divergent scenarios, e.g. Czech speakers on holiday in Asia discussing the challenges of international travel. To avoid stereotypical scenarios, I began searching for content that could be adapted to meet the needs of a more modern, transnational pedagogy.

Embracing a transnational approach led me to rethink my original concept of 'good content.' I began by admitting that my approach to materials design based on a pre-planned scope and sequence resulted in stereotypical, 'convergent' scenarios as described by Risager. I considered how user-generated content from the internet could be used to create a more accurate picture of Czech speakers. Eventually, I completely flipped my developer's script. I stopped designing content based on my preconceived ideas about the language and culture. In contrast, I began to rely on open media created by native Czech speakers themselves about their own reality. In other words, this newly discovered content began to shape the curriculum, rather than the pre-packaged curriculum shaping the content. This led me back to the *Reality Czech* interview videos. While filming these videos, I had noticed that my interviewees used all sorts of constructions and vocabulary that I had not originally included in my scope and sequence. In other words, the speakers in the videos were choosing non-canonical ways of expressing ideas that no Czech textbooks included in their grammar lessons. Just like my experience with user-generated content, I found that the best way to approach this was to let the materials speak for themselves and to provide the proper scaffolding around them to help students to learn to talk like their native speaker guides.

The result was an expanded OER that made room for many unexpected vocabulary and grammar items. Students learning from the *Reality Czech* curriculum are exposed to more authentic, unscripted language than any other Czech textbook in existence. Today, *Reality Czech* relies heavily on open content of all kinds – photographs, drawings, audio recordings, videos – as a way to provide authentic input to learners. In summary, as an OER developer, I came to realize that open content was the key to avoiding the linguistic and cultural stereotypes so prevalent in commercial textbooks. As a consequence, I realized that my real job was to find the best open content available on the internet and to decide how to use it as the basis of a coherent Czech curriculum.

Open Licenses

The most important knowledge that I gained early on was how to read and understand open licenses. Instructors new to the design of OER must learn that the term 'open' is related to two different meanings of the word 'free'. Much of the work in OER development has been mirrored by earlier work in the free software movement that resulted in products such as the Linux operating system. In the free software movement, the two senses of the word 'free' were neatly captured in the aphorism 'Free as in free beer vs. Free as in free speech.' No one pays for free beer. It is free in the sense of the Latin word *gratis*. There are many internet services that one can use without any payment, such as watching videos on YouTube, reading articles on CNN, or looking at Flickr image galleries. The mere fact that no money is exchanged for these services has no bearing however on the rights entailed with the use and reuse of the content. However, while users may access the content, they do not necessarily possess the rights to re-use it. In fact, re-use and re-distribution of much freely accessed content is prohibited. This represents a sort of elephant in the room that is frequently ignored by instructors creating pedagogical materials for their courses.

In contrast, the second sense of 'free' ('free as in free speech') is captured by the Spanish or French word *libre*. This sense of the word is synonymous with the adjective 'open' as commonly used in the open education movement. Open in this sense refers to one's rights. For instance, by placing a work under an open license, the copyright holder can share rights with end users such as the right to make derivatives of the original work. Materials under these licenses are considered 'open' because users are 'free' to Retain, Reuse, Revise, Remix and Redistribute the content. This bundle of rights is commonly referred to as 'the 5Rs' (see Wiley, 2014). Open licenses, such as Creative Commons licenses, exist on a continuum of openness depending on how many of the 5Rs are shared with the end user (see Figure 11.1).

Openly licensed materials have reached a critical mass, both in terms of their availability and the sheer number of people creating and contributing content. According to statistics provided by Creative Commons, there has been a tenfold increase in the past decade in the number of works put under a Creative Commons license, with numbers exceeding 1.4 billion individual works on such platforms as YouTube, Wikipedia, Wikimedia and Vimeo (see Figure 11.2).

Even a few quick searches of these archives reveal that there is a wealth of high-quality language materials available for use. Moreover, many of these openly licensed materials may be easily repurposed by language instructors. Nevertheless, educators who embrace the philosophy of using OER can still face obstacles in locating appropriate content. While there are vast repositories available on the internet, instructors may still feel insecure about finding 'the good stuff' and understanding open licenses. This became a problem for me as well as I began to incorporate more openly licensed materials into my curriculum.

As I began creating *Reality Czech*, I naively combined content that was copyrighted under different open licenses, not realizing that several of the more restrictive licenses can present difficulties when incorporating them into OER projects. I discovered that the ShareAlike licenses that

Finding and Using the Good Stuff 251

CC license	Terms	Description
![CC Zero]	Public Domain	Free to be used for any purpose without attribution to anyone for any purpose.
![CC BY]	Attribution CC-BY	Attribution to originator required but may be used for any purpose.
![CC BY-SA]	Attribution-ShareAlike CC-BY-SA	Attribution required and derivative content must be placed under an identical license.
![CC BY-NC]	Attribution-NonCommercial CC-BY-NC	Attribution required and no commercial use allowed.
![CC BY-ND]	Attribution-NoDerivs CC-BY-ND	Attribution required and the work must remain unchanged.
![CC BY-NC-SA]	Attribution-NonCommercial-ShareAlike CC-BY-NC-SA	Attribution required, commercial use not allowed, derivative content must be placed under an identical license.
![CC BY-NC-ND]	Attribution-NonCommercial-NoDerivs CC-BY-NC-ND	Attribution required, commercial use not allowed, and the work must remain unchanged.
![GFDL]	GNU Free Documentation License	Attribution and sharing of derivatives under the same licensing provisions. The terms are largely similar to a CC-BY-SA. Originally created for software documentation, though some cultural works have also been placed under this license. These works are typically also concurrently licensed under CC-BY-SA terms.

Figure 11.1 Open licenses

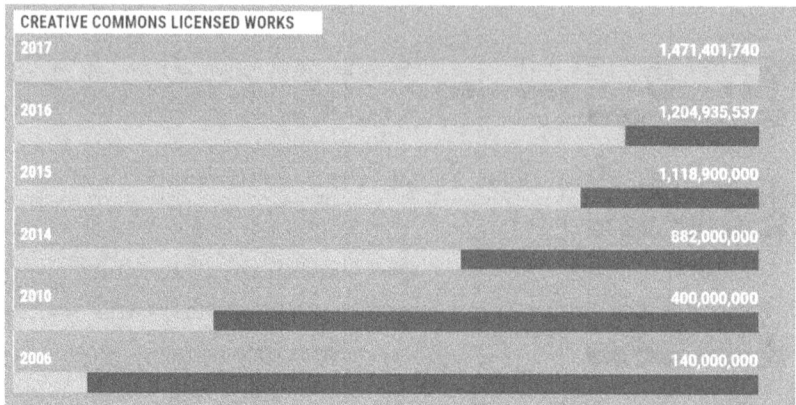

Figure 11.2 Creative Commons Licensed Works – CC-BY 4.0 from https://stateof.creativecommons.org/

require derivatives to be published under an identical license can make integrating content into an OER more difficult, especially if there are multiple works with different ShareAlike licenses. A project cannot be composed of both materials under an Attribution-ShareAlike license and materials under an Attribution-NonCommercial-ShareAlike license since the resulting work could not simultaneously meet the contradictory terms of both licenses. The *Reality Czech* curriculum uses significant amounts of open content from Wikipedia and Wikimedia Commons. These two resources host content frequently licensed under a CC-BY-SA license. Given the advantages of using these resources, the decision was made to place the entire project under a CC-BY-SA license to meet the licensing requirements of the content. However, this also prohibits the use of audio recordings from other resources such as *Forvo* (https://forvo.com) that often contains high-quality recordings in hundreds of languages but whose content is licensed under a CC-BY-NC-SA license. While there are workarounds, such as publishing a separate standalone resource under a compatible license, these different license restrictions can impose significant hurdles to adapting these types of open content.

Other license restrictions such as 'Non-Commercial' (NC) and 'No Derivatives' (ND) present fewer barriers to use in OER projects. OERs are often deemed 'non-commercial' resources since they are offered under an open license for free. Moreover, open content that carries a 'Non-Commercial' license may be used in a derivative without requiring the user to adopt the same license. For this reason, the content under a CC-BY-NC license can be used in most OER projects. However, the 'No Derivatives' stipulation places sizable restrictions on the use of open content, since a developer may wish to crop, retouch, or add content to an image. These actions are expressly prohibited by a 'No Derivatives' license. It is therefore imperative that beginning users understand the terms of these licenses since their work may otherwise have content which cannot be incorporated into the larger work. At some point in the creation of the *Reality Czech* textbook, it became apparent to me that numerous photos had to be replaced because of license compatibility issues. It is best to avoid these problems by having a clear understanding of open copyright licenses prior to development.

Finding Images for an OER

Images have long been an indispensable part of the FL curricula. They provide a window into the target language and culture by providing a visual representation of such basic things as food, clothing, weather, sports and holidays. Additionally, research indicates that images facilitate vocabulary learning by aiding the retention of new lexical items (Kost *et al.*, 1999) and by providing useful context for textual interpretation (Omaggio, 1979). Moreover, images prove useful in a variety of contexts, from grammar lessons to online cultural activities.

There are times when authentic images from the target culture are essential for the curriculum, for example, when representing well-known people and places or capturing the many manifestations of everyday cultural practices. Examples 1 and 2 illustrate how presenting the look and feel of a Czech pub or Czech money demands authentic images. The ways in which we search for authentic images can frequently vary depending on the image archive; some repositories contain more cultural realia than others. In many instances it is possible to find images of realia by searching directly in the target language. Flickr and Wikimedia Commons are two prime examples of sites where one can search in the target language for titles and descriptions of photos. Czech speakers and visitors to the Czech Republic have posted numerous photos to these two repositories. Moreover, given the robust Wikipedia offerings for numerous languages of the world, Wikimedia Commons will likely serve most LCTL instructors as a good source of culture-specific images.

Example 1 – Public domain image found on Wikimedia Commons of a typical pub scene

Example 2 – Wikimedia Commons images of Czech currency

I discovered, however, that searching in the target language is not always a reliable strategy. For example, the website Pixabay contains over 1.5 million public domain images that have been rigorously tagged to include various types of metadata about each image. However, these metadata have been translated into 26 languages. This means that when I search for *pivo*, the Czech word for 'beer,' I am likely to find images of beer from many different countries. Of course, this makes searching more time-consuming. That said, Pixabay remains an excellent resource for high quality images of culture-specific realia. The point is that one's search strategy must be decided on a language-to-language and culture-to-culture basis. For instance, a picture of any Western-style dinner table might suffice to illustrate the corresponding Czech vocabulary item. However, it is easy to imagine a country such as Japan where a common dinner table may be too low to the ground than those found in the Czech Republic. At times, however, a culture-specific image may be unavailable, and a generic image will have to suffice. Clearly this issue must be decided on a case-by-case basis. These points are illustrated in Examples 3–6. While the images in Example 3 come from a Czech archive, it would be equally possible to illustrate 'Czech clothing' using images from many other European countries. Similarly, Example 4 demonstrates how simple clipart images of analog and digital clocks are sufficient when illustrating a lesson on time. In contrast, Examples 5 and 6 point to areas where culture-specific Czech realia are essential, such as illustrations of holiday customs and local transport options.

Bára málokdy nosí kraťasy
Bára rarely wears shorts.

Kolik je hodin? - What time is it?

When stating what time it is, we will use the word hodina - hour with various numerals. Take a look at the following forms below.

Je jedna hodina. | Jsou dvě hodiny. | Jsou tři hodiny. | Jsou čtyři hodiny.

Example 3 – Here multiple photos from a single account were used to exemplify the vocabulary used when talking about clothing wearing habits

Example 4 – These images, from the public domain archive https://openclipart.org are instrumental in complementing a unit on telling time

Prodej kaprů na parkovišti | Kapři se kupují z velkých kádí

prodávat - to sell
prodávat se - to be sold (lit. to sell themselves)
káď - tank, tub, vat
odnášet - to carry off

Cvičení 2 - For this last exercise you will be planning routes to travel by bus and by train to and from various Czech cities.

České dráhy

https://www.cd.cz/eshop/ | https://www.regiojet.cz/

First, let's make sure we have some vocabulary in order. What do the following mean?

1 odjezd _____
2 příjezd _____
3 přestup _____
4 volné místo _____

Example 5 – Public domain images illustrating the sale and butchering of Christmas carp

Example 6 – Public domain images of Czech public transport

The above examples illustrate that the choice of an appropriate image depends on multiple variables that raise questions about the concept of cultural authenticity. Foreign language specialists often judge cultural products to be authentic when they are created by a member of the target culture for another member of the same culture. However, when it comes to images used in pedagogical materials, the concept of authenticity requires a more flexible approach. It is often sufficient for the developer to ask a native speaker whether the image is a 'reasonably authentic' representation of a culture-specific item. In the *Reality Czech* curriculum, images are used in a variety of ways and the various illustrations cited throughout this chapter are representative of this. Photographs and drawings populate the entirety of the curriculum. The absence of cost associated with open media allows OER developers to use many more images than would be feasible in a commercial textbook. Additionally, since OER projects are frequently hosted online, space limitations usually associated with print textbooks do not apply. In general, grammatical concepts or vocabulary items may be profitably illustrated with multiple images. These images not only help the student evoke the concepts and words more easily, but they also break up the monotony of black and white text.

Examples 7 and 8 demonstrate the use of images to illustrate basic concepts at the beginning of a lesson. Neither of these images is drawn from target language realia. Nevertheless, they serve to enrich the learning experience by providing visual associations for grammatical topics. Additionally, images can be used to inject humor and whimsy into a lesson. In *Reality Czech*, this is frequently achieved through the use of online memes that are popular in many forms of digital culture. When using memes, developers must make sure that the image does not violate its license restrictions. Examples 9 and 10 demonstrate the use of memes for giving hints or for serving as a mnemonic device. Memes have the added advantage of exposing learners to informal registers used by younger speakers.

Examples 7 and 8 – Public domain images from Wikimedia Commons to illustrate vocabulary and grammar items (i.e. numbers and indefinite expressions)

256 Part 3: The Exosystem: Developing Knowledge in the Field of L2 Education

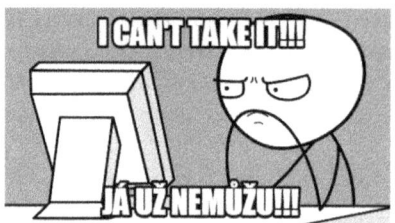

Example 9 – Informal language as a pervasive feature of internet memes

Example 10 – A meme that plays on the irregular 3rd-plural form *jedí* 'they eat' in Czech

Finally, the use of memes in pedagogical materials helps to foster a learning environment that is informed by the participatory culture of the internet (Jenkins *et al.*, 2006). The term 'participatory culture' is often used to refer to the production or creation of some type of published media on open platforms such as Facebook or Instagram (Fuchs, 2014). In general, the concept of participatory culture is meant to stand in opposition to 'consumer culture' in which producers and consumers are viewed as playing mutually exclusive roles (Willis, 2003). In contrast, members of the internet's participatory culture are viewed as both consumers *and* producers. In essence, the use of internet memes within the context of OER can be viewed as an OEP since the goal is to promote language learning. Ehlers (2011: 4) defines OEP 'as practices which support the (re)use and production of OER through institutional policies, promote innovative pedagogical models, and respect and empower learners as co-producers on their lifelong learning path.' Memes are typically meant to be recycled and shared with group members. As such, the use of internet memes in pedagogical materials can serve as an impetus for learners to create their own memes in the target language to be shared with their peers.

Image Repositories – Public Domain Images

There are numerous advantages to using public domain images. As the least restrictive of openly licensed images, public domain images can be edited as the user wishes. Moreover, they require no attribution, and are compatible with all licenses including commercial or non-commercial licenses. In the *Reality Czech* curriculum, I have selected images from the public domain in several cases because they require no citation. This includes certain website images used for page navigation where providing an appropriate attribution would negatively impact the visual appearance of the website. Similarly, activities such as games, as in Example 11, also benefit from not needing attribution. These concerns are primarily

Example 11 – Examples of public domain images that require no attribution

aesthetic in nature, and it is possible to use images that carry CC licenses for these purposes as well.

Pixabay (https://pixabay.com/) is one of the largest archives with over 1.5 million public domain images. While much smaller, OpenClipArt (https://openclipart.org/) is an excellent resource with 145 thousand public domain clipart images. The following sites do not publish information about how many images they contain, but are nevertheless fruitful archives for public domain images:

- Pxhere – https://pxhere.com
- SVGSilh – https://svgsilh.com
- Pexels – https://pexels.com/
- Public Domain Pictures – https://publicdomainpictures.net
- Max Pixel – https://maxpixel.net/
- LibreShot – https://libreshot.com/

Image Repositories – Mixed Licensed Content

There are also numerous repositories that carry user-generated images under a variety of copyright licenses, such as Flickr (https://www.flickr.com/) and Wikimedia Commons (https://commons.wikimedia.org/). At the time of this chapter, Flickr holds nearly 200 million images that are either in the public domain or that carry a Creative Commons license. In contrast, Wikimedia Commons holds over 48 million images that are either in the public domain or that carry the two most open Creative Commons licenses (CC-BY or CC-BY-SA). When searching for images on these two sites, instructors must pay careful attention to the copyright restrictions that have been selected by the owner who has uploaded the image. Moreover, since users from around the world upload and tag their images with metadata in their native languages in these archives, users can often find culture-specific images by using a target language word to conduct the search. Additionally, since the originator/owner of a posted image in Flickr and Wikimedia Commons is identified, a browser may wish to search more images uploaded by the same person by simply clicking on the individual's account name. While this can take more time than searching for individual images, it often reveals interesting content.

Google Images

While Google's image search (https://images.google.com/) may not be as efficient as other resources such as Flickr, it can yield interesting results. By selecting the search filter Tools > Usage Rights, one can limit the search to images offered under a specific open license. There are two important caveats to searching on Google. First, while it happens rarely, Google will occasionally return images on websites that contain no license information regarding the image. In these cases, it is advisable to err on the side of caution and not use these images. Second, Google translates native language metadata and tags into other languages when searching for images. For this reason, it can be somewhat more difficult to locate authentic realia on Google if generic search terms are used. Placing quotation marks around target language search terms helps to overcome this obstacle. Finally, creativity is necessary for conducting a successful Google image search. If you are unsure about how to conduct your image search, it is always advisable to read the tips provided by Google.

Videos

Videos are extremely useful media well suited to any language curriculum. Commercial textbooks are frequently accompanied by videos that are professionally produced and integrated into the textbook content. OER projects typically lack the financial resources to attain high-production values. Nevertheless, there are many high-quality open videos available on major video sharing websites. In fact, some open videos are professionally produced, especially those shot and edited by news services or non-profit educational organizations. While open videos may require some additional editing, this task pales in comparison to the shooting and editing of videos from scratch. The two most fruitful platforms to search for open video content are YouTube (currently 49 million CC-BY videos) and Vimeo (currently 6.6 million videos under a variety of CC licenses as well as public domain content). Many students are already avid users of these two media platforms and frequently use them outside of the classroom for both entertainment and educational purposes. Alm (2006), Brook (2011), Jones and Cuthrell (2011) and Terantino (2011) highlight the advantages of utilizing online video platforms such as YouTube for their ability to foster online communities and motivate independent learning. The potential for YouTube is particularly high in this regard given the near saturation of everyday life by clips from this video sharing site. Moreover, YouTube is an effective tool for fostering OEP, as discussed earlier, because it gives students opportunities to share their own content with fellow students.

So how do content creators go about finding high-quality, open content on these sites? Both YouTube and Vimeo allow for content filtering so that only videos with an open license are listed in search results. YouTube allows users to place their content either under a Standard YouTube license, under which the copyright holder retains all rights to distribute content, or a CC-BY license. To search for content, simply run a search as normal and then click on the search filter to limit the search to Creative Commons content. Vimeo requires that users first run a search and then filter the results for open content. Vimeo allows for a number of different license options for their users, from public domain declarations to more restrictive CC licenses, such as CC-BY-NC-SA or CC-BY-NC-ND licenses. There is no direct way to search for all licenses on Vimeo, and so one must filter the results according to these individual licenses. This can represent a benefit to those seeking content under a specific license (or trying to avoid specific licenses), but it also creates a complication for users who wish to search for open materials in general. For example, the *Reality Czech* curriculum (under a CC-BY-SA) license, can use content in the public domain, CC-BY, CC-BY-SA, but cannot utilize content under a CC-BY-NoDerivs, CC-BY-NC licenses, CC-BY-SA-NC or CC-BY-SA-ND license. Therefore, in searching for videos, one is often required to search for content by clicking on multiple licenses that are compatible with a particular project.

There are, however, some caveats to consider when searching for and using videos found on sites such as YouTube and Vimeo:

(1) YouTube and Vimeo are massive repositories. While most of the content is properly licensed, there are problems. On several occasions, I have found videos that violate copyright. For example, I have come across videos with a CC license that have obviously been derived from a copyrighted source such as a feature film or a television program. Therefore, a discerning eye for mislabeled copyrighted content is necessary. Users should avoid any video that they suspect of violating copyright law.

(2) Sometimes user-generated videos may contain small elements of copyrighted material. For instance, it is not uncommon to find a popular song used as a soundtrack or other snippets of commercial content in a user-generated video. Educators must take precautions when using such problematic content. In these cases, they should remove the copyrighted content by muting the songs or by replacing them with open audio content. Open music and audio files may easily be found on SoundCloud, an online audio distribution platform and music sharing website based in Berlin, Germany.

Unfortunately, since September 2017, YouTube no longer allows users to download videos licensed under a Creative Commons license. YouTube's new terms of service state 'You shall not download any Content unless you see a "download" or similar link displayed by YouTube on the Service for that Content.' Currently, YouTube advises users to contact content creators directly: 'You can send a private message to the uploader if you find a video that is licensed as Creative Commons, to ask if they could share the original video file with you.' These problems are not as formidable on Vimeo. Certain premium accounts allow content creators to provide direct download links to users. Moreover, as of this writing, the terms of use for Vimeo do not expressly prohibit downloading of openly licensed content. While the number of videos on Vimeo is far surpassed by YouTube, some of the best content I have found for the *Reality Czech* curriculum has come from Vimeo.

Finding Good Video Content

How does one go about finding good video content? I was able to find several strategies that turned me from a doubter into a believer, when literally in the course of a single evening I stumbled upon a vast array of openly licensed videos. I found that one of the most fruitful ways of discovering videos is to search using specific terms that frequently appear in videos posted by users from around the world. One can search for videos using these specific terms in addition to a target language specifier. Here are some of the most fruitful terms:

(1) **Vlog** – Vlogs are the video analog to written blogs. Begin by combining the term *vlog with a* keyword from the target language (e.g. vlog pivo, vlog Prague). You might also run searches that combine vlog with English key words such as *vlog apartment, vlog Christmas, vlog travel, vlog workout, vlog restaurant*, etc.
(2) **Timelapse** – Time-lapse videos are created to present a geographical location such as a city over a given time period. The element of timelapse gives viewers a chance to understand the time-related characteristics of a location. These kinds of videos do not usually contain written or spoken language. Nevertheless, these kinds of videos may prove useful at multiple levels of language instruction. At the novice levels, timelapse videos can be used to elicit responses at the single word level; at the intermediate levels, students can talk about what they would like to do or what they would like to see at the location; at the advanced levels, students can create a narrative based on the video; and at the superior level, students can discuss the social implications of surveillance cameras or the benefits of watching a live video feed of a particular location. Clearly, these ideas represent only a fraction of what is possible for time lapse videos.

(3) **Haul** – Haul videos are demonstrations of a person trying on clothes or using various consumer products. In this genre, the person describes what they like and dislike about the product. These videos can be especially helpful for units focusing on clothing. They are also a good source of comparative language input.
(4) **Unboxing** – Unboxing videos show a person opening a new product that they have purchased. The object being unboxed is often some sort of technological item such as a new phone, computer, camera, etc. though it is possible to find other products being unboxed such as clothing or food.
(5) **Room tour (Roomtour)** -–These kinds of videos feature someone who describes various facets of their room, house, or apartment. A major advantage of room tour videos are the vocabulary used to describe living spaces that proves particularly useful at beginning levels of instruction. Some room tours focus on aspects of the room, such as clothing or furniture, making them useful for particular thematic units.
(6) **DIY** – Do-it-yourself (DIY) videos, often include running commentary and instructions on how to complete a task. While such videos are most easily adapted to intermediate levels and above, one can even find uses at the novice level with a bit of creativity. DIY videos can address many different topics such as making holiday presents, cleaning a room, preparing a dish or, completing a project.

After finding a particularly useful video, I learned that it is often a good idea to click on the creator's name in order to browse other video content created by the same person. Using this method, I have been able to find dozens of videos after finding a single video through a search. In some cases, I have been able to locate professional video channels from independent media companies and various cities and small towns. In other cases, I have discovered passionate individual posters of vlogs and similar content. In fact, by using the above search terms and conducting searches of individual's work, I have found an abundance of useful videos for language instruction. For language educators who know how to conduct internet searches, the problem soon becomes how to incorporate all the excellent content that is readily available.

Google Docs

Dissemination is also crucial to an OER project. Content creators must consider how to disseminate their OER in a way that allows others not only to access the materials, but to exercise their rights as outlined by the 5Rs (Wiley, 2014). Most educators are at least familiar with Google Docs if not active users of the platform. However, many world language educators are unaware of how easy it is to use the Google Docs toolset to share information with a large number of users. With Google Docs, educators can share vast amounts of materials with anyone who has internet access. Google Docs allow users to publish their works in various forms by choosing from different menu options (File → Publish to the web). In addition, Google Docs allows creators to share their materials by choosing different menu options (Share → Get shareable link). If a creator shares their work with the public, anyone can copy the content to their own Google Drive or download the content in a number of different formats to edit as they wish. In the *Reality Czech* curriculum, all documents are available on a Wordpress site with direct links to the editable Google documents. Students can not only make copies of documents, but they can mark them up with notes to aid their learning. Finally, Google Docs can be edited from any computer or even a smartphone. Thus, while Google Docs is itself not an open source platform, it can be leveraged by OER creators to help them accomplish their goals.

Quizlet

Quizlet has existed for over a decade as a free platform for providing vocabulary learning tools such as flashcards, interactive exercises and games. Instructors can create numerous lists and choose pictures from the Quizlet database to accompany vocabulary items. Quizlet contains several features that facilitate sharing content, including exporting sets as CSV files or directly copying a list to another user account. A list can be modified in many ways to meet the user's needs. While the Quizlet platform is not strictly open, it allows for use consistent with the 5Rs. Moreover, users must pay a fee of $3 per month for Quizlet Teacher that gives them access to additional features such as the ability to attach sound recordings to vocabulary items and upload other images to a vocabulary set. The *Reality Czech* curriculum takes advantage of the following Quizlet features:

Flashcards	Students see a flashcard accompanied by a picture and the target language word, then flip to see English word
Learning Exercises	A two-part activity that begins with multiple choice options – target language word matched with English word + image; after several iterations, students then practice typing some of the words in the target language
Listening/Writing	Students hear a target language word write in a target language word; one can optionally create a list with no English definitions to focus only on sound to word correspondence
Matching with English	Students match target language word with an image and the English translation
Matching with Picture	Students match target language word with an image

In addition to the above activities, Quizlet offers games that can be either completed independently or as a classroom warm-up activity. Additionally, Quizlet can be leveraged to provide grammar exercises such as verb conjugations, noun declensions, and other activities given a little creativity on the part of the content creator. Finally, OER Commons and Merlot are two platforms/repositories which allow content creation that is directly integrated into searchable databases of OER content. While they do not offer the niceties of other platforms such as Google Docs, they still are a versatile option for creators of open content.

Conclusion

This chapter has followed my journey as a creator of a Czech textbook that relies heavily on openly licensed images, videos, texts and other materials. While developing my materials, I have often been inspired by the analogy of going to the farmers market. As anyone who frequents a farmers' market knows, there is no guarantee that you will find exactly what you are looking for. For instance, the tomatoes may not look very good, but the peppers and eggplant may look fantastic. If that's the case, it's time to cook with peppers and eggplant! In this chapter, I outlined some of the key strategies that I have learned through trial and error for finding excellent open media and for developing materials around such content. Today, I select my content based largely on what looks appealing rather than what fits a planned scope and sequence. With the 'good stuff' in hand, I curate the content and craft lessons and activities to accompany them. While many FL educators may not wish to undertake a large-scale OER such as the one described in this chapter, they will likely want to engage in some form of content creation during their careers. By understanding the affordances of OER and OEP, L2 educators can develop a richer set of tools for use inside and outside the classroom. It is my hope that a greater knowledge of the OEP described in this chapter will help world language educators to 'find and use the good stuff' and to share their OER with the world.

References

Alm, A. (2006) CALL for autonomy, competence and relatedness: Motivating language learning environments in Web 2.0. *The JALT CALL Journal* 2 (3), 29–38.
Belikov, O. and Bodily, R. (2016) Incentives and barriers to OER adoption: A qualitative analysis of faculty perceptions. *Open Praxis* 8 (3), 235–246.
Blyth, C. (2013) LCTLs and technology: The promise of Open Education. *Language Learning & Technology* 17 (1), 1–6.
Brook, J. (2011) The affordances of YouTube for language learning and teaching. *Hawaii Pacific University TESOL Working Paper Series* 9 (1,2), 37–56.
Creative Commons. 'Frequently Asked Questions'. See https://creativecommons.org/faq/ (accessed August 8, 2018).
Ehlers, U. (2011) Extending the territory: From open educational resources to open educational practices. *Journal of Open, Flexible, and Distance Learning* 15 (2), 1–10.

Florida Virtual Campus (2016) '2016 Florida student textbook survey.' Tallahassee, FL. See https://florida.theorangegrove.org/og/items/3a65c507-2510-42d7-814c-ffdefd394b6c/1/ (accessed August 8, 2019).

Fuchs, C. (2014) Social media as participatory culture. *Social Media: A Critical Introduction* (pp. 52–68). SAGE Publications.

Hilton, J. (2016) Open educational resources and college textbook choices: A review of research on efficacy and perceptions. *Educational Technology Research and Development* 64 (4), 573–590.

Jenkins, H., Puroshotma, R., Clinton, K., Weigel, M. and Robison, A. (2005) Confronting the challenges of participatory culture: Media education for the 21st century. White paper. See http://www.newmedialiteracies.org/wp-content/uploads/pdfs/NMLWhitePaper.pdf. (accessed August 8, 2019).

Jones, T. and Cuthrell, K. (2011) YouTube: Educational potentials and pitfalls. *Computers in the Schools* 28 (1), 75–85.

Kost, C., Foss, P. and Lenzini, J. (1999) Textual and pictorial glosses: Effectiveness on incidental vocabulary growth when reading in a foreign language. *Foreign Language Annals* 32 (1), 89–97.

Nicholls, N. (2009) The investigation into the rising cost of textbooks. White paper. Scholarly Publishing Office, University of Michigan Library. See https://www.lib.umich.edu/files/SPOTextbookBackgroundStudy.pdf (accessed August 8, 2019).

Omaggio, A.C. (1979) Pictures and second language comprehension: Do they help? *Foreign Language Annals* 12 (2), 107–116.

Risager, K. (2006) *Language and Culture: Local Flows and Global Complexity*. Clevedon: Multilingual Matters.

Risager, K. (2007) *Language and Culture Pedagogy: From a National to a Transnational Paradigm*. Clevedon: Multilingual Matters.

D'Antoni, S. (2009) Open educational resources: Reviewing initiatives and issues. *Open Learning: The Journal of Open, Distance and e-Learning* 24 (1), 3–10.

Terantino, J.M. (2011) YouTube for foreign languages: You have to see this video. *Language Learning and Technology* 15 (1), 10–16.

Wiley, D. (2014) The access compromise and the 5th R, *Iterating toward Openness*. Blog post, March 5, 2014. See https://opencontent.org/blog/archives/3221 (accessed September 9, 2018).

YouTube Help – Creative Commons. See https://support.google.com/YouTube/answer/2797468 (accessed September 9, 2018).

YouTube Terms of Service. See www.YouTube.com/static?template=terms (accessed September 9, 2018).

YouTube Video Editor. See https://support.google.com/YouTube/answer/183851? (accessed September 9, 2018) – Content since removed, but accessible at the web archive – https://web.archive.org/web/20171027154236/https://support.google.com/YouTube/answer/183851

Image Attributions

Figure 11.2
Title: Creative Commons Licensed Works
Source: https://stateof.creativecommons.org/
License: CC-BY 4.0

Example 1
Title: Example U Fleků, waiter, 2006.jpg
Author: Bruce Tuten

Source: https://commons.wikimedia.org/wiki/File:U_Flek%C5%AF,_waiter,_2006.jpg
License: CC-BY 2.0

Example 2 – Images of currency from https://cs.wikipedia.org/wiki/Koruna_%C4%8Desk%C3%A1

Example 3

Title: 'barin' Author: Petr & Bara Ruzicka Source: https://www.flickr.com/photos/pruzicka/275910659/ License: CC-BY 2.0	Title: 'B u poliu' Author: Petr & Bara Ruzicka Source: https://www.flickr.com/photos/pruzicka/275910659/ License: CC-BY 2.0
Title: 'Ja a B' Author: Petr & Bara Ruzicka Source: https://www.flickr.com/photos/pruzicka/337787082/ License: CC-BY 2.0	Title: 'bara a koule' Author: Petr & Bara Ruzicka Source: https://www.flickr.com/photos/pruzicka/278029678/in/album-72157594211582126/ License: CC-BY 2.0

Additional Images

All images in other examples are from the public domain and therefore do not require attribution.

Appendix

Language Learning OER Featured in the Book

Acceso http://acceso.ku.edu/
Antología abierta de literatura hispana https://open.umn.edu/opentextbooks/textbooks/antologia-abierta-de-literatura-hispana
Busuu https://business.busuu.com/education
Chqeta'maj le Qach'ab'al K'iche' https://tzij.coerll.utexas.edu
Cultura https://cultura.mit.edu/
Duolinguo https://www.duolingo.com/
eComma https://ecomma.coerll.utexas.edu/
Foreign Languages and the Literary in the Everyday (FLLITE) https://fllite.org/
Français interactif https://www.laits.utexas.edu/fi/
Le littéraire dans le quotidien http://goo.gl/VurRFE
Reality Czech https://realityczech.org/

OER Repositories

Global OER Graduate Network https://go-gn.net/
Languages Open Resources Online (LORO) www.loro.open.ac.uk
MERLOT https://www.merlot.org/merlot/
MIT OpenCourseware https://ocw.mit.edu/index.htm
National Foreign Language Resource Centers (US Department of Education) https://www.nflrc.org/
OER Commons https://www.oercommons.org/
OpenDOAR http://www.open.ac.uk/
Open Course Library http://opencourselibrary.org/
Open Learning Initiative (Carnegie Mellon) http://oli.cmu.edu/
Open Textbook Library https://open.umn.edu/opentextbooks/
Openstax https://cnx.org/
TES https://www.tes.com/en-us/teaching-resources
Wikiversity https://en.wikiversity.org/wiki/Wikiversity:Main_Page

Articles/Blogs/Books/Websites about Open Education

Accessibility Toolkit https://opentextbc.ca/accessibilitytoolkit/
Cape Town Open Education Declaration https://www.capetowndeclaration.org/
Case Studies of Openness in the Language Classroom https://research-publishing.net/book?10.14705/rpnet.2013.9781908416100
Creative Commons https://creativecommons.org/
Digital Pedagogy in the Humanities https://digitalpedagogy.mla.hcommons.org/
Languages Open Resources Online: Fostering a Culture of Collaboration and Sharing http://oro.open.ac.uk/31504/
New Case Studies of Openness in and Beyond the Language Classroom https://files.eric.ed.gov/fulltext/ED596829.pdf
OER Creation and Adaptation Pressbook https://pressbooks.bccampus.ca/oerworkshop/#main
OER Handbook https://wikieducator.org/OER_Handbook
Open Pedagogy Notebook http://openpedagogy.org/
Open: The Philosophy and Practices that are Revolutionizing Education and Science https://www.ubiquitypress.com/site/books/e/10.5334/bbc/

Open Educational Institutions and Organizations

Center for Open Educational Resources and Language Learning (University of Texas, USA) (https://www.coerll.utexas.edu/coerll/)
Creative Commons https://creativecommons.org/
Department of Educational Technology (US Dept of Education) (https://tech.ed.gov/open/)
Digital Humanities Now https://digitalhumanitiesnow.org/
LangOER http://langoer.eun.org/
OER Hub (Open University, UK) (http://oerhub.net/)
Open Access 2020 https://oa2020.org
Open Education Global https://www.oeglobal.org/
Open Education Group http://openedgroup.org/
Open Language Resource Center (University of Kansas, USA) (http://olrc.ku.edu)
Open University (UK) http://www.open.ac.uk/
SPARC https://sparcopen.org/

Open Tools/Platforms

Annotation Studio https://www.annotationstudio.org/
Audacity https://www.audacityteam.org/

Canvas LMS https://www.instructure.com/canvas/
Cityscape Project http://cityscape.lrc.columbia.edu/
Charlie Archives http://cahl.io/
Curriki https://www.curriki.org/
Drupal https://www.drupal.org/
Flickr https://www.flickr.com/
Flipgrid https://info.flipgrid.com/
Forvo https://forvo.com
Gephi https://gephi.org/
Google Docs https://www.google.com/docs/about/
Google Images https://images.google.com/
G Suite for Education https://edu.google.com/products/gsuite-for-education/?modal_active=none
Hylighter https://www.hylighter.com/
LibreShot https://libreshot.com/
Lino https://en.linoit.com/
Max Pixel https://maxpixel.net/
Omeka https://omeka.org/
Open Clip Art https://openclipart.org
Open Broadcast Studio https://obsproject.com/
Open Shot https://www.openshot.org/
Open Journal Systems https://pkp.sfu.ca/ojs/
Padlet https://padlet.com/
Palladio https://hdlab.stanford.edu/palladio/
Pexels https://pexels.com/
Pixabay https://pixabay.com/
Public Domain Pictures https://publicdomainpictures.net
Pxhere https://pxhere.com
Quizlet https://quizlet.com/
Rebus Community https://press.rebus.community/
Scalar https://scalar.me/anvc/
Shot Cut http://www.shotcut.org/
SVGSilh https://svgsilh.com/
Vimeo https://vimeo.com/
Voicethread https://voicethread.com/
Wakelet https://wakelet.com/
Weebly for Education https://education.weebly.com/ed-features.php
Wikimedia https://www.wikimedia.org/
Wikimedia Commons https://commons.wikimedia.org/
Wikipedia https://www.wikipedia.org/
YouTube https://www.youtube.com/
Zooniverse https://www.zooniverse.org/

Open Journals (L2 Teaching and Learning)

Journal of Digital Humanities http://journalofdigitalhumanities.org/
Journal of Interactive Technology and Pedagogy https://jitp.commons.gc.cuny.edu/
Language Learning & Technology https://www.lltjournal.org//
L2 Journal https://escholarship.org/uc/uccllt_l2/
Open Accessible Summaries In Language Studies (OASIS) https://oasis-database.org
Open Journal Systems https://pkp.sfu.ca/ojs/
Open Linguistics https://www.degruyter.com/view/journals/opli/opli-overview.xml
Open Journal of Modern Linguistics https://www.scirp.org/journal/ojml/
Reading in a Foreign Language http://nflrc.hawaii.edu/rfl/about.html
Second Language Research and Practice http://www.slrpjournal.org/

Open L2 Corpora

Chinese corpus http://corpus.leeds.ac.uk/query-zh.html
English-Corpora https://www.english-corpora.org/
Lextutor (English) https://lextutor.ca/
Multilingual Corpus of Second Language Speech (MuSSeL) https://l2trec.utah.edu/multi-Lingual_Speech_Corpus.php
NINJAL (Japanese corpora) https://www.ninjal.ac.jp/english/database/type/corpora/
Southeast Asian Languages Library (Sealang) http://sealang.net/library/
Talk Bank (English) https://talkbank.org/

Index

Affordances 3, 5–7, 12, 17, 28, 42, 47, 60, 131–134, 162, 175, 183–197, 200, 223–224, 245, 263
Agency 5–6, 104, 146, 219, 232–233, 238
Applied linguistics 15–17, 138, 154, 164, 169, 181–183, 191, 193, 196
Authentic (experiences, resources, speakers, texts, etc.) 8–9, 14–15, 19, 31, 37, 41, 111, 122, 141–142, 162–163, 167, 172, 219, 232–234, 248–249, 253–255, 258

Communities 3, 13, 18–19, 28–29, 31, 62–63, 70–72, 76–77, 83, 87–93, 104, 154, 198, 201, 219–221, 225–233, 236–238, 258
Complexity/complex systems 1, 3–4, 6, 202
Creative Commons license(s) 8, 37, 43
Critical reflection 15–16, 158, 160
Crowdsourcing 14, 88, 92–96, 100–104, 153, 227, 235
Cultural knowledge 59, 70, 76–78, 81, 173, 228

Digital humanities 2, 5, 16, 18, 219, 220–222, 227–228

Ecological framework 1–5

Freemium (business) model 13–14, 87–92, 94–98, 100–102, 104

Generative scholarship 18, 226–227

Heritage language(s) 4, 8, 12, 26, 62–63

Indigenous language(s) 13, 69–72, 74–78, 80, 83

Intercultural (communication, competence, education) 12, 47, 49, 55, 57–59, 61, 65, 94

Journal(s) (reflective, scholarly, student) 2, 6, 17, 91, 97, 147, 183, 185, 188, 190, 191–193, 196, 222, 268

Knowledge ecology/ecosystem 3–5, 14, 17, 19, 176, 183, 191, 194–196

Language play 160–165, 168, 170–174

Multiliteracies 11, 25–28, 30, 31, 36, 41, 43, 159, 164–166, 176
Multilingual 3, 59, 163, 165, 223, 229, 268

OER lifecycle 18, 198–199, 202, 205–206, 208, 209, 211, 214–215
Open access 4–5, 9, 11, 13, 17, 78, 81, 83, 96, 183, 185, 190–191, 195–196, 222
Open content 9, 14, 17, 19, 87, 89, 96, 103, 245–247, 249, 252, 259
Open education 5, 7–10, 14, 20, 28, 42, 64–65, 109–111, 123, 125, 131, 146, 151, 162, 220, 246
Open educational practices (OEP) 7, 9, 10–11, 14–15, 88, 110, 130–131, 134, 138, 140, 142, 150–154, 160, 199, 220, 238, 245–246, 256
Open educational resources (OER) 2, 25, 37, 65, 69, 71, 87, 109, 110, 130, 140, 158, 198, 219–220, 245
Open license(s) 15, 19, 83, 87, 142, 144, 149, 151, 175, 198, 237, 249–250
Open pedagogy 7, 9, 48, 55, 65, 111, 229, 231
Open washing 13, 88, 95–96, 102

Participatory culture 19, 229, 256
Privacy 219, 229, 233

Repositories 2, 4, 9, 10, 15–16, 142, 195, 245, 250, 253, 256–257, 263

Social network(s) 6, 41, 87, 91, 131, 144, 229

Tacit knowledge 16, 18, 198, 201–202, 206–207, 245
Teacher cognition 14, 16, 135, 174, 176, 201–202

Teacher development/education 16, 159, 167, 176
Telecollaboration 12, 48, 61, 64–66, 94
Transnational 19, 88, 249

User-generated 14, 19, 92, 102–103, 133, 167, 245, 247, 249, 257, 259

Variation (dialectal, regional, social) 62, 64, 69, 71–74, 78–79

Weak ties 16, 18, 220, 225

For Product Safety Concerns and Information please contact our EU Authorised Representative.

Easy Access System Europe

Mustamäe tee 50

10621 Tallinn

Estonia

gpsr.requests@easproject.com

www.ingramcontent.com/pod-product-compliance
Lightning Source LLC
Chambersburg PA
CBHW070556300426
44113CB00010B/1269